OPEN TV

Open TV

Innovation beyond Hollywood and the Rise of Web Television

Aymar Jean Christian

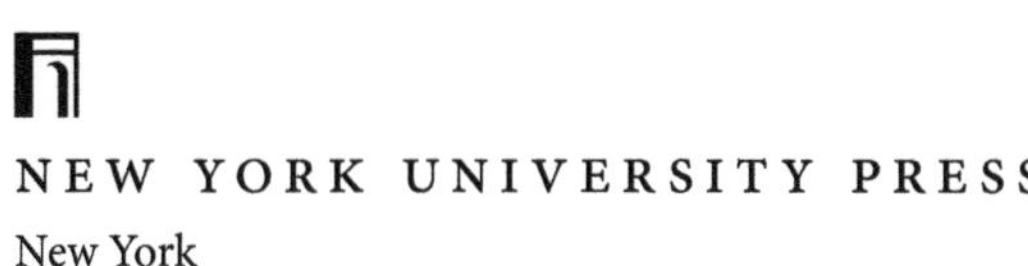

NEW YORK UNIVERSITY PRESS
New York

NEW YORK UNIVERSITY PRESS
New York
www.nyupress.org

References to Internet websites (URLs) were accurate at the time of writing. Neither the author nor New York University Press is responsible for URLs that may have expired or changed since the manuscript was prepared.

Library of Congress Cataloging-in-Publication Data
Names: Christian, Aymar Jean author.
Title: Open TV : innovation beyond Hollywood and the rise of web television / Aymar Jean Christian.
Description: New York : New York University Press, 2017. | Series: Postmillennial pop | Includes bibliographical references and index.
Identifiers: LCCN 2017012922| ISBN 9781479874224 (cl : alk. paper) | ISBN 9781479815975 (pb : alk. paper)
Subjects: LCSH: Internet television—Production and direction.
Classification: LCC PN1992.926.P76 C55 2017 | DDC 791.4502/32—dc23
LC record available at https://lccn.loc.gov/2017012922

New York University Press books are printed on acid-free paper, and their binding materials are chosen for strength and durability. We strive to use environmentally responsible suppliers and materials to the greatest extent possible in publishing our books.

Manufactured in the United States of America

10 9 8 7 6 5 4 3 2 1

Also available as an ebook

CONTENTS

This book culminates years of work that started in 2009 when I first discovered I could write about "web series" as scholarship. Learning to take television seriously was a longer journey. I grew up in the 1990s and spent most of my free time watching cable television. I didn't have a lot of friends, or least friends who would have me over for parties, which I attribute to my being both shy and one of very few black kids in the neighborhood. At the time, I didn't know why I was so engrossed in TV. Now I realize I was being socialized into believing that television should speak more specifically and directly to its audiences than it had in previous generations. *In Living Color* had me sniping "hated it!" and tormenting my little brother with a sock hammer. I jumped to sing along to the themes of Nickelodeon's *All That* and *Roundhouse*, declaring, "I know that I can find a friieeeeend . . . down at the Roundhouse!" Television filled a space friends could not. My attraction to these shows certainly related to their diverse casts. Seeing black boys do sketch, playing different characters and gender expressions, must have spoken to my not-yet queer self, socialized into performing differently in my Caribbean household than in my predominantly white classrooms. So, I begin these acknowledgments thanking the many cultural producers who have pushed the boundaries of representation as far as they could in a system that undervalued their labor. I must also thank my parents for providing a relatively stable household and allowing me to explore all the media they could afford, from cable to video games to the Internet.

This book asserts the importance of understanding production and distribution in theorizing media and culture. Conversations about media representation often hinge on value: why and how does this story matter, or not? I believe we cannot address issues of representation without understanding the ways in which stories are valued through labor and capital. To do this I needed to know the stories of people working toward change. This book is indebted to the scores of producers, executives, journalists, and exhibition organizers who worked hard to transform television and lent me their time and access to their workspaces.

Writing this book showed me the deep investments I have in television and new media. I am forever grateful to the Annenberg School for Communication for giving me the time and space to explore my interests. I first have to thank Katherine Sender, the perfect advisor for me, both in terms of my need for structure as a student and in scholarly practice. Through Katherine I came to see television as an industry based on representation and learned research tools, including field methods and production as research. John Jackson helped me further develop those methodological tools and offered a way to think about identity that I still draw on today. Joseph Turow pushed me to understand the histories, practices, and theories of creative industries—an understanding that remains essential. At Penn I broadened my expertise with visiting scholars Mark Anthony Neal, Graeme Turner, Yeidy Rivero, and John Caldwell; scholars at Penn outside the School for Communication, including Heather Love, Timothy Corrigan, and Peter Decherney; and faculty in my department, including Barbie Zelizer, Elihu Katz, and Paul Messaris.

I have been fortunate to engage a host of scholars as I developed this work. A number of senior colleagues offered essential guidance and mentorship throughout this process, including Ralina Joseph, Roopali Mukherjee, Sarah Banet-Weiser, Stuart Cunningham, David Craig, Jonathan Gray, Denise Mann, Vicki Mayer, Lisa Henderson, Lisa Nakamura, S. Craig Watkins, James Bennett, David Hesmondhalgh, Bambi Haggins, Mimi White, and Alisa Perren. My peers were similarly critical in pushing me to think more deeply about my areas of interest. In terms of cultural production, I remember fruitful and formative conversations, debates, and written exchanges with Al Martin, Racquel Gates, Melanie Kohnen, Chenjerai Kumanyika, Lori Lopez, Mecca Jamilah Sullivan, Adrienne Shaw, and Latoya Peterson. I further honed my knowledge of media industry with Kristen Warner, Josh Braun, Myles McNutt, Ethan Tussey, Liz Ellcessor, Courtney Brannon Donoghue, Karen Petruska, Suzanne Scott, Miranda Banks, Brooke Duffy, and Devon Powers.

It is hard to finish a scholarly book without also successfully navigating the academy and its institutions. I must thank administrators Michael Delli Carpini at Penn and Ellen Wartella and Barbara O'Keefe at Northwestern for providing institutional support. At Northwestern, E. Patrick

Johnson and Pablo Boczkowski offered invaluable mentorship, while C. Riley Snorton, Joshua Chambers-Letson, Miriam Petty, and Jasmine Cobb offered advice and guidance. At Penn I was further assisted by staff members Brendan Keegan and Waldo Aguirre, particularly in production, and Paul Messaris, who along with Katherine and John helped me with the basics of filmmaking. Finally, I would not have made it through Penn without the marvelous Beverly Henry, who helped me build community and always had my back, along with Deb Porter and Sharron Shepherd, who run Penn and Northwestern, respectively, with aplomb.

It took a small community of people to produce *She's out of Order*, the case study that introduces chapters 2 through 4. My partner Derek McPhatter deserves the highest praise for bringing me the story, writing the script, assembling the team, and tolerating my moods throughout the entirety of my career, whereas Teresa Lasley's ingenuity in creating the show and courage in acting in it, along with Rhonney Greene's direction, were integral. I thank the crew and cast, notably Amber Efé and Rocio Nuñez, along with our Indiegogo contributors and key financiers Dionna McPhatter and Yanru Chen. Many thanks to my Philadelphia friends Jeff Gottfried, Connor Krone, and J. T. Christensen for offering up their homes and gallery. I am also indebted to the late Jiwon Lee, a brilliant comedian and friend, who acted in my first web series.

This book would not exist without great editors who helped shepherd it through production, most notably Alicia Nadkarni at NYU Press, who faithfully kept in contact with me from the moment I finished my degree and offered useful advice throughout. I'm indebted to series editors Henry Jenkins and Karen Tongson, who made sure this book did not get lost in the process. I must also thank Katie Day Good and Northwestern undergraduates for their assistance in data analysis and collection. Carol Stabile, Dawn Durante, Alex Juhasz, and Ramzi Fawaz were instrumental at key stages in the process. I wrote hundreds of blog posts about web series in graduate school and thank editors at more popular publications for publishing some of this work, including Liz Shannon Miller, Bryce Renninger, and Joshua Cohen. Many thanks to Cathy Hannabach for copyediting this manuscript at a critical time in its development.

Thank you to my friends in academia who supported me emotionally and intellectually throughout this journey: Khadijah White, Madison Moore, Karl Swinehart, Heidi Khaled, Brett Bumgarner, Dayna Chatman, Faithe Day, Dan Berger, Shawnika Hull, and Robin Stevens. Thank you to my collaborators on Open TV (beta) who helped me build the platform that extends the ideas in this book, thus motivating me to complete it: Elijah McKinnon, Stephanie Jeter, Nicole Morse, Kemi Adeyemi, Robert Smith, Mark Díaz, and Chris Walker. Without you I would not be here. You were there for every crisis and accolade, and I love you all.

Lastly, parts of this book have been published previously. Parts of the introduction were published in "Indie TV: Innovation in Series Development," in *Media Independence: Working with Freedom or Working for Free?* edited by James Bennett and Niki Strange, 159–81 (New York: Routledge, 2014). Parts of chapter 2 were previously published in the article "Fandom as Industrial Response: Producing Identity in an Independent Web Series," *Transformative Works & Cultures* 8 (2011). Parts of chapter 4 were previously published in "Beyond Big Video: The Instability of Independent Distribution in a New Media Market," *Continuum: Journal of Media & Cultural Studies* 26, no. 1 (2011): 73–87 and "The Problem of YouTube," *Flow*, February 11, 2011, http://flowtv.org/2011/02/the-problem-of-youtube.

Introduction

Independents Change the Channel

A hot and sweaty crew films a teenage woman for a low-budget pop music video outside a home in Westchester, a New York City suburb, in the second episode of Adam Goldman's indie web drama *Whatever this is.* Oscar, the head of production, sends one of his assistants, Ari, into the kitchen for a different camera lens after the teen requests more shots. The teen's father and video's financier, Ken Priest, stops Oscar: "Should he be going in there *alone*? . . . Isn't he a little . . . *brown*?" Later he calls Ari a "wetback," and Sam, Ari's roommate and coworker, says nothing to defend him. After the shoot Sam apologizes, but racism on set provokes Ari into educating Sam on his everyday struggles with gender, race, and sexuality as a gay man of color:

> You're my best friend and you say nothing to that shithead. . . . Sometimes, before I meet a guy, in the dark times when I used to meet people . . . I have a full-blown panic attack because I have no way of knowing if he's only meeting me because he's like *into* Latin guys, and he wants me to be some like macho fucking *papi*, because I am *never* macho fucking *papi* enough for those people, never. And then I come here. I come to fucking Westchester because it's all part of Sam's Big Plan to make us have a career and Ken fucking Priest acts like I just hopped the fucking border fence to pick fucking oranges in fucking California or some shit. . . . You know, sometimes I look at you and I'm like, "What problems does this straight, white guy have? Does he have any? Is that a word with any meaning to him?" Apology accepted.

By turns poetic and frank, *Whatever this is.* uses[1] dark humor to reveal how the television and media market fails to protect workers from wrongful termination, excessive overtime, and consistent humiliation or discrimination based on gender, race, and sexuality. We see how unstable media distribution is today, how it prevents young, aspiring creative talent from meaningful work, and how it generates cheap, vacuous stories for audience consumption. *Whatever this is.* creator and writer Adam Goldman unspools this narrative slowly and lyrically, in six half-hour episodes, showing how characters survive or succumb to the trials of youth, compounded by poverty. Crowdfunded by fans, Goldman's meticulously written and produced show critiques our appetite for cheap content while showing the personal, political, and social consequences of a free market.

How did Goldman independently produce a series with half-hour episodes about how market inequalities affect diverse workers? He used the web to intervene in representations of gay and New York life. In 2012, Goldman was an underemployed Bard graduate living in Crown Heights, Brooklyn. Around him were writers, musicians, actors, and cinematographers with lots of talent but no space to unleash it. Goldman saw opportunity. He wrote *The Outs*, a drama about a group of young, sad, broke Brooklynites searching for connection and same-sex love, which the press frequently compared to HBO's show *Girls*.[2] *The Outs* stood out in an already crowded online market for gay web series for its polished cinematography and sound, confident acting and direction, and for focusing on gay men not seeking marriage, a dominant theme on TV. After a second season that explored nonmonogamy, John Sherman wrote in the *Los Angeles Review of Books*, "*The Outs* represents a plurality of queer politics with a greater breadth than in a show in which gay characters are shunted off to the side or fettered by the traditional boundaries of same-sex relationships and parenthood."[3]

Goldman uploaded to Vimeo the twelve-minute pilot for *The Outs*, "State of the Union," which he used to raise $1,000 on the crowdfunding site Kickstarter to make the next two episodes. His pitch? Help a team of creatives transform television with a sincere story about underrepresented experiences:

Finally, you know that TV show you hate? No, not *The Good Wife*. The one with the stupid people and the bad actors spouting dialogue that makes you cringe? Less of that, please. Vote with your dollars. Then maybe next time someone's going to put something like massively offensive, short-lived sitcom *Work It*[4] on the air, they'll think twice and produce something you'll actually enjoy. Makes sense, right?[5]

The pitch laid bare legacy television's failures in representation, and it worked. Goldman beat his goal by $600. Three months later, Goldman went to Kickstarter again to raise $8,000 dollars to finish the six-episode first season. He ended up raising $22,000, enough to produce a forty-five-minute "Chanukah Special," which premiered half a year later to a crowded room at Public Assembly in Williamsburg—*Good Wife* regular and *Outs* guest star Alan Cumming attended, along with famed queer director John Cameron Mitchell, who told Goldman after the screening that the show "makes me proud to be a New York faggot." Goldman's success granted him rare and limited access to corporate development. At the same time that Goldman took meetings with television producers to bring *The Outs* to a major cable or premium channel, he wrote *Whatever this is.* "I would love for the *The Outs* to be on TV but I also find this space that we're occupying really exciting, because we're something that people can't get on TV," Goldman told me. When he launched his third Kickstarter campaign to raise funds for *Whatever this is.*, he beat his goal and raised $171,000, much of it before the pilot aired in August 2013. Seeing the power of his fan base, Vimeo greenlit a second season of *The Outs* two years later in what would be its second original series after *High Maintenance*; creators of both series retained their intellectual property.

Goldman's story illustrates independent television's bottom-up approach to development, in which creative workers, fans, and new sponsors pilot new stories, represent new experiences and communities, and at times generate earnings, adulation, and experience for producers. Goldman joins a generation of creative workers who raised tens of thousands—and at times, millions—of dollars through crowdfunding for shows about gamers, black women, Asian Americans, Jane Austen acolytes, homophobic lesbians, and countless other underrepresented communities and brilliant personalities. They were years ahead of more established directors and producers like Rob Thomas, Spike Lee, and Zach Braff in discovering that fans could finance media independent of corporations.[6]

This book focuses on a generation of creative producers and entrepreneurs working to reinvent a medium that has never fully represented the United States: television. I argue that the Internet brought innovation to television by opening mass distribution to those excluded from legacy development processes, fostering new ways of creating and marketing series. Web series are television because stories are told episodically, in seasons, or through channels. Yet they are different from what people understand as "television" in the way series develop. This book contrasts "open TV," web or networked distribution, with "legacy TV," linear or traditional network distribution, arguing that the former fosters innovation and diversity in series development. Legacy television is characterized by scheduled and time-based distribution via broadcast, cable, or premium (subscription) networks like ABC, TNT, or HBO, respectively. Most people understand the legacy system through multinational conglomerates composing "Hollywood," which yields power as "one of the focal points of the culture industry" that "has moved . . . beyond the silver screen" to encompass a wide range of cultural production and distribution globally.[7] The legacy system is one-to-many; we often call it "traditional," since its roots stem from the very beginning of American television in the mid-twentieth century. The development process is controlled by teams of network executives who solicit, license, and produce a select number of series.

By contrast, open or networked television distribution occurs via Internet or web protocols. It is digital, on-demand, and peer-to-peer, meaning any participant in the web—a producer, a fan, a sponsor—can directly connect to another at any time, eliminating the need for legacy network executives. In this book, "open TV" will refer primarily to independent web TV production and distribution. "Legacy TV" will refer to broadcast, cable, or premium channels or distributors who, during the period this book covers (the mid-1990s to mid-2010s), largely kept in place development practices from the twentieth century. Many of these distributors have started networked, or "over-the-top," applications—CBS All Access, NBC's SeeSo, and HBO Now—while tech companies like Netflix and YouTube are now using networked distribution to revive some legacy practices, including live-streaming, up-front ad sales, long-format programming, and re-airing of legacy TV series. It remains to be seen to what degree and in what ways networked distribution will continue to shift legacy development practices. Because of corporate dominance in both legacy and open TV markets, I will often refer to web-distributed series as independent or "indie TV." Most of the book focuses on indie producers because their precarious status and access to distribution compels them to execute new ideas and strategies, the core of innovation.

To survive in an incredibly competitive market for television programming, open TV producers have to take risks and pilot projects by and for creative workers, sponsors, and fan communities, advancing innovation. Digital networking facilitates connections among television's core value creators—producers, fans,[8] and sponsors—more quickly and deeply than legacy distributors created in the mass media era. Open access to distribution gives producers a platform for creative expression and ownership, enables diverse storytelling for marginalized fan communities, and produces more dynamic ways of releasing, showcasing, and rewarding shows for brands, sponsors, distributors, and exhibitors. On the basis of over one hundred interviews with writers, producers, filmmakers, and network executives, I argue that the open TV market demonstrates the value of more open access to distribution in industries where access has been historically restricted.

In our networked economy, major studios and networks are struggling to meet rising demands from consumers, ease pressures on workers, and maintain cultural relevance. Twentieth-century legacy processes for developing, financing, rating, and rewarding art are confounding media conglomerates. They focus on maintaining their brands and profits, empowering top producers, executives, and shareholders while releasing a few quality but many more cheap programs that fail to represent a diversifying nation. Meanwhile, media workers face underpaid, temporary work. Audiences have exponentially more options but fewer real choices.

Left behind, independent producers, entrepreneurs, and fans are creating their own media system. For two decades, scores of producers have been making television independent of legacy television distribution, creating their own shows—"web series"—to create value as major distributors extract it. YouTube alone hosts hundreds of thousands of showrunners, comedians, talk show hosts, video game commenters, makeup and shopping gurus, and pop culture and political commentators, each with millions of followers. Beyond YouTube, producers from diverse communities make series for platforms like Vimeo and Funny or

Die and multichannel networks like Maker, Machinima, and Fullscreen. Netflix and Amazon reimagined original series development by giving producers more autonomy while incorporating viewer taste through big data. Social media platforms like Facebook, Snapchat, Twitter, and Tumblr give creative workers tools for speaking to and organizing fans. Kickstarter, Indiegogo, and other crowdfunding sites provide platforms for efficient financing campaigns that bring fans into the production process. New advertising technologies allow video distributors to make money for pennies per view. Productions shoot all around the country, with hubs in New York and Los Angeles but outposts in Atlanta, Chicago, Washington, DC, New Orleans, and college campuses across the nation.

In *Open TV*, I focus on how and why a specific set of practitioners participated in the early years of the rapidly expanding television market. In doing so, I combine a growing body of research in innovation studies with critical media industry studies.[9] I think of the web as a distribution platform where individuals and groups try to profit from new opportunities, a space where "cultural workers seek to negotiate to their own purposes."[10] Workers and entrepreneurs produce value for the economy but also for the public, expanding dominant notions of innovation beyond pure efficiency and investment. I rely on interviews, on-site observation, and my own indie TV production, supported with analyses of websites, advertisements, and marketing materials.[11] In this I follow longstanding traditions of ethnographies of subcultures and industries.[12] Because indie producers and markets are marginalized, much of the evidence for my claims is narrative-based, because few institutions or researchers systematically quantify this activity, perpetuating its marginalization. For me, understanding how producers make these digital objects, under what constraints and to what ends, is critical to understanding what, if anything, is new in new media. Innovation is never all good or all bad, progressive or regressive. This book focuses on value creation, but value is not limitless. Indeed, as the book progresses from production and representation to independent and corporate distribution—where strategies must generate revenue—we see how open markets challenge innovators and how conglomerates still dominate in this period. For indie producers and their fans, "open TV" is both an ideal and a demand, always already foreclosed and in process, enabled by networked distribution but shaped by the cultural, political, and organizational realities of the early-twenty-first-century media.

Open TV builds on scholarly research about the value of independent production to creative industries—music, radio, television, and film—as well as how indie production fosters new products, addresses markets underserved by mainstream industries, and broadens society's base of producers. Few studies exist on how these producers use media distribution to develop communities and markets for alternative practices. S. Craig Watkins and David Hesmondhalgh's work on hip hop and punk music, Susan Douglas, Christina Dunbar-Hester, and Michael Keith's histories of amateur and independent radio, Devorah Heitner, Gayle Wald, and Deidre Boyle's work on alternative and community television, and Alisa Perren's work on independent film have influenced this book's strategy of examining how independent agents work to improve the industry through new narrative, production, and distribution practices and strategies.[13] Yet most of media studies, particularly television studies, still privileges projects from corporate distributors as a basis for theory. This is untenable in a networked economy where independent agents are constantly organizing, albeit with less capital than corporations.

The open TV market is massive, comprising thousands of series, and by the mid-2010s, its most innovative projects have inspired some legacy television networks to develop them. While increasingly common, particularly for cable networks like HBO, Comedy Central, MTV, and IFC, few indie web series transition to legacy television. The case studies throughout focus on indie producers developing work for the open, web-based market, even if they "sell out" down the line.

Open Development: Indie Innovation for the Networked Era

I often describe web series as independent television or "indie TV" to account for the way network*ed* distribution—as opposed to linear network distribution—allows producers to function independently of the legacy development system. This is different than "web TV" or "IP [Internet Protocol] TV," more general terms that focus on the changing distribution *technologies*—networked, many-to-many connections—and not the changes in *production* and *development* practices new technologies facilitate, namely, increased opportunities for small-scale independents. Web and IP TV describe platforms like HBO Now, where distribution is networked but development still occurs through a cable channel and studio primarily invested in legacy, linear distribution in this period. In theorizing open TV development, I focus on the independence made possible with web or networked distribution compared with legacy TV development.

Open TV focuses on series produced and distributed wholly independently of legacy distributors. Independent of legacy development processes and linear cable exhibition, open TV development renders visible the stakeholders necessary to create television: producers or creators who write, act in, and film series; distributors, which curate, aggregate, and/or market series; sponsors—chiefly, brands and advertisers—who finance shows; and fans, who give their attention. In this book I use the term "fans" to denote communities of viewers who mobilize around texts and "audiences" or "viewers" to describe those communities as constructed by producers, organizations, and institutions who seek to profit from their attention and activity. I use "indie" and "independent" interchangeably in an attempt to expand "indie" beyond a genre category—as Alisa Perren and Michael Newman describe in film culture and industry[14]—to the practices and values promulgated by those who work outside of corporate development.

The reach of the indie TV market is wide. This book focuses on an undercounted segment of producers who create mostly short-form, scripted comedies and dramas and release them through online platforms. They are somewhat different from what most people define as producers of "user-generated content." Like consumers who choose to produce, most web series producers use corporate open-upload websites like YouTube, Vimeo, and Funny or Die. Unlike consumers who chose to produce, web series producers are more likely to be committed to production as a career—unlike early vloggers (video bloggers), who because of the newness of that form routinely described their initial participation as accidental. Indie TV creators include amateurs, film students and graduates, and television professionals[15] who produce video for themselves, for their communities, or, most rarely, for independent and corporate online and TV networks. In the early 2000s and 2010s, this sector got by on limited financing, chiefly algorithmic advertising, licensing, crowd-financing, subscription, or sponsorship—a greater range of options but smaller pools of revenue than those available to legacy television networks during the period of this book.

The open TV market is unstable—in concept, production, distribution, consumption, size, texts, and value. As I elucidate in chapter 1, the market emerged in the mid-1990s and grew in the mid-2000s. Its styles vary widely, following and breaking visual and narrative conventions of web video, television, and film. Most stories are told in short episodes, usually three to fifteen minutes in length, though many are longer or shorter. For example, the creators of *Teachers*, a YouTube series picked up by cable channel TV Land, produced many popular episodes running under one minute, while Goldman and other ambitious producers told stories in long format, with thirty-minute episodes. In the open TV market, episodes can range from just one scene to a feature-length film. Critically acclaimed New York indie series *High Maintenance*, *Broad City*, and *F to 7th*, all of which secured legacy development deals, had episodes whose narratives run for one scene, shot in one location, in under ten minutes. Coquie Hughes and Kalup Linzy's epic black queer dramas are over two and a half hours long—Linzy packaged seasons two and three as a ninety-minute movie, whereas Hughes grouped the first three episodes into a ninety-minute film and later released an hour-long finale. Many shows are bounded by seasons, though some publish continually (like the news and soap operas) or sporadically. They are also distributed through a number of creative deals that send content to mobile phones and televisions, as well as film and industry festivals that place them on a big screen and around the world. Some are structured like TV pilots broken into pieces, others like deconstructed feature films, and yet others exist in between and outside of established forms. Web series span and integrate an array of genres, including comedy, drama, soap opera, sketch, vlog, and talk.

The open TV market's diversity reflects the newness of the form and the freedom with which producers operate. Even so, by many measures, it is not small. Efforts to quantify the sector are in their infancy. Trade group Film LA now counts digital pilots, and production budgets for companies like Netflix and YouTube are widely reported. But few accepted figures exist on how many indie TV series have been made or how much money has been invested in them. Compared to the corporate American television market, which generates roughly $70 billion each year in advertising revenue, the web series market is no doubt smaller. The International Academy of Web Television (IAWTV), the market's first trade group heavily represented by indie creators, estimated that web series would see $250 million in production budgets in 2013,[16] almost double its $135 million estimate for 2012, which itself was a threefold increase from the year prior, calculations based primarily on submissions to their awards.[17] But the IAWTV's figures did not include Netflix's investments in original programming that year, valued at over $100 million, nor YouTube's short-lived investments, valued at several times that, though most of it in marketing support and not direct investment.[18] By 2016, Netflix earmarked over $6 billion for six hundred hours of original programming, half for U.S. release, and its competitors in the short-form market moved into ordering long-form series, including YouTube. Moreover, trade groups and analysts cannot account for independent series whose budgets are unknown or measured in time volunteered, which is the vast majority. In terms of audience, estimates by web analytics firm Visible Measures suggested that in 2010 the top ten series garnered well in excess of one hundred million views per month; it is safe to assume that the entire market, from the YouTube hits to the little-seen indies, now amounts to many times more than that.[19] By 2013, many of the top YouTubers had reached over one billion cumulative views on their channels, and an estimated two thousand had over one million subscribers. As corporate web TV distributors flex buying power, the indie web series market was seen as small only because of a lack of investment from brands, advertisers, or the state, not for lack of production activity or fan interest.

Who makes indie series and for how much? Again, calculations are difficult. Most indie TV creators are either amateurs or skilled professionals with degrees or experience in film and television. They come from all races, sexualities, ages, and geographic areas, though most productions are based in Los Angeles or New York, where industry workers live. Most of them are made for little or no money; most of the programs I profile in this book had budgets in the thousands to tens of thousands, compared to legacy TV budgets that routinely cost between $500,000 and $1 million for each episode. Independent television series are comparatively "cheap" television, and, as such, are generally considered "bad." Yet I argue that assessments of production value must consider available resources and cultural context. Corporate legacy and web television networks maintain quality standards through development investments, marketing, and a small pool of highly skilled technical crew. Even then, the public only sees a small percentage of the productions developed. Of those, even fewer are considered "good" by critics or Nielsen TV ratings. At their best, indie series producers can bring together passionate and skilled workers who are willing to sacrifice time and money for an artistic, social, political, or market-based project. Within these tremendous limits, independent television producers generate considerable value in production, storytelling, and distribution, not to mention more than a few superbly executed series.

Frustrated by legacy development, major brands and A-list talent have always been a part of the market, from BMW's *The Hire* to Joss Whedon's *Dr. Horrible's Sing-Along Blog* and Ben Stiller's *Burning Love*. Hollywood directors, producers, and actors in search of creative freedom or extra work have developed web shows and networks since the late 1990s. Major advertisers have consistently used web series to sell products, before and particularly after the rise of streaming video, including Unilever's *Evan and Gareth* to sell Axe deodorant and Toyota's *Pool* made for mobile phones and publicized via TV commercials to promote the Camry. Major studios like Paramount and most major television networks have used them to create series for digital consumption. These tend to have higher production budgets. Nonprofits occasionally produce web series, either to solicit donations or to advance their missions.[20] Without a doubt, independent production comprised the bulk of new series, even if few were mass marketed, in the period this book covers.

As the open TV market developed, new institutions arose to define and assess it: conferences, award shows, and trade group meetings have become key information-gathering sites. There are a growing number of web series conferences and festivals, most notably the New York Television Festival (NYTVF), the International Television Festival (ITVFest), LAWEBFEST, and HollyWeb Festival. Film festivals screen episodes and host panels, and niche festivals cover specific aspects of the market—for example, the gay web series festival Out of the Box, and the gay black film festival Queer Black Cinema. Private trade meetings, including quarterly meetings of the International Academy of Web Television (IAWTV), also serve this purpose. In recent years, film festivals have increased their involvement in the market, led by the Tribeca Film Festival, which started a New Online Work program in 2014 and introduced a curated marketplace of online writers and creators in 2016.

Awards for indie TV arose shortly after YouTube and the rise of streaming video. The Streamy and IAWTV Awards, explored in chapter 4, have been recognizing both corporate and indie web series since 2009 and 2012, respectively. Two of Hollywood's major guilds—the Writers and Producers Guilds of America—recognize web production. In 2010 the Writers Guild started giving awards to "original" and "derivative" new media, as well as video games, before changing the award to "short-form" new media, in part to allow big distributors of long-form TV like Netflix to compete with legacy programs; most of the WGA's short-form awardees were indie series, including *High Maintenance* (explored in chapter 2) and *Anyone but Me* (chapter 3).[21] The Producers Guild has been nominating a mix of indie and corporate digital series since 2012, from *30 Rock* webisodes to *The Guild* (chapter 2) and *Video Game High School*. Both the Primetime and Daytime Emmy Awards have recognized web programming since 2008, though both awards initially focused on series distributed by corporations.[22] In 2016 the Primetime Emmys, arguably television's highest honor, expanded web categories to include acting for men and women, and variety programs, but the only independent series nominated was Jen Richards and Laura Zak's *Her Story*, the first television series written by and starring transgender women.[23] That year, Netflix ranked third in overall Primetime Emmy nominations, nabbing fifty-four, just two less than FX but much less than HBO's ninety-four. Yet Netflix's haul was a near 60 percent increase from the thirty-four it received the year prior, whereas HBO fell 25 percent from 126 in 2015; Hulu received two, and Amazon received sixteen, up from twelve the year prior, when it won five for *Transparent*, the first television series with a transgender protagonist.

How did the open TV market come to exist? A number of developments influenced web series production, including lower prices for equipment (cameras and editing software, primarily), the mass adoption of broadband, the advent of streaming video distributors (chiefly, YouTube), declining interest in broadcast television, especially by younger viewers, the rise of niche marketing (to the segments important to advertisers), and the digital convergence of industry operations. Indie producers justify their market participation in many ways. They experiment with genres, forms, and platforms; create work samples to raise their industry status; or work to build an enduring business for audiences underserved by market-driven narrowcasting. As with any new market, individuals and young institutions compete and experiment to generate formulas, models, best practices, and breakthrough innovations. The quest for dominance—through fame, fortune, community, or visibility—is a rough one. Failure is high and payouts are low in markets for innovation. Yet creative autonomy (production), community value (representation), and the chance to connect with viewers (distribution) are enough to motivate producers and entrepreneurs. They work hard to master the metrics for success in an open field. This desire is the fuel powering Hollywood and Silicon Valley, keeping workers happy by offering an outlet for their passions and driving innovation for companies to develop when they care to.

Scholars have underestimated the value of the open TV market because it has far less cultural and economic capital than legacy TV. It has been largely small scale, because legacy television distributors controlled processes for finding, financing, and rewarding higher-budget shows at the beginning of the networked era. To understand the value of the open TV market, one must understand how legacy distributors profited from the old system. The next section explores the pilot process and up-front financing, which supported legacy TV distributors' access to billions in video advertising during the period this book covers. I show how pilot production and up-front monetization are ill suited to an age of social media and rising indie production, and how legacy TV distributors' control over programming falls short of balancing art, culture, and commerce. I argue that networked distribution supports innovation in series creation by empowering producers, fans, and brands frustrated with legacy distribution. Throughout the book I explore how open TV production creates innovative television in three interconnected ways: creative expression supported by "free" labor, a "highly ambivalent" political project counteracting exploitation in corporate employment (chapter 2);[24] diversity in representation, through self-representation and fan-led development (chapter 3); and flexibility in development and marketing, where open TV distributors work with sponsors and fans to support producer-led stories (chapter 4). These dynamics are in stark contrast to the closed legacy development system.

Closed Development: The Politics of Legacy Television Distribution

The open TV market developed at the turn of the twenty-first century in response to two opposing trends: the tightening of the series production market despite a greater number of distribution channels, and the opening of new TV markets through the Internet's decentralized distribution system. Networked or web distribution creates more choice and opportunity for both audiences and producers than in the broadcast TV era (1950s–1970s, characterized by the dominance of three linear broadcast channels) or the multichannel transition era (1980s–2000s, characterized by a rise in cable channels). The Big Three—CBS, ABC, NBC—controlled the broadcast era. A greater number of distributors—Fox, TBS, CNN—rose to power in the multichannel transition after the government opened TV to cable. Today, the web, the newest distribution technology, frustrates executives at legacy broadcast and cable channels: producers, advertisers, and consumers have more options. So, legacy executives focus on managing and generating hits on a cost-effective basis, as increased competition for advertising dollars, viewer attention, and new productions put pressure on revenue. These dynamics gradually led to a crisis in legacy television distribution during the 2000s and early 2010s.

The core of the crisis was the development process, the way legacy TV network executives selected new shows and financed them through sales. In development, executives solicited and licensed series pitched by writers, producers, and their companies. Scripted comedies and dramas were most important to legacy development, because they commanded high ad rates and branded TV channels as destinations. Despite the incredible rise of fandom and open TV production, a small group of executives continued to hold sway over the supply (creative production), consumption (fans or audiences), and financing (brands) of television content as we entered the networked era. The power imbalance between executives on one side and producers, sponsors, and fans on the other were less visible before deregulation expanded options for developing and distributing TV through cable in the 1970s and through the Internet in the 1990s. By the 2000s the system's inefficiencies irked nearly every major player in television, including the decision makers themselves. Studying the mid-2000s up-front buying process, Amanda Lotz found it in "crisis . . . with many in the industry expressing open dissatisfaction in public forums, one-on-one conversations, in trade press articles and as evidenced by the creation of an industry discussion group to formally reconsider the process."[25] By 2014, Fox's Kevin Reilly openly expressed a desire to "cancel" pilot season.[26] Central to the crisis were the vast number of pitches for extremely limited slots (constrained production), declining ratings for new shows (the challenge of creating new fans), and brand dissatisfaction with the reach and attention of commercials.[27]

Television development differs in scale according to distributor: broadcast, cable, and premium versus the kind of open or networked distribution that is the topic of this book. Traditionally, the pilot process included the pitching of new series to development executives[28] and the presentation of the first episode to brands and advertising agencies at the up-fronts in May, where 75–90 percent of advertisements are sold to finance the rest of the season. Piloting and up-front ad sales governed nearly all of U.S. broadcast scripted television development—that of CBS, NBC, ABC, Fox, and the CW—during the period this book covers. Sales for those networks represent half of all TV series monetization, totaling around $9 billion annually.[29] Cable channels comprised the other half of the annual haul, evidence of rapid growth in brand and advertiser interest in narrowcast programming over the 2000s.[30] Cable channels, most owned by conglomerates with ownership stakes in both broadcast production (series) and distribution (channels), increased market share by controlling costs, filling schedules with cheap reality television produced with nonunion contracts[31] while greenlighting a few costlier, more often union, productions to attract big financiers and critical attention. In the latter case, they tended to give producers more creative control (in shows like *Louie* or *Portlandia*) or develop series with passionate fan bases in other media or markets (for franchise shows like *The Walking Dead* or *Battlestar Galactica*). When cable networks released original shows, they piloted fewer shows and were more likely to commission straight-to-series.[32] Premium subscription distributors like HBO and Showtime operated similarly but did not need to court advertisers, allowing for some more risk in development.

For several years, corporate networked TV distributors like Yahoo and Hulu replicated up-front selling through the NewFronts, run by marketing firm Digitas in its early years and later moving to the Interactive Advertising Bureau (IAB). The online networks' lack of brand recognition as original program distributors, however, meant that channels catered heavily to brands' perceived needs, producing shows too uninspiring to excite fans to watch or brands to pay for video ads. The IAB estimated 2015 Internet advertising revenue at $59 billion, more than legacy television's $40 billion. Most of this was search and display. Online *video* advertising, which delivered high rates for open television producers, comprised just $4 billion.[33]

Despite increased competition from the web, legacy distributors maintained and, in some years, increased the size of the pilot market and up-front ad sales. Lotz found up-front financing of series "remarkably steadfast" in the mid-2000s because of decades-old client relationships between channels and ad agencies, the perceived value of linear television compared to other advertising channels, and the ability, albeit challenged, for legacy channels to attract larger audiences.[34] The up-front process started in the 1960s to accommodate the needs of channels, brands, and their agencies. It favored legacy TV distributors: brands purchased time on series that had not been tested with audiences and without data on what rates other brands were paying; each channel established base rates for brand clients to guarantee stable annual sales; programming options were scarce, particularly for channels with hits, incentivizing agencies to spend high and bid quickly; and each channel used scatter markets to monetize slots that had not sold up front or if programs underperformed.[35]

Buoyed by the up-front market, legacy TV development executives increased the size and scale of pilot production, even as success rates for pilots did not rise in kind. The number of scripted series rose to a record high of 455 in 2016, two and a half times the number in 2002, with most of the increase from cable and streaming services.[36] Most shows still failed, but the pilot market stayed intact. Film LA, which coordinates and processes film and television permits in Los Angeles, has counted the number of television pilots in production since the 2004–2005 season. That year, 124 pilots were produced, 101 of them in Los Angeles. Pilot production dropped to under one hundred from 2007 to 2009, following the recession and Writers Guild of America (WGA) strike. Yet by the 2015–2016 season, production rebounded to 201 pilots, near the record 203 broadcast and cable pilots in 2013–2014.[37] Accounting for the remaining jump in production were dramas, the vast majority of which were shot in New York, Vancouver, Toronto, and Atlanta, which offer financial incentives: "Often, this means financial concerns trump creative concerns when deciding where to shoot."[38] These tax incentives do little to provide stable employment to local producers; studios, investors, and real estate developers benefit the most.[39] The total amount legacy distributors spent on pilots remained stable, despite increased competition for brands' campaign dollars. Film LA estimated pilot spending in Los Angeles at $309 million in 2005, dipping to $207 million in 2009 after the strike but rebounding to $296 million in the 2015–2016 cycle.[40] Later, Film LA started tracking a shift in pilot production: an increase in straight-to-series orders across broadcast, cable, and digital channels, up to fifty-seven (eleven broadcast, twenty-four cable, and twenty-two digital) in 2015–2016, compared to just eight (seven cable, one broadcast) in 2010–2011. The pilot system finally started to break in the 2010s. Yet unbeknownst and of little interest to corporate players, open TV creators had been developing straight-to-series since the 1990s, as will be shown in chapter 1.

Broadcast channels historically release the highest-value productions but have the least managerial and artistic freedom. Still beholden to advertisers and looking for security in a competitive market, legacy networks have focused on owning their own shows to protect their revenue from advertising sale declines. But brands still invested billions in legacy channels. Continued brand investment in legacy television, along with licensing fees from new distributors like Netflix, buoyed the market for financing and producing new shows, allowing legacy distributors to control who got to make television and what kinds of stories audiences saw. Legacy distributors have had this power for most of their history, and it has been fraught with uncertainty and conservatism about what kinds of shows audiences want. Because of this uncertainty, networks "develop[ed] ways to control both supply and demand—supply to smooth its workings, demand so that it remains of a sort the networks are set up to satisfy."[41] By controlling television's supply (production) and demand (advertising, range and type of stories audiences can see), legacy distributors avoided drastic shifts in revenue year-to-year and prevented advertisers from migrating to other platforms. But the process is antithetical to story creation. In his analysis of television development during the beginning of the multichannel transition, Todd Gitlin characterized the pilot process as a "slow 'no' . . . the business of satisfying executives who have to satisfy other executives—all with opinions about the mass market."[42] Because of limited distribution through broadcast, legacy control in series development historically has limited storytelling possibilities, with networks copying existing hits and working with established producers.[43] In the 2000s, broadcast executives' risk avoidance declined after they saw competition from cable series, paving the way for morally and narratively complex series like *Arrested Development*, *Community*, *Lost*, and *Scandal*.[44] But an unconventional program receiving a series order remained an exception to the rule, and was typically possible only when pitched by elite producers with lucrative multiyear development contracts or with multiple projects in development or production.[45] Why? The loosening of program and network ownership rules through the slackening of Financial Interest and Syndication Rules of 1970—which were eliminated in 1995 and prevented broadcast distributors from owning programming—and the passage of the Telecommunications Act of 1996—which accelerated media conglomeration and vertical integration—increased the number of executives who could say "no" to projects while limiting the bargaining power of the independent producers who wrote them because conglomerates owned multiple channels.

The Telecommunications Act, in particular, structured media distribution in favor of large media, telecommunications, and tech conglomerates, privileging incumbent and well-heeled stakeholders over firms invested in the public interest and the cultural possibilities of technological innovation. As Patricia Aufderheide writes in her extensive account of the bill, "[T]he shape of the industry was changing most rapidly through financial, not technical, convergence, as large firms got larger and more multifaceted."[46] Conglomerates in media like Viacom and Time Warner, and in tech like TCI, argued successfully "for concentration and cross-ownership relaxation. They could also argue that the high-stakes, high-cost new network paradigms could only be accomplished by the very rich and powerful."[47] Among a host of complex provisions, the act allowed broadcasters unlimited rights to enter the digital space, companies with broadcast stations to own cable channels, and cable and telephone to combine services (as opposed to competing), all while nonprofit, public-access, and educational organizations and distributors were given very little in the way of new investments or support. Shortly after its passage, phone and cable operators rose in power as service fees increased—rising three and four times the rate of inflation in 1996 and 1997—and as broadcast ad revenue increased as well.[48] Communications and media companies have been surviving, even thriving, during the digital transition. As broadcast ratings consistently declined over the 2000s and early 2010s, revenue did not decline as quickly; for the 2016–2017 season, broadcast and cable networks saw double-digit increases in advertising rates at the upfronts.[49] Regardless, since the owners of broadcast networks also had cable and web holdings and investments, they had protection from market fluctuations, risk, and thus also innovation.

Centralized control over production kept diversity stagnant among writers and producers, even as the number of scripted series soared to record highs. Women and minorities made indie TV in part because they were not able to get employment in Hollywood. Employment for women and racial minorities barely rose as we entered the networked era: from 2007 to 2014, women composed 27–29 percent and racial minorities just 10–13 percent of all television writers, according to the Writers Guild, despite composing about 50 percent and 36 percent of the U.S. population, respectively.[50] Top writers with more control over story and employment—showrunners and executive producers—were even less diverse, with only 5.5 percent of positions going to minorities in 2013–2014.[51] This was despite the growth in series production and creation of network diversity programs in the wake of the black TV bubble in 1990s.[52] Three years after the Telecommunications Act passed, broadcast networks infamously debuted an all-white season of primetime programs, spurring protests and calls for reform from advocacy groups like the NAACP. In 2006, after UPN merged with the WB, the number of black writers fell sharply and rebounded slowly.[53] From the 2001–2002 to the 2013–2014 TV seasons, the number of black writers actually decreased from 6.1 percent to 5.4 percent, according to the Writers Guild, despite a dramatic increase in scripted series production.[54] Inequalities persist across all positions, including directors, a position that a *Variety* study found white men dominating, notably on cable.[55] By the mid-2010s, industry leaders were openly working to correct the problem: Ava DuVernay, herself a pioneer in networked black film distribution with her ARRAY network, hired only women to direct her cable drama *Queen Sugar*, and FX CEO John Landgraf raised the percentage of women and directors of color on his network from 12 percent in 2014–2015 to 51 percent the next year: "[E]quity matters. . . . There is a privilege in American society to being male and being white, and I think it's hard for white males to understand that privilege, because we've never experienced the opposite," Landgraf told *Variety*.[56]

It is no wonder, as we see in chapters 2 and 3, that women, people of color, and queer producers enthusiastically embraced indie TV. Most of their projects could not make it into or through legacy television development. Deregulation protected legacy TV companies from market fluctuations, and they found ways to profit from niche audiences through cheaper reality programming or by focusing on wealthier audiences, as NBC did successfully in the late 1990s.[57] Corporate development processes make it difficult for executives to satisfy multiple constituencies—producers, brands, and audiences. Balancing what is marketable, engaging, and artistically or culturally valuable, development executives only occasionally satisfy all three criteria, prioritizing marketability and profit potential.

The Value of Open Development

The Internet attracts independent producers because they can make more connections—due to many-to-many networked distribution flows—to develop new and different ways of creating, supporting, and financing new stories than in the legacy system. Open development only creates value when key constituencies can connect: writers who want to tell original stories, crew who want to support its creation, fans who want to engage with it, and sponsors who need those stories to find new customers. In their effort to connect different constituencies, independents shift our understanding of television development away from a top-down, bottom-line-driven activity to serial storytelling supported by fan publics. Of course, since they are developing new intellectual property, web series creators can sell their work to legacy distributors in "development deals," where a network or studio agrees to finance a pilot or order a series. In this way, indie TV is not too different from indie film, where festivals provide spaces for film distributors to buy and license or, as it is colloquially called, "pick up" indie films for mass distribution. Yet open, networked distribution means producers can release productions independently, find audiences, and attract financing without the major studios, distributors, and festivals.

An active independent media market is critical to innovation in a networked era. In the indie TV market, development begins with artists or creators and their ideas. First episodes or seasons of indie TV shows are best thought of as pitches and pilots, which, if successful, can sustain themselves through producer, fan, or brand support. The open TV market intervenes in legacy control over producers in the pitch process, intellectual property and labor once the series airs, what audiences watch through pilot selection and series renewal, the process of monetizing audiences through up-front financing and brand sponsorship, and systems for rewarding series with independent festivals and award shows.

In each segment of the market, indie TV offers an "innovation." Here, I am extending Stuart Cunningham's argument that innovation in creative industries is best defined beyond traditional terms of new products and modes of production to include "the application of those ideas for *realized or potential* economic, social or public benefit."[58] This framing of innovation "provides a value-driven orientation to productivity and, ultimately, quality of life, rather than merely a cost-efficiency driver for intervention," a foil to investment-driven innovation that dominates corporate tech and television development.[59] Our competitive commercial market incentivizes corporations to purchase existing productions and platforms rather than create new ones, as seen in the rise of TV network ownership of individual series (e.g., ABC Studios coproducing with Shonda Rhimes), of companies owning multiple channels (e.g., Disney owning ABC, ESPN, Freeform, etc.), and of media conglomerates purchasing networks of channels across broadcast, cable, and the web (e.g., Comcast owning NBC and Bravo while sharing Hulu with Disney, 21st Century Fox, and Time Warner).

In its ideal, the open TV marketplace values creative producers first, who then inspire fans and sponsors to support new projects. In this way, indie development reorients the value of television away from network intermediaries and toward those who drive the commercial television system with their labor, attention, and capital. Within the open TV market, producers labor to create value for writers, producers, and actors, through ownership of intellectual property, narrative experimentation, and producer-focused organizations like festivals; audiences, through community-shaped and -financed storytelling; and brands, through stories that appeal to communities specific enough for complex and targeted marketing and publicity campaigns.

While online indie TV producers focused on maximizing creative value, legacy TV networks valued advertising volume and price, both threatened by digital distibution.[60] Legacy TV distributors in the United States historically have profited from advertising. Advertising agencies' clients (brands) pay distributors for time (ad slots) within series. Distributors must value this time more than the agencies to command the highest price. By paying for time, brands get the audiences they value more than the network (potential customers), and agencies get fees for brokering the deal, solidifying their relationships with their clients and the legacy networks. As digital technologies allowed audiences to bypass commercial spots, and as ratings on broadcast networks declined due to audiences having more options,[61] brands started to question the value of legacy or linear TV time. The threat—the heart of the television "crisis"—is declining value for advertising from brands and viewership from fans. Both influence each other, driving revenue down, albeit slowly. It is a crisis of commerce, not of television's cultural value. Independent producers flipped the script by releasing shows largely without demanding financing up front, instead seeking it mostly after series have been published openly and have demonstrated some value.

Media studies scholars have explored challenges to legacy network processes in financing, audience behavior, and distribution.[62] Yet scholars have understudied the role of independent production in bridging competing industry stakeholders' needs through alternative practices and values. By considering alternatives to the pilot process, I expose the limits of corporate television's power to raise capital while supporting writers, audiences, and innovation. Lotz argues of proposals to restructure up-front financing that "a different method of purchasing [e.g., an all-'scatter' market] would reallocate capital and value throughout the television industry in ways likely to affect the programming produced."[63] I argue that indie TV creators are already reallocating capital and value, responding to Hollywood's tightening labor market on the supply side along with demand from brands and audiences. As will be shown, the types of narratives independents produce are often different from legacy television, including a consistent theme of individuals struggling and surviving, often humorously, under the pressures of contemporary corporate capitalism.

U.S. scholars and policymakers have not completely understood the breadth of creative industry innovation enabled by open, networked distribution. Creative innovations have been, as Cunningham argues, "hidden."[64] Economists and social scientists, particularly in Australia and the United Kingdom, have attracted attention and investment from governments and universities for arguing that our perspective on innovation gives too much credit to corporations, venture capital, and STEM (science, technology, engineering, and math).[65] As Paul Stoneman argues in his theorization of "soft innovations,"

> To date . . . the concept of innovation has primarily been centred around the scientific or technical, with the significance of new products and processes being judged upon the basis of improvements in functionality (technological product and process [TPP] innovation). Innovation that encompasses the artistic, formal (as in the contrast between form and function), intellectual, or aesthetic, has largely been ignored in the mainstream literature on innovation.[66]

For Stoneman, soft innovations are widespread and manifest in production innovation or differentiation (i.e., changes in creative products like films, music, etc.) or in the "aesthetic/intellectual dimensions of products in other industries" (product design, branding, etc., in noncreative industries).[67] To be sure, STEM fields drove innovation in the late twentieth century, allowing for the creation of tools that independent creators needed to open TV—the Internet and its applications and platforms chief among them. STEM innovations tend to focus on efficiency and scale, yet creative cultural production requires risk and experimentation, which legacy TV distributors have developed processes to minimize. The U.S. market-competition model has proven ineffective at fully valuing the talent and skill of the country's media workers.[68] Thus, the Internet's technical efficiencies and innovation—the focus of most new media studies—cannot alone describe its role in transforming media forms, markets, and institutions. As S. Craig Watkins found in his study of hip hop and black cinema, individuals motivated by broader social, political, and economic conditions "adopt and manipulate technology to accommodate their intentions."[69] Independent producers use networked distribution to develop television on a smaller scale, equally valuable to society but undervalued by the market and state. In networked television, creativity from a broader base of producers, in cooperation with sponsors and fans who participate or fund production,[70] "reverses the increase in scale that has long characterized research and innovation," as participants "undertake large projects on the basis of many small contributions."[71]

Television's indie web producers are innovators taking risks in a creative market whose vast inequalities and new technologies encourage value creation outside of it.[72] Lured by the chance to transform a powerful culture industry, indie producers framed their work as necessary for social change: "[E]conomic risks are socially constructed," as Gina Neff argues of dot-com workers who supplied Silicon Valley with "venture labor."[73] Unlike corporate tech workers, however, independent media workers used the web's technical efficiencies to generate value for themselves, communities, and other market participants amid persistent corporate control over processes of media distribution—product development, financing, and marketing of original series. A broader perspective on innovation would help legislators and reformists "attend to evidence of system failure, not only market failure," and realize how much vitality exists outside risk-averse power centers.[74] In an open, digital economy, we have to study independent production in markets that confound old ideas about media—"television" outside of cable, journalism outside of print, gaming outside of major studios, film without celluloid, radio without broadcasting. At the beginning of the twenty-first century, entertainment businesses look healthy, if we only consider the stock prices and products of conglomerates. A broader view reveals evidence of declining value for producers and consumers but also sources of innovation in the face of systemic revolution or evolution.

How do we integrate and value these markets? Examining indie production directs studies of innovation beyond new products and efficiencies toward the way open markets encourage agents to generate value for society at large. Contemporary media and cultural studies works have been calling for expanded analyses of media production, including Henry Jenkins, Joshua Green, and Sam Ford's *Spreadable Media*, John Caldwell's *Production Culture*, Vicki Mayer's *Below the Line*, Pablo Boczkowski's *Digitizing the News*, Christina Dunbar-Hester's *Low Power to the People*, and Derek Johnson's *Media Franchising*.[75] While I agree with scholars like Angela McRobbie, who argues that "the call to be creative is a potent and highly appealing mode of governmentality . . . whose main effect is to do away with the kind of welfare rights in work by means of eclipsing normal employment altogether," I argue that we need to understand how and why workers engage in this kind of risky work in order to map progressive alternatives.[76] If worker exploitation also exists within the legacy system, we must see what value is created outside of it. Web series are television, despite their development outside of legacy distribution. They represent economic activity but also deliver social and public benefits to workers, citizens, and communities to help them endure the tough cultural economy and forge alternative paths.

Open TV investigates innovation, serving as both an ethnographic production study about market activity and a cultural and political critique of the current American media market. Out of necessity and inadequate resources, indie innovation tends to be more informal than functional, more exploratory than practical. The market for indie scripted comedies and dramas is small, experimental, and fraught compared to that of higher-budget legacy series. But this small corner of the Internet is rich with ideas, producing clear public benefit. For the likes of Adam Goldman and his contemporaries, these benefits could spill over into the larger economy if existing institutions would support them.

Studying Open TV

Open TV is based on one-on-one interviews with writers, producers, exhibitors, and development executives, mostly on the phone, though also in person and occasionally via e-mail. When possible I visited sets, studios, and postproduction offices. I interviewed 136 individuals for *Open TV*, with each interview lasting twenty to ninety minutes. I interviewed a wide array of web series producers, from seasoned TV professionals like Marshall Herskovitz (*thirtysomething*, *My So-Called Life*) to producers unknown to anyone but their few fans. Most of the producers I interviewed share a general orientation toward "professional" scripted series: projects using semitraditional film and television equipment and production roles—director, screenwriters, editors, boom operators, etc. (though it will be shown that those roles are routinely reconfigured). Most of these producers distinguish themselves from "amateur" or "YouTube" creators.[77] Beyond their tendency toward professionalism, they vary widely. I followed producers and marketers of comedies and dramas targeted at advertiser-friendly audiences, as well as those whose series are explicitly aimed at underrepresented (i.e., less advertiser-friendly) audiences. That said, most of the creators profiled in this project have been marginalized by the industry in some way and entered the open TV market because Hollywood undervalues their labor.

I selected the key case studies in this book for the data they could provide: productions lasting more than one season and attracting fans or sponsors offer more insight into how open TV works. At the same time, I supplement these cases with insights from lesser-known or less popular series to show what practices and ideas extend beyond clear successes. Most web series are not clear successes, yet I find continuities in production and distribution practices.

In addition to interviewing producers about their work, I became one myself by coproducing an indie series. Production is as much a methodology as a form of economic activity and cultural critique. I begin each chapter with insight I gained from coproducing, with a small nonprofit, a sitcom, *She's out of Order*, by and about a black female journalist, Tara, played by creator Teresa Lasley. These prologues provide a grounded view of innovation and offer critical insights into the limits of open distribution and independent production. Like most series, our show did not reach as many viewers, or attract as many sponsors or development deals, as we had hoped. Therefore, while key case studies are slightly biased towards successes, *She's out of Order* provides a rare glimpse into the kind of precarious production that typifies the open TV market and how value is nonetheless created.

I used a matrix of news sources for greater context and data on trends in the market. Several blogs have regularly covered the web series market: *Tubefilter* focuses on web series and *GigaOM/NewTeeVee* focused on video in convergence culture. Throughout my research I constantly discovered new sites: *New Media Rockstars* grew quickly with its coverage of YouTubers, and smaller sites and podcasts like *Indie Intertube, Placevine, We Love Soaps* (which had its own award show), and *The Tangled Web We Watch* (*LA Weekly*) made it easier to keep abreast of new series. Major trade magazines and outlets, from *Deadline, The AV Club, Variety*, and *The Hollywood Reporter* to *paidContent* and *MediaPost*, occasionally reported on the market. Mainstream media publications also covered shows on occasion—the *New York Times* and *USA Today* have had regular columns on web video. Niche blogs are crucial to publicizing series to interested audiences. *Shadow and Act* and *Clutch* played pivotal roles in showcasing black web series; *Queerty, AfterElton, AfterEllen, SheWired, Deep Dish*, and *One More Lesbian* were regular champions of gay, lesbian, and queer shows; and *NBC Latino* and *Latino Rebels* published on the Latino market. Meanwhile, many individual members of the web series community, particularly those involved with IAWTV, blog about the market and invite others to comment and debate. A lot of information about the market came from press releases—which, like most releases, rarely get reported. In my research, press releases were useful tools for seeing how video networks and series creators communicated with the public about the importance of their activities.

I found a challenging production market, with frustrated, eager, and often talented people keenly aware of the limits and value of their work. No one was ever getting paid enough, many not at all. Everyone was pressed for time, hungry for recognition, and taking on considerable personal and financial risk. Yet in the open TV market, I also saw innovation.

The open TV market is a robust and complicated media world, complete with a rich history of development (which I explore in chapter 1), innovations in production (chapter 2), representation (chapter 3), distribution (chapter 4), and a rising tide of conglomeration (chapter 5). Chapter 1 focuses on the history of the "web series," how producers and organizations excluded from legacy television development used the Internet to create models for narrating and financing new stories. In chapter 2, I chronicle the greater degrees of creative freedom and fulfillment producers had in the market. I show how indie producers experimented with giving both talent and audiences creative input, giving writers more creative control and integrating cultural identity into production and storytelling. These production contexts supported narratives better attuned to the lives of those historically excluded from legacy TV, particularly black, Latino, gay, and lesbian populations, explored in chapter 3. In chapter 4, I show more agency for producers working with distributors, exhibitors, and brands that adapted legacy models for series release, recognition, and financing. Independent web channels and awards institutions arose to curate stories for fans, sponsors, and critics. They worked to be more accountable to producers and fan communities than legacy TV, even if a lack of resources often impeded their efficacy.

Chapter 5 explores the "scaling" of web television—the growth of corporate online distributors like Netflix, Hulu, and YouTube's "multichannel networks" (MCNs) that bundle channels from hundreds of creators. These networked TV distributors harness the web's vast information capacities to create epic productions or massive collections of small productions with dedicated audiences, or what I call "big data television." Corporate web TV distributors support some independent creators but focus on delivering high margins to shareholders, replicating legacy television's development inequalities by focusing on increasing scales of production.

The open TV market may not survive the growth of the video economy. This is a problem for those who have seen how the web democratizes distribution. If we want fair marketplaces in the twenty-first century, we have to start with what workers and consumers desire and what benefits society at large, not just corporate intermediaries. In the epilogue, I interrogate the networked television era and introduce my next research project: Open TV (beta), a platform for queer television designed as a system intervention. Independents have changed the channel. Will we watch and listen?

1

Developing Open TV

Innovation for the Open Network, 1995–2005

How did the Internet become television for Hollywood, Silicon Valley, and independent agents? Announcing American Cybercast (AMCY), one of the most significant early web TV channels, former cable television executive Sheri Herman imagined in 1996 a clear shift from television to the web: "[E]yeballs that once were in front of the TV are now in front of a PC."[1] AMCY debuted to attract and profit from those eyeballs in all the ways legacy networks do: licensing original series, promoting them to fans, and courting interest from advertisers to finance more. AMCY positioned itself as television, and yet its shows were not video based but rather text based. Even without video, Herman still believed web distribution could rapidly transform television development: "The system has proven it works. The networks still have a lock on the business, but they also gave birth to the dozens of channels on cable TV. . . . The gateway model will work on the Internet because of the absolute proliferation of content. People want choice, but network-branded content can help sort out all the choices."[2] Herman tried to reconcile the advantages of networked distribution, its breadth of production and greater consumer choice, with the advantages of legacy television's billion-dollar, advertiser-based business model. Throughout the 1990s and into the 2000s, executives like Herman differentiated the web from legacy network development practices by emphasizing greater choices for consumers and freedom for creators. They bet that preaching creative freedom, diversity, and choice could entice brands to shift campaign funds from legacy television to the new, open network.

AMCY betrayed these ideals by growing too quickly and top-heavily. Although they started with a mission to "husband their resources and grow slowly over a period of years, perfecting their shows, allowing the technology and business models to work out," they decided to "build rapidly" and shoot for an initial public offering, which never materialized.[3] Intense competition for small amounts of advertising, attention from passionate fan communities, and large investments for digital projects pushed networks like AMCY toward amassing scale and away from nurturing those who are essential to open TV series development: producers and fans, whose freedom and choice were essential to their pitch as better than television. Indeed, open TV distribution historically favors ingenious programs that producers can execute cheaply, fans can engage with immediately, or brands can use to tell more nuanced stories than in thirty-second spots on linear television.

How then does one distribute television via open, networked protocols? Legacy media companies like ABC grew into television "networks" by connecting broadcast stations across the United States in a tightly controlled system of licensing airwaves; owning and operating a station was costly and regulated. The Internet is different; its network is wider, with more access points. It is networked. By the mid-1990s, access to the web became available to the public, prompting media companies to experiment with ways to serve audiences entertainment through networked, peer-to-peer distribution. Entrepreneurs have been trying to develop television for the open network since it went public in the 1990s, long before streaming video. Most efforts lasted just a few years, as expected for new markets experiencing rapid innovation, particularly when venture-backed projects transferred legacy practices wholesale to the web.

In general, innovative open TV networks, start-ups, and programs harnessed the web's decentralized nature of distribution—as opposed to legacy networks' centralized distribution—to support a broader base of producers and fan communities than legacy television did. Web TV network executives and entrepreneurs adapted perceived weaknesses in legacy television: network control over monetizing viewers (namely, marketing and up-front buying) and the development system (namely, the pilot process and ownership and licensing of programs). The web opened the door to companies and individuals outside Hollywood, in Silicon Valley specifically and throughout the United States more generally, to experiment with series development. An unequal competition between distribution technologies ensued. Media conglomerates combined assets via mergers and acquisitions and refocused legacy television channels on owning intellectual property, reducing costs, and maintaining as much control as possible over audience attention.[4] Stakeholders who lost power and access in this period—independent producers and brands—flocked to a new distribution portal that could one day surpass television. While broadcast networks have released and produced web programs since the beginning, some of the greatest, most enduring innovations came from those disadvantaged in the legacy system.

This chapter explores the history of episodic web programming—variously called web series, webisodes, bitcoms, web television, and, in its earliest form, cybersoaps—as producers and entrepreneurs developed channels and programs indebted to but also distinct from legacy television.[5] From the time the Internet became available to most consumers, companies from Microsoft and NBC to independent production outfits and advertising firms have consistently declared the web the newest form of television. "Television" became a malleable concept through which Hollywood insiders, outsiders, financial backers, and artistic leaders expressed their hopes of media domination in a period of technological change and conglomeration among entertainment corporations. What they often meant was that the Internet would eventually amass a large, dedicated audience they could sell to advertisers to finance new productions outside the major studios.

New media markets emerge slowly and progress unevenly. From the telephone, radio, and film to the earliest forms of television, each medium has developed in fits and starts, responding to industrial, political, and cultural shifts. In new media moments, independents attempt to master new distribution technologies, promoting the possibility, however improbable, that the new medium might accommodate a broader base of producers and communities.[6] The writers, executives, and producers of web entertainment are very aware of this history. Press accounts of new web series in the 1990s are littered with references to the early days of television and radio. The trajectory they describe is simple and inevitable: scrappy beginnings to market dominance and cultural hegemony for a small group of players. Despite the common narrative, this did not happen as quickly as open TV's early entrepreneurs predicted. Instead, the largest surge in series production started over ten years after most Americans could access the web, long after large corporations and Hollywood producers like Steven Spielberg had attempted to turn the new distribution platform into television. The story behind that surge, starting shortly after YouTube's 2005 debut and lasting until the 2013 premiere of traditionally formatted comedies and dramas on corporate web channels (Netflix, Amazon, Hulu), composes the bulk of this book.

This chapter is organized in four parts, grouped both thematically and chronologically. In the first section I briefly explore why television became a frame through which web producers viewed their efforts. I then narrate the development of web programming in roughly four key periods from 1995 to 2011: the 1995–1999 beginnings and first boom, when excitement over the web led to multimedia experimentation; the period preceding and following the dot-com bust; the 2000–2005 period, when short-form comedy and short films created by producers and curated by brands and networks seemed best positioned to revolutionize TV programming; and the post-YouTube era starting in 2006, in which streaming video developed and a broader base of producers created filmed content. The chapter concludes with what the history of web programming says about the possibility and meaning of innovation in television.

The Web after Television

Why television? At the time of the Internet's introduction to the public, television was undergoing a revolution. Despite periodic shifts in business practices, the transition to cable made clear the stability of the "network era" of the 1950s through the 1970s—what we commonly understand as "television," with its tight, central control of advertising and content—and opened the door to the "networked" era of the new millennium. This period of instability, the "multichannel transition" of the 1980s and 1990s as narrated by Lotz and John Ellis, marked a transition from mass audiences and scarce programming to niche audiences and available programming through pay cable (versus free, "over the air" broadcast). Television has expanded and fractured, from its production to its content and the ways in which its practitioners and executives understand and organize audiences. Television today can no longer hold one theory: "Now it presents a diffuse and extensive process of working through. This takes the form of a constant worrying over issues and emotions . . . the presentation of a riot of ways of understanding the world without ever coming to any final conclusions."[7] This process of "working through" has been documented by scholars like Henry Jenkins,[8] John Caldwell,[9] Vicki Mayer,[10] and Amanda Lotz,[11] but few scholars have examined the myriad ways in which web-based producers participated in this process by creating programming that borrowed from genres and formats established in the classic network era while experimenting with new storytelling and distribution practices from other media and technologies.

New media producers organized networked television in similar ways to network television, including adopting many of its genres and its tradition of serialization, to keep new audiences consuming on a regular basis. They also borrowed legacy television's core business practices, including the formation of networks, sponsorship, branded entertainment, and licensing programs. Genres made web programming intelligible to viewers as TV. Dominant genres grew and declined as the online markets changed, as producers responded to technological and funding changes, and as fans directed their interests to new storytelling experiments. Producers and networks invested in genres based on their need to raise money, raise cultural awareness, or conform to technological constraints: "[W]e need to ask what a genre means *for specific groups in a particular cultural instance.*"[12] For web creators in each period outlined in this chapter, different genres took on particular significance according to a range of factors: soaps in the 1990s gained prominence as companies sought to capitalize on the genre's declining audiences on linear TV and harness serial dramas' ability to attract regular viewers to a new medium; sitcoms and animation became popular in the early 2000s as technology allowed streaming video but bandwidth was still limited; and a broad range of programs took off in the late 2000s as new networks premiered and advertisers financed video to target various niches.

Web shows combine the modus operandi of scripted television programming (series and serialization) with new formats (primarily shortform, due to fewer resources and perceptions of audience attention). With the exception of events, specials, and movies, most television programs are structured around a series, ranging from the nightly news to weekly sitcoms and sports. Serialization, connecting narratives from episode to episode, has been an enduring and profitable staple, particularly with drama.[13] The series and its serialization provide television its stability: narratives without closure keep viewers engaged.[14] This lures advertisers in search of consumer attention.

Television's standard formats, half-hour and hour-long runtimes interspersed with ad spots, were not common on the web until later in its development, when NBC, Fox, and ABC banded together to create Hulu to combat the piracy of their programs on YouTube and exercise greater control over their content. The original text-based web programs arose from producers' need to relate long narratives with consumers possessing relatively slow modems, while the later trend of short, comedic videos and cartoons reflected the need for cost efficiency on the production side and a similar efficiency on the reception side as modem speeds climbed. If there is a consistent aesthetic of early web programs, it is, in the words of Max Dawson, an "aesthetic of efficiency, characterized by streamlined exposition, discontinuous montage and ellipsis, and decontextualized narrative of visual spectacle."[15] Producers needed to be efficient because the potential payout was low, often nothing at all. Throughout the 2000s, advertising agencies shifted campaign funds very slowly to web-based distributors, and even more slowly to web video (most ads were text and image, not moving image).

The web as a home to short-form, "cheap" programming is largely a result of technology. As bandwidths have increased, so have episode lengths and narrative complexity. By 2012, enough Americans had broadband for web-original full-length (twenty-two- and forty-four-minute) episodes to premiere on channels like Hulu and Netflix in 4K "ultra high definition" streaming. The Pew Research Center's Internet & American Life Project found that broadband quickly outpaced dial-up: in 2013, 70 percent of Americans had broadband at home, compared to just 3 percent in 2000.[16] Program length, like genres, has ebbed and flowed. Early text-based stories were not limited by runtime, only by how quickly fans could read. The advent of streaming video introduced runtimes to online video: "Viewers could watch video as it was being transmitted rather than having to wait for the completion of the entire process. Because of Microsoft's aggressive pre-installation of streaming video players, they quickly became an indispensable accessory to personal computers."[17] While some of the early 2000s animated projects were rather short (under five minutes), high-profile projects existed with higher production value and longer runtimes (e.g., BMW's *The Hire*). Still, the dominance of the short format had a number of effects. Most importantly, it encouraged a diverse group of producers excited about cheaper production, and it contributed to the discourse of the web as "low quality," since brevity worked best with brash—often infantile—forms of comedy.

Outsider efforts to reinvent television coincided with persistent anxiety among legacy development executives over who audiences were and what they wanted, starting in the 1990s as new media technologies—games and virtual reality, cable, DVRs, VHS, and DVDs—gave audiences more choices and as legacy networks' "tight-fisted grip on their domestic audience had slipped."[18] Audience construction has been an essential function of financing media since the advent of advertising. Audience construction grew in sophistication throughout the 1970s and 1980s, as advertisers armed with more information looked for opportunities to sell to various audience segments, mostly defined by age and gender but also by sexuality and race.[19] Despite these goals, television audiences have been "an imaginary entity, an abstraction constructed from the vantage point of the institutions, in the interest of the institutions."[20] For entrepreneurs and indie producers, the Internet, with its ability to combine interpersonal communication, multimedia elements, and entertainment programming, was an antidote to the crudeness of legacy television's audience construction. Viewers' desires and vernacular practices could be seen and measured on an integrated platform, and short-form content, rapidly consumed on slower information lines, would allow for greater "engagement," rendering plain audience taste and disposition. Anxiety over audience value and retention was at the core of television's crisis as legacy networks entered the networked era. Mass audiences, along with mass distribution, are at the center of legacy television's identity, "because of the necessity for programs to be widely shared within the culture."[21] The Internet became television freed from its legacy of mass marketing.

Web production developed as the once-stable legacy TV business gradually morphed and fragmented. In the 1990s, organizations producing for the web relied heavily on TV traits—genre (soap), serialization (heavily serialized content), business (web extensions of on-air shows, sponsorship)—but with some experimentation, mostly in distribution and exhibition—i.e., where audiences might engage with brand-sponsored content. With bandwidth speeds low, producers could not replicate precisely the linear TV experience, so they created multimedia experiences, integrating text, photo, video, and audience participation. During the second phase of web programming development from 2000 to 2005, ideas about television expanded as cable channels started producing original shows. Even after the 2000 dot-com bust initially scuttled online development, producers continued to experiment with television form, moving into Flash animation and brash and ambitious short-form video, while leaning heavily on television's core business practice of creating channels to curate programs (the rise of "netcasting," to be explained). After 2005, widespread adoption of broadband Internet and the debut of open-upload platforms like YouTube spurred a broader swathe of indie producers and entrepreneurs to create original programming and channels, reimagining television as more open, diffuse and niche driven. As the next section indicates, one cannot understand the transformation of television at the turn of the century without the companion story of web production.

Tweaking Television, 1995 to 1999

In 1997, NBC made an entree into online storytelling with a companion web series to one of its marquee procedurals. *Homicide: Second Shift,* considered the first major web series from a legacy network, was a year-long experiment in networked storytelling, with interactive games and TV/web crossover characters and plots. A spokesman at the time told *USA Today* that NBC saw the web as the future, a way to strengthen television as ratings declined: "You're in the same milieu, the same genre, getting the same kind of look and feel that you come to appreciate on air. . . . But now we're extending that experience where fans can go online . . . and extend their connection with these new stories and new characters. They can participate in the investigation of a mystery and then try to unravel clues."[22] As spin, this statement positions *Homicide* as a silver bullet for a new medium, one that replicates television—"the same genre . . . the same kind of look and feel"—but delivers added bonuses, primarily audience interaction. It perfectly encapsulates much of the discourse on web series at the time: the new medium was television but also not. "This is a distinct medium, not television," NBC digital productions head Edmond Sanctis said in the same article.[23] The "not television" aspect was important. *Homicide: Second Shift* had little video, and used text-based cues and on-set photography to tell the story of the "second shift" of detectives of creator David Simon's show. *Homicide* was essentially a serialized novel, a century-old form of storytelling, with additional elements to keep readers interested. How did it become valuable to a television network?

When the web was new and legacy television in flux—but still relatively strong—individuals and companies producing for the web relied heavily on TV's most stable traits, while experimenting where they had to: in aesthetics. Thus, producers made online experiences with varied audience engagement within enduring serial genres—soaps and mysteries—securing audiences and extending traditional network brands online.

The question of why the Internet became a new kind of television for Hollywood and Silicon Valley is crucial for understanding why scores of producers would spend millions creating web programming from 1995 until the present. Contrary to claims that the Internet democratized production from its start, many early productions came out of conglomerates and well-connected independent media companies and firms. The text-based stories of the mid- to late 1990s often cost tens of thousands of dollars to sustain, with resources coming not from Random House or Hachette, but from America Online, MGM, Microsoft, and Lifetime, as well as aspiring directors and TV writers, bringing together the marketing muscle of the country's largest cultural producers and distributors. This period in new media history is often framed as a failure, most likely because so much money was lost after the dot-com bubble burst in early 2000. NBC axed much of its online staff not long after the *Homicide* series ended.[24] Yet it was also a period of tremendous innovation, creating stories hundreds of thousands of people read, watched, and interacted with.

By 1995, tech companies like Microsoft and America Online (AOL) started to create new entertainment channels for the web, while big movie studios and legacy television networks were creating promotional websites for franchises. Still, it was boutique ad agency Fattal and Collins's *The Spot*, an episodic soap in the style of *The Real World* or *Melrose Place*, that gave the web its first hit series. The first phase of web programming saw numerous, fascinating experiments like *The Spot*, visibly "not television" while relying on television genres, serialization, and business practices (sponsorship, primarily). Soap operas and mysteries allowed producers from within and outside the industry to tweak television for audiences and advertisers in a shifting marketplace.

The Spot was the first major project from creator Scott Zakarin, whose Prophecy Entertainment was a subsidiary of Fattal and Collins, since his first feature film went to Cannes in 1989. In a significant shift from his roots in cinema, *The Spot* was a text-based series about the lives of a group of twenty-somethings living in a Los Angeles beach house. Coinciding with the rise of blogs, *The Spot* featured individual web pages or diaries for each of the house's roommates. An early *Variety* article likened it to a magazine, but said it had "what in a film or TV show would be called production values."[25] Limited by traffic constraints on the web, each page included text, photos, and, eventually, short videos.[26] All this cost $500,000 to start and up to $100,000 a month to sustain, which it did through lucrative sponsorships by top brands like Hugo Boss, Honda, K-Swiss, and Sony Pictures.[27] The show, produced in-house at an ad agency, became popular rather quickly, logging hundreds of thousands of visitors a day. Like *lonelygirl15* ten years later, *The Spot* also benefitted from initial confusion over whether or not the characters were real, and user engagement was high. It ran for two years, winning the first Webby for a site in 1996. It spawned a companion book and eventually provided the catalyst for American Cybercast, which secured investments from the likes of Creative Artists Agency (CAA) and Intel Corp.

As for why the trade press depicted *The Spot* as the cutting edge of television, as opposed to magazines or literature, there were numerous reasons. The simplest answer was its serialization in regular installments, an old concept whose contemporary (profitable) equivalent was TV. As Hollywood aspirants, however, Zakarin and his collaborators actively compared their efforts to television, touting the web's interactivity as an innovation akin to "the early days of radio and television": "If you want to yell at your TV set because Heather Locklear is going to sleep with the wrong guy on *Melrose Place*, she's not going to listen to you, but if you say, Tara [a lead on *The Spot*], don't do that, she just might listen," he told *The Record* in 1996.[28] He was not the only one. Dean Vallas, creator of *Whodunit*, another important serialized mystery series from 1995, positioned his series as reinventing television as an industry, not just an art form: "All these media mergers, they're just rearranging the deck chairs on the Titanic. . . . We don't have to plead with a network to get it on the air, or get the 8 p.m. time slot. We can go straight to the audience."[29] In what would become a familiar move in the late 2000s, Vallas started his own channel, called the NETwork, to release independent shows funded through advertisers and sponsors, but it never took off. Even as he sought to lead a TV revolution, Vallas and many other cybersoap producers proposed more evolutionary tactics that nonetheless positioned producers and audiences as key agents in series development.

From film studios' interest in radio in the 1920s and television in the 1940s to their subsequent interest in cable, pay cable, and VHS, new media have both frightened and also spurred interest from Hollywood.[30] The 1990s rise of cable programming precipitated a slow siphoning of younger viewers from NBC, ABC, and CBS that would continue through the 2000s. Threats to legacy television business sparked interest in the web from its executives. In news stories, legacy TV executives continually cited the Internet as another cause for ratings declines, particularly for daytime soaps, which is why NBC quickly signed a deal with Zakarin and partner Troy Bolotnick to do a web series and script a pilot.[31] Early on, legacy broadcast distributors embraced the web, hoping not to be left behind, while Warner Bros., Paramount, and MGM studios created "interactive" divisions.[32] Text-based web stories served media conglomerates' broader, conservative mission to diversify by buying out competition and owning programming, made easier by the Telecommunications Act of 1996, which loosened ownership restrictions across the media industries, including ownership of TV channels and individual programs. Their efforts were not limited to the Internet, as they included games, CD-ROMs, and various digital "walled gardens" like NBC's SuperNet and most of AOL. All these production-side efforts spawned digital experiences aesthetically different from on-air ones, like *The Spot* and *Whodunit*, but they nonetheless supported Hollywood conglomerates, nearly all of which had ties to the legacy, on-air business. "Hollywood," moreover, extends beyond content providers and distributors: even talent agencies like CAA, barred from investing in legacy networks to avoid conflicts of interest, took advantage of the less regulated Internet when it invested millions in new media network American Cybercast.[33] As Todd Gitlin theorizes, the business of television is plagued with uncertainty, and digital convergence merely provides another reason to worry: "Uncertainty is the permanent condition of show business. . . . As soon as capital pays lip service to risk (for which profit is its just reward), it gets busy trying to minimize it."[34] This sense of uncertainty historically motivates the industry to develop new technologies. As Janet Wasko writes about Hollywood's relationship to technological innovation: "[T]here were a variety of reasons why the industry was not always successful in initially dominating or controlling these new technologies but there was nearly always great interest in the possibilities of exploiting them and some successful efforts to do so."[35]

Meanwhile, the perceived weaknesses of the legacy television business enticed dozens of noninstitutionalized producers to enter the market, many of them small communications, advertising, and production companies with well-heeled conglomerate and private investors. *The Spot* inspired many to copy both its premise and the format, especially after the NBC deal. For most of these smaller creators, the web represented a purer, less expensive (though still quite pricey) form for television that bypassed legacy intermediaries. "You don't have to sell it to anyone but the audience," said a representative from Marinex Communications, which produced *The East Village*, often referred to as *The Spot*'s East Coast equivalent.[36] The exciting rhetoric of remaking television spawned a diverse array of programming from producers small and large, including the gay series *Gay Daze*; sci-fi shows like *Madeleine's Mind* and *The Pyramid*; traditional soaps like *As the Web Turns*, a play on classic legacy drama *As the World Turns*; youth-oriented *Spot* riffs like *The Squat* and *Virtual Dorm*; and interactive experiments like *Ferndale*, a show about a therapy group that encouraged audiences to work through their personal issues. By mid-1996, an estimated sixty cybersoaps were online, though probably there were many more that were unable to get the trade press's attention.[37] Niche targeting through series, by then a common practice on linear TV, along with continuities to TV in genre, gave web producers enough television-like security to counteract their text-based peculiarities.

That said, web programs broke with TV's traditions by utilizing features only available online that supported greater producer creativity and further enabled fan participation and engagement. Cybersoaps enticed the press with their ability to incorporate audience interaction with producers through nonlinear storytelling. Press reports highlighted interactive features, primarily e-mailing and chatting with characters and producers, who adapted plots to the opinions of viewers.[38] *The East Village*, which eventually coaxed Time Warner into publishing and selling ads for the series on its Pathfinder website, featured music for users while they browsed, "micro-dramas" they could download, and "cliques" they could join with the characters, giving them access to rumors and insider information other viewers would not receive.[39] *KAPOW*, a mystery series, incorporated live theater and real-world participation at events like the Republican National Convention; other series like *Union2* were photo heavy, or photonovellas. Such innovations fit comfortably within the rhetoric that legacy television needed reform: "It's never going to be completely passive, not like television. But it gives people something that television can't," an *East Village* spokesperson said in 1996.[40]

The importance of the soap opera genre cannot be overstated. Soaps became important to radio in the 1930s because of their effectiveness in selling domestic products; this continued on television in the late 1950s and 1960s.[41] Robert Allen notes how soaps were integral to broadcast television's pre-Internet competitor, cable: "As the economic hegemony of the three American commercial television networks has been challenged by new technologies, soap operas have become programming innovations used by cable television services to lure viewers."[42] Soap operas' ability to hook audiences into narratives, through which sponsors can sell products, have made them integral to the success of new media, even as they remain one of the United States' oldest media genres.

The immersive, immediate quality of serialized web video lends itself to fan participation and spreadability, as users share cultural products to reflect on themselves and spark conversations in their communities.[43] But participation is contextual and *The Spot* arose early, in a less corporate web TV market. "The ways in which people can connect with each other is revolutionary," said Marshall Herskovitz, co-creator of *thirysomething, My So-Called Life*, and the short-lived 2007 web series, *Quarterlife*, which premiered online to much fanfare only to be canceled once NBC aired it to low ratings. In the post-YouTube marketplace, scripted series producers have used direct address and social media platforms and functionality to engage fans and sell them to sponsors. Zakarin's work presages the rise of social media platforms and scripted/vlog hybrid series. As web video entered its third phase after YouTube, having attractive women engage users directly—direct address—became a trend: mostly popularly with *lonelygirl15*, then with Marshall Herskovitz and Edward Zwick's *Quarterlife*, NBC's *Gemini Division*, MTV's *Valemont*, Day's *The Guild*, and Pemberley Digital's *Lizzie Bennet Diaries*, the first of five vlog adaptations of late-nineteenth-century novels with women protagonists. In her study of the *Lizzie Bennet Diaries*, Louisa Stein finds it "works within and plays with the language and logic of YouTube vlogging culture and millennial fandom," exuding at key moments an "expansive, mediated emotional intimacy" emblematic of what she calls the millennial "culture of feels" among its young women fans.[44] Many of the post-YouTube serial hits are extensions of Zakarin's gendered address, crafted to appeal to men who desire women or with the presumption that women will see themselves in the leads; as in legacy television, normative gender appeals dominate and sexuality is largely heterosexual, such that not until *Carmilla*, a 2014 vampire drama sponsored by feminine-hygiene brand Kotex, did vlog series explicity explore queer sexuality.

The praise of the cybersoap in the 1990s as a new and better form of television was consistently tempered by its obvious limitations. Users needed specific technology, both hardware and software, to view some of the stories' nonserialized extras. The need for certain processors, browsers, and media players (by Real and Microsoft) were all cited as reasons for the form's eventual demise. "Unlike TV, they make certain demands of their audiences," the *Globe and Mail* lamented.[45] Audiences for a few series were respectable, given these limits. Both *The Spot* and *East Village* drew in "thousands" of weekly viewers—up to fifty thousand by some estimates. High costs and declining advertiser interest eventually caused most to shutter by the end of the 1990s. Nonetheless, these constraints advanced innovations by early web producers and introduced audiences to the possibility of television outside of the legacy networks.

As both the dot-com market and cybersoap production expanded, efforts to tweak television redoubled. For a brief moment, web-based channels emerged online from legacy and non-TV companies alike, both looking to curate audiences as their options multiplied across cable and web entertainment. The creation of independent TV channels online reemerged in fuller force in the early 2000s at the same time as legacy television channels took a brief hiatus from web development after the dot-com bust. In the late-1990s, Internet ventures built on the genre-driven stories of 1995 and 1996 by organizing them with channels, looking for continuity between the new medium and the old through distribution. However, most of these would not survive due to lack of advertising, which legacy television distributors still dominated through the upfronts and established institutional relationships. While web distribution offered opportunities for creators to release new stories and audiences to experience those stories in new ways, effective development remained the province of legacy, linear media.

At its peak in late 1996, *The Spot* encouraged companies and entrepreneurs to increase their involvement in the web, creating channels and putting more original programs on preexisting properties. Perhaps the most ambitious of these efforts was American Cybercast (AMCY), which aimed to be "the Web's first episodic entertainment network." Premiering in October 1996, by November it was laying off staff and by January it filed for Chapter 11 bankruptcy.

The stories of these short-lived channels show how the fervor for new media technologies—the belief that they can replace and improve legacy media—often meets the cold realities of the market, where consumers and financiers adapt too slowly to technologies and replicating previous business models fails to work. AMCY's rapid rise represented large companies trying to cash in on comparatively cheap entertainment and establish early dominance in a new medium. AMCY counted as investors CAA, cable television provider Tele-Communications Inc., investment bank Allen & Co., and Japanese media company Softbank. It also attracted major Hollywood players, including former Columbia Picture TV head Scott Siegler as its president.[46] Additionally, it had major advertisers, including Sony, Kodak, Apple, Toyota, and Visa. Yet among AMCY's missteps was its implementation of an "old media" bureaucracy: hiring "executives upon executives"—mirroring developments in newly deregulated legacy television—without focusing on production and reception.[47] Critics claimed that the network had forsaken the storytelling of its marquee series (*The Spot*) by adding too many additional shows, a planned fifteen.[48] All in all, AMCY tried to become a full-fledged television channel too quickly, and its investors, previously shut out of becoming major television players, were too bullish about the pace of media change. "The real problem seems to be that AMCY believed its own hype," one critic said at the time. "The company seemed to buy all that stuff about the Web replacing TV. They started to talk about themselves as a channel."[49]

Yet AMCY's demise did little to slow legacy networks' interest in programming for the web, and, weeks after AMCY's bankruptcy filing, NBC announced it was creating *Homicide: Second Shift*. NBC part-owned *Homicide: Life on the Street*, which is why they opted to try original programming online. Other networks like CBS and Fox did not follow suit. For the next year, NBC created online offshoots of a number of other series it coproduced, including *Profiler* and *The Pretender*, in addition to *Nash Bridges*. *Dawson's Creek*'s web content built on on *Second Shift*'s narrative innovations but invited greater fan participation: *Dawson's Desktop* took fans into the minds and proclivities of the characters.[50] Anxious about the web as a new challenge to television, legacy network executives squeezed out as much value as they could through brand sponsorships and ambitious crossover storylines between the TV and online shows. "We believe we've got to get in the game because we don't know where it's going," said NBC Entertainment president Warren Littlefield, underscoring the sense of exploration and uncertainty with which networks like NBC approached the web.[51] Unlike AMCY, however, NBC had the benefit of preexisting franchises with built-in audiences and advertiser relationships, and the emphasis on creating synergies on the cheap: NBC's web programming was light on props and sets.[52]

While NBC and other legacy channels like Lifetime, HBO, and Showtime produced small projects from within Hollywood, tech conglomerates looking to break into entertainment programming invested heavily, resulting in new partnerships between Hollywood and Silicon Valley, or "Siliwood."[53] Tech companies hired film and legacy TV executives to create and curate programming for new ventures. Intel created an Intercast system that brought live television to computer screens. Bell Atlantic hired *Aeon Flux* producer Japhet Asher to create programming for its video/transmedia project Tele-TV, which never aired. Sony created the Station, which featured some original dramas and soaps along with websites for popular game shows *Wheel of Fortune* and *Jeopardy*.

By far the most ambitious efforts to break into online entertainment came from Microsoft and AOL, both of which spent hundreds of millions of dollars creating web-based channels to compete online. AOL's Greenhouse Networks bought Scott Zakarin's Lightspeed Media and launched Entertainment Asylum, run by powerful television executive Brandon Tartikoff and Zakarin. "Conquering and co-opting Hollywood was what the Entertainment Asylum was all about," wrote John Geirland and Eva Sonesh Kedar in their definitive account of late-1990s Siliwood.[54] AOL produced mostly nonscripted programming focused on celebrities and news, while adding some more creative programs like Zakarin's *Grape-Jam*, a comedy site. An expensive venture in "interactive webcasting," incorporating live video and chat with movie premieres, interviews, and oddball programming, Asylum did not last long. It was expensive, and Tartikoff's sudden death before its launch did little to help.[55] Meanwhile, Microsoft started working towards television as early 1994, seeing its Microsoft Network as a way to eke out more profits and challenge television—MSN's use of the terms "network" and "channels" was deliberate.[56] But the effort to produce programming through M³P (Microsoft Multimedia Productions) proved expensive and unpopular, and by early 1998, MSN shuttered as an entertainment network. At its peak it carried thirty shows, mostly nonscripted but including a few soaps.[57]

MSN's demise was the beginning of the end for many large-scale web entertainment initiatives. "Original programming dried up with the demise of Microsoft Network," one Sony executive said in 1998.[58] Once major media companies realized that online profits were years away and legacy television was still relatively strong, many packed up and cut their losses, a trend accelerated by the dot-com bust. In the meantime, smaller entrepreneurs, individual advertisers, and even a few amateurs filled the vacuum.

Pushing Television with More Producers and Channels, 2000–2005

As they approached the new millennium, producers and entrepreneurs moved on from tweaking television to trying to push it forward by showcasing a broader, more diverse base of producers making shows for more varied niche communities. After early web programming adapted to the web's recognizable genres, and its practices of curation and serialization, the next phase of online programming emerged as core legacy television businesses faced more uncertainty, and bandwidth speeds gradually increased. This led to increased experiments in comedy, less dependence on serialization, and more one-off shorts, along with netcasting.

A visit to the Sync's website in early 1998 led users to a limited but eclectic slate of programming: the Aikman Film Archive, showcasing classic horror films in the public domain like *Nosferatu* (1922) and *The Cabinet of Dr. Caligari* (1920); the Sync Online Film Festival, where viewers could watch shorts from the festival circuit; *CyberLove*, a dating talk show; and the *JenniShow*, a twice-weekly vlog from the famed Internet lifecaster Jennifer Ringley and her webcam, *JenniCam*. "ABC could not have come up with the JenniCam," Sync cofounder Carla Cole told the *Washington Post* in a lengthy profile. "[T]he Internet stars are going to be more accessible to their audiences," her partner Thomas Edwards added.[59]

As the dot-com bubble came close to bursting, open TV entrepreneurs started to push television beyond its previous aesthetic tweaks, incorporating a broader array of producers and a simpler, edgier form of video (webcamming or vlogging). Encouraged by users' steady adoption of the web and large companies' investments, entrepreneurs like Cole and Edwards started flocking to the web in the late 1990s. Like Microsoft and AOL, they had a mission to replicate television for the web, yet they also wanted to open it up to a wider array of producers, stars, and genres: from gay Sync star and pioneering vlogger Terry Crummit, aka SnackBoy, to independent filmmakers looking for distribution for their shorts. The Sync would eventually become a leading "netcaster," a trend that would boom and bust between 1999 and 2002. But unlike its progeny in vlogs, discussed in the next section, the Sync integrated into its mission to reinvent television a desire to incorporate outsiders, a narrative the mainstream media picked up:

> Though megamedia monsters are rushing headlong onto the Internet. . . . They are liable to get lost in the lotus fields. This is, after all, the medium of the common man. . . . In fact, anybody with a few thousand dollars worth of machinery and a killer idea can be a player on the Internet. Some of the smartest, tartest material is being fashioned by folks who are not in it for the money or the mass audience, but just for the hell of it.[60]

Accounts like these reflected the story of web "democratization." The advent of video streaming along with broadband diffusion refocused the utopian rhetoric of the web as enabling a broader base of producers, who created not for advertisers or expected audience size, but for the art of it or the connection to fans (a false dichotomy, as the Sync was a business like any network). Webcamming, performed by individuals who streamed their lives, reached a peak in the late 1990s.[61] The Sync and related efforts turned webcamming—a starker aesthetic genre break than soaps and mysteries—into a kind of television, with regularly scheduled, short-form episodes curated for advertisers and sponsors.

The Sync was not alone. Numerous networks aspired to reinvent television in slightly more dramatic ways. Pseudo.com had eight "channels" of reality-based programming, with hip hop DJs injecting product placement into programs, along with a similar relationship show: "When Evil D says 'Buy Sprite,'" Pseudo CEO Josh Harris explained, "it's far more powerful than when Michael Jordan says 'Buy Sprite' to our audience."[62] Here we see independent web channel executives focusing on the connections fans have to new media producers who have creative control. Meanwhile, TV on the web purported to give users serious programming in the style of C-SPAN. The audiences for these online channels, many based far outside Hollywood in places like Maryland and Virginia, spanned from the tens of thousands to the low millions, according to their founders' public statements. These were small audiences by television standards, but there was hope, if little evidence, that smaller Internet audiences could be monetized.

Entrepreneurs also held out hope that smaller films had a market online. This was the premise behind AtomFilms, which started as an independent netcaster distributing short films and animation. It eventually became the channel that film studios and brands would look to for the next wave of televised content. AtomFilms, which became AtomShockwave and then Atom before Viacom-owned Comedy Central folded it into the cable channel's online brand in 2013,[63] was an early entrant bringing cheap content and emerging filmmakers and producers into the market for television from which they had been excluded for years.

When Mika Salmi, previously a business development executive at streaming video company RealNetworks, created AtomFilms, he might not have guessed it would become one of the few web networks to endure the dot-com crash and much of the 2000s. Premiering in 1999 and acquiring investors annually for the next few years, AtomFilms embodied several trends in the second wave of programming web-based series. If the 1990s focused on replicating television's reliance on tentpole series—series that "carried" the channel with dedicated audiences and strong revenue—and an integrated business model (the one-stop channel), the next wave of the web focused on commissioning, licensing, and releasing short, quirky humor and alternative videos that these web networks could syndicate to other media, including television, film, and branded websites. As technology improved—chiefly higher broadband adoption and Flash animation—viewership rose from the tens of thousands to the hundreds of thousands and often millions. "Web television" could stand on its own, but the ailing economy and growing skepticism of dot-coms' financial stability meant entrepreneurs primarily had to rely on each other. After the dot-com bust, broadcast networks and large tech companies cooled many of their investments, paving the way for semi-independent networks, individual Hollywood producers, film studios, corporate brands, and cable channels to experiment with web programming, primarily in animation and comedy. Producers balanced experimentation in genre and form with continuity in content delivery (the "network" or channel); because of the brief retreat of legacy TV organizations from web development, we also see experienced producers and executives in Hollywood invest more in original web entertainment.

That comedy became the dominant style in this period is easy to understand. Brevity in comedy is an asset—a joke merely requires a set-up and a punch line—and comedy in general and animation in particular allowed producers to push the boundaries of representation and storytelling further away from legacy television. The ability of humor to attract attention, entertain efficiently (at low cost), and encourage participation and sharing underscores its distinct importance in the development of web programming. As Nick Marx states in his study of post-2005 web video, comedy is "distinct and disruptive, ushering in innovations at a time when existing media industry practices are undergoing change and instability."[64] Comedy is easily combined with other genres and can accommodate industrial self-reflexivity at critical moments in industrial change. For example, scholars have highlighted *Soap* in the 1970s and *The Simpsons* in the 1980s as evidence of comedy's importance in reinventing genres and media distributors.[65] As market players saw the coming of streaming video in the mid-2000s, legacy TV distributors started to embrace short-form humor on the web as a cheap way to extend on-air brands and claim a foothold in a new medium.

By positioning AtomFilms as a "next generation distribution platform," the founders revealed their desire to expand the meaning of "Hollywood" as video became increasingly possible through networked distribution.[66] "Definitely Not Hollywood" read the covers of AtomFilms' first two compilations of shorts in 2000, touting its renegade image with "dark comedy" and "extreme comedy" DVD editions. The title is an exaggeration. With early investments from Frank Biondi, former chief executive of Universal Studios, and Warner Bros. Online, AtomFilms could hardly claim independence from Hollywood.[67] AtomFilms pioneered a number of online business practices: acquiring content from independent production companies through film festivals and by reputation;[68] cutting deals with such disparate exhibitors as local malls, airlines, handheld devices, and other web networks;[69] and, most interestingly, offering equity in the company to filmmakers whose work it licensed, in contrast to legacy corporations who were starting to take ownership stakes in programming it licensed.[70] The site's initial focus on shorts and eventual emphasis on animation and comedy mirror those of other companies from the late 1990s to the early 2000s. It was Hollywood, but a marginally different kind of Hollywood.

The organizing of online shows into channels advanced series development experiments. To justify their online existence—it had to be "new"—netcasters employed a diverse array of producers, new technologies (Flash) for animation, edgier (often ethnic) humor, and audience interactivity, all under the umbrella of a network. AtomFilms claimed to receive five hundred to one thousand short submissions every week, putting it at the top of over one hundred websites releasing short films online.[71] Its reliance on film festivals, and its solicitation of prestige directors like Bernardo Bertolucci and Jim Jarmusch, brought independent filmmaking and short-form video to the web and television. AtomFilms also syndicated shorts to IFC, HBO, Cinemax, Fox, and the Sundance Channel over the years, fostering an underexplored market for short film on television.[72] Throughout its history it partnered with major brands like Ford and studios like Paramount Television to produce and release short films featuring branded integration, abstract themes, and animation. It also partnered with film festivals and released VHS tapes and DVDs: "AtomFilms' varied associations demonstrate how thoroughly involved new digital companies are with existing enterprises, just as these enterprises strive to have a presence in emerging markets."[73] As advertising and venture capital for digital entertainment slackened around 2001, online networks hoping to distribute video had to diversify revenue streams and sell content to whomever would buy it, and brands looking for an injection of "hipness" into campaigns became useful sponsors: "For businesses interested in new entertainment channels as additional venues for advertisements, the film short provides a subtle means of assisting their goals."[74] After the dot-com bust, web channels like AtomFilms faced more pressure to partner with brands, film studios, and new media companies to survive. Concurrently, the market for pre-roll and banner advertising slowly took shape.

AtomFilms debuted among hundreds of web channels from roughly 1999 to 2003.[75] Many of these networks, while nominally independent, were well financed by former Hollywood executives, film studios, and venture capital firms. Most did not survive long. The channels focused on comedy, although some, like AtomFilms, also distributed dramatic shorts, docu-series, and other reality-based programming (increasingly popular in legacy TV as well). Because of technological constraints—broadband was still in its infancy—most focused on animation, much of its supported by Macromedia's Flash.[76] In the early 2000s, Flash was important enough to web programming that Macromedia created a network for showcasing its technology, Shockwave.com, and, before Shockwave merged with AtomFilms, enticed Hollywood heavyweights like Matt Stone and Trey Parker, David Lynch, Ben Stein, Stan Lee, Tim Burton, and Jim Belushi to create content.[77]

Animation offered web channels "a more offbeat version of television," as *Variety* put it, "more profane and always less formulaic than its broadcast and cable counterparts."[78] Animation not only played better on slower Internet connections, but cartoons allowed producers to be edgy and still advertiser friendly, all of which helped attract the young male fans that advertisers and networks feared losing to the web. Many of the successful series from this period stoked controversy, including a number of "ethnic" cartoons, some of which inked movie and TV deals:

Lil' Pimp (Mediatrip.com, straight-to-DVD), *Mr. Wong* (Icebox.com, straight-to-DVD), *Undercover Brother* (Urban Entertainment, released in theaters by Universal), and *Queer Duck* (Icebox.com, screened on Showtime). Legacy distributors, looking for edgy content and experiencing an on-air "toon boom" with shows like *Futurama* and *King of the Hill*, licensed some of these series, despite frequent declarations that they were too controversial for legacy television.[79] Other programs sold to legacy media as well. Icebox's sci-fi series *Starship Regulars* sold to Showtime, which had previously licensed the woman-led sci-fi series *WhirlGirl* online. Despite these counterexamples, on the whole, legacy television networks were wary of the new players, and public spats between the online upstarts and old media occasionally erupted.[80]

The presence of former and current Hollywood powerbrokers managing or advising the most prominent web channels helped the netcasters effect some changes in industry practices while allowing them to claim that they were pushing the medium from "outside." As larger institutions took a step back from the web, industry veterans looking to gain a foothold in the "new television" stepped in. The trend led *Variety* reporter Marc Graser to speculate as early as 2000 that the wave of new media democratization was already over: "The doors for Hollywood newbies are closing. The way the dot-coms are dispensing money recalls in fact the way old Hollywood worked: The big names pocketed most of the dough while struggling writers and actors slaved away as an underclass. So much for equal opportunity on the Internet!"[81] This was not an exaggeration. By the early 2000s, individuals connected to legacy television executives and companies started to enter the web market. Early entrant iFilm was the brainchild of Kevin Wendle, who founded CNET and was among the founders of Fox Broadcasting in 1986. Icebox was started by a group of TV writers, including two *Simpsons* alums, with funding from a former Disney executive and the founder of EarthLink. *Seinfeld* creator Larry David sat on its board. AntEye, which funded TV pilot ideas, was run by a former USA executive; EzFlix, by the former head of DreamWorks and Columbia TriStar; Nibblebox, by director Doug Liman and HBO producer David Bartis; and the Romp, by Eric Eisner, son of Disney CEO Michael Eisner, who would go on to launch his own new media studio years later. Some, like Stan Lee, Ben Affleck, and Matt Damon, started their own websites and studios. Talent agencies stepped in to broker deals and, like CAA with American Cybercast, fund online networks: CAA, William Morris, Endeavor, and 3 Arts all supported the netcasters in various ways.[82]

Despite such prominent names involved, most hits came from companies with slightly less well-heeled founders creating brassy shows that could never make it to broadcast channels. A former executive director of the Los Angeles Independent Film Festival started MediaTrip, which distributed *Lil' Pimp*. Comedy network Newgrounds was the spawn of Tom Fulp, then a high school student in Pennsylvania, and innovative cartoon site Joe Cartoon was founded by Michigan-based comic artist and toy designer Joseph Fields. Other networks that stayed independent, like Heavy.com and Break.com, did not have enough A-listers and honchos to get press at first, but their focus on steadily building audiences helped them weather the dot-com bust and become leading YouTube competitors later in the decade.[83] Unlike the more Hollywood-like networks, which licensed and commissioned programs like legacy TV companies, smaller networks gained notoriety on the basis of one or a few hit videos produced by independent or amateur creators whose formulas they could replicate: Mediatrip made its mark with *George Lucas in Love*; Heavy.com with *Behind the Music That Sucks*; Joe Cartoon with *Frog in a Blender*; and Urban Entertainment with *Undercover Brother*. Like the failed new media studios of the 1990s, netcasters proved how starting a channel without an online hit was precarious, no matter how powerful one's backers. For many, the fall of the Digital Entertainment Network, a product of NBC, Microsoft, Dell, and former Warner Bros. chairman Terry Semel, signaled the demise of pseudo-Hollywood netcasting.[84] Yet this brief period showed how deviating from legacy television production in genre and serialization while retaining its role of developing and curating programs could yield results in a more open market.

The effort to push beyond legacy television's programming traditions included major brands, film studios, and those working in television left disempowered after the elimination of the fin-syn rules in the 1990s, which allowed legacy TV networks to own and coproduce programming (think of ABC Studios making shows for the ABC broadcast network) at the expense of production companies not owned by legacy TV distributors.[85] The mixed success of TV-style netcasting did not deter producers outside the legacy system from funding original web shows.

Then-current mega-producers from cinema invested heavily as legacy TV stepped away from the web. Looking for new opportunities, studios from Warner Bros. to DreamWorks (led by Steven Spielberg, Jeffrey Katzenberg, and David Geffen) sought out the web to "make Internet viewing competitive with television."[86] As an executive for Warner Bros. Online's main web network, Entertaindom, said in 2000, "We want to be leading the curve, not falling behind it. Right now, we compete with television, which spends so much money to get good production quality and good writing, but we want to be there when convergence happens."[87]

Hollywood entrepreneurs prospected for sites for distribution in the digital landscape rather than investing in a new generation of creators or cultivating specific fan communities. Focused on distributing original short-form comedy and light Hollywood-focused programs, their channels were short-lived. Relying too heavily on busy producers making most of their money in big-budget films, they were unable to generate hits fast enough to satisfy uneasy investors. Pop.com, from DreamWorks and Imagine Entertainment (Ron Howard and Brian Grazer), spent nearly a fifth of its $50 million venture capitalist funding before folding into iFilm.[88] Z.com, originally from CAA, then 3 Arts, along with Basic Entertainment (Brad Grey) and Idealab (Jerry Bruckheimer), folded shortly after.[89] Along the way, however, they provided some healthy business for a small number of larger independent studios, animation outfit Mondo Media and Brilliant Digital chief among them.

Eyeing the rise of netcasting and questioning the return on investment of lincar TV spots, brands started producing their own shows with vigor in the early 2000s. Advertisers wanted to bypass television entirely and reach consumers with more targeting and greater control over the message. By 2001 this was far from new: sponsored programming has always existed, both on TV from its earliest days in the 1950s and in web programming, with big advertisers like Calvin Klein producing interactive cybersoaps in the late 1990s.[90] In the 2000s, budgets and scale rose with interest in video. Brands like Altoids sponsored programs from Mondo Media and Volkswagen in shorts from Atom; Dial pumped a reported six figures into a small channel for talk shows aimed at mothers and grandmothers.[91] By far the most influential brand to jump into original transmedia programming was BMW, which in 2001 recruited leading and emerging film directors, including Ang Lee, Alejandro González Iñárritu, Wong Kar Wai, John Frankenheimer, and Guy Ritchie, and actors Madonna, Mickey Rourke, and Clive Owen to make *The Hire*, a series of short films about a driver (obviously of a BMW) played by Owen who is thrown into crazy situations by passengers. Produced by David Fincher, the series gave directors "full creative control" to "merge art, entertainment, technology and commerce in a way never seen before."[92] The project was so successful that BMW commissioned another set of shorts in 2002 with directors John Woo and Tony Scott. The use of prestigious film directors shifted the discourse of the web toward "cinema,"[93] a way for the brand to assert the cultural importance of nonlinear online media. Still, the video series eventually fed back into legacy television distribution: its second season was quickly sold to Starz! and led to pronouncements in the trade press about the web as "just another channel to surf."[94] *The Hire* was part of a larger move by advertisers toward branded entertainment, going "beyond traditional TV."[95] It spurred a host of imitators, especially from other car companies like Jaguar, Mercury, Mercedes-Benz, and General Motors (Pontiac).[96]

The branded entertainment trend as antidote—or addendum—to television commercials continued throughout the 2000s, when American Express sponsored *The Adventures of Seinfeld and Superman* in 2004, encouraging more programming with high-profile casts and storylines supposedly less traditional than legacy television. *Seinfeld and Superman*, starring Jerry Seinfeld, arguably legacy television's biggest star at the time, was directed by Barry Levinson and produced by commercial company @radical.media with help from Ogilvy & Mather. It featured Seinfeld and a cartoon Superman voiced by Patrick Warburton doing "banter in an edgy fashion."[97] Ostensibly a challenge to linear television—i.e., brands making their own ads instead of paying for thirty-second spots—the series eventually aired on NBC after *Friends* and on TBS after reruns of *Sex and the City*. Brands consistently noted how their online content was "opt-in," actively viewed, compared to linear television's short ad units passively consumed by increasingly distracted viewers: "'You've got to attempt things where people will opt in.' . . . While TV can be great for getting short messages out to lots of people . . . the Internet can create messages that engage consumers for longer periods of time."[98] Brands broke away from legacy television, only to return to boost audiences, cultural awareness, and return on investment.

To avoid being shut out as other producers pushed from all sides, legacy television networks adopted a piecemeal approach to their digital efforts throughout this period, picking up original series from the net and transmedia companies. In addition to NBC and TBS, ABC, Spike, Sci-Fi, Oxygen, and UPN all picked up short web series, while a few, like Fox and Cartoon Network, created web properties to promote on-air shows. One of the most active was Showtime, which, looking to compete with emerging original programming juggernaut HBO, aired a number of web originals on air and online, starting with *WhirlGirl* and followed by *Whatever* from MGM (and Goosehead on the net), and *Starship Regulars* and *Queer Duck* from Icebox.

Web and transmedia programming continued with and without legacy television's participation. As 2005 approached, the next wave included a rapid increase in independent, original production through open-upload streaming sites like Blip and Vimeo, experiments from social networking site MySpace and, most critically, YouTube. Video streaming was the "critical juncture," the great opening legacy television's challengers hoped for.[99] Broadband adoption and streaming technology encouraged a broader base of video producers, each working in a variety of genres and storytelling modes (serialized, nonserialized), and under a variety of distribution structures, ranging from web-grown independent networks to legacy TV networks and large "anyone can upload" networks like YouTube. With television entering the networked era—as ratings declined on broadcast channels, series development and ad sales flat-lined, and users had more ways to access programs—the web became what my interviewees often referred to as a "Wild West," a complex free-for-all of amateurs, independents, and corporations competing to shape it into a form of television increasingly unrecognizable from its network-era past. This period saw a considerable diversification in the types of producers and productions.

The rest of this book focuses on the period of rapid growth of video storytelling following the advent of streaming media. With YouTube, next-generation television reached new heights. The number of market participants grew exponentially: by 2010, dozens of hours of video would be uploaded to the site every minute, videos produced for anything from zero to millions of dollars. By 2015, four hundred hours were uploaded every minute, or sixty-five years' worth of video every day.[100]

Aside from omnibus video sharing sites, YouTube was joined by a resurgence of comedy sites, old and new, allowing users to upload videos. Networks from the late 1990s, including Atom, Break, and Heavy, started to promote user-generated programming, marketed as "a simple way for users to interact with brands."[101] Newer sites, most prominently Will Ferrell and Adam McKay's Funny or Die, combined the star appeal of Hollywood with the spreadability of user-generated content.

Understanding Television's Transformation through Open Distribution

"The internet is a place where they can't maintain control," screenwriter George Hickenlooper said of the film and television studios and distributors during the 2007–2008 Writers Guild of America strike, a pivotal moment in the history of web programming. "They are trying to introduce an old-school control-orientated way of thinking into a system that rejects and repels that tradition of control."[102] Hickenlooper's statement idealistically pits legacy media against web media. Believing in the power of the web's more open market, WGA writers quickly organized a new online network, Strike TV, to distribute the short videos being produced by Hollywood's out-of-work casts and crews—including Joss Whedon's *Dr. Horrible's Sing-Along Blog* and Tina Cesa Ward and Susan Miller's teen lesbian series *Anyone but Me*. Inspired by open TV distribution while the powerful Alliance of Motion Picture and Television Producers (AMPTP) fought to avoid paying writers residuals for content delivered via the Internet,[103] the strikers realized within a few months that access to distribution did not mean access to consistent audiences or the capital that viewer attention can bring (explored in chapter 4).

The open TV market's agents historically framed their activities in opposition to legacy TV, but they also affirmed legacy TV's value as they adapted its core practices. Throughout web programming's history, legacy television's allure has been its consistency in practices, forms, and institutions, along with its robust resources: a hit legacy TV show can provide steady employment for years through the syndication market, even after new episodes stop airing. Television's above-the-line workers can build massive fan bases—think of Whedon—while its below-the-line workers can practice and hone their crafts over the same amount of time. Television's reliance on advertising and its control over distribution have enriched corporations for decades, while occasionally allowing for creativity, especially with the "quality TV"[104] developments of the 2000s.[105] Producers, workers, and entrepreneurs placed hopes of new profits and consistent creative production in networked distribution. Even as they experimented with serial storytelling and fan engagement, they pursued continuity in legacy business practices. The Writers Guild strike laid bare their investment in the status quo: the AMPTP and WGA both fought for control over the legacy media practice of granting residuals.

Corporate TV distributors, from legacy media in Hollywood to new media companies like Netflix and Amazon in Silicon Valley, profit disproportionately from open distribution, leaving most independent producers to innovate with fewer resources. During the strike, Hollywood workers created dozens of projects. After the strike ended, however, most workers went back to their Hollywood jobs (if they still had them), and the A-listers who dabbled in next-generation television went back to collect paychecks from their well-heeled employers. Still, the strike instigated more web-based, independent productions in subsequent years, with nonguild members in Los Angeles and around the country creating their own stories and networks, a small number of which would become successful and an even smaller percentage of which would get picked up for broadcast, cable, and premium television. The writers received many of their demands from the AMPTP, including concessions on digital residuals, but it is too soon to tell whether their dream of an open market for television will be realized. The web has birthed a new crop of production companies and distributors, which around 2009 started to invest a lot of money in producing content. From Netflix and Crackle releasing original TV-length programs, and YouTube's hiring of development executives for comedy and reality programming, web producers and distributors have come closer than ever to securing consistent investments from sponsors and fans.

Whether, in Scott Zakarin's words, we will "see massive changes in how the mainstream media operate" remains an open question. What the history of web television shows is how new distribution technologies did not break entirely from television. Instead, television has been an object of both desire and abjection for those seeking to reinvent it online. During a period of uncertainty over the efficacy of its development practices, legacy television inspired web producers and entrepreneurs to create channels and hew to its established genres and storytelling modes. Within these constraints, producers tweaked, pushed, and at times attempted to revolutionize the medium from its margins as well as within Hollywood's increasingly complex production economy. The promise of innovation via the web—television production independent of legacy television distribution—is that new markets can support a broader array of stories, content creators, fan communities, and industry practices.

2

Open TV Production

Revaluing Creative Labor

Prologue: Producing *She's out of Order*

July 2011: It is 8:00 a.m. and hot. We are late—again. We are filming in my friend Jeff's studio apartment on the twenty-ninth floor of a luxury condo building in Center City, Philadelphia. Since it is only one room, we are using my apartment down the street to prepare the "talent" (the actors) for hair, makeup, and wardrobe. My apartment is also an office: Jeff is using my bedroom to work while I work in his bedroom. Because it is ninety degrees out and we don't want our actors sweaty or their makeup to run, we pick them up from my apartment and drive them to the set. Once they arrive, though, there is not much relief. Jeff has air conditioning in his studio, but the sound affects our audio, and we don't have funds for extensive postproduction. I'm waiting on Jeff's bed for the talent to arrive. I have set it up for a dream sequence that we eventually shoot but cut from the final series. Editing that scene proves too complex. I could have slept in.

Open TV production foregrounds the value of creative freedom and ownership, but, while this is a source of innovation, it also is fraught and costly in time and resources. Small-scale video production is mundane, even boring, yet stressful and thrilling. Mostly, it's exhausting. Never have I expended so much energy achieving rudimentary tasks: getting coffee, sending e-mails, picking up objects, and dropping them off. This was not what I expected when I set out to coproduce an independent web series. The sixteen-episode comedy *She's out of Order* was my first narrative production with a crew larger than two.[1] We had nine crew members on set, including four producers, three from Under the Spell Productions, a 501c3; Teresa Lasley, the star; Derek McPhatter, the writer; and Rhonney Greene, the director. They had worked together for ten years doing independent theater, mostly in New York; their biggest production, *It Goes Unsaid*, explored the politics of skin color in black communities. As coproducer of *She's out of Order*, I used some of my research funds to pay for crew and food, and helped scout and secure locations, equipment, and crew. Writing for Teresa, his friend and creative partner, Derek crafted a forty-six-page script, most of which we produced over three weekends in July 2011—six twelve-hour shoot days, plus two production meetings. On weekdays we planned, prepared, and addressed emergencies. We spent just over $6,000 shooting, editing, and marketing the show: $2,700 on food, travel, and lodging during production; $1,000 on crew stipends; $2,000 on postproduction; and the rest on marketing (festival entry fees, Facebook and YouTube ads).

Americans romanticize independence, and while this book argues that indie web series production represents an innovation in legacy television development, innovation comes with considerable risk and cost, as well as personal and ethical quandaries due to lack of resources. For three weeks, Derek was my partner in life and work, and we bickered more in those three weeks than in our previous four-and-a-half-year relationship. Almost always we fought about roles. Who was supposed to do what and when? Independent production is problem solving. Production roles—cinematographer, gaffer, production assistant—help studios manage responsibilities and complete the tasks necessary to produce images and sounds. Nothing about web distribution changes this. The difference is resources. We were making *She's out of Order* because we could release it, not because we had all the funding we needed. Legacy television productions shoot because their networks have secured funding or are making it themselves. Indie television productions shoot because producers have vision, passion, and the ability to organize crew to accomplish the task. Without several thousand dollars in funding, at least, productions cannot afford to hire separate people for all the necessary roles, so workers naturally end up doing more than they signed up for. Preparation can minimize complications and confusion: writing a script with modest ambitions, soliciting favors, trading resources, or hiring crew with multiple skills can greatly reduce filmmaking's inevitable trials. Yet many web series creators, including us, use digital production as their film school, or as their first significant credit or production, so first seasons or episodes of a project are often the least sophisticated. You are always learning, which can be frustrating.

The managed chaos of our production mirrored its idiosyncratic development process. When producers want funding for a legacy television series, they hold meetings with development executives, typically set up by agents or managers. The pitch—the necessary first step toward a pilot—is at once formal and creative. There is an art to it, but its practice is restricted to producers who have been working consistently in the industry for some years—a vast majority of them of straight, white men. *She's out of Order*'s team had some industry connections; at the time our director, Rhonney, worked in New York and Atlanta in the costume department of various television series (*Nurse Jackie, Mercy*) and films (*The Avengers, For Colored Girls*), and as a costume designer for several Tyler Perry shows and films. Nevertheless, since none of us had writer or producer credits in legacy productions, we couldn't get meetings for *She's out of Order* and did not try.

Successful independent production involves harnessing all available resources, from skills to spaces. While *She's out of Order* was a collaborative enterprise, Rhonney's work in the industry proved invaluable. He scheduled the shoots, approved locations, hired crew, and compiled the call sheets so crew knew when to show up, who would be there, and how to contact them. Location scouting was fairly simple. Nearly all our locations came from my friends in Philadelphia. Our nonresidential locations included our offices at the Annenberg School for Communication and Studio Christensen, whose owner, J. T. Christensen, was a friend.

Our Philadelphia-based crew brought their own resources in materials, skill, and passion. It was not difficult to find talent, even with the low rates we were offering—around a hundred dollars a day—because they saw value in production beyond monetary compensation. The people we hired were at various stages in their careers. Some were getting into the business late and working on smaller projects or at low-level positions on slightly bigger films. Our director of photography, Arnold Lawrence, had the most experience shooting reality-based web video for brands and local Philadelphia spots. Our younger crew—including Temple University students Timothy Harris, Cameron Mitchell, and Jonah Cooper—were eager for experience. In interviews for these positions, most crew said they understood that indie productions usually do not pay, or pay very little. All of our camera operators used their own cameras, all Canon DSLRs (5D, 60D, 7D), despite my having access to cameras through Penn. Digital equipment was inexpensive enough that indie producers could get access. One prospect, I later discovered, had an equipment list on his resume, suggesting that investing in equipment was a way crew members got an edge in the market. Part of the reason we didn't have too much trouble, our main production assistant, Colleen Desmond, told us, was that Philadelphia did not have too many film productions available and New York was a more competitive market.

The Under the Spell team tapped into their New York network for acting talent; we paid for their travel and meals while on set. Casting was nerve-wracking for me. Days before we started shooting we'd only had two parts cast—Tara and her cousin, played by Amber Efé, fellow Annenberg graduate student and my only actor connection in Philadelphia. Nevertheless, despite the fact that we were casting the series as we were shooting it, all the roles were filled, because film work was still rare for actors. Our actors worked under the Screen Actors Guild New Media contract, which allowed us to pay far below union minimums.

The producers and crew did what was necessary to help the production along, transgressing roles regularly. Our photographers suggested shots to the director, our assistant director often captured sound, our production assistants served as boom operators. During shoots I held up a "flag," a large sheet used to dilute the light coming from one corner, or a reflector for daytime scenes, which was typically the work of a gaffer. I also did a lot of driving: picking up actors, picking up lunch, dropping Teresa off at the bus stop, getting supplies.

When I reviewed my production notes later, one trend became clear: as production continued we became less efficient. Shoot days started and ended later. Cast and crew disagreements and mishaps increased. "We didn't have much time. I think a lot of people weren't used to the fast pace. But they stepped up," Rhonney recounted. I take much of the blame. In preproduction I pushed Derek to write a lot of short episodes in a limited number of locations. I believed having more episodes would give us more time to market the show and find an audience. That did not turn out to be true. Instead, it meant we had a small margin of error during production and a lot of footage to edit in postproduction. For this reason, our last production day went several hours over schedule. Postproduction took almost two years to complete due to lack of funds.[2] Nevertheless, we did release *She's out of Order*, the cast and crew got their credits, and their capable work is on display and easily linkable to future employers.

The story of how we made *She's out of Order* offers a grounded view of independent web series creators' pursuit of creative freedom and expression. The power of the web is open access to distribution, where producers can produce new projects without corporate intermediaries (though they need them to distribute it). Without institutional support, however, most productions flout the rules, procedures, and structures—permits, union contracts, residuals—designed to ensure stability and living wages for workers. They can do this because of the incredible demand for creative work in the United States, the romantic notion of doing meaningful cultural work in a country whose cultural products are valued around the world. Major studios and networks have increased television production but not the kind of "good work" associated with creative freedom and job stability, as most media industries scholars argue, so workers seek it in independent spaces.[3] In very rare cases, a production team has the right idea (pitch), resources, and talent to express their idea effectively enough to secure crew, fan, sponsor, or distributor interest. Supported by interviews, this chapter focuses on case studies of innovative producers who, in revaluing creative labor in television production, executed a pitch successfully and found a market for their hard work, demonstrating the value of open TV production.

* * *

Comedy writers and performers are key sources of creative labor in both open and legacy TV, and their opportunities are critical indicators of the health of TV production markets. By the early 2010s, web platforms like YouTube hosted legions of indie comedy creators whose work legacy networks like Comedy Central, IFC, and MTV slowly started to develop and curate for both online and linear distribution. But long before the web, organizations like Upright Citizens Brigade (UCB) offered a consistent route to comedy writing and acting with networks like these. Like Chicago's Second City, New York– and Los Angeles–based UCB offers improvisation classes, where aspiring comedians signed up to learn, met other comedians, and earned a spot on a "house team," whose weekly shows allowed them to hone their craft in front of agents and producers. Aspiring improv comedians worked to get noticed by Lorne Michaels, executive producer of NBC's *Saturday Night Live* (*SNL*), and several late-night talk shows and sitcoms feature its alums, including *Portlandia, 30 Rock, Up All Night, Late Night with Jimmy Fallon*, and *Seth Meyers*. Michaels had been producing *SNL* since the 1970s, and despite massive changes in television distribution, his influence did not wane in the digital era. Known for discovering a major share of the country's bankable comedy talent, Michaels was a comedy market influencer by the late 2000s. At the same time, UCB and Second City students regularly churned out videos for the institution's YouTube comedy channels. Michaels saw this market and launched his own YouTube comedy network, Above Average, in 2012 to showcase digital talent.[4] In 2013, fending off charges of racism and sexism for not having a black female cast member to play key pop-culture roles like First Lady Michelle Obama and *Scandal* star Kerry Washington, *SNL* found a new cast member in Sasheer Zamata, who had made several videos with Above Average, including a critically beloved web series, *Pursuit of Sexiness*, costarring Nicole Byer, who went on to sell her own show, *Loosely Exactly Nicole*, to MTV.

To a casual observer in the 2000s, it appeared that the serial comedy market was open. Funny people could easily showcase their talent. But for young comedians like Rob Michael Hugel, Ilana Glazer, and Abbi Jacobson, breaking in proved daunting. Hugel, Glazer, and Jacobson all came to New York in the mid-2000s, took classes at UCB, joined practice groups, and formed independent comedy troupes while regularly auditioning for the house team, "Harold." Hugel and Jacobson met each other during auditions. "We also happened to not get on the team every time, so we shared that frustration with the system," Hugel said in an interview. His frustration went beyond his inability to break in. The house team affected the dynamics of independent groups. Hugel spent years trying to find a steady community of comedians: "I'd meet people I really liked and we would be in an improv group. They might get on the house team for the theater, and they would end up being more invested in that because that's the theater and we're an independent group. . . . That was many years of being in that zone." Around this time Jacobson and Glazer, similarly eager to showcase their talent, contacted Hugel about editing some comedy videos they produced. Hugel had advertised his editing services on the Improv Resource Center's online message board, citing his experience in UCB.

Jacobson and Glazer met in 2007 in an improv practice group and joined an independent team, Secret Promise Circle, where they were the only women. They performed with the group for a couple of years before planning their own web series, *Broad City*. YouTube was growing in popularity, and New York's competitive comedians were slowly becoming a major driver of sketch online. "It wasn't so much that way when we started. . . . It wasn't 'send me links! Send me links!'" Glazer told me. The two did not have much production experience, so they experimented. "You could just see how low-budget they were. One of them was just one take," Glazer said. Hugel came on to direct and, along with filmmakers like T. J. Misny, added some polish. Jacobson and Glazer started thinking of the videos as a television show. They added title cards at the end and adopted a regular release schedule. "We had to play with it for a long enough time," Jacobson said. They stepped up their game in the show's second season in 2011, adding publicity and marketing to blogs, no matter how small. Glazer said they knew their videos would never go "viral." They wanted a "low quantity, high quality" audience, she said. As Glazer wrote in an essay published on my blog, *Televisual*, which I maintained while researching the web series market,

> But the fuel that kept the fire going was the feedback. While YouTube is notorious for having degrading, sexist, and racist comments, Abbi and I found the response to our work to be quite the opposite—warm, embracing, and encouraging. It prodded us with this hunger, hunger for more love from our friends and, eventually, one-person-removed from our friends. Then, two-people-removed from the original friend, and so on and so on. We got to see and feel (and taste and smell and hear, of course) the exact rate at which our show became increasingly popular.[5]

The pair found a high-value fan in 2012 when *SNL* and UCB alum Amy Poehler (*Parks and Recreation*) saw the show, performed a cameo in the series's second season finale, and signed on as executive producer for a half-hour sitcom that eventually premiered on Comedy Central in early 2014 to rave reviews, evidence of Jacobson and Glazer honing their voice on the web. In 2016 Comedy Central renewed it for a fourth and fifth season, and in the same year the Television Academy nominated Jacobson and Glazer for an Emmy for Outstanding Short Form or Drama Series for a spin-off web series, *Hack into Broad City*.[6]

I narrate Jacobson and Glazer's story to show how indie web production expands legacy television's series development process. The television market's unequal labor supply chain instilled a hunger for creative autonomy and experimentation in creative workers. Shared conditions allowed producers to support each other, leading to idiosyncratic, collaborative productions. "It's like this great bartering system. . . . It's because we're lucky enough to be in a community that's full of talented people. The talented people stick around and make stuff," Jacobson said. Production creates bonds and encourages producers to push the rules of storytelling. From 2010 to 2011, *Broad City*'s online episodes riffed on a situation or punchline, told in variously realist or aburdist ways. This was before Louis CK's *Louie* on FX and Lena Dunham's *Girls* on HBO cemented that style as sellable on legacy television. "We got to play with anything we wanted to," Glazer said. Their efforts inspired collaborators, including Hugel, who would create and star in *I Hate Being Single*, a sitcom that found a large following through Tumblr:

> The more web series happen, the more people see "Oh, I can do that too. And I can bring my voice out of the crowd a little bit." I didn't feel like I had a voice until *Broad City*, and then on top of that I definitely didn't feel like I had a voice until *I Hate Being Single*. Doing *Broad City*, just being their main director-editor for the first season, I started to get positive feedback from people. . . . I'm here. I'm doing something and people look at what we do and admire it.

Hugel's emphasis on taking on more production roles and connecting his voice to communities of fans highlights a common reason producers cite for working independently of legacy television: creative autonomy as strategy for increasing their labor's value, even if compensation is nonmonetary in the form of appreciation, love, or respect. Of course, institutions connected to legacy TV like UCB, along with Lorne Michaels's production company Broadway Video and platform Above Average, help shape creators' aspirations and practices, but rising in the industry through these institutions involves years of work without creative freedom or autonomy. After gaining access, producers must meet the demands of the distributor, via network executives and executive producers. In contrast, independent production for the open TV market allows producers to develop their voice and experiment with television form, while providing work and training for other aspiring entrants. As they work to create for themselves, they can connect directly to their communities or fans of their genres.

This chapter probes three different groups of producers whose labor practices and production ethics broke from legacy television production and distribution practices. I discuss Felicia Day and *The Guild*, which set a number of standards for a successful filmed web show and was the most oft-cited inspiration for independent creators years after its premiere in 2007. Indie TV creators looked up to Day for her insistence on creative ownership, her deft cultivation of a fan base, and her securing of a brand sponsor and web distributor interested in preserving her autonomy and connections to fans. I then compare JankyClown Productions' *High Maintenance* and Offchance Productions' *Real Girl's Guide to Everything Else*, both of which scaled their projects to the needs of the talent and their fan communities. Each case study unfolds in two parts, the first exploring how producers executed their projects and the second exploring how they released them, demonstrating how their practices innovated television series development.

In interviews producers stress how open access to distribution allows for greater creativity and collaboration. Freed from the constraints of legacy television, producers are better equipped to tell stories sincerely and flexibly, adapting to the needs of their collaborators, fans, brand sponsors, and distributors. Each case study illuminates the different ways indie web producers contribute meaningfully new or provocative production practices to the television development process. I argue that producers are working through alternative ways of making media and connecting directly with those who could support it. Yet it is important to remember that this work is precarious. Like most indie web series producers, we were not able to offer talent and crew on *She's out of Order* health insurance, overtime pay, workers compensation, child care, or anything else by way of a safety net. If the rest of this chapter reads as if I am downplaying the downsides to this kind of labor, it is only because it was and is so pervasive. Precarity, on the rise in legacy TV production, structures and defines open TV production. It variably causes and limits innovation for those in the process of developing for the open market.

Understanding Open TV Production

Contemporary television production has grown more complex as new media transform the business. As John Caldwell describes in his landmark study of Hollywood production around the turn of the twenty-first century, "[P]roduction cultures are far too messy, vast, and contested to provide a unified code—to either job aspirants or scholars—for breaching its walls."[7] Responding to a tough and ever-changing market, TV workers think critically about television, its past and future, and imbue their efforts with meaning. I situate the independent television market within concurrent changes in legacy studio production. As production cultures decentralize, producers organize themselves to pilot new stories and new ways of producing them.

I use the term "production" to denote not only specific spaces and practices of filmmaking ("the set") but also the intellectual and physical work that precedes and follows the act—traditionally called pre- and postproduction. Historically, this work is divided by a "line": above the line are creative producers, chiefly writers, executive producers, and actors, and below it are craft workers like sound technicians, makeup artists, assistant editors, and production assistants. Above-the-line workers are typically paid more and have access to residuals (a cut of sales from later distribution windows like reruns) and "back end" deals that allowed them to profit long after the work was completed. Below-the-line work, as Vicki Mayer argues, is increasingly low-pay and unstable as competition forced legacy distributors to cut costs.

Indie TV series are driven by producers because writers craft the narrative, but, as the case of *She's out of Order* shows, producers and their collaborators often take on additional work to make the show happen: the one who writes or creates the show often ends up managing the entirety of its production cycle, from preproduction and production to postproduction and marketing. At the same time, any worker can take on outsized importance in the show's development, since most teams are small. Writers may make coffee; sound tech assistants might assist with set design. Because producers take on extra work, or creatively manage work, I refer to a variety of workers as "creators" and "producers" who often perform both above- and below-the-line labor, or what I call "off-the-line" production. In most independent series, producers take on the work of reaching out to audiences or fans, marketing, and securing intellectual property and licensing fees. Crew members can perform a variety of roles beyond the scope of their credit. New media production studies confirm the expansion of television labor even within the legacy TV's supply chain: Derek Johnson finds fans doing the work of franchise management, and Denise Mann uncovers a network of authors—including executives—in the production of ABC's *Lost* franchise.[8]

The indie TV market mirrors shifts across creative industries, with labor disorganized, minimized, and dispersed across a growing number of small firms and skilled laborers doing more work for less money and job security.[9] "Work in film, and, increasingly, in television and video, can be characterized as extremely precarious, generally freelance, project-based, involving . . . a 'roller-coaster atmosphere' of continual transformation and shifting uncertainties," Mark Deuze writes.[10] In film and television production, most of the pressure is exerted on below-the-line workers—laborers from boom operators to visual effects artists and acting extras—who execute the ideas of higher-value above-the-line producers but have no intellectual-property-ownership claims.[11] Labor's power decreased at the turn of the century. The production line became a marker of increasing inequality. But pressures did not dissuade workers from creatively and critically thinking about the industry and its limits while innovating progressive ways forward, off the line.[12]

The open market shows how workers create value as corporations continually extract it. Many makers of web series are current or would-be below-the-line workers, and for that very reason, venture off the line in search of creative autonomy and claims to intellectual property. Creative freedom is the strongest incentive to produce indie television. Of course, the tension between the need to control and execute production (i.e., to segment and value labor) and to foster creativity (i.e., support workers' agency) has always existed in television history. But tensions have escalated as laborers and their organizations face mounting pressure in a competitive, global market. As Vicki Mayer shows in her robust study on below-the-line workers: "This narrative [growing invisibility of labor] should be of particular concern at this conjuncture at which all of us increasingly define ourselves through our productive work while at the same time industries devalue our agency as producers through abstract quantitative measures, from stock share prices to advertising rates."[13] The power of a small stratum of Hollywood producers in a market with more distribution options increases the value of creative autonomy and accelerates the growth of independent production as workers strategize ways to fulfill creative urges and close the gap.

When Felicia Day says that web television is "an independent person's dream" against power-grabbing corporations, she implicitly invokes the problem of precarious labor and offers hope for a potential solution.[14] This new media dream may be displacing the old media dream of union-backed employment by corporate networks, but only because union employment is hardly keeping pace with the rapid rise of television production. Union-represented writers faced pressure after the 2007–2008 strike. As scholar Felicia Henderson described her own experience as a WGA writer, "[S]tudios are scapegoating writers to punish them for striking. This punishment has come in at least two forms: (1) decreased salaries regardless of salary history and (2) redefining compensation in nonmonetary terms."[15] John Caldwell finds a "race to the bottom" following the strike and global recession of 2008, with non-union workers taking the place of union workers, resulting in the "disaggregation of professional craft groups and labor coalitions" and "the spread of unauthorized 'worker-generated-content' (WGC) alongside user-generated-content."[16] Faced with declining labor value, workers embrace the opportunity to prove their value through digital, open distribution technologies.

While creativity and agency lure producers into a challenging online market, producer agency is not anathema to legacy television or any media industry. In the decades following television's mass adoption in the 1950s and 1960s, the industry accommodated producer-driven or "unconventional" programs, coinciding with early television's relationship to live theater and the advent of the hyphenated "writer-producer" on *I Love Lucy*.[17] At the beginning of the multichannel transition around the 1970s and early 1980s, certain independent production companies, led by writers like Norman Lear and stars like Mary Tyler Moore and aided by federal regulation protecting independent production (the Financial Interest and Syndication Rules), sold narratives that pushed the norms at conservative broadcast channels like CBS.[18] Throughout television history, then, legacy distributors have allowed creative professionals skilled at managing subordinates, developing marketable ideas, and navigating bureaucracies to develop narratives close to their dreams.

The scope of producer agency shifted at the end of the twentieth century: "[A]s 'true' independence became more exceptional, writers and producers complained of a return of classic broadcast network-era abuses: tightening financial and creative control, pickups conditioned on participation in program ownership, syndication rights self-dealt below market value between studio-network divisions."[19] Creativity and independence took on added value and urgency by the time producers could access web distribution, and writers implored the government to include more spaces for independent labor.[20] While "creativity is never a process of total freedom," as Robert S. Alley argues, choosing to work through constraints can create "special forms and meanings."[21] When producers work independently and release online, they circumvent legacy television's longstanding structures, opening up possibilities in art, production, distribution, and politics.

How can the American media market reconcile the bottom-up efforts of indie producers distributing series on the open network with top-down control of distribution by corporations? Throughout television history, writers have amassed power by organizing themselves (unions) and performing services—like the administration of residual payments or regulation of production roles—that help studios regulate labor.[22] In the early years of television following the 1950s, writers and workers made gains (like residual payments on syndicated series) alongside many other workers in a variety of industries. Independent production and relatively stable job security characterized the first (or second) "golden age of television" in the 1970s. Both corporate distributors and outside entrepreneurs pushed for deregulation soon after, resulting in an ever-increasing number of cable channels and low-cost genres like reality television, where labor was most precarious. The post-1980s market saw, for the most part, downward pressure on production costs and rising corporate flexibility in hiring and firing.[23] In response, small firms and craft producers, shut out of industrial production and profits, performed more roles, including those the industry could not or would not value. In contrast to corporate flexibility in hiring and firing, for example, smaller producers gave more flexibility to actors on set and to the audience in the show's release, blurring historical roles and hierarchies.

Production was "freed" from hierarchies and structures in these contexts, but governments did not expand the base of power. Accordingly, smaller producers collaborated and shared among themselves, producing innovations legacy institutions could organize: "[S]urvival can be the basis of innovation and risk spreading the basis for risk taking . . . for it is precisely in reworking the institutional materials at hand that actors innovate," according to David Stark and László Bruszt.[24]

Yet legacy television distributors have been slow to develop work created in the open market—HBO's development of *High Maintenance*, described in the last section of this chapter, or Comedy Central's development of web comedians represented a slight shift in legacy TV attitudes to indie labor. Historically, legacy networks have offered development deals to very few indie projects like *The Spot* in the mid-1990s and *The Burg* in the mid-2000s. Corporate neglect of open TV production has impoverished indie creators and their products, thus reaffirming the value of legacy television in both the culture and the market. Legacy distributors could develop a sustainable indie market if they extend ownership rights, license indie series with healthy fees, and open development.[25]

Faced with a closed development system, indie producers work among themselves and, with the right story, the right marketing plan, and a bit of luck, organize and maintain relationships with fans and sponsors directly, cutting out network intermediaries. Without legacy TV connections to finance and develop series, independent producers take on this labor, not only in story conception but also in production management, marketing, and fundraising. In doing so, as the following cases show, they innovate outside of legacy television development.

Revaluing Creative Labor in Hollywood

It is impossible to separate *The Guild*'s origins from the real-life story of its creator, Felicia Day. An actor who in the mid-2000s was best known for a short arc on the WB's *Buffy the Vampire Slayer*, Day started writing her web series after she found herself between jobs and playing dozens of hours of World of Warcraft, a multiplayer online role-playing game. Warcraft was not her first gaming experience; in interviews she has stated that she was a gamer from the age of six and has spoken about the online MUDs (multi-user domains) of the 1990s providing her a sense of community.[26] Frustrated with waiting for and pitching to Hollywood, she decided to go it alone and wrote a series about her experience as a serial gamer with help from producer Kim Evey, who was known for her comedic web series, *Gorgeous Tiny Chicken Machine Show.*

From its independent origins to its low-budget, corporate release, *The Guild* typifies how independent producers revalue TV labor. Day's origin story, frequently retold in the press, highlights her belief in the Internet as an antidote to legacy media. Her identity as an occasionally working actress incapable of landing lead roles and as a gamer "geek" misunderstood by older and out-of-touch executives underscores her argument for the web and against legacy television. "Unless you're in Hollywood, you don't really understand how actors are treated—either like dirt, or you're a god, and there's no in-between," said Day, who also recounted numerous instances of misogyny by studio executives.[27]

A comedy about a gang of socially awkward misfits, *The Guild* mirrors Day's own sense of feeling out of place in Hollywood. The show follows Cyd Sherman, player of an unnamed online role-playing game similar to World of Warcraft under the handle Codex; her "guild" is a group of players who collectively solve puzzles, complete tasks, and wage battles in a fictional universe. The narrative unfolds through their digital debates and squabbles; each character looks into a web camera (at the viewer) when talking to each other in the computer game. The relative simplicity of *The Guild's* narrative technique makes it at once intimate and cost-effective, which Day said allowed the show to connect to fans and deviate from legacy television norms: "Online video is the Sundance of our time, it's where people can take risks with material and find their audience."[28]

The "risk" is the topic of the show: gaming. Day wrote a script from her experiences and pitched it to a few legacy TV network executives, all of whom passed, saying that the gamer audience was not large enough for television: "[P]eople loved it, but said it was too 'niche.'"[29] Coloring Day's statement is an awareness of legacy media's tendency to pathologize and stereotype fans, gamers, and geeks.[30] This is another reason, alongside her critique of Hollywood misogyny and labor politics, that she pursued her own creative projects. Day consistently connects creativity to working outside the system: "There are a lot of gatekeepers in Hollywood, but there are a lot of creative people, too. . . . Now that there are ways to go around that, I'm really proud of having found a way, and shown a way to do it."[31] Even as Day asserts her own importance, her decision to self-produce a show she could not sell to legacy networks was creative and generated a successful model for many others.

Yet Hollywood was still critical to Day's success. Her small role on *Buffy* made her recognizable to its passionate fan base.[32] Later, her connection to producer Joss Whedon landed her a role on his popular 2008 web series, *Dr. Horrible's Sing-Along Blog*, amplifying *The Guild*'s already rising success. Moreover, Day's "niching" strategy existed in advertising and marketing practices for decades, as advertisers sought to reach consumers in smaller demographics and deliver more "personal" messages.[33] Lastly, *The Guild* is heavily based on a number of legacy television conventions. The cast consists of six leads (three male, three female) of various ages, ethnicities, and life circumstances, a version of *Friends* with more diversity. The storylines add a gaming component to sitcom tropes of unruly suburban households, nerds with schoolboy crushes, sexy next-door neighbors, and disapproving parents. *The Guild* is easily watchable, a familiar comedy with just enough tweaks to support Day's claim to differentiation. Indeed, many web series creators model their shows on previous successes and contextualize their pitches by citing on-air hits. *The Crew*, another geek show about a spaceship crew debuting shortly after *The Guild*, is a neo–*Star Trek* for *Star Trek* fans who want to see the backstage of the *Enterprise*: "As a kid, you want to be on the ship," creator Brett Register told me, describing his deep affective connection with the classic television series. Comparisons to classic hits were common, as when Tatyana Ali, producer of BET's first web show, *Buppies*, told me that her show was inspired by eighties primetime soaps, newly hip in the 2000s on networks like ABC: "It's kind of in the spirit of *Dynasty*, *Falcon Crest*, and all these great nighttime soaps that I used to watch when I was young, with outlandish comedy and drama." Direct spoofs, like the gay medical procedural satire *Gay's Anatomy* (a riff off the ABC hit *Grey's Anatomy*) or parodies of Fox's *24* (*00:24*, or twenty-four minutes, and UCB's *24x24*) are also common.

Creativity, though, involves more than stylistic innovation. Vicki Mayer argues persuasively that television studies focus an inordinate amount of attention on powerful showrunners, even as their work was so evidently constrained by the network and advertiser demands. In her study of assembly line workers who make television sets, she redefines the meaning of creativity for workers outside of Hollywood: "[E]ach worker sought ways to evade control and reduce stress. This is a different way of thinking about constraints and creativity. Whereas the history of television production sets these terms in opposition, indicating how constraints limit creativity, assemblers looked creatively for solutions to stressful limits because *they had no other choice*."[34] Here, constraints produce the need for creativity, to avoid injury or gossip. It is impossible to compare these conditions directly to those of open TV producers like Day. Day's own rhetoric, however, signals a related gesture. As professionals who work on better-capitalized productions on legacy television, workers like Day are close to more classically "creative" labor, the province of high-concept shows like *Buffy*. Yet as marginal players, their own creative energy is needlessly proscribed and relentlessly limited. Day's narration of her time as an actress made the sentiment clear:

> But being the kind of girl who is stereotyped as the secretary—or I've played a crazy cat lady five times, which is fine because I do that very well—but at a certain point you're like, "I am more than this." That's why I wrote Codex [her character in *The Guild*]. I sat down and was like, "What role would I have the most fun playing and would never be offered to me?"[35]

Day portrays her "industry time" as suppressing her creative instincts, narrating her exit with a sense of urgency; she reached a breaking point. Day's will to create stems not only from a desire for formal or stylistic innovation, but also from an unmet need to realize one's own value in a harsh development process. In fact, writing one's dream role is an extremely common practice among indie TV creators, particularly among women, minorities, and actors of all identities who are limited in the roles they could play. Add in the editors, film students, music video producers, postproduction supervisors, and all the rest of the industry's below- and above-the-line workers and a fuller picture emerges: producing a web show became the creative outlet for a mass of workers whose labor had been devalued, and the most successful of them connected to fans and sponsors who could support their work.

Independent TV producers face paradoxical labor conditions: as content owners, they have control but less support and security. Most web series producers are keenly aware of Hollywood's unequal labor market, but Day's commitment to addressing it is distinct. She emphasizes both her individual labor and the show's collective effort. Day's work on *The Guild* required taking on multiple roles in lieu of institutional support. Early in the show's development, Day did a lot of work not traditionally considered producer work. In an early interview with *Lifehacker*—itself emblematic of an environment in which individuals ceaselessly self-manage—Day sketched a production portrait familiar to many of her peers: "Out of necessity a web producer is forced to wear many different hats on a day to day basis; whether it's navigating a new social network, installing WordPress, learning about video cameras or doing a cast member's makeup. We're inventing it as we go along. Personally, I love the opportunity to constantly educate myself."[36] As outlined by Day, taking on multiple roles and constantly learning new ones typifies indie TV production. Day discussed doing "menial" tasks like installing web applications and below-the-line acts like handling cameras and doing makeup, jobs that would be staffed and stratified in corporate contexts.

Flexible, precarious labor is more pronounced in the early stages of an indie series's development, before producers secure a fan base or a sponsor to finance more crew and resources. Director Sean Becker, who joined the show in its second season after Microsoft came on as a distributor, noted the shift. In season one, "[I]t was a very, very skeleton crew. It was very basic," he told me. When the show got a sponsor and a budget, "they could afford a crew. And you didn't have people taking on five positions, five people filling those roles." *The Guild* is an exception that proved the rule. The vast majority of indie TV production resembles the show's first season, with small crews taking on multiple tasks and production lines blurring. This generates debate and angst among producers, who are aware that delegating roles raises quality but who lack the funds, experience, or, at times, humility to take on collaborators.[37] Those who do not want to delegate are best served by scaling projects accordingly. Elaine Carroll, creator of *Very Mary Kate*, a spoof of Mary Kate Olsen, wrote her show so she could shoot it with a crew of one: "I have to make sure that the scripts are tight." She did not use a stand-in when Mary Kate was talking to her twin Ashley, whom Carroll also played. Producers who want to make more sophisticated series need to collaborate. Matt Enlow, who created the award-winning indie series *Squaresville* and worked in development at Strike TV and AtomFilms, said he could not imagine going it alone, despite having multiple skills, because it decreases quality: "As you scale things down people have a broader range of skills. . . . If you cloned me . . . you would not have a good web show."

With funding in place, Day started delegating, using union workers whenever possible. "I want to set an example that unions don't necessarily have to be the bane of Web producers," she once said.[38] This was exemplary, especially at the time *The Guild* was being produced, when the video marketplace was less robust. So rare was union work in the independent web world that it was not until 2009 that the Writers Guild admitted its first writer for online work: Ruth Livier, an actor and creator of an early all-union production called *Ylse*. Livier saw value in union production so workers could get credit, or "points," for their work, and because it conferred legitimacy. As she wrote for my blog *Televisual*, "It was a personal honor, but it was significant in essence because it meant that the industry was acknowledging that New Media was in fact a viable alternative way in for the rest of us."[39] Most independent web shows do not employ union workers, and even if they do, "union work" in new media contexts should not be compared to that of network-era television.

Already facing pressure from a more concentrated conglomerate system, unions began offering "interactive" or "new media" contracts in the early 1990s—chiefly, the Writers Guild, Producers Guild, Directors Guild, Screen Actors Guild, and American Federation of Radio and Television Workers.[40] To encourage producers to enter into such contracts, unions allowed exemptions on minimum pay rates, meaning that workers were often paid significantly less, a cause of some consternation.[41] In some cases producers justified not using union labor in favor of more "creative" forms of payment, like revenue sharing with stars and above-the-line talent.[42] Creativity here is ambivalent: greater freedom, but often not better labor conditions. Indeed, for *She's out of Order* we hired actors under SAG's New Media contract to pay less than industry minimums; actors received rare credits but worked long hours and received no benefits.

Open distribution gives producers the freedom to create series without a "pitch." For example, in 2006 Matthew Kirsch created one of the first gay web series for YouTube with *duder*. A series about a young gay white man and his friends, *duder* was described by Kirsch as "anti-pitch," focusing on young college graduates who "spend their time overanalyzing the mundane. . . . I couldn't conceivably have my own TV show, but the web gave me the capability to have my own show." This kind of autonomy is historically anathema, rare among all legacy TV producers but rarer for those who are not straight, white men (à la *Seinfeld*, the paradigmatic show about nothing).[43] To make a show, creators pitch their workers—not executives—to kickstart production. Making television involves negotiating interests from people with different financial stakes and cultural investments: "Viewing television as an industrial— rather than merely artistic—practice shows television authorship to be inherently protracted, collective, and contested."[44] In Hollywood, texts are created through bureaucratic and occasionally personal conflicts over ideas and marketing, when executives pass "notes" to showrunners, a process much maligned by writers who desire creative freedom.[45] Free of executives, indie TV creators shape their series around resources and professional networks.

To retain intellectual property and produce their pitches without licensing fees from legacy distributors, producers must inspire workers with their creativity but also empower them to be creative. Yet executing a pitch without legacy TV support and funding comes at a cost. Becker frames the show's creative freedom as a compromise: "What do you have to give up in exchange for that? . . . It's all about sacrifice." Day has characterized *The Guild* as "a dream situation" creatively, but she hedged about financing:

> I would love to say that we're having such a horrible problem and we're rolling around in money but we aren't. It's a very funny place to be in that we're so well known yet our budgets are so small. We're still stealing shots in the alleys because it's too expensive to buy a permit. The profit margins are so small. . . . But at the end of the day I felt it was very important for me to retain the rights to the show.[46]

Like Day, Becker positions the realities of production against the benefits of relative creative freedom: "We do a lot of the season guerilla-style. . . . We're shooting ten pages a day. We don't have time to figure something out." Due to those constraints, Becker notes, he grew more adept at thinking on his feet and improvising quick solutions if, say, a location fell through; in at least one case of location failure, the solution was improvised product placement from a nearby store.[47] Day has emphasized in interviews that the basis of the show, the script, was firmly in her hands. Yet, production limitations could emerge sporadically and were even built in before filming started—every character's home, for instance, was filmed in Day's house, to save money on locations. Shooting in creators' homes is common in the indie space.

Given the precariousness of *The Guild*'s production, its distribution strategy is equally important. The tangible payoffs for open TV production are realizing one's creative goals, developing sincere connections to fans, and securing a contract for distribution. Day's success in these makes her indie TV's matinee idol. It is why she was invited to give keynotes at festivals like SXSW. It was also a source of pride. Perhaps the most pivotal decision Day made in her career, frequently cited in the press, was saying "no" to a host of unnamed legacy TV channels and corporate brands who wanted to sponsor and distribute *The Guild* but also wanted its intellectual property. The show had been popular for months before Day announced the Microsoft deal. She had the freedom to be picky. "I was adamant about holding on to the rights of my series," Day told the *Hollywood Reporter* when the deal was announced.[48] Under it, Microsoft had exclusive rights to release the show for a limited time across its online platforms, primarily MSN.com and Xbox, and rights to any gaming extensions—Sprint phones were also placed in the show—and in return Day got control of the narrative and rights to ancillary texts and sales—DVDs, comics, music video, etc.—allowing her to profit from her intellectual property.

Once Microsoft began releasing new episodes of *The Guild*, the work only continued. Without a robust marketing budget, the production team did a lot of its own promotion, which Day characterized as heavily fan- or community-driven. Day, as Elizabeth Ellcessor argues, was an ideal example of a star who managed her celebrity, fans, and marketing duties seamlessly, across platforms, enabled by social networking and its ability to facilitate conversations among various participants: "By forming textual, industrial, and personal connections through the use of online social media, the star text itself can be used . . . to smooth the convergences of aesthetics, audiences, and industries that complicate the contemporary media landscape."[49] A significant portion of *The Guild's* marketing power—its ability to deliver passionate audiences to Microsoft and sponsors—rested on Day, whose status off the line enabled a tailored and community-responsive distribution strategy.

Marketing is an important and underappreciated aspect of television development. Legacy television marketing historically uses personalities to brand channels and time slots, especially after the rise of magazine-style advertising in the 1960s gave networks more control over their schedules.[50] Independent television production challenges our understanding of the marketing of televisual texts. The vast majority of web series producers do their own marketing, leveraging whatever resources they have—stars, genres, awards, political topics—to attract fans. For *The Guild*, most of the promotion was funneled through Day, a relatable and charismatic personality to whom fans gravitated. Without the support of corporate promotional and marketing departments, open TV producers build support around themselves as stars and content creators: "It's all, basically, me behind the computer. When you see an update on the Facebook page, it's probably me or maybe a volunteer. Everything is done grass-roots because we're on web video budgets, so we can't afford to hire people to do stuff," Day said.[51] At the small-scale, low-risk end of the television market, the labor of promoting a show typically falls to the creative producer. This places a tremendous burden on that person, one most are unable to carry.

For *The Guild*, narrowing the gap between the production team and the audience lowers marketing costs. Most independent web series creators end up marketing their own shows, though very few are as adept as Day in maintaining such close and profitable ties among fans, advertisers, distributors, and producers, making it one of her most significant contributions to the way other creators conceive of independent distribution. Day's approach was integrated, parts of it unplanned. Marketing *The Guild* began in preproduction, with character development. As is typical in legacy television, and often true in the open TV market, Day wrote the show's characters to be broadly appealing[52] but to represent different gamer types. Day's self-deprecating, unassuming nature in interviews and on Twitter reinforced her connection to her character.[53] Day's appearance in person and in character as an "ordinary" woman cemented her sincerity with fans, an authenticity she positioned as anti-Hollywood: "I think Codex, in a mainstream world, would have a perfect nose and great highlights, but that's not reality. And I wanted to, somehow, infuse reality into what I was doing."[54] Ellcessor points out that in loving the show, one learns to love Day, both as a star and as a producer working outside legacy institutions.[55] This seamless integration of character, personality, producer, and marketer increased her legitimacy as a promoter: to most fans, Day *was The Guild*.

As the center of the narrative and its marketing, Day had remarkable control over the show's reception, but she also had more demands on her time and labor as a result. Especially in the show's early years, Day had to manage her fan community–building time rigorously:

> I have to prioritize because I could whittle the whole day away answering Facebook messages. I ruthlessly schedule my time with social networks, allotting an hour in the morning and an hour in the evening to deal with all of it in bulk. Important messages I forward to my Gmail account, tag them and deal with them on weekends. I try to read every message, but can only respond to about 20% of them, so any time I can answer something publicly is a great opportunity to head off duplications. That's why I love Twitter. It's an amazing tool to inform a large number of people simultaneously. I can see why people think they are a time-sink, but social networks have definitely made my show what it is because it's easy for us to deliver our content to fans and communicate en-masse on a semi-personal level.[56]

Here, Day connects the convenience and efficacy of social media with the tremendous amount of time and energy it takes to manage connections. Her invocation of social media as "semi-personal" signals that she understands the power of connecting her personal identity and labor to the show's creative success, but, unlike in one-to-one communication, she cannot respond directly to most fans. Instead, applications like Twitter and Facebook streamlined the show's fan management needs. Day's self-effacing personality on these platforms reflects and diffuses the otherwise bureaucratic nature of her involvement with fans, thus differentiating her from "corporate" television, as evidenced by the way the media and viewers perceive her.[57] Day and *The Guild* thus generate value from their sincerity.

Independent and legacy television producers harness fans quite differently, even at a time when most legacy television networks started integrating social media into their promotional campaigns. Indie TV fans perform much-needed labor and create value. *The Guild*'s fans helped produce the show, with about five hundred of them supplying much-needed funds in its first season, enough to shoot a few episodes before the team got distribution. Fans literally produced the show: according to Becker, many members of the crew signed up because they were fans. Jenni Powell, a well-known transmedia producer, got her start in video production when she met Day in a chat room and professed her fandom for *The Guild*. Powell started as a production assistant in season two and moved up to assistant director in season three (the kind of job mobility increasingly rare in Hollywood, especially for women). "Literally the show was built by the fans. . . . People see the people who create it as very approachable," Powell told me in an interview. Before working for Day, Powell worked on the set of *lonelygirl15*, and noted the similarities between the production of those early web shows, from the multiple roles crew members took on to the importance of intimate and flexible releasing strategies. Producers used Bree, the lead character on *lonelygirl15*, and her likability to cultivate fan enthusiasm. Amanda Goodfried, a senior producer on *lg15*, spent hours responding to YouTube comments as Bree. "Nurture your superfans," Powell said. "Bree became a part of the community. . . . In the beginning those hard-core people who were trying to help Bree and committed . . . a lot of those people who were there in the beginning, they're still there."

Crowdfunding significantly contributed to web series production in its early years, allowing fans to directly support and get involved in production. In 2010, I counted one hundred random web series campaigns over ninety days (the standard campaign length) on Kickstarter, the dominant crowdfunding site at the time. Fans donated $252,650 to one hundred projects, 38 percent of which were successful. Among those projects that reached their goal, producers earned on average an additional 26 percent more than their ask. From 2009 to 2013, Kickstarter reported that web series projects had attracted $6.8 million in financing out of a total $102.7 million pledged in the film and video category (its most successful), including narrative and documentary features ($74.4 million combined), short films, and animation.[58] The 2013 figures represented a threefold increase from two years prior.

Day's literal indebtedness to donors gave her added incentive to keep in close contact and occasionally create ancillary texts to satisfy their desire for more content. Throughout the show's run, producer Kim Evey and Day extended the *Guild* experience outside the series itself, including a "Do You Want to Date My Avatar" music video and a comic book published by Dark Horse and written by Day.[59] The comic explored the "in-game" world of *The Guild*, which, for cost reasons, is largely unexplored in the show, but a crucial part of the story for gamers. In 2013 Titan Books published an official companion to *The Guild*, with behind-the-scenes information and interviews, and in 2015 Felicia Day published a memoir, *You're Never Weird on the Internet*, with a foreward by Joss Whedon.[60] The show had also been a strong presence at various festivals and conventions, including the massive San Diego Comic-Con, BlizzCon, and Dragon Con, all of which are dominated by marketing from large studios and publishers.

Because Day owned *The Guild's* intellectual property, as noted above, she profited directly from its distribution. Day only had to make a few concessions to Microsoft, the most important of which was granting a semi-exclusive distribution window (up to four weeks until the end of the season), the primary function of linear distribution. This initially caused some confusion from fans, who were used to watching the show on YouTube, and led to initial concerns about "selling out": "It comes from having started on YouTube, and then all of a sudden you said, it's not on YouTube any more at all. . . . That was one of the requirements. That's the value, they're paying for the content," Day said.[61] *The Guild's* transition from pure self-distribution to restricted, corporate distribution was tenuous. After all, Microsoft's desire to build MSN and Xbox into entertainment platforms that could compete with television[62] was at odds with the producers' goal of providing the show via the most accessible platform at the time, YouTube, which professed a cultural politics of empowering independents and Hollywood outsiders. Yet it was Day's public explanations of the show's financial and creative situation that helped the transition, which most industry watchers agree she handled smoothly.

Years into *The Guild*'s existence, Day leveraged her position as the show's creative voice into not only a host of industry awards and high-profile roles on networks like Syfy and Machinima.com but also her own network, Geek & Sundry, initially part of YouTube's massive premium content initiative before eventually selling to Legendary Pictures in 2014. In 2016 Legendary Digital Networks announced a subscription video platform called Alpha, featuring exclusive new shows from Geek & Sundry as well as Chris Hardwick's Nerdist channel. Years after entering the web as a refugee from television, Day became a new media version of the decision makers who initially rejected her pitch: she was a network executive with a budget to develop a slate of programs targeted at nerds—particularly women. It is an inspiring tale of the power of retaining creative control relatively independent of corporate studios and distributors. As open TV's producers develop their own intellectual property, they pilot new shows legacy distributors can "pick up." The following section analyzes two indie series of disparate degrees of popularity and marketability to show how indie producers' pursuit of creative freedom and control in an open and precarious market innovates and intervenes in the legacy pilot process.

Indie TV Series as Open Pilot Development

By developing series as new intellectual properties without financing from corporate distributors, indie TV producers transform the market for "pilots"—the first episode of a series traditionally produced long before the rest of the season. They circumvent the process by which development executives dilute pilots' cultural specificity, and they prove the value of their story through fan engagement and producer-led development. In this section I contrast the story of *High Maintenance* with that of a lesser-known series, *The Real Girl's Guide to Everything Else*, to show how providing meaningful, artistically or politically driven work for creative producers creates value and supports innovation. Both shows serve as a counterpoint to legacy network processes, where pilots were designed to hook a large audience, increasingly rare in a competitive TV market. Instead, web series demonstrate how new series benefit from finding time to develop a voice through collaboration and introduce new characters and storytellers.

High Maintenance tells the story of an unnamed marijuana dealer who delivers product to stressed-out New Yorkers. It is an anthology series where every episode focuses on a different customer. In *Real Girl's Guide*, Lebanese lesbian Rasha is being forced by her publisher to write a straight, mass-market, chick-lit book instead of a political work on women's rights in Afghanistan. The story revolves around Rasha's venture into (presumably, white) heterosexuality as she sacrifices her political ideals to get the story she wants. A collective of queer women of color—led by writer Carmen Elena Mitchell, director Heather de Michele, and actor-producers Nikki Brown, Robin Dalea, Reena Dutt, and Jennifer Weaver—produced *Real Girl's Guide* as a response to *Sex and the City* and Hollywood's romantic comedy films. In this effort they contributed programming to new indie web TV networks, secured critical attention for its producers, and attracted interest from established producers with more funds for development. Both case studies demonstrate how, even with varying levels of success in the form of corporate development contracts, indie TV producers reorient pilot development toward stories with greater sincerity and cultural specificity, where actors and crew have creative ownership and distribution is flexible or community based. Indie production emerges as an innovative approach to series development attuned to the needs and desires of creators invested in telling new stories.

High Maintenance's "Helen" episode begins with a woman coughing as she lies next to her son in a cramped bedroom. She wants him to shave his beard, but he says he won't for another two to three weeks because his oatmeal-based shaving cream is on back order. In a montage, we see how consumption shapes the man's life. We see photos and drawings of Helen Hunt on the walls (hence the episode title). The man orders all types of goods online, and we see some delivered: shirts from J. Crew and groceries from delivery workers who clearly know him as a regular client. Suddenly, we leave the cramped apartment and we're outside in a street festival, with a bearded guy roaming the streets and taking in the sights. This is the man's next delivery worker, and he's delivering weed. The man puts on a new shirt and brings the delivery person peanuts, and they engage in idle chatter—the delivery person asks about buying a dreamcatcher from the festival—before the man asks for Pink Kush for his mother. When the delivery guy leaves, the man puts the Pink Kush in a box full of unsmoked weed: he needs the company more than the weed. The episode ends.

The episode does little to advance the plot of the series, nor does it do much to develop the central character, the Guy dealing weed, played by co-creator Ben Sinclair. Each episode introduces a new character, a New Yorker in search of marijuana for a variety of reasons, typically stress. Every episode is different except for the appearance of the Guy. Originally conceived as a vehicle for Sinclair, co-created with his life partner and casting director Katja Blichfeld, *High Maintenance* started production when the creators reconceived it as a more open, flexible character study: "We just want to get inside the apartment and meet these characters. And that was it," Blichfeld told me. "It's more intriguing, I think, to just speculate what's this guy's backstory than seeing it."

Blichfeld and Sinclair's approach to serial storytelling defies legacy television's genre categories (comedy and drama) and its approach to story development, where pilots clearly introduce and explain central characters, settings, and plots. The flexibility of their production and storytelling practices allowed the *High Maintenance* creators to develop a devoted fan base via Vimeo not because they aggressively pursued fans but because their show offered multiple points of entry beyond plot, be it identification with the characters, the city, or their situations. Episodes can be watched in any order. As evidence of open TV producers advancing innovation at a small scale, its earlier episodes were produced for $500 to $700 each. *High Maintenance*'s episodes are distinct and stand alone. As *New Yorker* critic Emily Nussbaum writes in her review of the web series, "Because 'High Maintenance' has no obligation to follow any one character, or make a season-long arc pay off, it can take different risks. Gradually, the episodes build up a detailed and empathetic image of a specific demographic slice of New York, one cramped apartment at a time."[63] Rejecting the pilot requirement of introducing the characters and plot, the creative team cultivated a realistic world based on their location, the actor, and social identity (primarily New York–based, upper-middle-class creatives). The production team responded as much to who and what was on set as to the script and overall identity of the show. For "Helen" they shot in the apartment of one of their producers, Russell Gregory, a talent manager whose clients were cast throughout the series. Gregory's apartment was small, traditionally considered a production constraint—legacy shows seek large apartments or studio sets for added production value. But Blichfeld and Sinclair, serving as their own art directors, stuffed the space with *more* furniture to give it a cramped feel. "I think really that's where the idea came from, was having the space first," Blichfeld told *Fresh Air*'s Ann Marie Baldonado.[64] Serendipitously, on the day of shooting, a street festival was rerouted to outside the apartment. Initially viewing this as a problem, they realized that it provided a cinematic contrast to the hermetic protagonist, as well as a sense of unpredictability and spontaneity characteristic of living in New York. "Helen" is also one of the show's most collaborative episodes; Sinclair and Blichfeld developed the story, but the script came from Michael Cyril Creighton, at the time known for his indie series *Jack in a Box*, one of the first indie series reviewed by the *New York Times*.

Years later, *High Maintenance* ranks among the most critically acclaimed independent web series. It achieved notoriety first by cultivating meaningful, if undercompensated, work for above- and below-the-line producers in New York. Rather than focusing on cultivating fans—as Felicia Day did—or continually developing new series—as Scott Zakarin did— Sinclair and Blichfeld worked with their collaborators on developing the tone and voice of their show. Their "series of shorts," as Blichfeld described it to the *New York Observer*, functioned as an extended pilot with a diverse array of characters, contexts, and plots.[65] Vimeo eventually picked up the show for its On Demand platform, but soon after, Blichfeld and Sinclair secured a six-episode series order from HBO, rare for the premium network accustomed to producing pilots before ordering a full season. The HBO deal was concrete evidence that indie TV series can function as pilots, developing stories from new groups of storytellers for specific communities of fans.

Indie TV producers reinvented piloting as building a community of producers. Traditionally, television comedies and dramas have one or two creators who produce a pilot based on a successful pitch. After a network orders more episodes, creators establish a "show bible" with characters and plots to be executed by a writing team led by a showrunner. The hierarchical structure ensures continuity in broadcast and cable shows whose narratives run for hours each season. With fewer resources and shorter run times, many indie TV creators find tight control over the story a luxury they cannot afford. Consider Daryn Strauss, whose drama *Downsized*, an online drama about the recession, earned her membership to the Writers Guild and shared WGA nominations with Creighton's *Jack in a Box* as well as higher-budget projects like AOL's *Aim High* (from studio director McG) and NBC's *30 Rock*. For her series, Strauss worked alongside underemployed actor-friends to develop storylines about the consequences of economic decline: "It was a very collaborative process. . . . We shoot in blocks. So we shot a couple of episodes, and then I would watch the footage and see what the footage is like and then I would write more based on what they brought," she told me in an interview. *Downsized* is led by a woman (Strauss) and features a racially diverse cast, all of whom feel the economic downturn differently.

Actors are television's most visible creative workers, but unless they earn a regular role on a long-running scripted series, they rank among the industry's least empowered. Pilot season makes inequalities clear, as legions of actors camp out in Hollywood to audition for a tiny number of roles. Moreover, actors rarely have input in their characters. New and emerging actors entrust their careers to the whims of development executives and executive producers. "It can take years for someone to even get a pilot made," said Vivian Kerr, co-creator with Heleya de Barrios of the 2010 comedy *We Are with the Band*, about two lost young women trying to figure out their lives in Los Angeles. *We Are with the Band* gave Kerr and de Barrios a chance to write lead roles for women where they did not have to play the "straight girl" to the funny man. "A large part of why we wrote kind of a female-driven comedy is coming out of a growing frustration with reading the straight-man always, even when we do get auditions for some of these bigger shows," de Barrios said. "Those roles that we wanted to play weren't readily available to us," Kerr added. The pilot production market establishes the lead roles for the primetime season, and it is where inequalities in role distribution take root.

Independent web series producers are more reliant on actors in new stories than legacy studios; actors' depth of participation greatly affects the way the story proceeds. An actor dropping out can halt a production without a casting budget. Because actors are essential on set and very often (but, depending on scale, not always) needed for large blocks of shooting, indie series creators ask more of their actors' time but often compensate by giving them more control over their characters and the story. For *High Maintenance,* even though Blichfeld and Sinclair wrote all episodes of the show other than "Helen," they continually redistributed creative ownership over the narrative. As a casting director who eventually secured an Emmy Award for casting *30 Rock*, Blichfeld said they were "super fortunate that we've all been in that community for as long as we have":

> We're really performance-oriented. Like more than anything. So, we're just interested in what's going to get the best performance from our actors. Which really informs our whole process. It's why we keep our sets to a very minimal group of people. It's why we tell actors, "Ok. Here's the script. Ultimately make sure you hit that and hit that. But if this doesn't sound right coming out of your mouth, just say it in your own words." We like really try to make them feel like . . . they have some ownership over their character. And we're asking them to do very little, usually. We're usually asking them to just kind of be themselves. Because we're usually writing for actors and hoping they're going to bring themselves to the character.

Blichfeld's description of their development process makes perfect sense for a series in which every episode rests on a small number of performances and whose producers all work with actors on a regular basis. With each episode consisting of just two or three scenes, actors drive the story. *High Maintenance*'s creators define independent production as the ability to best utilize talent, and it is not alone. In his own series, *Jack in a Box*, Creighton, their collaborator on "Helen," also wrote lean episodes where he could demand less time from guest stars—shoots lasted at most three hours—and gave them more agency: "I do tend to write for specific actors, and I've been lucky that they've all been able to do it," Creighton said.

Many independent series productions are produced by actors looking for better roles and more creative control, especially women. Ingrid Jungermann and Desiree Akhavan created their Brooklyn web series *The Slope* to mock their relationship and Brooklyn neighborhood while showcasing their own writing and directing talent. On the basis of that success, Akhavan financed a feature film she wrote, directed, and led, *Appropriate Behavior*, a semi-autobiographical story about a bisexual Arab New Yorker, which screened at Sundance, while Jungermann produced two seasons of a spin-off, *F to 7th*, showcasing numerous great women actors across generations, including Amy Sedaris, Gaby Hoffman, Stewart Thorndike, Janeane Garofalo, and Olympia Dukakis (revealing how age and gender intersect to produce inequalities in casting). Never a widely viewed series online, *F to 7th* secured a development deal with Showtime in 2016, when episode counts ranged in the low thousands and Jungermann's own feature film, *Women Who Kill*, made festival rounds.[66] Meanwhile, Julie Ann Emery (*Hitch*, *Fargo*) created her relationship comedy *Then We Got HELP!* to cast brilliant actors but also to produce the kind of work she didn't always get to do in legacy television and film: "I write for specific actors. . . . [T]hey're all people we've worked with. We respect their work, and like their temperament and would want to be stuck in a room for sixteen hours with them," she said. Several legacy soap opera actors migrated to indie production after their characters were written off or legacy networks canceled their series. In the case of two popular web soaps, *Venice* and *Eastsiders*, producers cast actors whose characters were marginalized as gay on legacy TV: costars Crystal Chappell and Jessica Leccia's queer romance on *Guiding Light* drew fans to *Venice*, which ran for four seasons, financed through subscriptions; *Eastsiders* creator Kit Williamson starred opposite Van Hansis, whose character on *As the World Turns* performed daytime television's first gay kiss only to end up tragically alone. *Eastsiders* aired its first season on Logo's website but crowdfunded its second and third seasons, available on Vimeo On Demand and later licensed to Netflix.

Blichfeld and Sinclair wrote for specific actors, revealing how indie production reshapes the legacy casting process. Rather than auditioning, the creators focused on getting to know the talent and building rapport to support sincere performances and ensure a smooth filming process. "We don't have a traditional audition process. But the thing that could be equated with that is just us hanging out with the person that we'd like to write for," said Sinclair, who cited the casting of Dan Stevens (*Downton Abbey*) in "Rachel," the episode that won them a Writers Guild Award. "We basically hung out with him a half-dozen times before we realized what character would fit best for him." The first episode, "Stevie," has Bridget Moloney, Sinclair's sister-in-law, as the lead (Blichfeld met Sinclair through Moloney). "Olivia," once the most popular episode, features Heléne Yorke, Gregory's client, and Max Jenkins, a friend of Sinclair and Blichfeld and star of Bobby Hodgson and Karina Mangu-Ward's web series *Gay's Anatomy*. Blichfeld cast both Yorke and Jenkins in very small parts on *30 Rock*. Yet casting for *30 Rock* was a challenge because Blichfeld needed strong actors who could keep up with career comedians Tracy Morgan, Tina Fey, and Alec Baldwin and also deliver laughs with just a couple of lines: "I started fantasizing—and strategizing—about ways that I could somehow . . . put a spotlight on some of these actors who I am obsessed with," she said.

Giving actors more responsibility also streamlined the production process for the producers of *Real Girl's Guide*. Lacking the clout of casting a broadcast television series, they conceived of their team variously as a "family" and a "collective." Everyone, from actors to producers, shared responsibilities on set. Weaver and Dutt were both actors and associate producers, with responsibilities on the set and before filming began: Dutt managed craft services, and Weaver helped out as a production assistant and with the art department. In preproduction, Weaver helped audition actors and find costumes; after production, she helped Mitchell research festival submission deadlines. Everyone helped with fundraising. The producers raised money by e-mail and through creative events, such as a karaoke night with a ten dollar entry fee and raffle. They asked three comedians to be *American Idol*–type judges but to only give positive feedback, in keeping with the project's progressive thrust. In the end, the team was able to raise half the project's budget, and they put in their own money for the other half.

In contrast to *High Maintenance*'s focus on television narrative as art, *The Real Girl's Guide* motivated actors to produce it because Mitchell focused the story on reforming the cultural politics of television production and narrative. Mitchell characterized *Real Girl's Guide* as a commodity intended to change "what's seen as marketable for women," and she praised progressive examples in the mass media, including writer-actor Tina Fey. In fact, all of the show's creators peppered our conversations with examples of what they saw as positive changes in legacy media, focusing on women actors who appeared to have agency in the production of their image. Associate producer Dutt cited South

Asian actors—*The Office*'s Mindy Kaling and *Scrubs*'s Sonal Shah—and black actors—Jada Pinkett Smith and Halle Berry—as examples of women who produced original material. Weaver, an associate producer who plays Liz (the lead's girlfriend), praised women's roles on Showtime's *Nurse Jackie* (Edie Falco) and CBS's *Good Wife* (Julianna Marguiles). Brown cited the diversity on *True Blood* (the lead's black best friend, Tara, played by Rutina Wesley), and Dalea highlighted roles for women and people of color on *Grey's Anatomy*, *Damages*, and *Mad Men*. But such roles "are rare, and a lot of them are white," she said.

The creators lamented the limits of the marketplace for actors, made clear by *Sex and the City*'s narrow (straight, white) representation of womanhood. Dutt bemoaned the lack of "fulfilling" roles for women of color, recalling personal incidents: "[M]ost of the time I'll walk into an audition office, and I'll get into character and they'll say, 'can you do this with an [Indian] accent?'" Brown, who is black, said nonstereotypical roles were hard to come by in Hollywood: "You come out here and it's not quite about talent. . . . The representations aren't as positive as I'd like them to be, for my own race." Dalea, who identifies as multiethnic and plays the lead, said the issue is supply and demand: there are many more actors than roles, and race and gender only exacerbate inequalities.

Research on television role distribution by gender and race in the late 2000s and early 2010s showed persistent inequalities, despite the appearance of some diversity, particularly on cable and on digital series. According to the UCLA Bunche Center's 2015 Hollywood Diversity Report, broadcast scripted shows became less diverse between 2011–2012 and 2012–2013, with nearly 60 percent of series having less than 20 percent of their casts represented by minority actors.[67] Over 60 percent of cable scripted series had the same level of representation, despite an uptick in the number of majority-minority series on cable, just over 10 percent.[68] Over 80 percent of roles on broadcast series were claimed by white actors and 54 percent of roles by men, with white actors claiming 77 percent of roles on cable and male actors, 58 percent.[69]

Mitchell, de Michele, Brown, Dalea, Dutt, and Weaver turned their disappointment with the cultural politics of Hollywood casting into a project to correct representational imbalances on television, starting with centering the story on an Arab lesbian and a multicultural cast whose actors could decide to what degree their race affected their character. For Mitchell, it was important to write scripts that did not force the characters to play up their race or sexuality. "I liked that Carmen wrote diverse characters where that wasn't the focal point," said Brown, who found it "refreshing" that her character, Vanna, "went to Columbia, is bossy, and happens to be African American. . . . You don't get that that often." De Michele, the director, who is white and identified as lesbian, liked that race did not drive the story, despite the cast's diversity. "The characters happen to be of color but it has nothing to do with the story," she said. Most importantly, the actors all said they could shape their characters and follow their instincts. Some participated in the project from its inception and thus had input from the beginning. Others contributed during shooting. Dalea said she changed dialogue that did not feel right; one of the more memorable lines in the series—when Rasha refuses to go for a bikini wax by saying, "I went to Columbia"— was improvised. Such connections between actors and their characters helped them feel connected to the work and the project. Dalea said of her character, "We have the same value system but she has the balls to go out and fight for it." Similarly, Brown said she related to Vanna's love of fashion and her diverse group of friends. Since Dutt helped initiate the project, her character hewed closely to Dutt's own off-screen personality as a "crazy, goofy" woman, and she found it a welcome change from her mainstream roles: "My last three auditions were medical practitioners . . . [but] Indian American girls can be different. They can be your best friend that's zany and not appropriate."

Beyond a focus on actors, indie producers must adapt to local conditions, the availability of crew, and even viewers' perception of the story. The *High Maintenance* producers noted how one week before shooting "Dinah," weather reports forecast a blizzard. In one week, they rewrote the episode so the lead, Chad (Chris Roberti), is stuck in town because of the blizzard, and they prepared to shoot in the snow. "They're small, flexible, and then they get really excited about what they've been flexible about. Then all of a sudden it's like, 'Oh my god, snow!' It's going to look amazing," Gregory said of the producers. Other episodes came together in postproduction. In one case, the actors they wanted were going away for the summer, so they shot something—a "cutaway scene," Blichfeld said—and sat on the footage for several months before writing around it. Filling multiple roles aided the creators' flexible style of production:

"We don't really write scripts as much as we write shooting drafts. . . . [I]t's nice that I'm an editor and when I'm on set, we can be like, 'Okay, we can make this work. We got it, we got it.' You know, we can move on," Sinclair said. The team was also open to working with crew they didn't know: they hired an eighteen-year-old British filmmaker who e-mailed them; he received an entry-level credit. Yet most of the crew were connected to New York's independent film and comedy scenes; the team shared crew and actors with other web series like *The Slope* and *Broad City*. As Ilana Glazer told me, "We were able to play with these different directors. . . . I know you don't even get to play on a bigger scale." Creators framed this ability to work with different crew, because of the inconsistency and low cost of production, as an asset.

Character-driven projects representing specific local or cultural experiences bring value to new online distributors. As noted above, in an unprecedented deal, Vimeo contracted the *High Maintenance* creators to write and produce six episodes to be sold on its On Demand platform. The team got a "nano-budget" from Vimeo to deliver more content to their "passionate, loyal following," as Greg Clayman, Vimeo's general manager of audience networks, told the *Los Angeles Times*.[70] After producing thirteen engaging character-driven stories off the line, the team secured their intellectual property and creative control, along with 90 percent of sales after Vimeo recouped its investment for a limited license. Episodes sold for $1.99 each or $7.99 for all six. "We were like artists in residence over there," Sinclair told me. "We had this repository of characters [from developing for FX] . . . we were just mixing and matching." With a clear production budget, Blichfeld and Sinclair expanded their series, bringing back fan favorite characters, including Yorke and Creighton, and adding locations to give greater character context.

Freed from the linear cable system, the creators kept open ended the episode length (newer episodes ranged between ten and twenty minutes) and release schedule (three-episode "cycles" every few months, instead of seasons). The flexibility of digital distribution made Vimeo more appealing than FX, where they first had a development deal, because for FX they had to construct the story around the commercial breaks that finance legacy networks. Moreover, they were already publishing the series on Vimeo, and their approach—a series of shorts—fit well with Vimeo's existing network development strategy based on "Staff

Picks" of the best videos on the site (overwhelmingly shorts). Vimeo's on-demand, shorts-driven strategy matched the team's personal taste: "That's definitely how we like to view media," said Blichfeld, referring to their on-demand viewing habits. "We spent two years building our brand and it would be kind of devastating if a marketing exec rebranded and took it out of our control," she said. What they wanted control over is the specificity of the characters and the time we spend with them, even if not every fan identifies with every character. Sinclair says, "With Vimeo we don't have to tell big stories. It's very niche. . . . We don't expect everybody to get every joke or relate to every character." The *High Maintenance* team cultivated their brand differently than Vimeo, however. While the network took out ads across the Internet—especially on New York–based sites like Gawker and IndieWire—and on public transportation in cities like New York and London, the team got most of their pre-development marketing muscle from Tumblr, where they posted GIFs and art related to weed, New York, and other artistically driven content.

High Maintenance's innovative release strategy shows how indie TV series, as pilots developed for an open network, adapt marketing and distribution to meet the needs of the story, the storytellers, and their fans. Indie series generally only find a market if the story relates to its communities of interest and the producers collaborate on getting the word out. As a result of the producers' passion for the project, *Real Girl's Guide* was able to achieve a sizable audience for a low-budget show. As Brown said explicitly, "Because you believe in it, you want to market it . . . I felt like it was a very collaborative effort." While Mitchell handled most of the marketing, some of the actors and producers pitched in, mentioning the show wherever they could, at festivals and among friends. Dalea worked in marketing and so offered to write press releases and blog posts for the series. "I offered that up. That's not something they requested of me." Her marketing efforts got them entry into a few festivals and stories on National Public Radio, *Jezebel*,[71] and *AfterEllen*.[72]

Real Girl's Guide's narrative connects with producers' outreach to fans. *Real Girl's Guide*'s central plot is Rasha's quest to write about a serious issue (Afghan women) and sell her work to the publishing industry (which is dominated by chick lit). This quest serves as a loose allegory for producing independent and fan-driven media in a conglomerate-controlled media system, which became part of its pitch to viewers. The central tension in *Real Girl's Guide* is between creating something culturally and politically important (the domain of the fan and the marginal) and creating something marketable (the domain of industry and the mainstream). In the end, Rasha compromises on her dream, writing the manuscript she wants but selling the book packaged with free women's products like cosmetics, a clear nod to dominant chick-lit culture. For Mitchell, this is an important compromise, a way to chart a third way in political and grassroots production, to take the "cultural economy" of marginal works and place it within industrial practice: "[We've] got to continue to write what we want to write and to find the stories that we want to write. And sometimes it's going to have to take some creative packaging to get the stories out there." For de Michele, compromises are intermediary steps in progress: "It's definitely a feminist story, and we're all feminists driving it. But we also recognize that we have to package something so someone will eat it. It's sort of like this stupid compromise that women have to make just to step ahead, but it just comments on the reality, while being smart within that reality." The tension here among reality, progress, and the compromises between them is significant. *Real Girl's Guide* is an unconventional story for legacy television. In its trailer, it introduces potential fans to a familiar concept—a story about four girlfriends trying to find love and success à la *Sex and the City*—before subverting it by referencing the "other girls" who do not want Prince Charming. Rasha complains about having to write a "Middle Eastern dating novelette" to save her women's history book and responds apprehensively after her friends rally for a makeover—"women of color unite and shop!" Riffing off *Sex and the City*'s breezy theme song, the trailer ends with a toast to Afghanistan and a shot of Rasha tripping on her heels as her girlfriends skip beside her.

The team consistently expressed their disenchantment with the raced and gendered dynamics of marketing. Most were fluent in marketing-speak, citing brands' and networks' desire for young white male viewers, the most coveted group in both film and television. Mitchell recalled the numerous times she had described her project to colleagues and felt quite marginalized:

Even right now, when we go out to plug *Real Girl's*, it's all guys. It's all white guys in their midtwenties to midthirties, and as soon as you say something with the word "girl" in the title, it's kind of like they don't hear anything else. They put you in a box: "Oh, it's a girl film." . . . There's also this understanding in that world that what really sells is work that is marketed to the eighteen-to-thirty-four male demographic, and [*Real Girl's Guide*] is deliberately going out of its way to not touch that demographic and basically market to everybody else. It's like, "Well, why would you deliberately write something that's not commercially viable?"

Mitchell's criticism of the television market is personal, political, and professional. She acknowledges who produces most commercial content, for whom the content is made, and reasons why women might not feel welcome promoting their own work in such a market. Then she uses this criticism to argue for *The Real Girl's Guide*'s importance, turning a pitch that would fail in the corporate market into one that might connect with fans. Their project for industry reform eventually became a practical sales pitch to potential investors and audiences: *Real Girl's Guide* is a women-produced series marketed to women and people of color who felt excluded by the market: "Guys in the industry, they think about the market first and the content secondly. . . . We kind of went the opposite way, which I think made our series really successful, because we focused on story, and we focused on interesting characters and we focused on going beyond traditional demographics," said Mitchell, formulating a way to think about marketing content as artistic, progressive, and, at the same time, fan driven.

A growing network of web distribution sites created for releasing independent and minority web series helped the series spread and reach potential fans.[73] The first site Mitchell approached for distribution was Strike TV, created by Hollywood professionals after the Writers Guild of America strike. The Strike TV executives liked the *Real Girl's Guide* script and told the team to send them the show after it was completed. As of this writing, the series has 150,000 views on its first episode and forty thousand on the finale on Strike TV's YouTube channel. Once the show went live in 2010, other sites started expressing interest: video sites DailyMotion, Rowdy Orbit, and KoldCast were interested, while lesbian entertainment sites *AfterEllen* and *One More Lesbian* redistributed the series through YouTube.[74] *AfterEllen* consistently supported lesbian web series to counter the dearth of legacy media programs, and

One More Lesbian held real-world marketing events for original web content. "The lesbian sites have been so incredibly supportive. They have gone out of their way to spread the word about us," Mitchell said. These networks tried to marshal the passions of marginalized communities into an independently sustainable commercial market, although their success varied. *Real Girl's Guide*'s diverse cast, political and industrial critique, and inclusive story, along with its invocation of a popular franchise, helped widen its distribution options.

It is hard to overestimate the importance of independent and culturally specific distribution networks, because web distributors are not immune to Hollywood's bias for young, white men. Describing why she built Digital Chick TV as a platform to distribute *Downsized*, alongside other shows by and articles about women producers, Strauss said, "I felt like at the time a lot of the distribution sites were really targeting that male demographic and it was really hard for women to find web series." The issue of discovery affected series like *Real Girl's Guide* more than it did other shows. The show found an audience receptive to its explicitly political and culturally situated story in large part by being redistributed through independent networks interested in cultivating underserved audiences. In turn, series like *High Maintenance* and *Real Girl's Guide* helped brand independent networks and made them relevant to those communities. While many independent networks were unable to sustain their enterprises in a tough online advertising market—explored in greater depth in chapters 3 and 4—they nonetheless served a vital function in the market.

The Value and Limits of Creative Ownership in Independent Production

While this chapter shows the value of indie innovation in an open market, the open market was limited by who could succeed and how far they could go without legacy TV's deep pockets. When I spoke with Abbi Jacobson and Ilana Glazer three weeks before they started shooting the *Broad City* pilot for Comedy Central, they were in good spirits, despite a hectic development year. Originally FX had optioned the show, but the network let it go. Comedy Central, whose programs skewed heavily toward the young male demographic, needed more programs that appealed to young women, as evidenced by its distribution of *Inside Amy Schumer*. Jacobson and Glazer conceived of the cable series as a bigger version of the web series, where the segments between commercials functioned like mini-webisodes, or skits. "I just want to try as best as we can to recreate what we did with the web series," Glazer said. "There was just something about it that was just a little bit different."

The pair no longer had pure creative freedom. Glazer compared working with FX to "Hollywood grad school or college," where they learned how to realize their vision and protect their voices within the legacy development process. Producing a web series helped them solidify their voice, particularly visible in experimental episodes like "Commute," a music video contrasting Abbi and Ilana's morning routines, and "Dream," a tight sketch about Abbi dreaming of Ilana. "Now that we made these decisions, we've proved that we know what's best for this brand by trying to stretch it," Glazer told me. But television development privileges continuity: "People like familiarity. Executives like familiarity," Glazer said. "We don't just have total control. . . . [Y]ou also have to sand those edges down so that more people can watch and enjoy it," she added. Judging from critical reception of the first seasons on Comedy Central, as well as the network picking it up for subsequent seasons, Glazer and Jacobson negotiated their creative needs and those of the network well.

Each of the producers in this chapter lived the dream, or, at least, some form of the dream. They were able to produce and distribute the shows they wanted with relative autonomy, and those shows found fan bases, small and large. What was missing from the dream was what only large institutions could provide: sustainability and legitimacy. Instead, these producers consistently worked across multiple roles, meeting the needs of sponsors and fans much in the way legacy network executives, showrunners, and marketing directors do. Until a corporate distributor stepped in, the reward for their labor was creative autonomy and flexibility in production and distribution practices.

Stability in the open TV market is elusive for most. Finding stability is challenging when labor is at a surplus—e.g., the incredible glut of skilled film professionals trained by accredited schools and universities.[75] As Christian Fuchs notes in his treatise on labor in digital capitalism, working in the creative industries in this moment in history means never fully living "the dream"—generating one's own capital consistently through one's own creative labor—but rather experiencing a constant back and forth: "[I]t is not a fixed, but a dynamic category, as many of these individuals shift from self-employment to temporary labor, unpaid labor, and back again, and so on."[76] In the face of uncertainty, individuals rely on themselves and small networks more than institutions like studios or the government to get work done. Life itself becomes a pitch, in the words of Rosalind Gill, where individuals "must be flexible, adaptable, social, self-directing, and able to work for days and nights at a time without encumbrances or needs."[77] Most web series creators would recognize this life.

Still, in their search for creative freedom and escape from the industry's cold marketing calculus and uninspiring labor conditions, independent television producers develop innovative strategies for releasing content: integrating audiences organically, experimenting with storytelling and release strategies, leveraging creative autonomy and seeking ownership, and seamlessly connecting production politics with brand and fan desires. Indie producers show how television can harness the affordances of an open distribution platform, with all the benefits that distribution autonomy can bring: off-kilter or specific stories, greater responsiveness to fan demands, and greater openness to the politics of cultural representation.

The web has been home to thousands of web series, few of which could boast the successes outlined in this chapter.[78] The chasm between the possibility of new media—which Day, the *High Maintenance* creators, and the *Real Girl's Guide* creators typified—and persistent challenges of an unequal and saturated marketplace—evidenced by the relative marginality of the rest of the market—completes the picture of independent networked television production. Indie TV production offers the possibility of fulfilling many of Hollywood's invisible workers' dreams. But conglomerates still control the vast majority of the media market. Legacy TV series garner the most attention from press and fans, set the standards for production quality and practice, and command the most funding from brands and advertisers. Web creators propose a different way of doing things, and, in limited cases, the corporations are watching and listening. In the next chapter I delve deeper into the issues of representation raised in this chapter to demonstrate possibilities for more sincere stories about those historically underrepresented on legacy TV.

3

Open TV Representation

Reforming Cultural Politics

Prologue: Representing Black Women in *She's out of Order*

Teresa Lasley conceived of Tara, star of *She's out of Order*, as a woman quick to anger but mindful of the "angry black woman" stereotype perpetuated by cable reality shows. Tara is confident professionally but struggles over how she represents herself to society. She is a relatively complex representation for a series with short episodes. Every line of dialogue, scene, and gesture matters more in short-form stories. Each scene composes a larger percentage of the whole. During our final shoot, a minor plot point caused a disagreement over Tara's representation, which delayed production. The ultimate question was one of sincerity: would a character with these identities really do this? In particular, would a bougie black woman get an attitude over a ticket fee for a fundraiser she agreed to attend? The answer is no, but on-set confusion over what was sincere versus stereotypical demonstrates sincerity's value to underrepresented creators crafting short-form representations of their communities.

Our final shoot took place at Studio Christensen, a gallery in Center City. We started filming the scene late—9:30 p.m.—even though we were supposed to start at 7:00 p.m. and the director had arrived at 8:15 p.m. At this point, everyone was tired, particularly Teresa, who had been in almost every scene for the entire three-weekend shoot. The hectic shooting pace was causing her to worry. Throughout the day, she had been struggling to get into character. Earlier, she mentioned to me a problem with the final scene: in it, Tara resists paying the ticket fee because she doesn't want to be at a gallery for a fundraiser, but Teresa said that Tara would not show up at the door (the beginning of the scene) if she was going to stiff a charity. She asked Derek to rewrite it, which he did. When it came to filming the scene, she stopped filming to say the line was changed, and Rhonney did not seem to understand. The two stepped out. At this point it was 9:30 p.m., and some of the actors told me they had 10:00 p.m. buses to New York to catch. While we all waited in the gallery for Rhonney and Teresa to talk it out, I called Derek to confirm the bus times. I told them the last buses were leaving in twenty minutes so we needed to shoot now or cut the scene. Rhonney asked about trains leaving later, and I found one closer to 11:00 p.m. for a steep seventy dollars per ticket. We quickly revised the scene, Derek bought three train tickets, and we shot everything in forty-five minutes, with myself and colleague Khadijah White chipping in as extras. The scene did not make it into the first season.

I narrate this scene to demonstrate how debates over representation take hold and drive costs in production, revealing how producers value and negotiate character, story, and reception. Because television is historically collaborative in the way it is written and produced, the process of crafting representations is necessarily complex. In the low-budget context of independent web production, where producers take on multiple roles, disagreements over representation can be more challenging to negotiate. *She's out of Order* had five producers, all invested in getting the project done but with their own assessments of the final product's value.

The question of "who is Tara?" weighed on all of us before, during, and after production. We constantly debated the consequences of not having enough storytelling time for a nuanced representation of a black woman. John Fiske noted how television narratives function on multiple levels: reality (environment, light, sound, bodies), representation (plot, costume, lighting, character), and ideology (racism, capitalism, misogyny).[1] A complex labor system supported Hollywood's representations, with production jobs to handle the level of representation and commercial imperatives on the distribution end (the network's programming and funding goals) shaping each representation's ideology. Independent television creators produced new realities, representations, and ideologies without a legacy development system with longer traditions and more rules. Our limited resources, fluid organization, and storytelling aspirations were in constant tension. Representing complex, historically underrepresented black women, we found resolving these tensions something of a challenge.

When asked why she created the show, Teresa told us she tended to be misunderstood in social interactions, and this misunderstanding related to her individual identity. *She's out of Order* offers the provocation of a black woman who is perceived as "difficult." Teresa wanted episodes to flip audience expectations: "She's not really out of order, it's just her environment. . . . She just acts on it," e.g., the impulse to call out impropriety or disrespect. Although she was nervous about the representation, this was personal as well as political for her: sincerely representing the complexities of identity and identification for black women was rare.

Because production and representation are so complex, many of the most successful independent series, as in film, come from actor-auteurs: producers who write and star in their series. By controlling as much of the story and its execution as is feasible, star producers like Felicia Day and Issa Rae keep the story sincere, allowing them to meaningfully connect with fans who shared similar experiences and spread the story to friends online. Indie TV series build community through shared recognition and social networking,[2] but rare is the producer who can write sincerely about his or her experience, act the leading role, mobilize a crew to shoot and edit it, market it, and reach fans. *She's out of Order* lacked a singular vision on the value of its representations. Teresa—a black woman—and Derek, Rhonney, and I—black men—had different investments in the representation of black women. Both Rhonney and Teresa expressed a desire to see more black women in comedy, but for different reasons. Rhonney stressed how *She's out of Order* challenges the industrial role of black women in comedy: "[I]n comedy usually the black woman is the stereotypical girlfriend," he said, adding that he was particularly proud of seeing the role performed by Teresa, "a woman of color that I knew, that I grew up with, put out there." For Teresa, comedy was an artistic impulse, a chance to connect with her own unique perspective on humor: "It was a chance to confront this impulse . . . something closer to me." Meanwhile, Derek wanted to support a broader community of artists of color, particularly guest star LaJune, who was pursuing a singing career: "It gave us a way to celebrate and showcase all these talented collaborating artists we worked with. We were trying to give opportunities to other talented actors, colleagues." As a researcher I was primarily interested in the particular dynamics of what it would take to produce representations of black women—our three leads and two supporting characters—along with their reception.

Our production delay offers insight into our issues with representation, which many productions have. Written with Teresa's feedback but not her precise voice, *She's out of Order* ultimately reflected multiple visions of the same character. At the same time, my suggestion to keep episodes short raised the importance of every single scene. In fact, most episodes were essentially one scene, and, depending on how a viewer found an episode, any episode could be his or her first—and potentially last—impression of Tara. Our production team had to grapple not only with what we wanted Tara to do or say but also how her character would circulate via open networks where fans had more control. Ultimately this proved moot, as our series did not substantially engage an online community. Our comments on YouTube were few, but generally supportive. I think part of the series's lukewarm reception could be attributed to this lack of specificity in voice.

In the end the production team saw value in the story. "I think what we set out to do we were able to accomplish," Teresa said. "It was great to see different levels for Tara, especially with the character Cameron [her ex]." So while each individual episode raised the stakes of the cultural and social importance of Tara's action, as a whole the series reflected different parts of her life. Episodes covered her professional challenges as a journalist returning to work under new management and interviewing idiosyncratic artists; her romantic struggle of still being in love with her ex, Cameron, while flirting with a new man, spoken word artist Ruzza Grey; and her social world of friends and family (the other two leads playing her supportive best friend and skeptical cousin). The breadth of episodes and their short length made filming hectic but also, Teresa said, forced her to focus every moment of acting on what would be "revealing": "I never really wanted to play her angry. . . . It's a nice luxury: revealing the moment of the character in that moment."

Questions of sincerity hover over every production. Telling a compelling story about a new character is a challenge. Short-form storytelling, as a strategy for dealing with constraints on resources, presents unique challenges but also opportunities for complex storytelling in the open TV market. Representing historically underrepresented people adds to these challenges and opportunities. In general, a creative team with a unified vision of the characters and of the community within and around the series can resolve these tensions. Open TV representations are most effective when they ring true to the realities or fantasies of a particular community, especially those for whom representations have been scant or inconsistent in the past. This is an innovation in television development, which historically sees audiences as markets first and networks of individuals and fan communities second.

Each case study in this chapter shows how stories produced for the open TV market advance representation in series development. Using interviews with producers and reports from the trade press, I focus on the production and release of four series and examine how creators made and marketed them through networked distribution: *No Shade*, a comedy about four black queer New Yorkers working to make it in the arts; *The Misadventures of Awkward Black Girl & Friends*, a sitcom about a black woman dealing with romantic and professional struggles; *Anyone but Me*, a web drama about a pair of star-crossed teen lesbians and their friends; and *East WillyB*, a political satire by and for Latinos about gentrification in Brooklyn. By addressing people as communities first and markets second, indie TV creators innovate about how to sincerely represent communities underrepresented by legacy distributors.

* * *

The pilot for Sean Anthony Torrington's *No Shade* introduces us to four twenty-something queer black New Yorkers coming back from the funeral for Noel Baptiste's mother. Throughout the first season we hear from Noel's mother, Patricia, but never see her face. She is unrelentingly homophobic and mean—later in the season she kicks Noel out of the house, yelling, "Get out, Noel, until you release those demons of faggotry!" Needless to say, none of the four protagonists appear sad about her death. Later in the episode we learn that this might be the case because they have another mother named Patricia: Pattie Alchemy. Kori, a dance instructor, is sleeping on Pattie's couch because he is homeless, a nod to the reality that a disproportionate number of queer youth of color face housing instability. Pattie loves Kori as if he were her child, but she is also intent on him being self-sufficient so insists his stay is temporary.

Who is this bottle-blond queer black mother? In a cut-away, Pattie introduces herself directly to viewers, echoing Pepper LaBeija in *Paris Is Burning*, Jennie Livingston's famed documentary about the New York ball scene:

Fierce. I'm not fierce. I'm Pattie Alchemy. The legendary mother of the House of Alchemy. Not the founder, no. Crystal. Crystal was the founder. I just rule it now. Soft love. I find it important that I be mother. There's so many little kids out there that need me to look out for them. Although they don't listen to me—they buck my authority—I still think I rule it pretty well. I'm one of the more popular ones. Been around for two decades. *Reigning,* that is! I've won more grand prizes than all the rest.

Black and brown queer viewers might instantly recognize the reference to Crystal LaBeija, legendary black transwoman who is widely credited with creating the first and longest-running house of vogue (fifty years old in 2016). But viewers unaware of voguing and ball culture might be confused by Pattie's introduction. She presents as femme but her voice is a cool baritone. What is her gender? What is "fierce"? How do mothers reign? Who are these "little kids" who need her help? What is the "house" in the "House of Alchemy"? What are these prizes she has won?

Kori clears up some of the confusion about her relation to him after her soliloquy: "You're lucky you're my *gay* mother or I would have read you for filth" (emphasis added). But this only raises more questions for viewers not in the community *No Shade* addresses: what is "reading for filth"? The answers to these questions index the particularities of a subculture that legacy television routinely fails to represent: how, in the face of persistent oppression, queer black and brown people have built alternative families, sublimating biological relation to cultural relation. "Reading"—put-downs and critique—is just one practice we share. Performers join "houses" for art practice (voguing), competition (ball prizes), and emotional and financial support, houses that are ruled by "mothers" who protect their "children."[3] The series is rife with phrases popular within, and originating from, black and queer subcultures: "the real tea no chaser," "yes gawd!" "head-to-toe overness," "kiki," and "oh my God New York is a kee." Indeed, the series title *No Shade* refers to a particular style of "reading" in which self-aggrandizement produces insult.

Torrington's use of black queer vernacular intervenes in a decades-long struggle over popular culture, particularly legacy television, when during the 2000s shows like Fox's *Glee,* HBO's *Looking,* and Logo-then-

VH1's *RuPaul's Drag Race* introduced black gay slang to white viewers, at times with no attribution.[4] The *No Shade* production team eventually launched spin-off series, including *Black Gay University*, releasing short films reclaiming black gay slang and desire. As Stuart Hall writes in his classic essay "What Is the 'Black' in Black Popular Culture?": "What we are talking about is the struggle over cultural hegemony, which is these days waged as much in popular culture as anywhere else. . . . [I]t is never a zero-sum cultural game; it is always about shifting the balance of power in the relations of culture."[5] *No Shade* shows how independent creators like Torrington produced television to shift cultural power away from the identity markets that corporations construct for profit toward specific communities whose full range of life is invisible, though critical, to cultural production in late capitalism. For *No Shade* this means counteracting broadcast and cable TV's use of "Black gay men . . . to symbolize the embodiment of turmoil and destruction in Black communities," as Jasmine Cobb and Robin Means Coleman found, by centering their diverse dreams and struggles.[6] Indie TV fans want representations by producers who understand their personal (intimate, idiosyncratic), social (connecting familial and filial networks), cultural (bridging and integrating identities and communities), and political-economic (intervening in struggles over capital) dimensions. This attention to the specificities of diverse experiences encourages online and word-of-mouth sharing by indie TV fans.

Open TV series rise and fall on their ability to connect with communities through producers and characters. Ball culture composes only part of *No Shade*'s narrative, because the culture of voguing encompassed only part of the black queer community *No Shade* addressed. Two characters, Kori Jacobs, the dancer, and Danielle Williams, a transgender makeup artist, compete in the ball scene for prizes, explained in the third episode, "No Roaches." The lead, Noel, is an artist struggling to paint while living with his homophobic mother, and bar manager Eric Stone grapples with his addiction to drugs, sex, and money. Throughout the show each of these characters struggles to find satisfaction in love and work, with varying degrees of success. Most fail. Noel learns the ins and outs of contemporary gay dating while failing to lose his virginity. Eric's hunt for sex and money leads to a host of questionable decisions, including shirking his job. Danielle looks for love while navigating the legal system to formally transition from male to female. Kori is trying to take his dance career national and international. Throughout the show we learn each character's thoughts on sex and relationships (some endorse promiscuity and "raw" sex, others don't), their struggle for happiness in global capitalism (they pursue sex, love, or enterprise), and their barriers to happiness (family, the state, employers, addiction).

No Shade represents black queer realities and fantasies by integrating different genres of television storytelling, particularly melodrama, situation comedy, and variety (music and dance). Noel narrates the story's drama in a way that, as Peter Brooks described of melodrama, "leads us in a movement through and beyond the surface of things to what lies behind, to the spiritual reality."[7] *No Shade* integrates intersecting emotional and spiritual realities to drive the first season's narrative of the tragedies facing black queer people, specifically how sex can thwart one's pursuit of romantic, creative, and professional fulfillment. But most of the show is comedy, in a variety of styles. "Reading," the style of verbal insult, is used consistently for humor, as it was in many black queer spaces, but *No Shade* also employs slapstick. When Eric pulls down a paramour's pants in the sixth episode, "Insensitive B*tch," and finds genital warts, we see him pull out successively more extreme "tools" to deal with it, from a hammer and nail to a blowtorch. To stop Danielle from fussing over a date with Winston, a handsome cisgender man she met in the subway, out of nowhere Noel whips out a giant red flag, because she has not "come out" as trans. After Noel's mother dies in the finale, a cut-away shows the four friends failing to bury her in the woods. Dance sequences, including an audition for a Grammy-winning artist and a voguing ball in the finale, dramatize Kori and Danielle's search for financial stability and pride in performance. In *No Shade*'s integration of drama, comedy, and music, we are reminded of Stuart Hall's assertion that black cultural production enables "other forms of life, other traditions of representation."[8]

Web creators often address communities underserved by legacy television development, and many of the most passionate producers create stories about those marginalized by race, gender and sexuality, and class in politics and culture. They utilize open distribution to create stories for communities perceived "too niche"—of too little value—for television and theatrical distribution. Niche marketing "targets" identities for product sales or branding, diluting representations because the marginalized are treated only as potential consumers as opposed to active community members. By contrast, indie producers release stories on an open distribution system where, with little to no marketing budget, they have to directly reach fans who will connect with and, ideally, share narratives.

Open TV fans primarily share series they find sincere, flipping their position from targets to participants in marketing. By invoking "sincerity" I borrow from John Jackson's description of racial sincerity as antithetical to image production, or "authenticity," which implies that identity can be categorized, policed, and managed: "Sincerity is a trait of the object's maker . . . but never the object itself. . . . Instead sincerity presumes a liaison *between subjects*—not some external adjudicator or lifeless scroll."[9] No representation is wholly sincere. Yet because indie producers release stories directly to fans, they are more accountable to communities and understand that TV narratives must ring true to those they represent in order to be seen and funded.

In the open TV market, intersections of race, gender, sexuality, and class become part of the way producers and fans understood a show's "production value," extending notions of "quality television" beyond directing, acting, and cinematography, where white men dominate, to the ability to write to and connect with communities, where deep experience with cultural difference matters. Despite lacking the technical sophistication of Hollywood series, indie producers make and release scores of sincere stories to fans.

There are hundreds of scripted series by and about black, Latino, Asian American, and gay, lesbian, bisexual, and transgender people. I spent years tracking the premieres of series by and about underrepresented identities. From 2009 to 2014, I counted and publicly listed on my blog 182 series addressing black communities, 154 addressing GLBT communities, 43 addressing Latino communities, and 34 addressing Asian American communities.[10] This was a conservative estimate, as some producers did not reach out to me or my sources (other producers, press, and social media accounts) for publicity. For example, in his 2015 catalogue, independent scholar Vincent Terrace counted 335 LGBTQ web series released from 1996 to 2014.[11] In my study I took a closer look at the size of *No Shade*'s black and GLBT web series markets, revealing considerable investment in the production of new stories. Black web series creators released more than 113 hours of narrative in the five-year period, while GLBT producers released over 637 hours. The season finales of these shows received on average 169 comments for black web series and 143 for GLBT series, with an average of 28,839 and 235,165 plays on various platforms for black and GLBT series, respectively.

Independent television is not independent of the market, and financing sources for production and marketing are limited for those marginalized by the industry, so few producers reach all of their desired fans and communities. Those who do master writing sincere stories, engage those represented, and direct their attention and funds to brands, channels, and producers. This is a different kind of commodification than in legacy television, with identities edited to attract corporate advertisers who are not typically participants in the communities they hope to monetize.[12] In legacy television, series can succeed with postracial, postgender, or postgay representations, despite their distance from lived experiences. Success for shows like those in this chapter, by contrast, is rooted in how sincerely—and entertainingly—producers address the personal, cultural, social, and political realities and fantasies of the communities they represent.

Understanding Open TV Representation

Sean Anthony Torrington and his peers emerged in a perplexing moment in television representation. During the industry's transition from mass to niche marketing, representations of historically marginalized communities rose to prominence because TV channels needed new ways to organize audiences, and advertising and marketing agencies saw new markets, in the face of new distributors on cable: think of the period from *The Cosby Show* through *Will & Grace*, which brought us Lifetime and *Oz*.[13] This period offered more, if not more realistic, representations of communities marginalized by identity, particularly race, gender, and sexuality.

Yet television distributors continue to discriminate. Although more visible, women, gay men, lesbians, and ethnic minorities are limited in the degree to which they can challenge stereotypes as characters and in their chances to lead franchises and marquee properties as characters and producers, making it difficult for creative producers who are not white and male to find consistent work and marginalizing sincere narratives about our diverse population. Fear of difference, inequality, and history blinds Americans to the reality of real strife and division along lines of race, gender, and sexuality. In this context, the rise of white supremacy in 2016 should have surprised no one, particularly the media.

The problems of diversity in the television industry reflect broader issues in post–civil rights America. After civil rights protests in the 1960s and 1970s foregrounded issues of inequality across lines of cultural difference, people in power started a backlash, policing women, queers, and people of color in a wide variety of ways. In the media, we find evidence of this in the demise of black public affairs programs like *Soul!*, which hosted vital conversations about black power and aesthetics, stoking fear in white funders and benefactors in the 1970s; thereafter, public TV took a sharp turn toward assimilationist and postracial representation.[14] In the corporate-run creative economy, acceptable identity politics were limited to messages that could be marketed, masking persistent social, economic, and political injustice. American media narratives emphasized postracial, postfeminist, and postgay characters and plots. Susan Douglas defines this odd tension between progress and its pitfalls in her study of contemporary representations of women: "[T]he media illusion is that equality for girls and women is an accomplished fact when it isn't. Then the media were behind the curve; now, ironically, they're ahead."[15] Douglas argues that corporate media producers, specifically in television, created "fantasies of power" in the 2000s, the illusion that feminism's work is over and that "we are stronger, more successful, more sexually in control, more fearless, and more held in awe than we actually are."[16] In practice, this ideology translates into a host of scripted shows about older women who are near perfect at their jobs (with unstable love lives, mostly), masking real-world workplace inequity; at the same time, reality television and youth media depict young women who are sexually empowered, masking the continuous power of the male gaze and threats to women's rights at local, state, and federal levels.

Representations of racial and sexual minorities followed similar trends toward normativity and mass marketability, including the steady dilution of real conflict and difference even amid the appearance of characters of color on legacy networks. As indie production expanded online during the 2000s, legacy television networks created "uni-cultural" spaces, where difference was visual, not cultural.[17] Despite the existence of dense prestige dramas like *The Wire*, *Treme*, and, later, *Being Mary Jane* and *Queen Sugar*, along with intermittent storylines on procedurals, legacy TV producers used "color-blind" casting, a trend best exemplified in the popular work of Shonda Rhimes.[18] Postracial politics reflected legacy networks' inability to represent characters' lives amid social realities, structural imbalances, and injustices. Identity became purely individuated, diluting structural truths about what makes people different.

Postracial representations fail to account for the full lives of marginalized people, assuming that specificity is not marketable and everyday experiences, not real. Scholars critique postracial representations on television and in the news, as they elide inequality and difference in service of portraying an overly optimistic, and therefore hollow, image of equality.[19] As Sarah Banet-Weiser states, "[L]ike consumer citizenship, postfeminist and postracial culture is profoundly, indeed necessarily ambivalent."[20] Catherine Squires, in her analysis of postracial discourses in news, finds that niche-focused blogs counteract legacy discourses: "Many [web contributors] argued the ambivalence of post-racial discourse leaves too much room for those who deny racism."[21] Eager to profit from diversity, but fearful of backlash from a white mainstream, entertainment media companies hired producers who could cast characters of color without grappling meaningfully with difference and oppression. Producers like Rhimes, among precious few executive producers of color in Hollywood, were largely shielded from structural imbalances like racism, giving them freedom to underplay it in their stories. Kristen Warner argues, "Rhimes' way of circumventing the very clear structural impediments to accessing industrial employment for women and . . . women of color is to displace the issue altogether. . . . [S]ystemic issues can exist but if she is immersed in her work, she cannot feel the effects of its limitation."[22] Warner shows how the industry enriched a few producers of color, whose success separated them from the realities of their communities, thereby erasing awareness of difference.

For gay, lesbian, bisexual, transgender, and queer people, the landscape was equally complex. After decades of virtual invisibility, the 1990s and 2000s saw a sharp rise of popular and niche media targeting gay men, lesbians, and, to a much lesser degree, bisexual and transgender people. Still, media representations focused almost exclusively on portraying gays and lesbians as "normal," eradicating the sexual revolution's promise of celebrating difference and confining GLBTQ politics to matters of the home, primarily love, marriage, and military service.[23] What was lost was the power of nonnormative sexuality to expand mainstream views of sex. As Michael Warner writes, "[N]onstandard sex has none of . . . this built-in sense of connection to the meaningful life, the community of the human, the future of the world. It lacks this resonance with the values of public politics, mass entertainment, and mythic narrative."[24] In contrast to this more expansive vision, television represents gays and lesbians as middle-class or rich, white, male, and generally unconcerned with much beyond finding a partner and settling down.[25] Across media, gay marketing stays away from politics.[26]

Producers of independent web series often challenge but also occasionally uphold postidentity values. What binds their series is a commitment to using representation to intervene in series development, proving the value of communities through storytelling. In making and marketing their own shows, they remind critics and fans that one cannot understand representation without grappling with the political economy of television and its effects on those the industry represents. As legacy television's ability to reach mass audiences decreases, its power to mediate images of "others" does as well, opening up the market to new storytellers and rendering visible the economy of TV characters.[27] Representation moves beyond vague and endlessly rehashed debates over "positive" and "negative" images—"the primary site of hope and critique," Herman Gray laments—toward employing producers and actors who create worlds and characters that communities recognize.[28]

Independent television creators challenge and participate in American niche marketing but demand greater investment in development—new series in different genres and styles representing a range of identities. They focus debates about cultural representation not on authenticity but on the decision makers, power, and the industry's tendency to devalue and stereotype the real lives of marginalized communities.[29] Making a web show allows a producer to be a decision maker, giving them a chance to fill a gap left by legacy television distibutors, which have been promising full diversity since the introduction of cable. The promise is partially realized. After a surge of interest in black—often coded "young and urban"—programming in the nineties, spearhead by Fox, UPN, and BET, large media conglomerates stepped away and refocused on wealthier audiences.[30] Racial-justice activists and black writers joined forces in the late 1990s and early 2000s to pressure broadcast networks to hire more writers and to buy pilots from black producers, which yielded some results, including the adoption of minority staffing programs by the major networks.[31] Similar efforts also yielded programs for Native American and Latino writers and producers, and for female and minority directors and actors.[32] From 2012 through 2016, racially diverse casting—but not necessarily writing—in legacy television saw a resurgence with strong ratings for primetime dramas, a genre broadcast networks had rarely developed with minority leads. But history tells us that racial representations occur in cycles. As Warner writes in her work on color-blind casting, "[O]utside of a systemic structural overhaul, my general prediction is that the cycles of underrepresentation leading to protests that culminate in periods of overrepresentation will continue."[33]

Even though niche marketing opened up markets for content geared toward diverse audiences, by the mid-2000s nonwhite, nonmale, and nonheterosexual creative workers started to feel that more could be done. Web distribution extended cable's long tail, reviving the midcentury ideal of channels for every cultural and identity affiliation.[34] By the time producers started releasing independent web shows in the late 2000s, a host of blogs had already challenged Hollywood to include more diverse storytelling. Many of these sites were eventually purchased by conglomerates and larger networks, including *Jezebel* (focusing on women, owned by Gawker Media, then Fusion), *Shadow and Act* (focusing on global black film and television, integrated into the IndieWire Network, then Blavity), *Women and Hollywood* (also integrated into IndieWire); and *AfterElton* and *AfterEllen* (focusing on gay men and lesbians, respectively, though both shut down in 2013 and 2016, respectively). The sites, along with dozens of smaller, less well-known publications, were key to publicizing independent web shows by and about people across identities.

At issue in representation are two, often opposing, ideals: communities and markets. Niche marketing purports to ascribe market value to communities, shading out differences to create a unified, comprehensible type that can be sold to advertisers:

Market segmentation involves the transformation of social groups, loosely organized around contingent identifying characteristics, into consumer niches, where those characteristics are assumed to be stable, measurable, and powerful in predicting consumer behavior. Like market research, audience research assumes that disparate individuals constitute a natural group, a "taxonomic collective," that is united by a single characteristic.[35]

The existence of market-based demographics is at the heart of the way legacy TV programs get financed and developed. Yet marketers' reliance on stability and measurability means that differences and nuances within communities disappear. Only the most marketable consumers get represented, or the most marketable aspects of particular subcultures and communities. This practice has kept alive large niche networks like Black Entertainment Television (BET), Logo, Women's Entertainment (WE), and other related affinity networks, all of which premiered with fanfare and excitement during the multichannel transition. As they matured, however, audiences started to realize that the diversity of their communities was not fully reflected on-screen, particularly identities intersecting race, gender, class, and sexuality. Lesbians found themselves disproportionately underrepresented—and often prematurely killed off—in gay programming, since men were presumed to have more disposable income and appeal for straight women.[36] Many black viewers harangued BET for focusing on cheap entertainment for young, male viewers.[37]

Indie web producers invoke diversity to address the incomplete representations they see in the mainstream media. They hope their work expands Hollywood's labor markets and helps better value their communities. They marshal their communities to advance this mission: tellingly, over the course of my research, each of the main case studies in this chapter orchestrated successful crowdfunding campaigns, demonstrating producers' ability to get fans invested in the development of new, sincere stories. In each series examined in this chapter, creators implicitly and explicitly critique dominant forms of marketing and representation. As entrepreneurs and marginal industry workers, however, open TV producers are aware that advertisers need commoditized audiences. So even as they advance production, storytelling, and marketing in various ways, some rely on established conventions to be intelligible to legacy market players—from writing broad characters in easily recognizable genres to employing dominant cultural frames and, occasionally, marketing practices. Crucially, producers' availability to fans, their need and ability to respond to fan investments as the show progresses, instills in their representations a sincerity that cuts through—perhaps, masks—their efforts to negotiate between what legacy distributors want and what fan communities need.

Producing and Releasing Representations of Black Women

Awkward Black Girl's first episode is a delicate balancing act between universal and specific black women's experiences. The show opens with the protagonist in her car in Los Angeles. "Am I the only who pretends I'm in a music video when I'm by myself?" narrates J, played by creator Issa Rae. J, a twenty-something, dark-skinned black women with a shaved head, is alone rapping loudly to an original song written for the show: "My booty shawts, booty shawts. . . . Niggas wanna fuck me from behind . . . niggas wanna feel up on this booty, they ain't got a chance." Suddenly a coworker drives up next to her car, waving eagerly. She waves back, as if to dismiss him politely, but they keep meeting at successive stop signs. It is a common and relatable "awkward moment," J says. In the next scene, J introduces herself: "My name is J and I'm awkward . . . and black. Someone once told me those were the two worst things anyone could be." In the four-minute episode we learn that J has recently been dumped by her boyfriend, D, twice: first for vague reasons, then, after a one-week reconciliation, because her shaved head freaked him out, triggering homophobia. Despondent, J copes by crying in the mirror, getting drunk at the office holiday party, and sleeping with a coworker, A. Her secret coping mechanism, though, is writing violent rap lyrics: "I'm a bad bitch. You're a pussy nigga," she says on screen. "What the fuck rhymes with 'pussy nigga'? . . . Burn in hell, nigga! Burn in hell, nigga!"

The pilot episode, which a year later had been viewed one million times, is masterful in its ability to signify black youth culture and awkward-comedy tropes of misrecognition and misinterpretation, breaking the rules of both the web and TV. Rae bookends the episode with excerpts from comically offensive hip hop, a nod to the most marketable black cultural form since the 1990s. But those lyrics are filtered through J, her individual awkwardness and her postbreakup anxieties: the rap is divorced from its masculine and corporate television context. Instead, J signals blackness by referencing its position in culture and the market (it's one of the "worst things anyone could be"). Rae integrates experiences specific to black women—most importantly, the politics of natural hair—with familiar plot devices from women's sitcoms and rom-coms, like getting dumped, crying in the mirror, cutting one's hair, and sleeping with a loser.

I narrate the first episode of *Awkward Black Girl* not only because it is the series's most-watched episode—as is the case with most TV series—but also because its explicit appeal to black women worked: *Awkward Black Girl* retained over half its large opening audience. Within a year, Rae had been profiled by a diverse group of media outlets, from mainstream outlets like CNN and the Associated Press to black media like *Essence* and *The Root*. Media mogul Arianna Huffington asked her to write an inaugural post for the *Huffington Post*'s new site targeting black Americans.[38] When Rae started a thirty-thousand-dollar crowdfunding campaign to complete her first season, she raised fifty-six thousand dollars. After she pitched the show to networks, *Awkward Black Girl* landed on a premium YouTube channel, iamOTHER, headed by Pharrell Williams. Two years later, after the Shonda Rhimes–produced *I Hate LA Dudes* faltered in development at ABC, Rae secured an HBO development deal for a series about young black women, *Insecure*, premiering fall 2016 with Larry Willmore attached. Rae's success hinged on her sincere use of and innovation on black culture and sitcom genre conventions, all filtered through black feminist cultural politics. She created an original representation and then experimented with distribution in ways that deviated from and continued a tradition beginning with BET. *Awkward Black Girl* proposes to represent its community of fans—primarily but not exclusively black women—in a way unseen on legacy television, and does so convincingly.

Whereas legacy TV representations of black women are constrained, the indie TV market features a breadth of representations of black women, each differently tied to black feminist politics, across genres. In fantasy web series, producers literally realize black women's empowerment. Series like the postapocalyptic *Vexica* and action comedy *Sheroes* use the visual conventions of video games and comic books, respectively, to represent black women with complete mastery of the art of fighting and vanquishing men. Character-driven series connect personal with cultural struggles. Inspired by the creator's own life, *Chick*, a comedy from actor Kai Soremekun (*Monk, Fresh Prince of Bel-Air*), follows a woman who, after leaving a philandering and abusive boyfriend, goes on a mission to find her inner superhero. *Chick* borrows from images of empowered, afro'ed blaxploitation-era heroines to sell a fantasy of empowerment, complete with superhero costumes and lo-fi special effects. As Stephanie Dunn argues in her study of blaxploitation, these images appeal to a broad base of black women, yet Soremekun's "girl power" ethos—the theme song is "I'm a *one* girl revolution!"—appeals to women generally.[39] The show's marketing campaign includes a website intended to bring together a community of empowered women, a place "where *every* woman is a f*@cking superhero!" For Soremekun, fantasies of power allow escape from and mastery over historical injustice: "I'm not a fan of 'oh woe is me I'm a woman, oh woe is me I'm a black woman,'" she told me.

Many of the earliest and most popular black web series starred women in dramas achieving or losing professional success amid broader inequalities. Popular queer ensemble series like Michelle Daniel's *Between Women* and Coquie Hughes's *If I Was Your Girl* combine complex romantic associations with struggles against the state and capital. *Between Women*'s characters contract work with the state (Atlanta) but also cope with imprisonment. Kim Williams's *Unwritten Rules* follows a young woman recently hired in a predominantly white office and offers a comedic and pedagogical view on how she survives micro-aggressions. Dramas like *Kindred* and comedies like *Jenifer Lewis and Shangela* showcase women who have already achieved success and have to maintain it or pay it forward. Robert Townsend's *Diary of a Single Mom*, a serialized web series about a single mother named Ocean (Monica Calhoun) who moves to a new neighborhood to manage an apartment building filled with off-kilter characters, uses melodrama to promote social justice and community. Produced by a nonprofit, One Economy, for three seasons, the series explores Ocean's struggle for professional advancement and family stability, raising issues of housing and renters' rights, illiteracy, and poverty, all of which disproportionately affect black women. To do this, it focuses on the personal dramas of an ensemble cast. Producers depict Ocean's life as a series of dramatic events, including surprise visits from deadbeat dads and the arrival of a niece she suddenly must parent. "Monica's going through so much. . . . Oh my God, do you want to root for her!" Townsend, the show's director, told me.[40] Producers make series to connect with the struggles people face in their everyday lives. "I wanted to keep my audience engaged and give them something to talk about," said *If I Was Your Girl* creator Hughes. Hughes made *If I Was Your Girl* by drawing from some personal experience but also from others' as well, seeing undertold stories about state and domestic violence in a black lesbian community with different gender expressions and sexual politics.

Producers creating series about black women frame their representational strategies differently from each other. Some producers explicitly focus on empowerment; others want to write morally complex characters. Series like *Blue Belle, Left Unsaid,* and *Celeste Bright* portray black heroines as antiheroes with complex storylines told with the muted drama emblematic of critically acclaimed cable dramas.[41] For producers like *Celeste Bright*'s Sonya Steele, a veteran writer on television (*ER*), legacy quality television series are well produced but almost exclusively star white men. The heroine of Steele's series, Celeste, is a banker enmeshed in a political and financial scandal in which she may play a part. "I wanted to be able to show us in the totality of our humanity," Steele said. "I can do my part to counter that and produce images of black women that are multidimensional that are based on other attributes than being a black woman." From the trailer to the first episode, Celeste is portrayed as a mysterious woman whose innocence is suspect. Here, Steele markets difference by placing a black woman's body in a genre historically resistant to those characters, and, it should be noted, two years before Rhimes's *Scandal* did so on ABC.

While black women have a long history in the comedy genre,[42] *Awkward Black Girl* advances a new, complex, and occasionally divisive perspective that challenges and innovates within legacies of their representation. When viewers first see J's boss, Boss Lady, a white woman, we learn from J that she is "an offensive dumbfuck of an idiot." The boss goes on to utter a number of truly offensive things, including commenting on J's natural hair, which she compares to pubic hair. *Awkward Black Girl* explicitly calls out racism, and does so by putting the viewer in the position of a black protagonist facing discrimination, a direct challenge to television's postracial politics. Seconds later, though, viewers are introduced to the other characters in J's office, and Rae leaves no target unhit. We meet individuals who embody racial stereotypes (J: "the loud black bitch"), gender stereotypes ("drama queen who never shuts up"), generic social types ("guy who can't take a hint"), and peculiar pastiches ("the space-invading germ chick who probably has AIDS"). *Awkward Black Girl* defines itself as a political work whose agenda is both counter-cultural and familiar, wrapped in the political incorrectness kept safely in J's thoughts. Indeed, Rae said as much after a controversial episode in which Cece, J's best friend, calls another woman a "tranny bitch," which fans interpreted as transphobic.[43] Members of the Crunk Feminist Collective penned an open letter accusing Rae of marginalizing those who are already marginalized:

> For those of us, the awkward black, queer folks who have lived at the intersections of our awkwardness, our blackness, and our transness, words like "tra**y" erase our lives, and our humanity. Phrases like "No lesbo" and the use of affected speech to imitate hard of hearing people detract from the vision of creating representations for the rest of us who are all too often maligned in mainstream media.[44]

Despite the show's attempts to shock—or, as Rae says in response to the letter, "poke fun at ignorance"[45]—the show refracts it with an interesting narrative device: many of its most charged statements, including its profuse use of "bitch," occur in J's head, through her narration. In the show, J presents to other characters as a kind, if awkward, regular black woman. In her head, she is often upset, vengeful, and powerful. Thus, she both embodies and resists legacy representations of black women. In short, J cannot be placed in a box.

So goes Issa Rae's balancing act. The web space allows her creative freedom to include narratives and jokes too edgy and niche driven for larger TV markets. Yet ultimately, the web series is a commodity, one Rae said numerous times she hoped would make it to legacy TV and show mainstream networks that black people can be "relatable" too.[46]

Despite its newness, *Awkward Black Girl* is a hybrid: it speaks to its core audience of black women as sincerely as a show produced to sell can do. "Black women really aren't accurately represented," Rae told me in an interview. "This extremely aggressive, ghetto girl or the best friend. My character is a middle ground." J is aggressive, but only to herself; she could be your best friend, but she's awkward. Rae took television's types for black women and extended each as far as she believed she could. In doing so, she built a market, employing black actors and crew members, while organizing a community that marketers and network executives have been missing. "Issa is telling universal stories with characters we're not used to seeing," said Andrew James, who plays A ("guy who can't take a hint"). "I believe black people and nonblack people are yearning for these characters without even realizing it."[47]

Racial sincerity is personal, political, and contextual, a level of complexity that legacy networks find hard to represent. Consider the case of hair diversity in representations of black women. In her 2015 memoir, *The Misadventures of Awkward Black Girl*, Rae pens a hilarious and incisive chapter on growing up and learning to love her hair. Rae notes how when she was living in an ethnically diverse community before moving to Los Angeles, she was proud of her hair, because she stood out among her peers. Moving to a black community in LA, she encountered the "hair hierarchy": "[T]he hair hierarchy rates worth by length and texture of hair. . . . The shorter, kinkier, and more African your hair? Kill thyself."[48] Ultimately Rae reclaims self-esteem by cutting off all her hair, just as in *Awkward Black Girl*'s pilot. When Rae initially received interest in adapting the web series to TV, legacy network executives suggested she make it pan-racial and cast a lighter-skinned lead with straight hair.[49] Their suggestions miss a central goal of *Awkward Black Girl*: to represent the complexities of being a dark-skinned woman trying to take pride in her natural hair, a form of black pride with deep roots in black feminism.

What fans of black television yearn for, I argue, are shows that explicitly deal with race, without the necessity of irony or color-blindness, while also demonstrating a range of individual subjectivities across and within identities in the community. *Awkward Black Girl* cuts through ambivalence, most visibly in its title, calling out race explicitly: "[S]ome people can't get past the 'black' in the title," Rae wrote after the show received an unexpectedly racist reaction to its winning a Shorty Award.[50]

Its explicit addressing of race and racism charges the series, amplified by its flagrant use of profanity, including "bitch" and "nigga." That Rae, as J, utters those profanities underscores the point. Very few black female leads in television or in films in the early 2010s had dark skin or natural hair, let alone hair cut short, perhaps because natural black hair historically evokes counterhegemony and black pride, at odds with postracial cultural politics of color-blindness.[51] Rae is attractive, but not by Hollywood standards, which favors lighter-skinned women with weaves, wigs, and perms:[52] "If *Awkward Black Girl* could make it to HBO starring a dark-skinned black girl, that would be revolutionary," Rae told *New York Magazine*, five years before it did.[53] The implication in Rae's comment is that even HBO—whose motto proclaimed "it's not TV"—has not done enough to engage racial politics.[54] Publishing on the web gives Rae license to push the boundaries of normative black female representation. Still, after HBO premiered her series, Rae told *New York Magazine* that the main note she received from the network was to focus the series on the central friendship between black women.[55]

The web show's gender politics are as explicit and complex. J's employer, Gutbusters, makes its money selling "basically . . . bulimia in pill form to women." In the first season, women run the office (season two replaces J's white female boss with a Latino, Jesus), though J ranks as one of its worst employees, a plot point that endears her to us, since the product literally attacks women's bodies. Beyond a clearly feminist narrative that critiques the commodification of women's body dysmorphia, *Awkward Black Girl* renders complex black women's representation by showing different types, at which J throws varying levels of shade: "drama queen," "loud black bitch," "space-invading germ magnet," and Nina, the "light-skinned bitch" who is her greatest adversary. J's best friend, Cece, provides the kind of support and kinship J needs from women of color, as well as quirky comic relief, whereas the women in the office are frequently adversaries or nuisances, if only because they take their jobs at Gutbusters seriously. Through this network of women, *Awkward Black Girl* cleverly integrates and critiques a range of legacy TV representations. It draws on fans' nostalgia for stories about friendships between women of color seen in long-canceled nineties sitcoms like *Living Single* and *Girlfriends*, even as it twists the trope of black women as adversaries prevalent on on contemporary cable reality shows like *Love*

& Hip Hop, Basketball Wives, and a host of others, by basing disagreements not solely on men but also on ideological, political, and interpersonal differences.

Still, legacy television retains much of its cultural cachet. Years before the HBO premiere, when I asked her about whether she wanted to make the move to television or stay on the web, Rae was conflicted. Labor and capital were primary concerns. She did not make money from *Awkward Black Girl*, her third web series after *The Fly Guys* and *Dorm Diaries*. A brand sponsor could finance a web show, but no advertisers or online distributors were calling—as Microsoft did to secure *The Guild*'s coveted gamer fan base. Corporate TV, meanwhile, provides capital but less creative freedom:

> I'm sort of struggling with that . . . I want to keep it completely on the web, and make the space my own. . . . [But] it would be completely great to have a show on HBO or Comedy Central. . . . That would be amazing. Whether it's *Awkward Black Girl* or not . . . if this show can inspire the creation of that, that would be amazing.

Although she enjoyed the creative freedom the web afforded, Rae was aware of television's power to create cultural awareness and markets, which in turn creates demand for more producers like herself. Concerns about representation shifted her thoughts the other way, however. Rae lamented the medium's tendency to place black women in stereotypical roles (as side characters): "The show deals with an everyday person. . . . I'm not sleeping with lots of men or dealing with all my baby daddies." Freed from television's constraints, Rae could develop J's complex inner life and politics, alongside cultural and political struggles.

To make the show legible to legacy development executives, Rae constructed *Awkward Black Girl* as a classic romantic comedy about a professional woman trying to choose between two men. The series begins with J getting dumped, and the main narrative unfolds as a love triangle between her and two men, one black—Fred, the boyfriend of a coworker—and one white—"White Jay," a counselor J meets when sent to anger management classes—a satire and critique of the stereotype of the "angry black woman." *Awkward Black Girl* employs some sitcom tropes but filters them through black women's bodies.[56] Throughout, however, Rae's pitch—"the show deals with an everyday person"—retains its validity. The love triangle is coded racially and culturally—J and Fred, for example, share a facility with music and hip hop—but in general, J is just looking for a man she feels comfortable with. When the triangle reaches a breaking point, the show pivots to common issues in heterosexual love: "Every time I get comfortable with a guy, it blows up in my face," J tells Cece in the penultimate episode. "I suck with guys. I always have." The twenty-minute finale, the show's longest, focuses solely on resolving the romance. J picks White Jay. Race does not disappear, however: when she rushes to his house to declare that she is "in like" with White Jay, J narrates that she "hopes White Jay is cool with me rolling up like a nigga." Ultimately, though, J's choice has nothing to do with race; she chastises herself in front of White Jay for reasons concerning her personality, regardless of race—"I've been insecure, selfish, ungrateful, and other bad adjectives. Through all that, you've been there." The first season concludes by mirroring the beginning, but this time we learn that J being "awkward and black" might not be a big deal: "My name is J and I'm awkward . . . and black. Someone once told me those were the two worst things anyone could be. But when you meet someone *who likes you for you*, none of that matters." In the series's TV-length finale, racial issues fall aside in the wake of personal connection. The show appears to endorse legacy television's view of race as individualized, but the story goes on, and in the second season White Jay and J must continually work to bridge differences in culture and politics.

Awkward Black Girl signaled to fans independent TV production's potential to narrate a fuller range of life, culture, and politics around black women. As one writer opined,

> She makes the New, NEW Black Woman for all those reasons and more. She has harnessed her creativity, humor and social circle to produce what might one day be a huge money-maker, and stick Hollywood in the eye, because it will show that you don't have to be a mammy, Jezebel, or a b*tch to make a good black female character on the TEE VEE.[57]

For most of *Awkward Black Girl*'s fans, the show was valuable not only because its lead character broke and experimented with stereotype, but also because it challenged the industry. Black women could produce their own programs in the face of widespread neglect and misunderstanding by legacy television executives. Yet *Awkward Black Girl* also shows how the definition of a marketable representation belongs to legacy television; outsiders can deviate, but not too far. New media can allow for more specific representations of black women, but in the end, radical representations remain a challenge for indie producers looking to sell or license their intellectual property.

To sell their stories, producers and entrepreneurs balanced marketing to black women as a community and as a market. The signature line from *Awkward Black Girl*—"I'm awkward . . . and black. Someone once told me those were the two worst things anyone could be"—was the product of a real-life exchange. "I made a Facebook status one day that said I was awkward and black. . . . [M]y now producer replied with 'those are the two worst things anyone can be' and I was like 'haha bitch' but it got my gears turning," Rae told *Clutch*.[58] It was a significant moment. It prefigures Rae's marketing philosophy of maintaining a dialogue between producer and community about blackness and society. Marketing *Awkward Black Girl* would involve marshaling viewers' desires for representational change: "People sort of marketed it as a movement on their own," Rae told me, with a message of "if you don't support this you can't complain about the images you see of yourself on TV." Rae would go on to create a community around the show, a community she could use to show demand for representations to an advertiser or major network. Fans in turn revere Rae as an entrepreneur representing the concerns and desires of black people, women, and marginalized groups.[59]

American media has been here before. In fact, it is easy to place Rae within a long tradition of black entrepreneurs entering the television business using community empowerment as their rhetoric. The clearest case is Black Entertainment Television (BET). BET arose in a similar period of hope for new media. It debuted in the early 1980s after the federal government, led by consumer and corporate activists, spent years deregulating the television industry in the hope of creating a more diverse marketplace. Community groups wanted more "democratic" programs, political debates, and local news coverage. "Discourses surrounding the medium were filled with optimism about its potential to provide specialized content and to serve minority and niche audiences," Megan Mullen recounts.[60] Economists and alternative video activists joined this discourse of increasing diversity and competition.[61] Cable would be a "cure for the ills of modern urban American society."[62] Techno-optimism, the kind that would resurge with the advent of the Internet, was rife. Yet belief in cable's community-building possibilities —the kind of noncommercial discourse attracting black Americans—stood opposed to cable's financial incentives. Public demands for cable dovetailed with the interests of tycoons and businessmen, who were eager to break into legacy network television. Introducing cable to the American public was part of Presidents Nixon and Ford's effort to deregulate various industries, including the three-network broadcast model.[63] Waiting in the wings were entrepreneurs like Ted Turner and BET's own Robert Johnson gathering funds to bring cable television to the cities and suburbs.

BET was a product of a strong belief in the power of new media technologies to correct representational imbalances: "[F]or people of color and those concerned with their representation, cable was marketed as the cure-all for a very white television world."[64] In her exhaustive study of the network, Beretta Smith-Shomade highlights the peculiar faith in a fairer form of capitalism that led to BET's creation. BET had a tall order. BET would function as a hub for the black community, but it would sell that community to advertisers, and, eventually, cable operators. This commoditized community could boost minority labor and correct representation, particularly given the unsteady images of black people from the advent of broadcast television.[65] In the 1990s, BET offered some representations of black women in music videos that allowed them "to voice and visualize themselves differently" from broadcast sitcoms by showcasing artists like Janet Jackson and En Vogue.[66] But pay-cable distribution's need to syndicate older shows to fill schedules (reruns), and BET's eventual purchase by Viacom, limited its ability to serve the black community: "[W]ith much of its programming coming from off the [broadcast] networks, the offerings reflect the same one-dimensional notions of Blackness and gender that networks already employ. . . . And . . . despite BET's Black-business status, African-American communities receive little tangible benefit from supporting it."[67] Moreover, for most of the 2000s BET "had not surged ahead with creative risks," despite being one of Viacom's most profitable divisions.[68] Its lack of experimentation, coupled with the dominance of misogynist images in male-driven music videos, makes BET's ability to represent the black community fraught.

Nearly forty years later, a new crop of entrepreneurs created their own indie channels online to showcase series like *Awkward Black Girl*, which premiered soon after these networks started to arise. For black open TV network executives, however, the drive to create television online is about more than pursuing higher advertising rates. Online network executives continually espouse, like Johnson before them, their support of the black community, while also promoting the representational and labor possibilities of web distribution: hiring black filmmakers to create new black stories. The online channels curate (select programs relevant to a particular audience) and market (promote those programs to viewers and advertisers) the series being made by the likes of Issa Rae, Al Thompson (*Johnny B. Homeless*, *Lenox Avenue*), and Anthony Anderson (*Anacostia*).

Rowdy Orbit, among the first of such networks, is an excellent case study in how digital media entrepreneurs deploy discourses of community, representation, and labor in new media distribution. Debuting in 2009, Rowdy Orbit is the brainchild of Jonathan Moore, a copywriter with seventeen years in the advertising business and seven as a "multicultural marketing consultant." Moore started Rowdy Orbit because he was frustrated by his inability to hire directors of color for advertisements. Working with agencies was a challenge, because they primarily worked with directors they already knew—and their social contacts privileged white men. The mission of Rowdy Orbit, then, was to "give creators of color a place to create," Moore said in an interview. "We know they're out there, we're just out to find them."

New media distribution ignited interest in serving marginalized groups in the black community. Black women have historically pushed forward discussions of marginalization and identity, so it should not be surprising that they excitedly took to the web to distribute stories about what it means to be a black woman or how black women should be represented.[69] For black audiences especially, the historical failure of mainstream networks like BET to encompass the community's gender diversity makes the possibilities of online self-marketing more enticing. Dozens of web series starring, produced, or written by black women exist online. In 2011, one of the first online networks started to market these series to audiences and advertisers: the Black Women's Entertainment Network. "As black women . . . seeing people that look like us is really uplifting," founder Camille Irons-Coakley, herself a traditional media participant with former projects at HBO, said in an interview. "We cater to advertisers, and we cater to the community as a whole." Black women, then, have tried to reform "narrowcasting," expanding beyond the limitations of the mainstream media, whose ownership structure has barely changed and whose business models seldom accommodate marginalized identities.[70]

Awkward Black Girl's concept and story resonated with black women, who evangelized for the show. Rae, reading user comments and e-mails, sensed the fervor she created and built campaigns to keep viewers engaged, channeled through Rae herself. She was active on Facebook, with pages for the show and herself: Rae could count five thousand friends and three thousand subscribers on Facebook by early 2012, while the show's Facebook group had nearly sixty thousand fans at the same time.[71] By 2016, *Awkward Black Girl*'s Facebook page had over 180,000 fans. A similar dynamic—accounts for both Rae and the show—could be seen on Twitter.[72] Facebook and Twitter pages, by 2010, were perfunctory components of most web series's social media marketing campaigns. Rae went beyond that with a personal Tumblr blog, on which she directly promoted both her show and related projects. As we saw with Felicia Day in the previous chapter, Rae's ability to use her personal brand as a member of the community she represents greatly enhanced the show's marketability, but this level of fame is relatively uncommon in the open TV market and typically reserved for creator-writer-stars like Rae and Day.

Rae's blog provides an interesting glimpse into how she promoted *Awkward Black Girl* as a community- and market-oriented project. The blog highlighted the show's merchandise, including t-shirts stating "I'm Awkward . . . And Black" or "I'm Awkward . . . And Mixed."[73] Rae also posted artistic and cultural recommendations and contributions from fans.[74] Much of the blog's space went to supporting projects that shared *Awkward Black Girl*'s mission of reforming Hollywood, including, for instance, the *Black Girl Project* celebrating classic black TV programs[75] along with clips and media by and about Hollywood producers combating the system.[76] Outside her blog, Rae positioned herself as a thought leader on race in Hollywood by penning a number of opinion pieces on black representational politics[77] and embarking on a nationwide college screening tour.[78] Consistent with the show's simultaneous commitment to humor, many of Rae's publications and blog posts had no obvious connection to race or gender politics.[79]

Indeed, a lot of *Awkward Black Girl*'s early marketing success came through traditional media channels or niche-driven sites that focus on Hollywood. Rae has credited blogs like *Shadow and Act* and *The Loop21* for helping drive views and fundraising.[80] The show even collaborated with *Vibe* magazine, historically the community's main source for news and views on hip hop, for an *Awkward Black Girl* contest, the winner of which would be a guest star in season two.[81]

In the years following *Awkward Black Girl*'s finale in 2013, Rae escalated her distribution efforts by releasing series from other writers, mostly in Hollywood. As she worked with HBO on her series, in 2014 she launched an initiative to allow fans to support programming through the Color Creative initiative, administered with Patreon, a start-up that manages regular contributions. Along with Issa Rae Productions, Color Creative extends Rae's practice of releasing romantic comedies from other producers on her YouTube channel, including *The Black Actress*, featuring cameos from talented but undercast actors like Tatyana Ali, Naturi Naughton, and Jenifer Lewis; a romantic comedy, *How Men Become Dogs*; a gossip talk show, *Let Leslie Tell It*; and *Roomieloverfriends*, a collaboration with Dennis Dortch and Numa Perrier. Dortch and Perrier, with Jeanine Daniels, launched their own network, Black & Sexy TV, as a spin-off of Dortch's Sundance film *A Good Day to Be Black and Sexy*. Through 2013 the Black & Sexy team released seven series, including an Issa Rae collaboration, *The Number*, a spin-off of *The Couple*, which they developed with Spike Lee at HBO in 2014.

Rae, Dortch, and Perrier's distribution activities reflect both Hollywood's tough labor market for black writers and the studios' lack of investment in popular genres like romantic comedy and drama, proven marketable in the 1990s. Rae's launch statement for Color Creative explicitly frames the enterprise of correcting conglomerates' activities by mobilizing fans through open distribution:

I'm a fan, first. Everyday I am inspired by amazing content in all forms and mediums. For me, it started with the 90s era of film and television. That era not only made me want to tap into my own creativity as a writer but also be an active supporter of great content. The diversity of representation was prevalent back then in a way that it isn't NOW.[82]

Here, Rae connects the movement for diverse representation with the need for communities and producers to work together to effect change, as Rae's activities did: one of *Awkward Black Girl*'s writers, Amy Aniobi, went on to create her own series, *The Slutty Years*, and found positions on NBC's *The Michael J. Fox Show* and HBO's *Silicon Valley* before becoming a producer on *Insecure*. In 2016 Issa Rae Productions partnered with Adaptive Studios to develop a series by women writers of color and launched *Fruit*, a podcast exploring black masculinity and sexuality.

By 2014 Rae had already undergone (unsuccessfully) developing a show, *I Hate LA Dudes*, with Shonda Rhimes at ABC. So Rae started Color Creative as a pilot incubator, starting with a slate of three half-hour comedies in 2014: *Bleach*, about a black serial killer who takes on a white assistant; *So Jaded*, about two stoner black women; and *Words with Girls*, Brittani Nichols's comedy pilot based on her web series about Los Angeles's queer community. "It came from my place of frustration having gone through the pilot process with ABC and then currently with HBO," Rae said. "The process just felt really, really outdated to me, and really inefficient for writers." Yet by releasing pilots in a format that only legacy television development can support, Rae and producing partner Deniese Davis find themselves reliant on the old system. Says Rae,

> To legitimize the program, we have to sell something. . . . We're still depending on these old television networks who are still using this old pilot system to say "we'll buy it from you" when that would be admitting that this pilot system is stupid, and that's kind of weird. We want to be able to have a relationship with internet networks or work within the system to be able to say this is a new model.

Rae expresses disenchantment with legacy television development and hope for new networks like Netflix and Hulu—though in chapter 5 I express skepticism at these networks' ability to support open TV. Davis cites the Black List as an inspiration;[83] the Black List started as a list, compiled from a survey of top agents and managers, of the best unproduced scripts in Hollywood. It grew into a platform to promote those works. Selling a pilot to a legacy TV network would "validate us as an incubator, as a program," Davis said. Indeed, HBO reportedly signed a deal with Rae to bring two series to the network over two years.[84]

Ultimately, though, Rae, Perrier, and Dortch understand that they need fans for distribution: without corporate marketing and development, rarely bestowed on creators of color, they need fan communities to ensure that their series get attention in a networked economy. Patronage turns fans' affective attachments into investments supporting labor and story creation: "People don't want TV on the web. They already have TV. They want something that feels a little closer to their lives. . . . We're building that trust," Perrier told me. In 2014, Black & Sexy TV started charging for content, putting the new season of Lena Waithe and Ashley Blaine Featherson's *Hello Cupid* under a paywall administered by VHX after the premieres aired on the Tribeca Film Festival's website.[85] It worked, and they soon started a subscription platform. When I spoke to Dortch and Perrier a few months after the launch, they said sales were strong and VHX viewed them as a key asset. By 2016, after syndicating three series on BET's cable channel, Black & Sexy significantly increased original production and licensing, adding comedies, dramas, and reality shows: *Rider*, a comedy about a driver, running for two seasons with episodes from fourteen to forty minutes; *Sexless*, a comedy about a woman's sex hiatus running for three seasons with episodes running from twelve to thiry minutes; *Chef Julian*, a spin-off of *Sexless*, running for two seasons with episodes from fourteen to thirty-six minutes; a reboot of *The Number*; and a number of *After Party* series in which their stars recap shows for fans. The Black & Sexy TV team delivers hours of original programming directly supported by fans, and then they engage those fans on social media (primarily Twitter) by encouraging simultaneous viewings of episodes.

Releasing diverse representations of people of color by producers and executives of color has been a political quest for decades, and black entrepreneurs have historically claimed access to capital and cultural legitimacy by working with legacy distributors. The capital demands of original film and TV and the dominance of postracial cultural ideologies limits the power of alternative distribution, benefiting a few producers, like Tyler Perry, who own their intellectual property and have audiences large enough to catch the attention of studios.[86] Open distribution allows community-engaged creators to monetize and market to their respective niches. The work of Issa Rae and her peers is among the most successful models for this new form of television. Through representing and producing for the black community, they show how television distribution can incorporate and more accurately value the communities it represents, even if ultimately its distribution power does not approach that of legacy networks.

Producing and Releasing Queer Representations

In the opening and closing scenes of *Anyone but Me*, two attractive young women sit together in Battery Park, at a crossroads. Vivian, the show's teenage protagonist, has to leave New York because her father, a 9/11 first responder, got sick from the attacks. They are moving to Westchester, a New York suburb, to live with her aunt. Aster, Vivian's girlfriend, mouths the question, "Why?" and Vivian kisses her head. Shot at sunset in Battery Park, the scene is quiet, intimate, and moving. It sets the tone for the series: subtle and personal, showcasing realistic drama, with politics referenced openly and slyly.

When it premiered in 2008, *Anyone but Me* broke a lot of barriers. It was one of the earliest and most successful lesbian web series. It was an outgrowth of the 2007–2008 writers strike—one of its writers, Susan Miller, wrote for Showtime's lesbian drama *The L Word*. Its release also marked a return to web drama or soap opera, last seen in the 1990s, with its story progressing slowly and quietly. Over the years it steadily racked up award wins and nominations, including ones for writing, acting, and directing (Writers Guild, Streamys, IAWTV Awards, Indie Series Awards, Webbys), overall drama (Clicker, Indie Intertube), and marketing (We Love Soaps). It was one of few diverse indie series to reach a distribution agreement with Hulu; later, the multichannel-turned-subscription-network fullscreen also redistributed their show. When the creators started a crowdsourcing campaign to produce its final season, it raised over $30,000 from fans. By its conclusion, *Anyone but Me* had been viewed fifty million times.[87] As this book went to press, the creators released a fourth season of *Lost Scenes* with over four hundred thousand views and counting.

Anyone but Me's original tagline positions the story's central relationship as a byproduct of post-trauma New York: "The world changed and so did they. . . . Introducing a new generation searching for love and belonging in the post 9/11 age."[88] The show was always political, but by season three, the series's pitch would shift more explicitly to representational politics: "introducing a new generation: gay, straight, and ethnically diverse, struggling with identity and modern relationships."[89] This shift is partially borne out in the narrative as well. Like *Awkward Black Girl*, *Anyone but Me* straddles the line between legacy television representation and a more fine-tuned and explicit sense of cultural politics. Wrapping the story in a conventional drama about growing up, *Anyone but Me*'s producers also have a mission of proving that a drama about teens who are other than white men could be sold to a broad base of viewers. They marketed it as a movement: television in the image of those marked by cultural difference, centered on women's queer sexuality.

The central narrative of *Anyone but Me*'s first season is Vivian's coming out as a lesbian in a new place, the suburbs. A testament to the writers' commitment to subtle storytelling, Vivian's conflict plays out over nine episodes, and only in the final moments does she finally decide to be "open" about her relationship with Aster in New York. Differences in identity—sexuality primarily, but also race and gender—unfold slowly. The series's showrunners, Susan Miller and Tina Cesa Ward, portray the nuances of personal relationships; sociological differences emerge in ways intended to seem organic and surprising: "*Anyone but Me* shines a light on identity—coming to terms with who we are as gays, African Americans, women, and citizens of the world. I'm drawn to the fragile, social balancing act of young people because we've all been there. Life at sixteen is fraught and fertile for drama," Miller told me in an interview. For most of *Anyone but Me*, producers couch problems of cultural difference within broader discourses of growing up and discovering one's place in the world.

Anyone but Me, like many other series about marginalized groups, tries to balance the marketability of broad "universal" storytelling with the demands of community-focused niche storytelling. The writers are quite aware of prejudice and discrimination. Vivian takes a long time to "come out," and viewers have to endure her lengthy period in the "closet." We are put in the place of someone who feels marginalized. *Anyone but Me* represents hegemony but contextualizes it as a symptom of youth. As Miller said,

> The thing is, no matter how accepting modern urban teenagers may be of "difference," there's such a deep ambivalence they feel about themselves on so many levels, that each time they think they know who they are or who other people are, it's going to change in the next instant. So it's tough to come out about anything. Not just sexuality. Being gay at this moment may be less lonely than it ever was, especially with access to the Internet and to a show like ours, but it's still a stigma. And in some places, a danger.

Miller acknowledges the persistence of oppression—and of outlets to counterbalance those forces—and the possibility of danger—hence Vivian's reluctance to declare her sexuality in the first days of school. Ward said she wants "a more relevant take on coming out," showing how gay- and lesbian-identified individuals have many coming out stories. Vivian spends the entire first season, and parts of the second season, declaring and hiding her sexuality to the people close to her. In the penultimate episode, Aster takes issue with Vivian's secrecy about her sexuality while talking to Archibald, Vivian's suburban friend (who is black). Archibald tries to reframe the discussion around personal idiosyncrasies: "You know who you are and she knows who you are. So what else is there?" Aster responds, "Pride," a nod to "gay pride"—or, given that she's talking to a black man, pride in cultural difference generally. In the next episode, Vivian kisses Aster in front of her classmates.

Anyone but Me endorses Eve Sedgwick's thesis that "the closet is the defining structure of gay oppression in this century."[90] It argues for an explicit assertion of gay identity, particularly where environments are generally nonhostile, as it frames Westchester. It asserts that postgay culture is a myth, perhaps a nefarious one.[91] At the same time, the show warns that the closet and coming out are "now verging on all-purpose phrases. . . . so close to the heart of some modern preoccupations that it could be, or has been, evacuated of its historical gay specificity."[92] Indeed, all the *Anyone but Me* characters have secret desires, wishes, and stigmas they are attempting to resolve: Archibald grapples with his desire to draw comics against his parents' wishes and racial expectations; his girlfriend, Elisabeth, is trying to be an actress, against some odds; Sophie, Vivian's friend and possible love interest, might be coming out herself, but also has an older boyfriend she's hiding; Aster has a terrible relationship with her parents and a bit of wanderlust. *Anyone but Me's* narrative balances young people's common desire to "fit in" with the knowledge that they have so many media choices after which to model their identities: "As a teen the last thing you want is to be different from everyone else, and now because of our visibility you can see that there are other people like you," Ward said.

So, despite its explicit mission to bolster lesbian representation, *Anyone but Me* cast a wide net as a way to appeal to legacy television and sponsors, which did not materialize. Part of that is probably due to the show's slow pacing, which allows the producers to stretch out political representations and focus on more universal drama. Plot points hinted in the first season go unresolved for several episodes. One, Archibald's peculiar relationship with the principal and schoolwide drug use, takes two seasons to resolve. Slow pacing allows the writers to focus on tender moments in the narrative, but it also disperses plot points about race and sexuality. The series's most explicit plot development centered on cultural identity does not occur until the second half of the second season, when Vivian and Archibald produce a comic for the school newspaper. The comic focuses on two superheroes trapped in an alternate universe of "truth," according to Vivian: "And our characters, the fierce lesbian journalist and the black dude with super drawing powers, are the first inhabitants to actually live there. . . . [T]hey have to get people to live there or their world dies. . . . [I]t's about taking people to a place where it's safe to be yourself." The comic serves as a metanarrative for independent production and explicitly claiming identity in a way legacy media properties rarely do. Other plot points deal with politics directly but also through dreams and in-show representations: the season two opening scene dramatizes antigay bullying, for instance, but it is literally a nightmare.

It is impossible to deny that *Anyone but Me* is a lesbian series. Its focus is clear: even though two of its characters are straight white men, they are marginal to the narrative. Its creators are invested in declaring that lesbian identity matters. At a pivotal moment in the show, Vivian comes out to her friend Sophie. She tries to dismiss it as immaterial, but Sophie disagrees:

SOPHIE: I saw you kiss a girl! Okay. That's new information. So: who the hell is this person I'm supposed to be getting to know again?
VIVIAN: That blows. I'm sorry. [*sincerely*] But it doesn't change who I am.
S: It kind of does! I mean, not "who you are" like "now you're a bad person," but . . . I kind of told you things about me and Jonathan. And you were just holding back. It changes . . . us.

Here, Ward asserts the importance of gay identity—it is not, as post-gay cultural politics suggests, just about individuals and preferences. Though not wholly individualized, sexuality nevertheless changes the shape of social relations.

Representing lesbian identity runs against conventional television and advertising marketing wisdom. Mainstream media institutions generally lack interest in the lesbian market for a variety of reasons, including the contrasting marketability of the gay male stereotype and the history of women's consumption as heterosexual.[93] Moreover, throughout the short history of lesbian marketing, marketers "feminized" lesbians to appeal to straight men and women, an image advertisers associate with postidentity progressivism. Katherine Sender shows that "marketers and critics alike have tended to characterize the lipstick lesbian as the newer, apolitical or postfeminist lesbian consumer, contrasting this image with the older, feminist, anti-consumption stereotype."[94] This trend is best exemplified by *The L Word*, arguably one of the earliest and largest investments in lesbian programming, initially marketed as a West Coast *Sex and the City*, replete with gorgeous, consumerist, feminine women: "Same Sex, Different City," the tag line stated.[95] *Anyone but Me*'s producers are acutely aware of this dynamic and try to split the difference. Aster is quite stunning and feminine, with the look of a younger Angelina Jolie. Vivian is attractive but unglamorous in her fashion sense, revealing the kind of realism and creative freedom the web affords. *Anyone but Me* reflects the representational paradoxes of the networked era. Even as gays and lesbians were visible on television, many programs showcased characters whose concerns were identical to those of their straight counterparts; by comparison, web production emerged as spaces for self-representation, especially for gay youth outside of urban areas.[96]

Much like web series produced by and for black women, independent productions addressing gay and lesbian viewers implicitly reference legacy media texts and genres: lesbians are seen as less marketable, and intersections between race and sexuality are infrequent, so series producers trying to value undervalued identities hew closely to proven formulas, at least initially. The popular black gay series *Drama Queenz* follows the "young thespians in New York" conventions of *Fame* and *Chorus Line*, yet invites melodrama like series made by black women, adding subcultural style to an identifiable genre. For instance, *Drama Queenz* began with a conventional tale—"you're young and determined that you're going to make it in New York City"—and then adds cues that black and gay audiences quickly recognize, including the camp overuse of the word "bitch" and a number of shirtless men. Similar strategies are used in the web soap *In the Moment*, which cast across ethnicities, and *Chump Changes*, an urban soap that was among the first black web series. Black lesbian web series, like *Th3m* and *The Lovers & Friends Show*, function more like traditional soaps, with sprawling casts focused on friends and family. *The Lover & Friends Show*, the most popular of such early shows, kicked off its second season with a trailer that foreground the show's nucleus of four girlfriends—"whatever you need we got your back," is the opening line—before defining itself as "a show about . . . friendship . . . relationships . . . family . . . and all the drama that goes between." This is a fairly traditional pitch, using keywords central to most on-air dramas. Throughout the series's trailer, however, are dramatic scenes of couples crossing lines of class and race, with different gender expressions, all of which firmly mark the show as "black lesbian."

Anyone but Me's peers delicately balance universal themes with community-specific narratives. Other indie series lie on both ends of the spectrum, pushing representations to finer specificity and political potency or creating series where sexuality is only occasionally at issue. Queer series *The 3 Bits*, created by Margaret Singer and Max Freeman, features three separate storylines in three genres: a lesbian thriller called "Roman," starring Singer; a gay male rom-com called "Henry," starring Cole Escola; and a Park Slope mommy blog, "Madison," starring performance artist Erin Markey (also costar of Wifey TV's feminist comedy *Rods and Cones*, with Jibz Cameron). All the characters are related but exist in their own series, where they challenge norms around acceptable relationship structures (monogamy vs. polyamory), labor (illegal vs. legal), parenting (type-A mother vs. slacker mother), and representations of race (a storyline about opposing queer gangs). "It's obviously an absurdist version of reality, two lesbian gangs warring over Brooklyn, that's not the reality," Singer said, but "racism still exists, and we can try and set up this world so we can explore that." Freeman noted how Roman's story has no men: "It's not a world you see very much of, and that's very intentional." On *Hunting Season*, created by Jon Marcus, characters engage in explicit sexual action and debate racial preferences in online, app-based dating: "I want people to respond and identify," Marcus told me. Broadcast shows and series on cable networks like Logo, he added, "weren't entering into the conversations that I was having with people, with what they were watching." Freeman characterized legacy TV's representations of the intersections of sexuality, gender, and race as "safe and dumb," echoing sentiments among queer and of-color producers.

Whether queer or gay, indie web series variably embrace and shirk the burdens of legacy TV representations. As Brian Jordan Alvarez told *Paper* about his artistic comedy series, *The Gay and Wondrous Life of Caleb Gallo*, which joined Kit Williamson's *Eastsiders* and the second season of *The Outs* in exploring nonmonogamy among gay men, "I don't really think about how I'm supposed to be representing gay people, but I know that I am one and I know a lot of them, so I do it based on my real life experience." This focus on sincerity from gay producers leads to wide-ranging representations. While Marcus's series is sexually explicit as an homage to 1990s queer cinema—fans could purchase uncensored episodes with shots of penises, a rarity on legacy television—series like Adam Goldman's *The Outs* and Kieran Turner's *Eastsiders* excited fans with flawed gay characters unable to secure love in their lives, a contrast to homonormative, happily married gay leads on popular television series like *Modern Family*. "The relationship is a character," Goldman said of *The Outs*. "The community needs complex characters." Black gay dramas like Deondray and Quincy LeNear Gossett's *Chadwick Journals*, Band of Artists' *Freefall*, and Anthony Anderson's *Anacostia* offer complex characters within the genres of crime and drama, speaking to black communities' struggles with violence. New York and Los Angeles producers, inspired by the likes *Seinfeld* and *Louie*, created series about individuals whose distance from mainstream, marketable gay and lesbian identities informs the narrative. In Ingrid Jungermann's *F to 7th* and (with Desiree Akhavan) *The Slope*, Amy Rubin's *Little Horribles* and *Boxed In* (produced for IFC.com and later IFC), Alexandra Roxo and Natalia Leite's *Be Here Now-ish*, Matthew Kirsch's *duder*, and Brent Sullivan and Eliot Glazer's *It Gets Betterish*, characters fail at same-sex dating as often as they fail at relating to gay and straight family members, strangers, coworkers, and each other. "There are a ton of gay guys who aren't the slightest bit fierce. I think it's important to remember that you don't have to be a porn star or wear body glitter to feel accepted within the community," Glazer and Sullivan wrote in a joint interview.[97]

Declaring cultural difference more explicitly than series on legacy television became a defining aspect of gay online representation during the 2000s and 2010s. However, sliding too far off into in-group specificity and politics limited their appeal to legacy distributors. As of 2016, few gay and lesbian series secured legacy development deals, and as of this writing all have yet to go to series, including Lena Waithe's *Twenties* (a pilot presentation in four parts produced by Queen Latifah, picked up by BET), Benjamin Cory Jones's *Bros* (also a pilot presentation picked up by HBO), and Jungerman's *F to 7th* (Showtime). Nevertheless, Amy Rubin's *Boxed In* did screen on IFC as part of a licensing deal with its Comedy Crib platform, and Alvarez's *Caleb Gallo* got him meetings with networks as MTV's Logo hired him for their comedy series *Gay Skit Happens*. The creators of *Anyone but Me* and the many productions following it want to strike a balance: marketing stories that both gay and lesbian communities and the industry might accept. That proved a tall order, one that only exists on the open market.

By the end of its second season, *Anyone but Me* had achieved a sizable audience and critical recognition. As with *Awkward Black Girl*'s niche-driven strategy, *Anyone but Me*'s producers focused on reaching lesbian drama fans through new and old media. Ward and Miller interacted intimately with their communities, but they also worked through semitraditional networks, many of them products of the broader gay marketing trend. That Miller and Ward were both television and theater veterans helped in their niche marketing efforts. In the early months of the show, before and after the premiere, their campaign focused on getting established personalities and publications to legitimate the series as something worthy of the gay, lesbian, and black communities' attention. "I just started calling on people I knew or worked with," Miller said. One of those individuals was Kate Clinton, a prominent lesbian comic and actress. Later, the show promoted endorsements from other cult figures like Eric Stoltz (*Caprica*), Zachary Quinto (*Star Trek*, *Heroes*), and Liza Weil (*Gilmore Girls*, *How to Get Away with Murder*). Clinton announced the series in her newsletter, after which the Viacom-owned lesbian media site, *AfterEllen*, reviewed the show and posted each episode as it aired, giving *Anyone but Me* consistent publicity. Independent gay publications like the *Windy City Times*, *Curve*, and *Autostraddle*, along with *Advocate* site *SheWired*, promoted, embedded, and reviewed the show. "I took wild stabs at reaching out to every link appearing on every niche site I could find—the equivalent of cold calls. And I still do," Miller said. For a very short time during season two, however, they did also have the aid of a PR firm to arrange interviews and handle releases.

Some of these tactics are familiar to legacy networks; in fact, most of the media outlets featuring *Anyone but Me* spent a significant amount of time covering the products of companies like Viacom. And new media marketing strategies were already integral to niche cable networks like Logo and larger channels like Oxygen and MTV.[98] Ben Aslinger argues that the Internet, with its interactivity and community-building tools (forums), was vital to the creation of Logo, which Viacom hoped would represent "televisual queerness in the age of the digital," thus explaining why the conglomerate purchased *AfterEllen* and *AfterElton* a year after Logo launched.[99] Indeed, for a small licensing fee, Logo occasionally distributed independent web series on its website Logo.com, but only those about white gay men, including the first seasons of WGA Award–nominated *Vicky & Lysander* and Indie Series Award–winning dramas *Hunting Season* and *Eastsiders*; however, for their second seasons, all three opted to forgo the Logo's website and distributed independently on YouTube and Vimeo On Demand.

Series like *Anyone but Me* cannot rely solely on legacy press and marketing to generate interest and audiences; they also need to actively mobilize and demonstrate the value of their communities through new web-based tools for raising funds and awareness. After two seasons of releasing episodes on Strike TV, Hulu, and Blip (a YouTube competitor), *Anyone but Me*'s producers lost their primary investor and had to raise money for a third season. The pair hoped the press they could generate by raising over $100,000 for another season would elicit interest from television or sponsors;[100] they did not want to finance *Anyone but Me* through exclusive subscriptions, a model that had worked for another lesbian series, *Venice*. Their season three fundraising drive was the show's most visible evidence of its community. They demonstrated the value of their fans as fans valued the show with their money. The team was already used to releasing bonus footage and providing fans access to stars;[101] this time they produced a three-day, ninety-minute web-a-thon with special programming: interactive sessions with the cast and crew, an eBay auction, tours of the set, readings of fan letters, and quirky videos.[102] Following in the footsteps of *The Guild*, the producers also released an exclusive music video from indie singer Rachael Cantu, which featured an appearance from the two leads (in a nod to the second season's finale cliffhanger, in which the couple broke up). "You have to be as creative in your strategy to survive as you are in your storytelling," Ward said in an earlier interview. What made *Anyone but Me*'s crowdfunding campaign work was its deft citation of viewers' desire for lesbian representation on television through a larger discourse of community-produced online media. The team skillfully connected supporting the show with representational struggle: "We know you sacrificed something to express your love for *Anyone but Me*. And your love makes us fierce!" one campaign e-mail stated. In this, *Anyone but Me* employed a decades-old discourse connecting community formation to market recognition.

Such appeals are common in the gay web series market, as evidenced by the premiere of independent web TV networks targeting black LGBT and lesbian communities. Unlike networks for black women, intended to expand existing legacy television representations, black LGBT and lesbian-focused networks focus on bringing communities out of invisibility into the gay market. Maurice Jamal, one of the few working black gay directors in the 2000s, with films like *Ski Trip* and *Dirty Laundry*, started a pay-TV network, GLO, in 2010, to distribute his own series along with other scripted and docu-shows about lesbians, gay men, and trans individuals: "In communities of color, we rarely see these images. Or hear these stories. And we need to. That's how we affect change, by breaking down the barriers," he said.[103] Like other niche network producers, Jamal positions distribution as a way to commoditize communities seen as less valuable in mainstream markets. He told me, "[A]s a community I think it's been a challenge to show that we have the economic power and the business sense. . . . The urban community is one of the largest, if not the largest, consumers of media and culture."[104] Jamal supported this community-building mission by including programs about HIV/AIDS, allowing subscribers to interact with filmmakers, and openly soliciting program ideas and pitches. While not as robust, other networks did some of the same: No More Down Low distributed its own half-hour news program about the black gay community, and social networking (and "hook-up") site Black Gay Chat (BGC) Live, distributed web series like *The Chadwick Journals* (from Quincy LeNear and Deondray Gossett, showrunners of *The DL Chronicles* on gay premium cable channel Here! TV) and *Drama Queenz*. In the mid-2010s, new subscription-based distributors in the black LGBT market developed artistic, complex, and dramatic representations, each channel buttressed by a hit indie show and running subscriptions and on-demand sales through VHX (purchased by Vimeo in 2016): Michelle Daniel, creator of black lesbian series *Between Women*, started Between Women TV in 2015 for the show's third season, along with short films and docu-series; that same year *Freefall* creator Lamont Pierre started The Arthouse, for new seasons of that Atlanta-based drama about black gay men, along with at least four other series, shorts, and feature films; in 2016, *No Shade* creator Sean Anthony Torrington started SLAY TV, with four original series and twenty-three re-releases of indie black LGBTQ series, with some, like Dwight Allen O'Neal's 2006 drama *Christopher Street TV*, among the oldest black gay shows.

Like many independent networks distributing queer programming, GLO did not last, but it was not the first subscription-based independent queer web TV network. It was preceded, for example, by tello films. Founded in 2007 by Christin Mell and Nicole Valentine, tello successfully created original dramas and comedies for lesbians through subscription rates of four dollars each month. Until the network merged with lesbian film site *One More Lesbian* (OML) in 2013, creating a kind of "lesbian Netflix," roughly a thousand fans paid for comedy western *Cowgirl Up*, teen drama *The Throwaways*, and Chicago comedies *#Hashtag*, *Roomies*, and *The Neighbors*.[105] In 2013, tello mobilized fans on Indiegogo to resuscitate *Nikki & Nora*, a police procedural that UPN had passed on a decade earlier.[106] Tello's key producers, Julie Keck and Jessica King, helped grow its subscriber base by using social media. Keck and King got their start by working in queer communities, producing films about sex and relationships with and for friends in Chicago: "[T]hey were just comedies with social commentary. They actually explored some interesting issues," Keck said. King describes their early years learning to engage people through crowdfunding, production, and screenings: "[P]eople just wanted to be part of this little community and this play and engagement online." Over the years, tello's audience grew and the network was constantly producing more programs at higher levels of production value in both Chicago and Los Angeles. Keck and King describe tello's relationship to its audience as a romantic one: "You have to woo them; you have to spend time, like gaining their loyalty and gaining their trust. And so just getting a lot of views does not automatically translate into a lot of subscriptions," King said. "Asking people to give you their money does require a lot of trust," Keck said.

Distributing lesbian and gay identities neglected by legacy television networks involves a careful balance of making explicit appeals to difference while creating easily consumable commodities for complex communities. Black gay and lesbian series, far less present on television, share with lesbian series like *Anyone but Me* an intense desire to distinguish their products from the legacy media, utilizing creative and community-focused strategies for releasing content. Yet the goal of monetizing those shows—selling them to advertisers, television networks, or conglomerates—means that distribution portals often stray from pursuing anything too radical and instead focus on appealing to communities' desires for visibility.

Producing and Releasing Latino/a Representations

Visibility is necessarily fraught. *East WillyB* begins with a series of disagreements, all revealing tensions around race, ethnicity, class, and capitalism. The show starts in a local bar owned by Willie Reyes, a Puerto Rican everyman. He playfully bickers with Gisele, the local drunk, when his ex-girlfriend, Maggie, barges into his bar with a business plan: "You also need to start selling those six-dollar malt liquors.

Those rich white hipsters love that shit!" Maggie owns half the bar and has been taking classes at a local college. She thinks Willie should ride the wave of gentrification, transforming his bar's down-home feel into an ironic commodity: "I'm thinking we can make this bar more emo. . . . Slightly depressive, dive. We can have some eighties video games, some Confederate flags." Maggie's appeals are ignored, partially because she left Willie for another man, Albert, a white entrepreneur. "This is still a Latin bar. I don't know why everybody's trippin'!" Willie retorts.

Such is the central drama in *East WillyB*, a web sitcom about gentrification in the Brooklyn neighborhood of Bushwick, east of Williamsburg. Willie is the heart of *East WillyB* and a metaphor for the brand of independent entrepreneurship the show represents: a Latino businessman trying to preserve his specific, local cultural heritage against the encroachments of white money and cultural influence. The series premiered on YouTube in 2011 and instantly gained the attention of the New York and trade media because of its political narrative and "new" ethos for marketing to the diverse Latino community. The series creators, Julia Ahumada Grob and Yamin Segal, found a way to represent a diverse community. They focused on using "viral humor"—short and brash[107]—to sell to what they called the "new generation Latino," a generation of bicultural, bilingual, English-dominant, and urban young people with multicultural friendship networks and cultural tastes. The phrase "new generation Latino" is the producers' way of speaking to corporations and sponsors looking to invest. The show's marketing materials emphasize both its wider appeal and its niche focus: "In many ways I would say it's an American story told through Latin eyes, Latin voices. And I think it resonates as both those things, as incredibly Latino and as incredibly American," Segal said in a promotional video.[108]

East WillyB reflects the ability of the web to accommodate politically and culturally aware stories speaking directly to underrepresented communities. In a complex Latino media market dominated by Spanish-language television networks Univision and Telemundo, *East WillyB* as a text and commodity was an argument for reconfiguring or reframing "Latinidad" as a market more diverse and attuned to local politics and culture than was present in larger outlets. This move was not new—such media have always existed—but mass-market television has rarely been able to accommodate the rich complexity of the American ethnicity loosely defined as "Hispanic" or "Latino."[109] *East WillyB* offers a compelling alternative to legacy television marketing and programming, yet it borrows proven representational and distribution strategies to do so.

Each episode in *East WillyB*'s "pilot season"—a series of six two- to three-minute episodes intended to generate interest from audiences and sponsors—intervenes in debates about Latino representation and politics. In "Baseball's Dead," episode three, a debate about whether to show baseball in Willie's bar escalates into a comically thin disagreement about community diversity. A customer tells Willie to turn off the baseball game, while Edgar, another local, suggests he put on soccer to get Mexicans in the door. Annoyed, Willie calls Edgar "Pancho Villa," to which Edgar replies that he is Salvadoran. Willie retorts, "Tomato, tomato. Same shit! You wanna watch sports, you watch baseball!" Ceci, Willie's friend (played by Grob), intervenes, and the customer tells her to be quiet because she is half Mexican: "Plus, you ain't half Mexican 'cause you whiter than milk, yo!" She retorts that she is half Mexican and half Cuban. As Willie and the customer continue to argue, Edgar and Ceci agree: "Puerto Ricans are loud." The episode ends.

If "Baseball's Dead" sounds frenetic, a muddled cavalcade of cultural difference, that is probably intentional. Creators and writers Grob and Segal created *East WillyB* because the media marketed to them did not reflect their Latina experience growing up and living in New York. It also did not reflect their personal stories: Grob identifies as half Chilean and Jewish American; Segal is Nicaraguan. *East WillyB* roots its representation of Latinidad in New York, with its residents mostly speaking English: "We wanted the characters to reflect the diversity of the Latino community." By the late 2000s, Juan Piñón and Viviana Rojas found Latino TV distribution diversifying, with U.S. and Latin American conglomerates seeking younger, English-speaking, and ethnically specific populations.[110]

What "diversity" means in the Latino market is a vexing question, and television's representational flaws have complex histories. In her seminal study of Latino marketing, Arlene Dávila argues that Latino/Hispanic identity has been collapsed into a catch-all term by marketers seeking to create a monetizable community, erasing differences within. Yet even as legacy television networks and programs collapse distinctions among Latinos, "Latino" remains important to the way some individuals and communities identify. It wasn't always this way. Dávila notes how "Latino" marketing prior to the 1970s was largely local and regional, with centers in New York (Cuban and Puerto Rican) and Los Angeles (Mexican). This changed with the onset of national television, spurred by satellite technology and Mexican entrepreneur Emilio Azcárraga. Contrary to the notion of cable television as a new technology intended to increase diversity and niches, nationalizing the Latino market required moving away from targeting particular groups to "a distinct yet unidentifiable market": "Among the most prevalent are the presentation of a neutral or universal version of Hispanidad—the putatively neutral, 'nonaccented' Spanish and 'generic' Latin look—and ambiguous appeals to a Hispanic spirit, way of being, attitude, or morality, which are supposedly shared among all Latinas."[111] Spanish became the market's unifying characteristic, and with the rise of the language came the concurrent rise of a particular kind of marketer: Latin American (foreign born) and educated with perfect Spanish and English. Miami and Univision rose to the top, and Cuban Americans dominated programming and marketing discourses. New York–based Latinos—Dominicans in particular—felt neglected by "assimilationist" media: "[T]he transnationalization of media flows provides little space for material that fully addresses U.S. Latinas' concerns and sensibilities, particularly regarding issues of race and gender."[112] As a market, Latinos were "hybrids," and their "representational ambiguity" was useful to marketers who could commodify the conveniently postracial community.[113] As Mary Beltrán unpacks in *Dark Angel*, starring Jessica Alba, "The apparent vogue for mixed Latina/o stars follows the more general popularity in Hollywood and U.S. popular culture since the 1990s for ethnically ambiguous looks. . . . These trends have been prompted . . . by increasing ethnic diversity and cultural curiosity in this country."[114] Even though Alba publicly identified as half Mexican, marketing and mainstream press for *Dark Angel* featured little mention of it, even as ethnic media trumpeted her as a Latina star.[115]

Hollywood film and television disproportionately portrayed Latinos as undocumented, loud, violent, or overly sexual, all images Latino consumers and activists have consistently protested, probably a result of the underrepresentation of Latinos as show creators, writers, and lead actors.[116] As Frances Negrón-Muntaner notes, "[I]n the few instances when Latinos appear, they tend to embody many of the same stereotypes first visualized in cinema over a century ago: criminals, cheap labor, and sexual objects."[117] Her 2015 report found the community historically and consistently underrepresented by legacy television, where less than 2 percent of writers and producers were Latino during the 2000s, despite a brief rise in representation in the 1990s and early 2000s. From 2010 to 2013, during *East WillyB*'s online release, no Latinos played leading roles on top-rated legacy television shows: "[O]n camera representation in the 2000s was the same as in the 1950s, and significantly lower than in the 1970s" despite a dramatic increase in the U.S. Latino population.[118] From 2012 to 2013, during *East WillyB*'s second season, 24 percent of all Latino TV characters were linked to crime, four times the proportion in 1994. Moreover, "since 1984, 51.9%, or 14 of the 27 Latino main cast roles in the top ten scripted TV shows, have been related to criminal activities, law enforcement, or security."[119]

East WillyB's producers and actors pitched their series as a sophisticated and light-hearted corrective to these dynamics. Grob and Segal's "new generation Latino" is both broad and specific. Their clearest target is the dominance of Spanish-language Mexican programming on the major television networks. At the show's premiere event in New York, actress Caridad "La Bruja" de la Luz (playing Gisele) claimed that American television leaves out ethnicities other than Mexican: "There isn't enough Latino work done by Latinos, written by Latinos, actors. There's a lot of Mexican representation in Hollywood and on TV, but now I think it's time for other Latinos to come together and represent *la cultura*," she said. Grob and Segal's market is bicultural and bilingual, but English dominant, younger, urban, and multicultural. Appealing to a smaller market than that of television's Spanish-language stations, their work positions its audience as less mainstream, but younger and ascendant. "Spanish-language is not going away. . . . There's space for both," Grob said, adding that their audience is starved for content: "Because their world is moving in English, they want to see it."

Grob's critique of Spanish-language media reflects the way Univision and Telemundo have dominated Latino marketing and elided local differences, a result, in part, of the Department of Justice and the Federal Communications Commission allowing media mergers: "The size and market power of Univision are not only or even primarily an economic issue. . . . [T]he high levels of concentration of Spanish-language broadcasting coupled with its control by non-Latina/o entities constitute a violation of the speech rights of Latino citizens."[120] The dominance of Spanish-language media distorts marketers' and network executives' perception of the Latino community, resulting in a representational imbalance. Both creators spent the year before and after *East WillyB* premiered pitching ideas to on-air and online networks, but were told that they were "ahead" of the market. At the same time, articles were coming out about the growing Latino market online and shifts in cultural tastes. "It was important for us to come out as the trends were emerging," they said. *East WillyB*'s desired audience was not more authentic or truer than its mainstream counterpart, though the producers came close to implying as much. It should also be noted that, within Latino marketing firms, the Spanish- and English-language distinction falls along class lines, with the latter preferred for reaching educated and middle-class Latinos.[121]

The desire to see a "new generation Latino" onscreen reflects minority producers' disenchantment as they found legacy television stubbornly incompatible with the kind of intraracial and interracial representations in *East WillyB*. The show targets American media representations of Latino criminality in its second episode, which has two dominant storylines: one of Ceci's cousins stealing her Social Security number ("I am sending your ass straight back over the fence where you came from!" she tells him) and one of a white real estate agent, John Henderson, with blatant disregard for the mundane financial concerns of less-privileged Latino locals (he refuses to recycle, despite landlord threats of raising rents). The final episode brings the entire cast together for a showdown between Henderson and Albert (the shop owner who wants to sell to hipsters) and Willie and the diverse group of Bushwick locals, mostly Latino. Henderson is trying to lease a storefront to Albert: "Just picture it: you'll be the first businessman to take advantage of the new white people. . . . You could be the King of East Williamsburg." The scene jump cuts to Willie, who states, "Doesn't he know I'm the King of Bushwick?"—a politically tinged rejoinder; in the struggle over space in New York City, "Williamsburg" represents the newly gentrified, predominantly white Brooklyn, where "Bushwick" represents its ethnically diverse history and contemporary reality. The season ends with the locals outside Albert's hipster store rooting for Ceci and Willie to beat him down. In *East WillyB*, "Latinadad" is a nation within a nation, as Dávila describes it, but it is one with conflicting interests, both within itself and in relation to America and capital.

To harness the Latino community and connect with fan desires, *East WillyB* turned to crowdfunding. In 2012, after *East WillyB* released its pilot season, the creators started a fifty-thousand-dollar Kickstarter campaign to raise funds to make a full first season, complete with an opening musical number, celebrity cameos (*Coach Carter*'s Rick Gonzalez), and further engagement with the issue of gentrification. The campaign raised money for production but also kept fans interested in the series: "We knew we were going to have a big, uphill battle to get our fans back [after a hiatus post–pilot season]," Grob said. To rally support for the series, Segal and Grob sent thank you's via social media, a standard practice; music from the show, mostly hip hop from independent Latino artists; twenty walk-on roles; dinner with the cast; and party invitations. Celebrity endorsements helped attract attention. The team released support videos from Andre Royo (*The Wire*), Rick Gonzalez (*Reaper, Coach Carter*), Lin-Manuel Miranda (writer of the Tony Award–winning *In the Heights* and *Hamilton*), and John Leguizamo. It was important during the campaign to show as much of Grob and Segal's lived experience as possible, underscoring how indie series development involves making personal connections with distinct fan communities. Grob and Segal posted photos from their office in a New York creative hub and hosted culturally relevant events throughout the city. These included offering tickets to a Latino comedy showcase, a pub crawl on Cinco de Mayo, a salsa event featuring one of their actors, a fundraiser with domino playing at the bar where they shoot the show, and a "cut-a-thon" offering ten-dollar cuts at a Bushwick barbershop as a way to engage businesses in the community the show portrays. Inviting fans to events mobilized them; Grob notes how one fan they invited to an event, their thirtieth of 557 backers, "became a mouthpiece for the campaign" at the Tribeca Film Festival. They created a "Brand Ambassadors program" and offered associate producer credit to any fan who could raise money for the show; of the twenty they picked, only two raised a significant amount, but that totaled $5,000, or 10 percent of their ask.

East WillyB's explicitly political and community-based approach to marketing is not wholly representative of other online shows targeting

Latinos. A year after *East WillyB*'s first full season, for example, Hulu released *East Los High*, a Los Angeles–set drama about women in search of reproductive health and justice. It became one of Hulu's most popular series. Unlike *East WillyB*'s focus on how local economies affect Latinos, *East Los High* focuses on how sex affects relationships between and among families. Created by Carlos Portugal and Kathleen Bedoya for Population Media Center, *East Los High* is a nonprofit, independent production designed to deliver health messages vetted and funded by a nexus of global institutions. The show explores issues of rape, molestation, deceit, bullying, HIV diagnosis, and, of course, pregnancy and its termination. The show has various "teachable moments" giving concrete advice on pregnancy and sexually transmitted infection (STI) prevention and treatment.

Other series share *East Los High* and *East WillyB*'s desire to reflect the complications of Latino American identification, where the community is both "hot" and misunderstood. 2008's *Ylse*, arguably the earliest prominent Latino series, about a young reporter trying to make it in television journalism, brands itself as a workplace comedy at once "American" and "Latino." The show reflects universal ideals of "love, career, and family"—mainstays of mainstream Latino marketing[122]—but it also explores being Latina in a white-American-dominated industry. According to lead actress and creator Ruth Livier, "It's about a woman who's trying to succeed in the entertainment world. It's a push and pull that we face, particularly as Latinos but as Latinas, where part of our decisions are based on our American upbringing, then the other part still holds on to our cultural, Latina roots. . . . And I think it's funny."[123] *Ylse*'s underlying themes are about negotiating cultural difference—the first line of the first season trailer broadcasts Ylse's contempt at having to change her hard-to-pronounce Latina name for TV. But it also focuses on the story's broad appeal—Ylse is a "regular girl trying to make it as a serious journalist."[124] If mainstream Latino marketing demands "exotic and segregated others," *Ylse* attempts to use otherness through more classic comedic and ideological appeals.[125]

What *Ylse*, *East Los High*, and *East WillyB* collectively show is how web distribution created an opening for markets smaller than legacy television, allowing independent producers to create politically and regionally situated stories about their experiences. By creating commodities, they critique market imbalances: in these cases, the nationalizing of a "postracial ethnicity" in service of big-media dollars at the expense of local particularities. The characters in these shows are both specific and relatable: neither Willie nor Ylse are radical beyond the point of relatability. Their causes are personal before they are political; instead of overturning the system, they only want to keep it fair and open to diversity, a message not too out of step with indie producers' critique of legacy television's depiction of others.

To market their stories, these producers needed to be more creative in attracting interest from fans and brands. *East WillyB*'s 2011 premiere event was, by independent web video standards, a glitzy and well-orchestrated affair. I arrived at Manhattan's Anthology Film Archives, itself a landmark of independent production and distribution, to a large, young, and diverse crowd. A table on the first floor allowed press to sign in and directed them upstairs. Upstairs, outside the theater, Grob and Segal set up a step-and-repeat (a backdrop for red carpets), complete with a velvet rope, camera crew, and backdrop emblazoned with *East WillyB*'s bright green logo. At the other end of the small room was an open bar serving cocktails with Licor 43, a Spanish liquor popular in Puerto Rico and Mexico, produced by a company looking to break into the U.S. market. Inside the theater, each seat was draped with a bright yellow tote bag with branded products, including the national magazines *Complex* (targeting young, urban men) and *Latina* (targeting young Latinas); a Licor 43 pamphlet and keychain light; coupons for Refugio, a Brooklyn cigar house; a bottle of Palo, a Dominican/Caribbean iced tea marketed by a Pennsylvania-based company; and a flyer for Rebelution designs, a Brooklyn printing company.

East WillyB marketed itself as a movement, at once national and local, reflecting the producers' desire to speak to a specific New York niche while also claiming to represent a national, young, politically aware consumer. Indeed, the audience cheered during the postscreening Q&A when Grob mentioned the brands that "believe in a homegrown series." Members of their niche evangelized the show, building an audience the creators could sell to sponsors. "The exciting thing about sponsorship as well is a lot of brands are trying to reach this population that we're trying to reach," Grob said in an interview, noting that Licor 43 contacted them, not the other way around. These efforts could create a new, broader market for actors and producers, who find it difficult to get roles. Many of the show's actors have prominent film and TV credits, from Showtime's *Nurse Jackie* to the high-profile independent film *Gun Hill Road*, but find steady work elusive.

East WillyB's story and marketing counteract dominant representations of Latinos as family-oriented, politically correct, or stereotypical, but the show's outreach efforts also reified the idea of Latinos as brand loyal and understandable, despite tremendous internal diversity and tension. "Latinos in general are very accepting of new media trends," Grob told me. Many of its strategies for selling Latinos were mainstays of film and television marketing. Their premiere event at Anthology Film Archives mirrored standard award-show and red-carpet mainstays, including sponsored giveaways, SWAG ("stuff we all get"), and photo opportunities with the cast and crew. Diligent promoters, Grob and Segal sent out press releases, garnering them coverage in local media like Brooklyn's *L Magazine*, *Complex*, *Fox News*, and MTV Tr3s, Viacom's Latino-focused channel and entertainment website.[126]

The *East WillyB* creators leaned heavily on their fans in publicizing their series. At the premiere, the creators instructed the audience to share the series's short videos using the hashtag #EastWillyB. The videos racked up thousands of views in their first month. Key to the show's appeal is the apparent novelty of representing young, English-speaking Latinos from a variety of classes and cultural heritages. In promotional e-mails and press releases, the team took on the role of ambassadors for a hard-to-reach and profitable audience. The pitch had some success: of the brands participating in the series's premiere event, Licor 43 was not the only one to approach the creators.

Marketing a new group in a traditional way runs the risk of producing similar, reductionist effects. Is the community too diverse for representation? The small scale of web series production seems amenable to cultural specificity, but marketing requires more clarity and simplification. Bernadette Marie Calafell warns,

> [T]he adoption of a monolithic Latina/o consuming body by advertisers and companies is irresponsible and dangerous in cases such as this. The point then becomes for those of us who are concerned with constructing a "Latina/o" identification to work toward creating images or representations that are not reductionist, representations that allow for some con-

nection without homogeneity. In working toward this goal, however, I am sensitive to the ways that potential organizing terms such as women or Latinos can be simplistic, historically reductionist.[127]

Balancing the richness of representation and the simplicity of marketing imperatives is a challenge, in any medium. *East WillyB*'s producers bet on the promise that the web, as a new and loosely organized medium, could do what legacy television could not: "Web series are exciting in that way because they're filled with possibility but no one really knows how much it's worth," Grob said. Without set market value, the creators of *East WillyB* have room to maneuver, to focus on building different cultural formations of Latinidad, "based on affective connections rather than more typical identification markers."[128] Whether such a thing is possible—connecting the lived realities of communities with the needs of marketing—has yet to be proven, but *East WillyB*'s visibility campaign certainly shows that alternative representational and marketing options are available.

Indeed, the producers marshaled their success into lucrative opportunities in Hollywood. Julia Grob became a Disney diversity writing fellow and eventually landed her first staff position on ABC's *Galavant*. Yamin Segal became head of programming and development for Flama, Univision's digital video destination for the young Latino market. Grob and Segal were clearly ahead of their time. In addition to Flama, Univision started a channel for short-form web series, Udisea; meanwhile, upstart independent networks like Latino youth channel Mitú and multicultural channel MACRO acquired investments from marketing and telecommunications conglomerates and released ambitious original series like America Ferrara's Los Angeles–set gentrification dramedy, *Gente-fied*.[129] Even HBO Latino started ordering web series with two seasons of William Caballero's *Gran'pa Knows Best*, which also aired as interstitials on its linear channel.

Combining Community Representation with the Demands of the Market

Rapid changes in media technologies create excitement for broader social change, but producers inevitably have to balance progressive desires for community uplift and representation with the needs of the market.[130] Over the past few decades, independent media producers have bemoaned the loss of community ethos. Post-identity politics, combined with marketers' desires to reach loosely defined niches organized around race, gender, and sexuality, blur differences and suppress demand for minority labor. The independent web series creators addressed in this chapter reintegrate community ethos and labor fairness into debates over representation. In an interview with Diana Veiga, *Awkward Black Girl* coproducer Tracey Oliver points out,

> Hollywood largely functions on economics. There's undoubtedly racism still present in the industry, but we as African Americans have the power to be the change that we want to see in our own representation. We can do that by supporting fellow artists' projects that we respect, whether financially or just by spreading the word to others. *Awkward Black Girl* is bigger than Issa and I. This show's success really reflects all of the people who stepped up to support what we're doing. If we succeed, it's a victory for all of us who want to see change on-screen.[131]

Oliver mobilizes fans' desire for more finely attuned representation in service of growing a market. The market is, according to most cultural studies scholarship, supposed to be opposed to progressive cultural politics. Yet throughout history, companies and minorities have tried to harness the market for political ends, using marketing to assert the importance of cultural difference.[132]

What kind of liberation can come from this? Black queer theorists Isaac Julien and Kobena Mercer praised 1980s and 1990s black queer experimental films for reimagining genre and cinematic form to express the tensions and irreconcilabilities of being black and gay.[133] Those filmmakers did not have the audience access that digital practitioners have today. With profit in sight, open TV producers see little value in the less commercial forms of experimentation Mercer described, instead adapting legacy TV programs' notions of the self, genre, and form to carve a space in open markets. Web series production arose after the niche marketing and media conglomeration, which commoditized previously unseen identities from GLBT people (Viacom's Logo) to Latinos (NBC's Univision, HBO Latino). As Maurice Jamal, founder of black gay network GLO, said in an interview, "It's about economic empowerment, our community showing if we can flex our muscle not only creatively, but also economically."

Yet there are limits to visibility, as gay consumers realized after the 1990s emergence of the GLBT market. The fundamental problem stems from the difference between consumers and citizens, economic subjects and social subjects. As Rosemary Hennessey writes, "Not only is much recent gay visibility aimed at producing new and potentially lucrative markets, but as in most marketing strategies, money, not liberation, is the bottom line. . . . Visibility in commodity culture is in this sense a limited victory for gays who are welcome to be visible as consumer subjects but not as social subjects."[134] Written after the 1994 "Don't Ask, Don't Tell" policy, Hennessy's warning bears weight. Markets, indifferent to transformational politics, are hostile to marginalized identities. For Dávila, the rise in Latino representation around the same time holds little currency for true political change: "Latinas are undoubtedly gaining visibility . . . but only as a market, never as a people, and 'markets' are vulnerable; they must be docile; they cannot afford to scare capital away."[135] Smith-Shomade's work on BET shows how access to mass distribution for black communities did little to quell representational grievances.[136] Moreover, class remains as uncharted online as on-air: *East WillyB* has a number of characters who are not middle class, but *Anyone but Me*, *Awkward Black Girl*, and many other web shows focus on middle-class lives. Ultimately, as a market, communities must appeal to advertisers, who seek individuals with disposable income.

What this chapter shows, however, is that difference is not lost in transition. Lacking marketing teams, independents innovate market logics, and so adapt legacy television representations to sell less visible "others." Pure independence, then, is an illusion; aspirants cannot break completely from dominant frames and practices, where capital flows. Yet when producers create and market their own representations, they cannot erase their identities, and so bravely insert differences into stories to connect sincerely with their communities. This is meaningful. Independents are actively working to reshape the market to support the creative freedom necessary to sincerely represent the underrepresented.

4

Open TV Distribution

Struggling for an Independent Market

Prologue: Releasing *She's out of Order*

It is harder to market a web series than to make one. Releasing *She's out of Order*, we learned the challenges of open distribution, where legacy television's exclusivity, control, and scale in program development—exclusive licensing contracts, syndication windows and reruns, robust marketing budgets—proves difficult to replicate. Independent distribution—e.g., the creation of networks or "publishers" to select, finance, and market series—is the most challenging aspect of an open TV market. The web's openness challenges efforts to control how and when series circulate. Meanwhile, exhibiting indie series at festivals and award ceremonies, a way to value exceptional series for distributors, critics, and fans, disrupts the ideal of openness that draws producers to the web in the first place.

Our struggles around distribution highlighted the challenge of creating an open, sustainable independent market. It took us two years to edit, release, and market *She's out of Order*. The show was never a "viral" hit, but we did have some success. Our greatest achievements were a nonexclusive distribution deal and acceptance to the 2015 LAWEBFEST, an independent festival for web series founded in 2010. Its founder, Michael Ajakwe, claims that it is the first festival dedicated to web series, if you do not count the New York Television Festival (NYTVF) and the International Television Festival (ITVFest), which have screened web series since the mid-2000s alongside legacy television. Teresa received a nomination for outstanding lead actress in a comedy and LaJune Grant for outstanding guest actress in a comedy, which she won. Flattered by the recognition, the production team committed to attending the festival—Derek, Rhonney, Teresa, and I traveled to Los Angeles in April to sit on a few panels about web series, attend screenings, meet other creators, and visit the award show.

Yet in January we received a troubling e-mail from Ajakwe. He sent us a message reminding us of a new exclusivity clause barring us from participating in other web series festivals within thirty days of LAWEBFEST: "This clause was put in place to protect the life of this festival and to prevent our audience from being cannibalized by another local rival festival here in Los Angeles called HollyWeb and, later, to protect the festival from further encroachment from an award show called Indie Soap Awards or ISA."[1] Ajakwe accused the HollyWeb Fest organizers of deliberately scheduling their festival within a week of LAWEBFEST to poach their audience. Ajakwe said he was hearing from creators who were burdened financially by having to attend both. Two weeks later, Derek found a response on HollyWeb's page, suggesting that we were not the only creators affected. In fact, while we had submitted to HollyWeb, by January we did not yet know if we were accepted—they announced on February 10—and we were not up for any Indie Series Awards. Ultimately we were not accepted to either, meaning that Ajakwe's warning was premature. Nevertheless, it was confusing and, in my immediate opinion, not a good idea. Most aggravating to us, Ajakwe redesigned the LAWEBFEST website so it could not be copied and pasted, making it rather clumsy and unattractive, a poor exhibition platform for our series.

One month later, a few days before HollyWeb announced its acceptances, #clausegate erupted on social media, with many web series creators publicly shaming LAWEBFEST for demanding exclusivity.[2] Among the first was Anthony Anderson through his Twitter account for *Anacostia*, winner of multiple ISA awards and eventually a Daytime Emmy: "My fellow creators DO NOT take this abuse from the LAWEBFEST stand up for yourselves stand for something or fall for anything!"[3] Both the Indie Series Network (ISN), which produces the ISA, and HollyWeb dismissed Ajakwe's charges and encouraged creators to choose for themselves. ISN director Kevin Mulcahy tweeted, "[W]e absolutely condemn and diligently discourage any endeavor to limit or censor opportunities for creators to freely present and publicly celebrate their artistic creation." Within a week, journalists and creators wrote blog posts largely condemning Ajakwe.[4] Lisa Gifford, creator of *3Some*, which had screened and won awards at HollyWeb, LAWEBFEST, and the Indie Series Awards, wrote of her dismay over the clause damaging "our inclusive industry": "Web festivals are in their infancy, and although massive strides are being made, the industry is nowhere near that stage yet. Having several events in close proximity, like these, can only increase the number of attendees making the journey, and strengthen the community as a whole."[5] Many producers in the community echoed Gifford's sentiments on social media. They were similarly bemused by the call for exclusivity in an industry where most productions operate openly and most distribution agreements with indie TV networks are nonexclusive.[6] Creators saw exclusivity as a threat to community building, which was the real point of festivals in a market where the products have little value outside their ability to create fan networks and showcase talent.

Despite some mentions of LAWEBFEST as less well run than in the past, Ajakwe's critics still gave LAWEBFEST credit for helping build the community: "Your festival was never about competition, just celebration and inclusion. Awards for web series, especially new series, are very important. It gives opportunities for the series, its cast and crew to celebrate in their accomplishments," *Out with Dad* creator Jason Leaver said in a widely cited post.[7] Leaver noted how LAWEBFEST gave his show its first awards—"it was the pinnacle of my career"—but the Indie Series Awards was an "amazing . . . prestigious . . . glamorous . . . well-run event." Leaver's comparison presaged criticism from other creators that LAWEBFEST was not worth the trip because it was *too inclusive*. The festival is known for having upwards of a dozen nominees in key categories. Teresa was one of thirty-nine actresses nominated for comedy, while LaJune was one of eighteen nominated for guest actress. Jonathan Robbins, creator of *Clutch*, wrote on his series's Facebook page that he did not agree with Ajakwe's exclusivity clause, but reminded the community of Ajakwe's commitment to people over business: "He told me last year, after the awards, that he knew it wasn't working with so many awards being given out, but he didn't want to crush anyone's dreams and he didn't know what to do. . . . These are not the words of a terrible festival who is business first and people second."[8] Robbins's description of Ajakwe matches the impression I and others had of him. "He's been great about creating a web series community and supporting web series in general," Issa Rae told me in an interview during my festival trip. During the festival, Ajakwe and I had a brief meeting in his Hilton Universal Studios suite. We spoke about the festival's history and his motivations for keeping it going. He noted how NYTVF was "for the big guys" and how "nobody's really looking out for the independents," even though they create better work. Ajakwe sees in the web series market a corollary to American black experience—even most of the festival's staff is black. Creators are "talented . . . marginalized . . . underappreciated . . . underestimated." Our experience, he said, "has made us better and stronger."

Ultimately, however, Ajakwe fell into a trap of Hollywood distribution: the need to control what audiences see and to profit from production through exclusive contracts. Networked distribution, where fans can decide what to watch and when, is antithetical to exclusivity and control, the source of much of the industry's woes in the digital era. Ajakwe's open letter to creators is suffused with this idea, treating the creators who support festivals as a market he can control. He says of HollyWeb and ISA,

> [W]e believe they both covet the international audience we have spent the last six years growing. They don't feel we deserve our audience and our accolades, want this audience for themselves even though they haven't earned it, and will do whatever they have to (except go out on their own and create it) to secure it.[9]

By framing creators as an audience to be acquired and managed, Ajakwe cornered himself discursively. The other festivals and creators framed the controversy around giving creators the flexibility and choice to decide what is best for their productions, something impossible in the linear, corporate system built on exclusive distribution. This freedom to shape the marketing of their shows is an incredible burden to independent creators—from searching for viewers online to reaching out to distributors and applying to festivals. Indeed, the only written commentary not critical of Ajakwe that I could find came from Leesa Dean, creator of the animated series *Chilltown*, who questioned the utility of web series festivals generally: "[A]s I learned the hard way, it's mostly a waste of money and time to submit to these types of festivals in the first place," because potential fans don't go, only other creators.[10] The value of distribution spaces like web series festivals, and most independent distribution outfits online, is community building among those interested in the genre: getting advice, recommendations, and information. Ajakwe appeared to have forgotten this.

The *She's out of Order* creative team went to LAWEBFEST and represented the show proudly, but we were saddened that our participation and nominations were sullied by controversy. LAWEBFEST was an opportunity to post good news about the show and revive interest. We did, and our Facebook announcements of our nominations were our most popular posts of the year. Our fans—friends, family, and several others who found us through social media—were unaware of the intra-community struggle. But the real value of the festival is the connections made with other creators. While we met several other creators, participation at the festival, from my limited view, was light.

The marketing and distribution of *She's out of Order* never met our dreams, but it did provide opportunities for the production team to reconnect with personal networks. We posted the first two episodes in early 2013 as a teaser, then episodes three through sixteen from August to December. Our earliest supporters were friends and family of the cast and crew. Our social media strategy included YouTube, Facebook, and Twitter. Our viewership grew most in 2013 and 2014 as we published the series and targeted fans of black web series about women and classic legacy TV shows on Facebook.[11]

Our challenges marketing *She's out of Order* harken back to preproduction and our ability to connect with communities of black women, demonstrating the importance of writing, sincerity, and fan connection, and not just access to distribution, in defining success in the open TV market. Just as he had written the series, Derek also handled the marketing, largely on his own. While I offered advice and some graphic design—I designed the logo, title card, website, and social media pages—during the show's postproduction and marketing I was on the academic job market, then moved to Chicago and started a job as a professor at Northwestern University. Teresa started a family. Derek tried to promote the show to his friends, but only a few potential fans were part of his network: "I was getting frustrated that people I consider my best friends weren't pushing it. I was taking personal offense to a lack of a Facebook share," he told me. On YouTube, we received a few comments, with a couple of viewers identifying with episode plots. On "Space Disco Chump," where Sherrie sneakily beats Tara at a video game, one viewer noted, "Hilarious I gotta a friend like this she always 1 up on me everything i do. Crazy." Contrary to long-established YouTube best practices,

Derek did not reply to most of the comments: "It felt weird answering fans and not being Teresa." Indeed, the marketing of the show lacked a specific voice identifiable as the lead. Most of our social media shares pointed to black pop culture news items and referrals to our content.

Under my consultation, Derek wrote *She's out of Order*'s episodes to spread. He wrote short, relatable stories based on specific, mundane, and occasionally outrageous experiences that middle-class black women might face. Our model was Rae, a high bar to achieve, said Derek:

> "Going viral" might be a cliché now . . . but that was the plan. We hoped to get hot during Indiegogo, building an audience that could carry the show through season two, with *Awkward Black Girl* as the model/inspiration. Though we were even more optimistic, we believed we could crowdfund *during* the release of season one, which in hindsight was wrong.

Almost necessary for most series that make it past season one, our crowdfunding campaign was a moderate success, raising $1,850 from seventeen donors out of the $10,000 we hoped to raise. Where we were most successful was in raising funds from people within our community. Indeed, to finance season one we received support from the same sources: my best friend, Yanru Chen, contributed $1,000, as did Derek's sister, Dionna. In hindsight, perhaps there was a way to design both the story and its marketing for those closest to us, instead of the variety of communities on the open net. We also tried in our marketing to promote other web series with which we shared a similar perspective or potential fan base—*The Unwritten Rules, Nice Girls Crew, Jenifer Lewis and Shangela, Awkward Black Girl*. I wrote short blog posts introducing the series, but those did not spread, either.

We received scant attention from the press and distributors, as is typical for nearly all series in their first seasons. Our only dedicated article came via Sergio Mims of *Shadow and Act*, a leading blog for film and television of the African diaspora, reporting on a distribution deal we signed with the ClickFlick network.[12] Derek connected with Sergio at the Black Harvest Film Festival in Chicago and told him about the deal. The story went live a couple of weeks later, amassing hundreds of likes. Publicizing the story on social media generated significant engagement and well wishes from friends and family.

ClickFlick approached us looking for content. The deal was nonexclusive, meaning we could retain control over our intellectual property and our YouTube channel, and sell to other distributors. Nonexclusivity, in theory, forces the distributor to work on behalf of the creator. ClickFlick's founder promised to shop our show to distributors with funds to support further production. Yet ClickFlick never published the show, nor did they find another buyer. The show elicited interest, however, in another indie distributor, DVPN, a start-up focusing on finding financing for a small slate of shows from a select group of writers, most with connections to New York's theater community. DVPN found us through a friend of Derek's. While the Under the Spell team had several meetings and conference calls with DVPN, where they proposed editing our unreleased episodes and adding more to create a second season, funding never materialized.

Yet *She's out of Order* is still creating value for the lead producers. Teresa has an entire series showcasing her comedy chops. Rhonney is now perceived by peers as a director on set and has recently received new opportunities in his field. Derek has used *She's out of Order* to get meetings and interviews in Hollywood. He was contracted to outline a story for a web series to be distributed on a cable network's website and has served as a professional consultant on the practice and pitfalls of web production.

Why is it hard to market indie web series? First, creators are storytellers, often with little experience in marketing and publicity. They have good ideas but may have difficulty understanding how to communicate what makes their show special to the wider public. The most successful creators are sincere and indefatigable promoters of their own perspective on media and culture and can communicate to fans with wit or sincerity about what makes their show worth viewing. The best marketing for indie TV series comes from creators with social media savvy or who write and star in their series—they embody the community. The exceptions to the creator-star-marketer model from the likes of Issa Rae and Felicia Day are those well-executed productions that have planned publicity well in advance of their release, just as in legacy television. As Rhonney noted in our debrief interview, the film and television studio he works for integrates marketing while in production, such as inviting bloggers and press to the set. Having stars and a publicity budget helps.

Yet even with extensive planning and no shortage of sincerity, marketing online is a challenge for studios large and small, because competition for viewer attention in a networked economy is intense. TV fans have no shortage of programs marketed to them across broadcast, cable, web, and mobile platforms. The immense supply of web productions creates limitless opportunities for innovation, and new products can reach fans and sponsors directly. Risk and failure are inextricable from innovation, and the openness of networked distribution only intensifies these dynamics. Legacy networks have decades of experience minimizing risk, controlling what fans see and what sponsors can invest in, at the cost of innovation. The networked economy is slowly challenging these systems, but corporations' considerable resources—the ability to buy new channels to control distribution, acquire intellectual property rights, secure exclusive distribution rights—protect them from an open market—or help them close it. With fewer resources in the vast open market, independent producers, distributors (networks and channels), and exhibitors (festivals and award shows) are set up to fail.

* * *

Independent distribution and exhibition are the greatest challenges in the open TV market. While innovations in production and representation have been occasionally valued by legacy TV networks, innovations in distribution have a sobering history. Because web TV distribution is so open, efforts to curate and value its productions by indie network executives, along with festival and award show organizers, have routinely failed. Why visit an indie TV network when Netflix has thousands of Hollywood titles on one site, when YouTube has hundreds of hours of video uploaded every day, or when Hulu has a next-day exclusive window on high-budget legacy shows? Why visit LAWEBFEST or follow the Indie Series Awards when Sundance and the Emmys acknowledge indie and web production? Legacy distribution commands exclusivity, control, and scale, smoothing the process of value creation. Nevertheless, I argue that the web provided a space for small-scale indie TV distribution, and their smaller scale forced them to respond to the needs of producers, fans, and brands in an open market, producing innovations in the way shows are developed, financed, and rewarded.

This chapter argues that open distribution challenges the ideals and innovations of independent agents, using the stories of a handful of indie channels—Blip, Strike TV, My Damn Channel, KoldCast, Babelgum, and Quarterlife—along with exhibitors in web series festivals and award shows—the International Television Festival, New York Television Festival, Streamy Awards, and International Academy of Web Television Awards. The indie channels began as hard-nosed businesses looking to harness indie innovation on the web to make money in the growing market. These cases show how production can only sustain itself for so long without direct input either from major advertisers, from the kinds of relationships legacy television networks continue to exploit through exclusive licenses, or from fans in the form of subscription support. Without a clear, universally agreed-upon standard for monetizing and measuring web video, indie web networks during this period eventually did what television networks first did: created and distributed programs made with significant advertiser input. Supporting the kinds of independent production narrated throughout this book—diverse products as evidence of television's expansion—was hard to sustain in a new and growing market. Profitable independent distribution in new media requires significant compromise, yet in the conclusion of this chapter I explore how indie subscription networks, financed by fans as opposed to major brands or media conglomerates, are slowly forging a new path for distribution in the open TV market.

The story of Blip TV, which weathered the open TV market from 2005 to 2015, demonstrates both the peril and the promise of open access to distribution for independent networks. In 2011, Blip courted press with a new homepage redesigned to showcase independent web series creators. Blip had been trying to position itself as a YouTube competitor focused on more professionally produced shows. Anyone could upload his or her videos to Blip and generate revenue from in-stream advertising, but Blip's staff curated its programming and selected the best for the homepage and various topical playlists. On the basis of the sophistication of ad delivery on its video player, the network established a solid reputation for delivering high ad rates and syndicating videos across the web to generate impressions. Blip promised higher advertising rates than YouTube—because its videos were arguably higher quality and its targeting more sophisticated—but its homepage was not a destination like YouTube or Netflix. The new homepage prominently featured curated shows selected by its staff. "This ecosystem that we started working with in 2005 has finally come into its own," Blip cofounder Dina Kaplan told the *New York Times* in 2011.[13] The following year Blip moved into developing its own original content and intellectual property, putting its vice president of content, Steve Woolf, in charge of Blip Studios and signing exclusive contracts with three popular producers.[14]

Blip's attempt to develop an open network for professional web video lasted just two years. In 2013, Blip sold to YouTube multichannel network (MCN) Maker Studios, which was looking for its own video network to compete with Google's platform, which many MCNs alleged seized too high a cut of advertising revenue. Soon after its acquisition, Blip started to remove tens of thousands of videos and independent producers from its servers.[15] The following year, in 2014, Disney made a bid to acquire Maker Studios, and the year after, Maker shut down Blip and encouraged creators to apply to the Maker Gen Network, its vertical for emerging YouTube talent. Blip folded into YouTube's corporate offspring and Disney, one of the most powerful media conglomerates and owner of one of the oldest legacy networks, ABC.

Blip's founders tried to develop indie TV sustainably in an open market. Networks like Blip allow producers to upload shows, entrust staff to curate them for audiences, and then sell those audiences to advertisers via algorithms or in-house sales teams. These start-ups adapt legacy television's strategy of branding channels for audiences and advertisers: "Many of Blip's top shows are part of a network, the same way that MTV is an umbrella for all sorts of shows," the *Times'* Brian Stelter wrote of the site.[16] Blip tried to find a middle ground between legacy channels like MTV, which operated on a closed development system where producers needed agents and contacts to get their series made, and YouTube, a site too large and open to cultivate a community of series producers. Blip subsisted on intense interest by investors in developing a competitor to YouTube. Typical of the Internet, most of those companies folded. Surviving distributors like Blip had to grapple with a tough marketplace: how to make money off content created outside legacy media in a diffuse and complicated online market.

Distribution in an open market has continued to pose unique challenges for entrepreneurs. Distribution connects producers with consumers. In legacy TV, a distributor is traditionally called a "network" that finds new shows, markets them to audiences, and helps secure financing to make more. Legacy networks profit because linear distribution accommodates a limited number of channels, giving them more control over financing (brands, sponsors), "windows" for exclusive runs, and brand awareness among TV fans (scale in attention). In interviews, web TV network executives and producers of series, festivals, and awards shows expressed desires and plans to include a wider range of programs from independents than on legacy television. They pursued a range of series so fans and sponsors had choices, but the underlying flaw was, ironically, the fact of open distribution. With so many videos uploaded to the Internet every minute, indie networks could not profit from exclusivity like legacy television, nor did they have funds to control or scale programming.

Yet independent web networks are more accountable to fans, producers, and sponsors, because in new media markets all parties have a choice to take their work elsewhere. To grow the market for independent video, open TV distributors innovated in three separate aspects of the business: development (curating series and relinquishing intellectual property claims), financing (sponsoring series), and recognition (awards and festivals). Their strategies harken back to the network era, when broadcasters counted on large and sustainable audiences for content. Of course, since many indie TV channels premiered in the mid-2000s, that goal was elusive. With web video companies like YouTube, Hulu, and Netflix, along with television networks like Comedy Central and AMC, all investing in web video distribution as well, convergence stiffened the competition, especially for independent start-ups like Blip, whose investment capital ranged in the millions, not the tens and hundreds of millions like its larger competitors.

This chapter explores independent web series networks, festivals, and sponsored productions working to create a sustainable marketplace for independent productions. After providing a brief historical framework and theoretical trajectory for understanding open TV distribution, I start with the important story of Strike TV, an online network started by the Writers Guild during its 2007–2008 labor strike. Strike TV was an effort to create a "Hulu" for Hollywood workers looking to bypass legacy media channels but not lose their work in YouTube's vast sea. Then I discuss select creative producers who secure financing directly from sponsors by targeting legacy development processes—the securing of up-front advertising and the decline of producers' creative autonomy—while promising more sincere storytelling for sponsors looking to innovate in online campaigns. I discuss the difficulty of financing independent production outside of legacy media channels, using a few indie networks—My Damn Channel, Babelgum, KoldCast, Quarterlife, and WatchMojo, as case studies. Finally, I examine the effort to legitimate web series as an art form through festivals, including the International Television Festival and New York Television Festival, and award shows, including the Streamys and the International Academy of Web Television Awards. The story of independent distribution online is fraught, and the stories of some of these companies are ongoing. Distribution is where production meets the market, and despite all the rhetoric of democratization, the American media market still favors larger institutions. During this period, most efforts to adapt television distribution for smaller, more flexible productions did not survive or faced considerable challenges.

Understanding Open TV Distribution

Legacy television networks rank high among the United States' cultural distributors in capitalization, so it makes sense that entrepreneurs would try to adapt the TV channel model to the online space. Legacy television audiences are measured and specified by age and gender, at times race and sexuality, and supported by a ratings agency, Nielsen. The broadcast and cable channels command scale and attention, capturing a significant share of the public's attention and capitalizing on it for billions of dollars each year. Their historical power to finance and distribute cultural programming places them at the center of debates about democracy and cultural hegemony.[17] Most of their distributive power derives directly from relations with government regulatory agencies: the broadcast system, an outgrowth of radio, is part of a long relationship between large media companies and regulators.[18] Given access to distribution, early television networks first monetized content by allowing advertisers to control and sponsor programming, often with minimal interference from networks. This changed in the late 1950s and early 1960s for a number of reasons, including the quiz show scandals that showed sponsors rigging the games. Buoyed by public disgust at sponsor control over programming, the networks shifted from single-sponsorship to magazine-style advertising and eventually the ubiquitous thirty-second spot. The shift lowered programming time available for advertisers, giving networks more control over their schedules and enriching them financially even more: "Advertising monies pouring into the big content-production and distribution firms had helped them grow to the point that they could dictate terms to their sponsors."[19] Soon grew the syndication market, reliant on exclusive contracts for reruns, supporting independent TV stations and producers but not necessarily advancing innovation: "[T]elevision's lack of innovation is a natural outcome of the distribution logics that support the industry's economics and the persistent dominance of the major networks," Karen Petruska wrote of television in the 1970s.[20] When web video entrepreneurs discuss the power of television, they are often referring to the heyday of broadcast television that resulted from this shift, when three networks controlled both the audience and the financers of television, a power that started to erode in the 1980s with the rise of competition in distribution from cable.

The web series market arose with legacy TV's distribution power in flux. The multichannel transition gave advertisers more options of where to place their spots, and in return they started to demand better targeting, more product placement, and other efficiencies made possible by cable distribution.[21] Linear broadcast networks still developed high-value original programming, but they did so with more input from advertisers and worked harder to reach more specific target groups, especially with competition intensifying via linear cable channels focused on specific niche demographics. With the mass adoption of the Internet, and its promise of more refined quantitative measurements and greater interactivity, advertisers demanded even more information from web networks.[22] As noted in chapter 1, they started investing in branded entertainment, producing and distributing their own programs and fracturing the tense relationship between Madison Avenue and Hollywood.[23] Business experts declared the death of the thirty-second spot, and with it, presumably, legacy television networks' firm hold on programming and prices.[24] Of course, the reality was more complicated. Thirty-second spots still dominated revenue, and deregulation in the

1990s created large conglomerates scaled to cater to brand demands across media.[25] What the networked era shows is how traditional "networking" as a strategy is increasingly fraught as audiences and advertisers have more choice. The availability of television programming from the 1990s to the present—web programming being the most recent addition—means that its programming is too vast to be contained; the challenge of curating and monetizing programs increases as content spreads across channels and devices on broadcast, cable, and the web.[26]

Online, programming has multiplied exponentially. To understand networked distribution, scholars must determine, as Alisa Perren writes, "the full range of intermediaries involved in distributive processes, and the types of influence they exercise over content individually and collectively."[27] Following these intermediaries challenges our perception of networked distribution as immediate and "brings a host of sociologically interesting relationships into focus."[28] Networked distribution involves a complex set of players. After the rise of content aggregators with open-upload policies—YouTube, primarily—video producers with varying levels of skill flooded the web with content.[29] Around the same time, independent web series networks responded to producers' need for outlets specifically curated for serialized, scripted, or more professionally produced programs than the glut of "viral" or "spreadable" videos created by so-called amateurs.[30]

Financing online videos is difficult. For most of Internet history, networked distributors lacked legacy television's top-down, industry-certified ratings system and decacdes-old relationships with advertisers. Instead, throughout the 2000s, new advertising networks, exchanges, and ratings agencies managed the glut through opaque algorithms that producers feared were content agnostic. Ad networks and exchanges automatically matched buyers (brands) and sellers (publishers) of advertisements by estimating the audience for impressions (demographics, purchasing intent, etc.), often in real time. Distributors like YouTube, indie networks, and their producers lacked control over financing. Many creators were skeptical of automated advertising and argued for the value of smaller audiences: "Engagement isn't always about the numbers, or the cost per click," Andrew Lane, a consultant who advised productions on distribution, told me in 2009. "[Web series are] not really an industry that's based on numbers, that's quantifiable, it's sort about this emotional connection." The diversity of ad-selling technologies and the surplus of productions suppress advertising rates, making it difficult for networks to generate funds to green light productions and market to audiences. Josh Braun notes how these understudied intermediaries are part of a "sociotechnical system" of distribution, which even corporate distributors were struggling to navigate and control during this period.[31] Still, the plight of indie distributors reveals a "missing middle" between the long tail of millions of products uploaded to the web and the top tier of mostly corporate sites that command the bulk of audience attention.[32] Successful independent distributors were fewer and farther between. Those that survived or thrived eschewed these financing intermediaries for direct fan support, including the likes of Black & Sexy TV and tello films, discussed in the previous chapter, which for years have subsisted on direct subscriptions from fans.

Despite challenges to profitability, indie web distributors advance the rich and fractious tradition of independent production outside corporate media. Independent distributors work to merge the presumed benefits of independent creation with ultimately conservative strategies of curating, selling, and rewarding art. Past theories of alternative media have stressed "anticommercial" or "low-finance" aspects of distribution, but some scholars have noted the ways in which media distributed outside major corporations can move away from the "radical" and into the commercial sphere, where advertising is no longer anathema.[33] By moving into the commercial sphere, indie web TV networks challenge the "soft" or "representational" power of legacy media institutions, but do so by experimenting with the industry's own strategies.[34] They are not the first to try. They follow the strategies of independent film studios, whose auteur-driven narratives by the 1990s became partially subsumed in the movie distribution apparatus and marketed as "indie," "a familiar idea that evokes in consumers a range of emotional and symbolic associations."[35]

Because legacy television distribution is farther away from indie TV distribution than indie film is from the film studios, indie TV distributors discovered that curating and financing in an open TV market was quite precarious, requiring sizable financial backing and consistently threatened by developments outside of its control—including policies like net neutrality, Hollywood developments like Nielsen's integrated web and TV ratings system,[36] and programmatic advertising, to be explored in the next chapter. Distributors found themselves working within both the rules of the web (chaotic, open, in process) and those of television (streamlined, increasingly at the whim of advertisers). While theorists like Axel Bruns and Yochai Benkler have historically lauded the innovations resulting from openness, lack of exclusivity, and centralized control in networked distribution, the case of open TV distributors in this chapter and the next shows how data must be "big" in order to be harnessed and valued in a corporate-controlled market.[37]

Nevertheless, following independent film, a cadre of market participants tried to streamline open TV distribution by forming institutional pathways for recognition: award shows and festivals. Integral to the market for cinema and, to a lesser extent, television, awards and festivals allow participants to combine artistic and cultural value with the market. Cindy Wong notes that "festival organizers and programmers can attract people in the business to attend the market, while markets can build on the people who are there 'for art.'"[38] Festivals and awards legitimated independent and alternative cinema to consumers and critics throughout the twentieth century. For web creators, they separate "professional" productions from the glut of web content, set quality standards in a space with few programming rules, create stars for the press to laud, and provide opportunities for producers to make connections.

In their effort to recreate distribution practices online, open TV network executives, producers, and curators provided low-budget productions with distribution of moderate scale and occasional consistency. What they lacked were the institutional relationships with advertisers and the press, along with curatorial and cultural influence, which Hollywood retains. Their goal of transforming a new medium into an old one proved elusive in this period.

Open TV Curation: Distribution without Exclusivity

To understand why entrepreneurs expended great effort creating curated TV-like spaces for independent series, one must first understand the problem of YouTube. Since its early years, the site has had strong detractors and competitors, mostly from corporations seeking more control over their intellectual property and more advertiser-friendly spaces. The problem of YouTube has always been about who will curate the growing market for web video.[39] Years after Google purchased YouTube in 2006, a new group of YouTube detractors emerged: independent filmmakers and entrepreneurs. Their complaint was about control, but it highlighted broader qualms about the digital economy. Plainly, YouTube had come to represent the chaos of the web itself, a rambunctious home to amateurs churning out low-quality content to rack up views from low ad rates.[40] YouTube challenged legacy television's windows for programming, where distributors have time-limited, exclusive rights to release and profit from a curated slate of programs before passing it on to the next tier of distribution—traditionally, broadcast to cable, with the web companies like Netflix joining the market in the 2000s. What YouTube's critics wanted was a more sustainable and less "viral" way to fund noncorporate content: a sustainable market for independent web video by skilled professionals.

A flare-up in the summer of 2010 offers a glimpse into some of the problems posed by YouTube's ability to profit from distributing the work of millions of producers. In what had become its own genre of reporting, *Business Insider* published a list of "the richest independent YouTube stars," all of whom earned more than six figures.[41] The top YouTubers were personalities who video-blogged, with a handful of independent filmmakers making comedic shorts. *Business Insider*'s list set off a debate in the "other" web video community: professional filmmakers making more-expensive-to-produce episodic programs—web series. Web series news site *Tubefilter* said that YouTube's supremacy in releasing amateur programming created an "identity crisis" in the indie TV community. For Marc Hustvedt, one of the founders of both *Tubefilter* and the Streamy Awards, the success of YouTubers making "cheaper" shows pushed web series creators to break more rules and adapt distribution to an open market: "I think the savvy web video creators will indeed push the envelope. Or more specifically, play to the internet's built-in strengths—many-to-many interaction, global exposure, 24/7 availability, etc."[42] Indie series creators saw YouTubers as great at building audiences but not at producing the kinds of complex, scripted productions necessary to attract major sponsors and fund a greater number of independent professionals.[43] Scores of YouTubers benefited from the platform early on. They built up subscriber bases by producing lots of videos simply and quickly, but by 2010 they had not yet created anything like legacy television: advertiser friendly, capable of bringing in new professionals, advancing quality (production) and quantity (views).

Fear of YouTube's fast pace and openness sent both web video entrepreneurs and legacy media companies fleeing. Legacy media and its stars created anti-YouTube comedy sites. NBC launched DotComedy in 2006 before quickly shutting it down and launching SeeSo in 2016. Turner Broadcasting launched Super Deluxe in 2007, shuttered it, and relaunched it in 2015. HBO and AOL launched ThisJustIn in 2006 and shut it down the next year. A few YouTube competitors, like Will Ferrell's Funny or Die (in which HBO invested) and InterActiveCorp's College Humor, survived and thrived. Hulu was the most visible "YouTube killer."[44] None of these sites matched YouTube's dominance in video views or unique viewers, but they did make money, in part because they curated their content. As opposed to the vast sea of content available via YouTube, they gave advertisers a smaller pond, clean and closed.

Seeing Hulu's success, a handful of independent sites then tried to replicate its walled-garden model. Banking on low-cost, high-definition videos, they offered a chance for filmmakers to reach niche audiences and match them with advertisers, thereby functioning as a place for semiskilled artists rather than upstart creators. Many, like My Damn Channel and Babelgum, focused on comedy, while others, like Koldcast or Strike TV, focused on producers with interesting ideas across genres. After 2010, sites targeted at minorities tried to connect black-, gay-, Latino-, and women-produced shows with hard-to-reach audiences: Rowdy Orbit (multicultural), GLO (black LGBT), VisionTube (black), BetterBlackTV (black), and (later) celebrity-led channels like Rebecca Odes and Jill Soloway's Wifey TV and Elizabeth Banks's WhoHaha (women), Marlon Wayans and Randy Adams's What the Funny (black people), and Horatio Sanz and Fred Armisen's Más Mejor (Latinos).

YouTube, while diverse, remains a tough space for minorities to break out in. "I've been on YouTube but there's a limit to how much you can get out of it," VisionTube's creator, Charles Williams, a veteran local and national news producer, told me in an interview. He started VisionTube for multicultural web series and films after hearing the troubles faced by black filmmakers. "We would love to take our stuff off of YouTube," he recalls being told by multiple producers. "We actually professionally thought about this [their work], cast it and produced it," in contrast to YouTube, which allowed any producer to distribute. Many indie network entrepreneurs were like Williams: experienced, having held positions in television networks or advertising agencies. They used web distribution to get a head start on or usurp the power of their former employers.

After 2010, YouTube and the web video space changed drastically. YouTube gravitated to more professional content, working with large digital studios, brands, celebrities, and Hollywood TV producers to create original channels modeled after television. Google knew that to command television's advertising dollars, it had to promote higher-quality, regularly released video curated by channels run by the likes of showrunner Anthony Zuiker (*CSI*) and studios like Electus (founded by former NBC entertainment chief Ben Silverman). Meanwhile, other sites copied YouTube's strategy of relying on high-volume, ad-supported content, but sought to make it more amenable to the web series community. The most prominent of these was Blip.

Openness and control is the web's distribution paradox. Having more people produce media was inspiring, but the oversupply of content suppressed demand for individual series and small fan communities among marketers unaccustomed to so much choice and different systems of measurement. Networks like Strike tried to solve that conundrum by only accepting content from Hollywood's less empowered workers and distributing their works on a curated channel. The site had some success, expanding the notion of web video beyond a simple struggle between conglomerates and amateurs. The problem they ran into was financing.

Open Distribution without Control over Production and Marketing

The winter of 2009 brought the second season of *Anyone but Me*, the drama series about teenage lesbians set in post-9/11 New York analyzed in chapter 3. Distributed nonexclusively on Strike TV along with Blip, YouTube, Hulu, KoldCast, and, eventually, fullscreen,[45] the independently produced series would garner millions of views and several awards for web series. An outgrowth of Hollywood's writers' strike, *Anyone but Me* embodied the independent spirit of its original distributor, Strike TV, a network created to promote the writers and industry workers using the web to battle corporations over the right to profit from web distribution.[46]

Hollywood strikers founded Strike TV to create a place online for indie television. After the strike ended, however, its position in the market grew precarious. In 2010, two years after its creation, Peter Hyoguchi, Strike TV's indefatigable chief executive, was optimistic about the potentials of independent distribution, but sobered by years in the trenches. Referring to *Anyone but Me*, Hyoguchi said,

> The whole economy of filmmaking from production to postproduction to distribution is allowing for a show like this, that has a voice, that's different. . . . Quality isn't enough, and that's the one thing I discovered. Although we have the tools to make this great content and we can distribute the content, there's a little something that we forget about, which is marketing.

Hyoguchi's statement perfectly encapsulates the tensions in the new economy for independent content. Online, producers can wield an incredible amount of control over their individual stories, but streamlined distribution and marketing of those stories remain the domain of legacy networks. Independent web content needs support from institutions with visibility, brand recognition, and refined methods for releasing content. This reality eventually led Strike TV to consider going back to the system it originally opposed for help in distribution and marketing.

Before explaining Strike TV's failed plans to marry independent and legacy media, we must contend with the site's beginnings as a site of activism against an industrial apparatus seeking control over new media. On January 7, 2008, weeks into the writer's strike that waged from the previous fall to the following spring, the blog *United Hollywood* posted a notice about the first Strike TV meeting. As Miranda Banks found, *United Hollywood* "provided an important voice to counter [the studios'] public relations machines" and served as a nexus for information and talking points for those politically aligned with the WGA: "The AMPTP [Alliance of Motion Picture and Television Producers] would like us to sit around and wait for them. Well, we're tired of waiting. It's time to start doing."[47]

The Strike TV meeting mobilized producers to develop a diverse, egalitarian market for their work. According to Hyoguchi, five to six hundred writers, editors, cinematographers, directors, actors, and below-the-line crew members showed up to discuss new productions and "speed date" to find collaborators.[48] "For one hundred years, creative professionals have wanted to create their own content and own it and control it, but haven't been able to do that," Hyoguchi said, describing the pitch to the Hollywood strikers. It worked. After that first meeting, dozens of web series went into production. Hyoguchi estimates that the meeting produced two hundred series aiming for distribution on Strike TV. Not all the series came to fruition, of course. But some, most notably Joss Whedon's *Dr. Horrible's Sing-Along Blog* and *Anyone but Me*, did.[49]

For Hyoguchi, Strike TV was a third way for those looking to break the legacy networks' hold on content but not sacrifice their work to YouTube's diffuse, user-generated marketplace. He told me, "[T]here's not a lot of incentive . . . to put something on YouTube when it's going to be shoulder to shoulder with a cat jumping on a piano." YouTube-style web video focused on the spreadable nature of content, he argued. Instead, Hyoguchi wanted to provide enough consistency for advertisers to invest money: in other words, a true marketplace for video creators. Scale, along with consistency, is important. One show, *Imaginary Bitches*, he said, reached six million views, but only after a year. Advertisers said they could reach the same number in one night on traditional television. "We realized: wow, we need to advertise these shows just like everyone else advertises these shows," Hyoguchi recounted.

In Strike TV's earliest weeks, the tension between the realities of new media distribution and the advantages of legacy television distribution became apparent, though initially Strike TV's champions may have ignored these conditions. According to one report of the initial meeting, Internet entrepreneur Ken Hayes noted how online, "traffic . . . is king, not content," and traffic must be packaged to sell to advertisers (essentially describing how ad networks work). Yet "no other speaker exhibited Hayes's crass commercialism . . . [T]he Strike TV discussion had an air of self-delusion about it."[50] By late summer 2008, Strike TV had abandoned plans to publish programs online before securing advertisers and moved to a distribution strategy similar to that of the upfronts, looking to book major advertisers in advance of the launch while syndicating its shows to other sites like YouTube and Joost.[51] The strategy appeared to contradict a post on *United Hollywood* (not written by Hyoguchi), which described working with advertisers as anti-independent: "Shoot first, get advertisers later. This is a good thing. It means talent generate the ideas, not marketers. . . . Getting advertisers to finance production can be more hassle than it's worth."[52] The statement reflects disenchantment with the legacy development system and belief in the web as a producer-driven alternative.

Yet without a strong revenue stream rivaling that of the major networks, Strike TV could not keep its talent: its reliance on Hollywood professionals hampered its potential growth. After the strike's euphoria wore off, writers, actors, and other professionals went back to their legacy media jobs, the fount of salaries and the residuals writers fought hard to bring to the web. The talent drain left Strike TV with a number of quality pilots from big television names but without ways to turn them into series: "If you're not looking to be a flash in the pan viral hit, but rather a long-term success, you might reconsider the involvement of the truly famous," journalist Liz Shannon Miller wrote about web series's reliance on traditional media professionals.[53] By late 2009, Hyoguchi's enthusiasm for the viability of an independent digital economy was tempered by realism: "Strike TV would be out of business if we were actually a business," he said pointedly. Strike TV realized that it needed the legacy media much more than it had originally thought. Journalists like Miller were starting to worry that the site was "still stuck in the year 2008," flush with optimism but not grappling with an increasingly challenging marketplace.[54]

In this context, Hyoguchi hatched a new and revealing business plan. Instead of trying to raise millions of dollars in financing—"impossible in this economy"—he could rely on traditional media to handle marketing and distribution. In this plan, the site would syndicate its shows (with writers retaining ownership) to the websites of network affiliates—ABC-Los Angeles, Fox-Philadelphia, etc.—and local radio stations. In essence, Strike TV would follow the web legacy TV's entrenched syndication-to-affiliates model that arose in the 1970s, i.e., would do what Disney's ABC, Comcast's NBC, News Corp.'s Fox and CBS already do: act as a feeder for content to smaller stations. The affiliates would license Strike TV's shows and potentially share revenue. If this approach was successful, Hyoguchi imagined expanding to distributing to the websites of traditional newspapers as well. But the plan did not last, and Strike TV folded after a partnership with forum site Metacafe to harness that site's community of fans to pilot new programs, the first, *Dwelling*, a black-led series from *Office* writer Anthony Q. Farrell.

Surviving independently of legacy development proved too difficult. Though its tale may sound familiar, Strike TV's story is far from one of pure cooptation into television's established distribution portals. Strike TV advanced television development with creative ways of envisioning production. Describing his role developing *Anyone but Me*, Hyoguchi differentiated his job as an online network executive from that of the note-giving executives on legacy television: "I'm more of a facilitator than their overlord." He gave the creators notes on some aspects, such as music, but granted them final say: "As a studio executive the relationship is totally unique. I'm not funding the show. I'm just presenting the show. I love the fact they have total autonomy that they have. I love the fact that they can do whatever they want." As I show in the following sections, other independent network executives echo Hyoguchi's description of his role. This attitude is due not to kindness but to market realities. With less funding from sponsors and a seemingly limitless supply of new productions, open TV network executives are less invested in every single production and more focused on experimenting with new stories to attract—as opposed to retain—fans and sponsors.

Open Financing without Exclusivity

Fundamental to web distributors' problems was financing: the web developed a fractured and complicated advertising system, in stark contrast to the tested, if occasionally contested, decades-old legacy television system. Many of the early woes in the indie TV market concerned advertising. By 2010, the web content market had matured enough to allow for functioning advertising networks and exchanges alongside direct conversations among brands, ad agencies, marketers, and publishers about funding new content. Yet the market was still nascent. The same problem faced both distributors—known to marketers as "publishers"—and advertisers: how to reach an audience and effectively convey messages. Publishers had to amass the largest audience possible and argue for their value to brands, which pay for advertising. Brands needed ways to reach consumers and wanted assurances that advertisements were making it to them. Having satisfied patrons (advertisers, mostly) has remained of utmost importance for publishers.

Could the market support independent online video after YouTube's rise in the latter 2000s? Yes and no. Networks could make money online through ads, but not enough to support independent producers in the way legacy networks enjoyed after the advent of the thirty-second spot. Instead, the market was flooded with conflicting reports about the viability of a scaled advertising market. Ads served on websites were not appropriately valued, and audiences inaccurately counted, requiring extensive negotiation between the publisher and brand, as seen in branded entertainment. Some studies showed that video ads shown during online TV shows were more effective than television advertisements,[55] yet the ad network revenue was slow to lift even the largest video sites to profitability—the most notable case being YouTube, which was unprofitable for years despite its ever-growing base of viewers and programs. As late as 2010, audiences for online video were still early adopters.[56] Early reports of web video were decidedly optimistic, exhibiting enthusiasm for (mostly independent) web series as potential competitors to traditional television.[57] Such reports proclaimed that series could subsist on ad dollars[58] and showed user-generated networks as beating old media in audience share.[59] However, those reports elicited doubt from indie networks executives, who knew the limits of distributing programs produced without the legacy media's semi-exclusive contracts.

In stark contrast to legacy television, there was an oversupply of web productions and strategies for funding it. Advertising networks, the lifeblood of many video sites in this time period, amplified anxieties, providing an almost dizzying array of business models—too many to bring the kind of order necessary to raise rates to the level earned by legacy television. Ad networks sold placement on websites by aggregating content and delivering it to advertisers; publishers often complained that these methods did not appropriately value their audiences and/or content.[60] The digital arms of legacy media outlets like MTV and Sony responded to the ad networks' low rates (CPMs, or cost-per-mille, the amount brands pay for one thousand impressions) by essentially becoming branded entertainment production houses, tailoring websites and integrating products for brands, with some success.[61] Some video aggregators made similar shifts, as when Sony restructured Grouper, an amateur/user-generated site, into Crackle, a site for independent and Hollywood production companies to create (often) branded content: "We realized user-generated video is something everybody likes to watch but it's not a great business. It's too difficult to make money," said Grouper founder Josh Felsher about the shift.[62] Understanding the market's dependence on flawed ad networks, other video dubs integrated them into their businesses, as when Adconion bought out video channel Joost and literally made it a video ad network, with some initial success in 2009.[63] Meanwhile, the vast availability of cheap video online led to growing concerns over "content farms," in which topical content was published automated and en masse solely to garner ad-friendly audiences and amass revenue from low CPMs.[64] Industry stakeholders hoped for a more controlled marketplace in ad exchanges. Exchanges allowed for a real-time, auction-based marketplace between sellers (publishers, who know their audiences) and buyers (brands and ad agencies, who want to reach specific groups).[65] Such efficiency—a kind of "mass customization"[66]—could presumably raise rates for publishers while providing better targeting to advertisers. By the mid-2010s marketers found hope in "programmatic" online ad campaigns in their efforts to mass customize (a topic to be explored more in the next chapter).

Emerging open TV distributors were greatly affected by conditions outside of their control, conditions created by the open distribution dynamics that allowed them to challenge legacy television in the first place. The early years of any new media form are delicate, and these outlets were trying to carve a sustainable market for independently produced programs in an industry that profits from scale and control, the bailiwick of large companies.

Selling Authenticity Directly to Brands

Faced with low rates from algorithmic networked advertising, indie producers and distributors fled to branded web entertainment—programs made by or for advertisers or sponsors—cultivating an unusual relationship between corporate brand sponsorship and independent storytelling. It was one of the few arenas in which independent producers sometimes outperformed legacy television in creating successful franchises.

By the late 2000s, brands became an important source of financing for indie TV through sponsorship. Frustrated by viewers skipping expensive advertisements on linear television, brands began using the Internet to distribute their own programming at least as of 2000, when American Express financed *The Adventures of Seinfeld and Superman* and BMW released *The Hire*. Branded entertainment accelerated in the later 2000s after the recession tightened budgets, streaming video grew in popularity, and studies showed that online video viewers were more engaged with ads than on legacy TV.[67] Most of the recipients of these brand-allocated funds were short-lived digital studios, advertising and marketing agencies, and the independent production companies they contracted for work. Very often brands granted producers more creative control over narrative and character than they granted legacy TV networks, as they did in the early days of television, to support authenticity in the brand's campaign narrative.

In 2004, Illeana Douglas, an indie film fixture, pitched legacy television networks a series based on a short she produced with Jeff Goldblum, *Supermarket*, about almost-famous actors working at a grocery store. The series never made it beyond the pilot stage, but IKEA contacted Douglas after seeing it, expressing interest in "a new, hip approach to their brand," Douglas said. *Easy to Assemble* premiered in 2008, and *Supermarket* relocated to IKEA. The first ten-episode season, with episodes under ten minutes, cost IKEA around $50,000, a sliver of the furniture maker's nine-figure global marketing budget.[68] The per-season budget eventually increased to the mid–six figures, still a fraction of the broadcast sitcom season budgets, which regularly exceeded $10 million. In return for less money, Douglas got creative control. When asked by the *Wall Street Journal* if IKEA ever censored what she wrote, Douglas said the company told her to change a line from "ice cream" to "yogurt," since that is what the company sells. "The first season was wildly experimental," she said in the interview.[69] Their only note for the next season was to keep it "family friendly," which fit into Douglas's vision.[70] For Douglas and celebrity costars like Justine Bateman, creative control made up for the lower investment. "Honestly I would rather be on the Web than be on television because I don't have any illusions that if this got picked up and went to network I would lose the creative control," she told Reuters.[71] The series would eventually get a spin-off called *Spärhusen*, starring Douglas and Keanu Reeves as members of a fictional 1970s Swedish band. Within six months of its premiere, *Easy to Assemble* garnered eight hundred thousand views and two thousand blog mentions, helped by exposure on IKEA fan sites.[72] Subsequent episodes averaged views under ten million, and the show ran for four seasons.

Helping the series attract such a wide viewership was CJP Digital, a unit of New York marketing firm CJP Communications. Started by PR executive and actor Wilson Cleveland, CJP Digital helped launch and promote some of the best of branded web entertainment from roughly 2006 to 2012, including *Easy to Assemble*, *The Temp Life*, *Suite 7*, *Leap Year*, *Bestsellers*, and *The Webventures of Justin & Alden*. *The Temp Life*, created by, produced by, and starring Cleveland, and *Leap Year*, co-created by Cleveland with Yuri and Vlad Baranovsky, were its biggest critical and ratings hits. Funded by temp-staffing firm SFN Group, *The Temp Life* is a comedy about workers staffed through a "worst practices" firm, Commodity Staffing, which sends temps out on jobs like urinal maintenance and assisting a socialite with her webcast. When the recession hit, the series picked up as more people started temping, and SFN chief executive Roy Krause, who was hoping the series would reach younger workers, said the show was the company's top marketing ploy and contributed to a stock bump.[73] *The Temp Life* would eventually amass over one hundred million cumulative views across platforms.[74] Cleveland used its success to support other indie TV workers. SFN would order another series, *Bestsellers*, from Susan Miller, who co-created indie hit *Anyone but Me*. Cleveland later tapped Baranovsky, who had created the indie darling *Break a Leg*, to script *Leap Year*, a drama about a Silicon Valley start-up chasing a five-hundred-thousand-dollar pot of money, funded by small business insurance company Hiscox. Storylines were taken from traditional start-up struggles and led to an increase in interest in and sales of Hiscox products.[75]

Cleveland successfully pitched brands on original production with two strategies distinct from legacy network development practices: advocating that producers more actively control the story and avoiding advertising agencies for financing. Through CJP Digital, Cleveland approached the public relations departments of the brands he thought could sponsor his stories, since PR executives are constantly trying to "earn" media—as opposed to pay for media through ads. "It's a lot harder to tell [a brand's] story. . . . They will always be receptive to things like this. They never get to do anything cool like the ad agencies do, so give them something different to do," Cleveland said in a Writers Guild of America East instructional video.[76] Public relations firms and departments help brands shape the story they want consumers to hear, and Cleveland saw an opportunity for skilled writers, actors, and producers to help brands reach increasingly disengaged audiences through authenticity, the prime goal of brands in late capitalism:[77]

> The way to always approach it is: how will this brand benefit from the story I can tell? Nine times out of ten they can benefit from being associated with something that's not a shill, and just telling a story. They don't need you to sell more cans of soda. They don't need you to sell more packs of gum. They have plenty of people who are paid a lot of money to do that. What they can never get across—what's harder to get across—is that actual brand story that you don't necessarily see in terms of a logo.[78]

Cleveland's producer-centered pitch to brands through alternative financing worked, but the payout was small. SFN gave Cleveland less than $1,000 to make the four-minute pilot for *The Temp Life*.[79] Three seasons in, *The Temp Life* had a modest mid-five-figure budget.[80]

Independent series have been able to secure funding from nonprofits and smaller brands and companies, particularly for documentary, variety, and sketch programming. Scripted series with primetime aspirations found sponsorship more elusive. Still, series with strong community ties and clear online marketing strategies had moderate success attracting sponsorship from small and regional companies. Harnessing Blip and KoldCast's video distribution platforms, Tony Clomax successfully solicited several independent companies to supplement the investment he and producer Emelyn Stuart put in to produce their black romantic comedy, *12 Steps to Recovery*, including a t-shirt company, dating website, management firm, and romance novel author. "It's a constant running commercial for your product," Clomax told me. Anthony Anderson's *Anacostia* partnered with a number of sponsors in and around the Washington, D.C., neighborhood, including a local real estate firm,

Anacostia River Realty, which allowed him to increase production values.[81] Large nonprofits found significant audiences for dramas, as seen in Hulu's *East Los High* and One Economy's *Diary of a Single Mom*.

Efforts by sponsors and legacy networks to monetize the immediacy and affective connections of fan engagement with scripted series have a mixed history. Few brands matched BMW's ambition with *The Hire* in the decade after its release. Puma found great success on Hulu with *The LXD*, a beautifully photographed and engaging dance series directed by Jon Chu (*Step Up*), while telecommunications companies like Verizon, Sprint, and AT&T have consistently invested in producing and distributing relatively ambitious original series and programs derivative of legacy TV shows.[82] Consider MTV's 2009 Verizon-sponsored transmedia series *Valemont*, created by Brent Friedman under his independent production company, Electric Farm Entertainment. Friedman's 2007 *Afterworld* was a 130-episode dystopian sci-fi mystery using computer-generated animation, exhibiting "myst-like storytelling," with different layers of information and ancillary content, some available on its site, Afterworld.tv, and on Budweiser's short-lived Bud.tv network. *Afterworld* was a pilot project intended as an experiment to see whether the producers could successfully monetize and narrate a story across platforms in an affordable and "epic" way. After the success of *Afterworld*—which made its money back by licensing different configurations of the story to TVs and cinemas around the world—Friedman developed *Valemont* with MTV and Verizon as sponsors, both searching for engaged fans to interact with a series and its sponsor. "We are invested more and more in telling stories across multiple screens," said John Shea, who was executive vice president of integrated marketing and branded content when *Valemont* was in development. The series and its alternate reality game—a way for fans to follow and shape the mysteries behind the main narrative through transmedia engagment—ran from about September to November of 2009; after its run, MTV edited the early episodes into a one-hour pilot with the hope of garnering interest in a second season as a full TV series. Despite some promise, the makers of *Valemont* never produced another season. To date the series remains a unique experiment in integrated marketing and transmedia storytelling within legacy networks.

Valemont followed a linear narrative structure but also integrated other media throughout the story. Christian Taylor, who penned the master script, wrote the series knowing it had to be versatile. The show had a basic storyline: Sophie Gracen discovers her brother's death, goes to his university, and uncovers a university for vampires, while becoming enmeshed in it herself. Taylor paced it episodically like a television series, but Verizon's involvement as a sponsor gave the series a transmedia imperative. Each episode was introduced using the image of a Verizon phone that belonged to the presumed dead brother. Gracen opens the phone to reveal a video message or text relevant to the mystery—the same text or video users saw before watching an episode. The Verizon introductions gave *Valemont* consistency but also made the sponsor happy by encouraging users to view content on the company's phones and the branded ValemontU.com. Those platforms featured even more texts and video messages, which thickened the story by providing additional clues. Transmedia writer Nina Bargiel wrote web and mobile content for the series, all of it connected to its ARG. Though her content had to fit within Taylor's planned narrative, it also had to be flexible enough to respond to fans: "While I had my roadmap, I was changing and reassessing and writing the content as I went along," Bargiel said in an interview with me. Bargiel made it her task to respond to fans. Her activities expanded the narrative, but the series was already produced, the mystery solved. Unlike the work of Pemberly Digital, based on preexisting material whose fans took pleasure in the story's familiarity and divergence from century-old literature, *Valemont* had to generate interest in a world via MTV and Verizon, each with specific goals, using MTV.com's player, as opposed to a broader, more open platform like YouTube, and prominently displaying the brand as sponsor.

As this example indicates, legacy distributors have the upper hand in attracting campaign funds from brands, but they have not created long-running original branded series for the web. Both NBC and ABC created digital studios for this purpose, but each only produced one or two series before shuttering.[83] Fox quietly launched and quickly shuttered a digital studio, 15 Gigs, around the same time, but restarted its efforts with Fox Digital Studios, which continues to produce new series, though nearly all have lasted less than a year.[84] Cable networks experimented with releasing indie series, but without brand integration, including AMC's marquee network AMC (*The Trivial Pursuits of Arthur Banks*) and sister network IFC (Joe Swanberg's long-running *Young*

American Bodies, Lizzie the Lezzie, Green Porno). Networks have had an easier time finding financing for extensions of existing series, particularly NBC, which had extensive transmedia promotions for *Heroes*, and ABC, which did for *Lost*, along with a stellar but short-lived Suburu-sponsored series for *Happy Endings*.

Brand- and creator-driven financing in the open TV market demonstrates the limits, however small, of legacy television's up-front ad-selling process. With more channels releasing more stories, legacy networks are finding it challenging to make audience guarantees to brands; meanwhile, brands want more data on who's watching, because they don't trust that their messages—brand narratives—are getting heard. Frustrated, brands are moving to data-driven methods online, an approach that raises questions around legality and ethics to be explored in chapter 5.[85] In this environment, indie producers and brands forged a productive, if tenuous, relationship, where brands granted them creative control and a small bit of financing so writers could lend brands a sense of sincerity that might cut through the noise.

Indie Distibutors Sell Independence to Brands

My Damn Channel was the product of an industry veteran remaking the media with full knowledge of the challenges posed by independent production and the value of corporate financing. The web series comedy network premiered in 2007 on YouTube and with its own website, following the success of Will Ferrell's Funny or Die, and quickly earned the moniker "Funny or Die Clone" from industry blog *NewTeeVee*. The site did in fact debut with short-form comedy, entering a crowded field awash in online ventures from the mainstream media—TBS's Super Deluxe, NBC's DotComedy, and the HBO/AOL joint venture ThisJustIn—as well as a number of new or already entrenched Internet-spawned sites like IAC/InterActiveCorp's College Humor and Break Media. The mainstream media offshoots quickly shuttered, but My Damn Channel continued to develop new programs, including YouTube's first daily live comedy show and a game series, "Videocracy," for the HLN network.

My Damn Channel's claim to independence was complicated. A site at once promoting independent producers while creating content specifically for brands, My Damn Channel made a good amount of its revenue as an outsource studio for corporate marketers looking to capitalize on low-cost comedy. Unlike the grassroots-grown Strike TV, venture-capital-funded My Damn Channel was the brainchild of the suits: in this case, Rob Barnett, a former MTV and CBS Radio executive. From the start, My Damn Channel had to operate as a business. Barnett planned to "create multiple streams of revenue," he told me. "[I]t's about making money." Nonetheless, Barnett's history in cable and broadcast taught him, he said, more about the power of *not* acting like a corporation than about the advantages of being big. He stressed flatter bureaucracies, with fewer executives and the ability to go from an idea to a pilot in weeks, not months. He saw how dense corporate bureaucracy could stymie "the benefits of acting fast" and doing something creative: "Sixty percent of the time we spent in horrible fear that we're going to lose our jobs. And if we do something risky and it fails, we're definitely going to lose our jobs." Early on, My Damn Channel promised to give artists "100% creative control to develop their own brands."[86] An early press release stated, "My Damn Channel empowers professional filmmakers, actors, comedians, musicians and athletes to co-produce, mass distribute and monetize original, short-form video across multiple platforms."[87] The idea of "empowering" producers and "not driving producers crazy" was key to the channel's self-identity. My Damn Channel focused on giving creatives like director David Wain (*Wainy Days*) and personality Andy Milonakis their own shows. It also distributed off-kilter ventures like *You Suck at Photoshop*, a low-tech comedy featuring voiceover and screenshots of Photoshop. Within its first year, according to press releases, the site's videos had been viewed thirty million times and it had earned $1 million in revenue, according to Barnett.

To support such projects in the early years, My Damn Channel had to rely on ad networks, the main drivers of the web video market, and eschew direct sponsorship, which came with creative strings attached. But ad networks, despite offering creative independence by automating sales, were tough on publishers, offering rates (CPMs) many times lower than those sold through legacy television. Soon, Barnett realized that display advertising could not sustain an Internet business; it undervalued premium independent content. Of the site's three-pronged revenue model—algorithmic display advertising, branded entertainment, and developing/licensing programs—display was "not compelling," he told me. To be sure, the site syndicated its content across various websites—including Atom, Yahoo, MySpace, and YouTube—to amass ad revenue. But such a strategy, involving harnessing the web's capacity for spreadability, was limiting: "You've got to be one of the biggest, most trafficked sites in the world to get rich." The most significant piece of its revenue pie became branded entertainment. Branded entertainment deals were slower to materialize but offered potential windfalls, reaching into the six figures. Branded content was a pathway to artistic independence, Barnett said: "When major ad sales deals become a consistent reality on the Web, then our business model will become a sure thing for talent craving artistic freedom and a solid paycheck," he told the Associated Press in 2007.[88]

In my 2010 interview with Barnett, I heard a more nuanced view of branded entertainment, focused less on artistic independence and more on reassuring corporations, signaling how open TV distributors must negotiate the value of artistic innovation with demands of monetization. Describing how series were developed, he said the most important aspect of the process involved understanding "what the brand is trying to accomplish," its business cycle, and what audiences it was trying to reach. (Such brands included advertisers like Lincoln, Southern Comfort, and Puma.) Only rarely did My Damn Channel itself have an idea—developed either in-house or through pitches from independent producers—and produce a series without brand input. "More often than not," Barnett said, the site was "pitching and collaborating" with brands for their own needs. The best case scenario was not an idea conceived independently, but rather an advertiser having a specific idea for a series it wanted My Damn Channel to execute: "[T]here's already that creative buy-in." The site worked like a studio, on a project-by-project basis, hiring producers to execute brands' ideas. Less frequently did it hire individual creators with passion projects, which would put My Damn Channel in the hands of the ad networks, far away from the guaranteed and sizable revenue gleaned directly from corporate patrons.

Relying on brands for financing somewhat conflicted with the site's mission of empowering independents. Ideas developed outside the small list of powerful marketers with the funds to pay for production put My Damn Channel in the more precarious position of hoping content spread (amassing revenue from pre-roll and display with less-than-favorable rates). With its subscriber base on YouTube and a small, dedicated fan base for the home site, My Damn Channel could appease brands "by following some of the most old-fashioned rules in the book, which is guaranteeing deliverables, guaranteeing traffic, guaranteeing the metrics, and not guaranteeing buzz, and heat," as Barnett said. "Buzz and heat" were the domain of the spreadable, the user-generated, and it was unpredictable. My Damn Channel's ability to market its independent spirit to large corporations, while ultimately catering to their needs, allowed it to stay afloat, to the envy of the mainstream media.[89]

"This company is about the independent spirit, we don't have an overlord telling us what we can or can't do," Barnett proclaimed, with a degree of truth. From its David Wain series to IKEA's aforementioned *Easy to Assemble* (which itself had numerous distribution partners), a number of its series featured stars with relative creative control. But these series were made to enhance the My Damn Channel brand and were sometimes separate from the big ad deals that directly brought in cash. My Damn Channel, then, espoused the rhetoric of independence while realizing that independence came at a price, one ultimately recoupable by cutting deals with the same companies who subsidize the legacy media. In 2012 the network leveraged its track record of creating classy, creative, branded entertainment into a premium channel deal with YouTube for its first live comedy show, *My Damn Channel Live*. The next year, My Damn Channel solicited independent producers to submit their shows for distribution under the My Damn Channel Comedy Network in a bid to become a multichannel network—a platform to represent hundreds, if not thousands, of producers to sponsors and larger distributors.[90] But while media conglomerates bought other multichannel networks, My Damn Channel rebranded itself Omnivision in 2014 to focus on managing and cultivating talent with mainstream potential, but two years later Barnett left the video space for a job at audiobook company Audible.[91]

The network was not alone in its delicate dance between independent production and corporate marketing. Such arrangements were de rigeur among the site's peers, including Babelgum and KoldCast. KoldCast, which, like My Damn Channel, distributed web series to TV screens through deals with TiVO and Boxee, debuted in 2008 publishing and soliciting professionally made films and series by independent filmmakers, musicians, and entertainers. As with My Damn Channel, KoldCast's early deals included distributing web series produced elsewhere and signing deals giving Hollywood stars—like Mindy Kaling and Harland Williams—their own shows with the freedom to do as they pleased. In 2009, KoldCast announced an "original studio," hiring former Hollywood executive Marti Restighini to help cultivate and buy new web shows for distribution on the site. Restighini functioned as a more artist-friendly studio executive, fielding pitches and cultivating talent. Unlike executives at the major studios, though, she aimed to be accessible: "If a video is submitted, you will get a response, and you will get a response from me," she promised. Restighini said she sometimes would advise a filmmaker on how to improve his or her product, even if KoldCast did not plan to do business with the person. KoldCast was invested in the success of "the space"—quality web video—so the success of independents was better for everyone: "So many filmmakers are using this as kind of a training ground for themselves; it's really important for them to realize what their strengths and weaknesses are in terms of story, in terms of production, and in terms of marketing."

My Damn Channel received dozens of cold pitches every week, but the chances of making it onto the site were slim. Similarly, KoldCast's site was curated, but the network did have a system for taking on an independent filmmaker without a brand's sponsorship and placing him or her on the site. Typically KoldCast would buy a series, either already completed or occasionally by paying for production, and cultivate it for a season, hoping to build an audience and find a brand to sponsor its second season. Filmmaker Kai Soremekun, whose series *Chick* explored a black woman who slowly finds out she's a superhero, told me she submitted a trailer of her already-completed series to the site and heard back immediately. Tom Konkle, creator of a popular green-screen series *Safety Geeks SVI*, said the site picked up all his production costs, leaving him free to worry about the narrative and quality of the show. In each case, filmmakers without much industry credibility could craft shows and get them distributed on a curated site.

Of course, KoldCast was a business, not a charity. Using pre-rolls (ads playing before a video), overlays (banners over a video), and post-rolls (ads playing after a video) to generate revenue for nonbranded series was "sort of the old way," Restighini said. Instead, KoldCast spent months creating a section on its site called ShowShops, a place for brands to sell merchandise and advertise products placed in series cultivated through the network. The network would try to place brands within shows, either in its first season (if it was working from a pitch) or in its second. As much as KoldCast was a platform for new media auteurship, it also gave equal placement to major advertisers. Its plan to sell products alongside its series made explicit the kinds of compromises independent new media distribution engenders. KoldCast folded in 2014 after losing millions on financing and producing original programming.

Babelgum, a site nurturing a niche audience of independent film and music aficionados, quickly realized that producing for brands, as opposed to cultivating individual talent, was the wave of the future. "There's just more inherent value there as you integrate your brand across platforms," Douglas Dicconson, Babelgum's chief revenue officer, said: "We need less monetized ad units and more marketing partners," he remarked, comparing ads served on indie videos to sponsored and branded content. This did not mean that independent filmmakers went unrepresented on the site: the network annually brought on sponsors for an online film festival and produced its share of indie web series. Yet increasingly catering to brands appeared to be its strategy—but perhaps they did not do so quickly enough. Months after announcing a million-dollar investment in independent production, Babelgum started cutting costs and shedding offices before effectively shutting down.[92] For Babelgum, making content geared toward corporate sponsorship was a safer proposition.

In the early years of streaming video from the mid-2000s to the mid-2010s, independent networks hoped they could marry the creativity of independent production—the kinds chronicled in previous chapters—with the curatorial and financial advantages of a TV network. What they found was that legacy television networks earned their independence from advertisers slowly, over decades; further, legacy TV networks still benefitted from high-cost, magazine-style advertising developed in the mass media era, even as new technologies challenged that model in a networked world. In the open TV market, the possibilities of distribution were far more precarious, necessitating a move toward the legacy network practice of compromsing creative freedom for market demands.

Supporting independent creativity meant compromising producer agency for sites like My Damn Channel, KoldCast, and Babelgum. By contrast, web video networks that cared less about supporting independent artists fared better. One example is WatchMojo, a Montreal-based video production and distribution website focused on selling a large library of corporate-friendly informational and lifestyle videos. As About.com did with text, WatchMojo focused on providing informational video, explicitly staying away from fiction, narrative videos, and user-generated content of the YouTube variety. Debuting in 2005, it rose to prominence—over ten million monthly streams and viewers by 2010—riding a trend of nonfiction video sites. The pitch was simple: consumers want information but are fickle with entertainment. Corporations will always need video, and informational videos are safe, easy, and corporate friendly.

Before delving into WatchMojo, it is instructive to compare the site to a much-publicized network debuting in 2007: Quarterlife. *Quarterlife* was most commonly known as a web series, initially developed as a pilot for ABC, which passed on the show. Marshall Herskovitz and Edward Zwick (*thirtysomething*, *My So-Called Life*) took the show online in late 2007. It first appeared on then-popular social media site MySpace, but eventually the team developed an independent social network site called Quarterlife. They aimed to harness artistically minded amateurs to create content—visual art, video, etc.—for Quarterlife.com while fostering a community to discuss and promote the show. "I'm a big believer in independent production," said Herskovitz, noting how independent television—"his vision without an intervening force"—really did not exist. "The entire landscape's owned by six companies," he lamented. When *Quarterlife* averaged 350,000 views per episode, NBC decided to give it a chance on a bigger screen. On the night of its broadcast premiere, the series flopped with roughly four million viewers.[93] "That was kind of the end of the television life on *Quarterlife*," Herskovitz said. The advertisers he'd secured for the series, including Pepsi and Toyota, "didn't want to come back." Traffic to its social networking site, which had reached tens of thousands, started to decline. The site stayed up, even though no new episodes were posted, but a year later, it was begging for money.[94] By early 2010, the site had ceased to be independent, instead joining Ning, a network of social networks, operating essentially as a much more modest, user-led nonprofit. By July 2010, the site had officially shuttered.[95]

Quarterlife's story is a fascinating tale of the clash among new media, old media, and trials of independence. By making it onto legacy television, *Quarterlife* proved that users could propel something into the mainstream on their own, but once mainstream success proved unsustainable, most of the users left, and with them, the advertisers too. "I think we did prove something, but it kind of was the tree falling in the forest with no one there to see it," Herskovitz said: "Now it's very rare for something to take off without any marketing. There's just too much competition." *Quarterlife* struggled to integrate open and legacy distribution and marketing. Arising in a networked context where program circulation is decentralized, *Quarterlife's* embrace of linear, one-to-many marketing after the fact reset the terms of success. Had *Quarterlife* taken its four million viewers to cable first, and sustained itself there, its story might have ended differently.

For WatchMojo's chief executive, Ashkan Karbasfrooshan, sites like Quarterlife that focused on web series and user-generated content were not the proper response to the online video market of YouTube (volume-based) and Hulu (curated legacy TV). "If you are a producer that wants to make what he wants, that's great. But it's not scalable. There's no guarantee that anybody watches it," Karbasfrooshan said. "The kind of viewers who watch web series, they're going to watch that on television." Instead, WatchMojo focused on short-form, professional content. With a small in-house production team, the site made no claims to artistry or independence and explicitly produced content either commissioned by brands or made to sell directly to companies, which then would use the videos as entertainment—in shopping malls, in coffee shops, on their websites, etc. WatchMojo's videos included such how-to clips as "Cover Girl Tips for Faking It: An Eyelid Crease" and "American Classic Looks from the Gap" (the fashion and lifestyle pages were the most popular). If not branded, videos were informational, like "The History of the Waterways in US and Canada" or "Travel Guide: Luxembourg."

WatchMojo prided itself on its ability to attract companies willing to pay for its professional and brand-friendly content. Since 2006, Watch-Mojo slowly built a large library of thousands of videos, most of which were not likely to go out of date. It competed with a plethora of informational video sites, many of which were designed to be more corporate friendly than YouTube's user-generated production and low-budget indie

TV series. An entire league of how-to sites achieved some success acting essentially as houses for brands to outsource video production: HowCast, which has garnered as much as twenty-five million streams per month, made deals with companies like Kodak, 1-800-Flowers, and GE, making videos as part of corporate promotional campaigns.[96] WatchMojo's Karbasfrooshan, whose background is in marketing, knows that "marketers didn't want to necessarily associate themselves with user-generated. We wanted it be the About.com of video." Brands like Coca-Cola used WatchMojo's sleek, topical, and benign videos in special promotional websites; McDonald's used them for a site geared toward women. Bluefly, on the contrary, produced its own promotional videos in-house and needed a place to publish them—they used WatchMojo. Eighty percent of WatchMojo's revenue came from licensing and syndication, the rest from advertising; in other words, WatchMojo was paid directly for content instead of risking cash on quirky indie videos. The site coordinated with marketers swiftly and received ad rates twice as high as with the ad networks. "Ad networks are good for ad networks," he said.

WatchMojo's business model reflects a different relationship to new media production and online distribution. It suggests that what consumers often want is information related to living, and this happened to be the easiest and most corporate-friendly kind of content to sell. This focus allows the site to subsist by making the content it wants to make without either relying on legacy media or needing to compromise artistic vision. Everything it produces is for brands: it makes few claims to artistic vision or independence.

Opening Networks of Recognition

The challenge of marketing and monetizing independent series raises the issue of recognition. To challenge the surplus of video online, new exhibitors pursue ways to curate the best programs for legacy distributors, fans, and potential sponsors in the form of festivals and award shows. Festivals are spaces where distributors can find productions to release and producers can meet each other, whereas award shows signal to distributors, advertisers, and fans what series are "the best" in any given year. Yet this process of conferring status on quality productions is as fraught as raising capital.

Consider the International Television Festival, which got off to a rocky start in 2011, its sixth year and first under new executive directors Frank Zanca and Ken Nicholas. A long line stretched down the red carpet outside Drai's Hollywood, a trendy club at Hollywood and Vine, a famous intersection in film and television history, not least because of its proximity to Hollywood's Chinese theater and Walk of Fame. Several indie web series creators could not get into the club or onto the red carpet. The public relations manager handling the door and the carpet appeared to be focusing her attention on "minor celebrities" like porn star Mary Carey at the expense of independent producers, making them "feel like second-class citizens," according to one series creator I spoke to. Sean Becker, director of *The Guild*, left in exasperation, tweeting, "To everyone who couldn't get in to the #itvfest party, a bunch of us are going across the street to Dillons Irish pub. Come over-dressed." The chatter started to reverberate: "They just keep pissing people off . . . just search #itvfest and you'll see," wrote Allison Vanore, Daytime Emmy–nominated producer of a number of web series, including *Vanity*, *Anyone But Me*, *My Gimpy Life*, and *Cost of Capital*. The next day, *The Guild*, a vital participant in web series events, tweeted to tens of thousands of followers that it was "canceling its participation in #itvfest."

For a festival seeking to generate interest in and excitement about independent web series as a form, and to represent the best the market had to offer, any decreased participation from a heralded and popular show like *The Guild* was a setback. What went wrong? The tension between the web and television, independent media and Hollywood lay at the heart of the kerfuffle. The first problem was the locale, Drai's, which a number of producers characterized as incompatible with the scrappy, low-key web series industry: "Wait, so a party at the Hollywood douchebag hot spot Drais wasn't good?! I'm shocked!" tweeted Mike Rotman, known for writing for the Emmy-nominated *Politically Incorrect* and winning a Streamy for a web show with Kevin Pollack. Another producer, Vanessa Driveness, blamed the "Hollywood webtv bubble." Steve Lekowicz, creator of *Vampire Zombie Werewolf*, an official festival selection, wrote an open letter to the festival's organizers accusing them of caring more about press and Hollywood prestige than about independent creators:

Who was the party for? We had mistakenly assumed this event was for us, the participants, to kick off the festival and meet other folks involved. This was obviously wrong in hindsight. According to your letter from this morning, it was a success because the confusing and poorly-planned amassing of people brought press and dragged some executives back from Hawaii. Your defenses make it sound like gaining some cliché obnoxious Hollywood bragging rights helps us all. Exposure in 33 media outlets makes no difference if it comes with disrespect.[97]

Lekowicz's disdain for the tone of the event and the festival—aspiring to glitz, overreaching their position in the Hollywood economy—was echoed by other producers like Vanore and Joseph Saroufim (producer of *OB/GY*, an official selection and later a winner at the New York Television Festival). Eric Mortensen, then Blip's director of programming, focused specifically on ITVFest's adoption of Hollywood conventions: "I guess I have to wonder if you can have the red carpet without, at least, some degree of Hollywood douchebaggery."[98]

Concerns about the festival's direction ran deeper than hurt vanity at the premiere. When I met with Avi Glijanksy, a recent NYU film school grad whose 2010 comedy, *The Further Adventures of Cupid and Eros*, was an official festival selection, he said that a number of changes led indie showrunners to suspect ITVFest was trying to live beyond its web-based means. Creators were not given enough festival comp tickets, making it difficult for them to see screenings, which was detrimental to the goals of furthering artistic legitimacy and fostering community within the space. Another producer I spoke to mentioned the event's location, around the corner from one of Hollywood's glitziest hotels, the storied Chateau Marmont. The perception among many was that ITVFest cared more about being Hollywood than supporting independent television.

Participants in the web series market are aware of their position within Hollywood, particularly at festivals and award shows, which purport to present the diversity and best efforts of its talent to audiences, Hollywood executives, and advertisers. As demonstrated in previous chapters, they partially model their production ethics, storytelling methods, and distribution goals on legacy television. The web series market has an unstable relationship with the legacy industry: admiring its power but understanding its limits. In 2011, anxiety was rising. A number of industrial developments raised concerns among independent producers, including the announcement, which broke on the first day of the festival, that the Streamy Awards (which had been in hibernation after its own controversy the year prior, to be explained) would team with Dick Clark Productions and bring the award show to television, which eventually materialized in 2015 on VH1.[99] Producers were also concerned about the upcoming deadline for a new, rival awards show, the International Academy of Web Television (IAWTV) Awards, as well as the recent announcement that web networks like Crackle were abandoning short-form for legacy TV–length programming. Meanwhile, companies like Netflix started to spend hundreds of millions on original shows, and Nielsen accelerated its push to rate the web like TV while also offering "Total Audience" cross-platform measurement for broadcast and cable distributors.[100] Simply put, hopes that short-form, independent creators could run alongside legacy television content were put into question: was indie TV splitting in two, Hollywood-lite versus indie upstarts?

In many ways, it was. But Hollywood studios, networks, and producers always participated in the new media economy, and independent entrepreneurs always tried to upgrade to the big leagues. Most individuals in the open TV market understood the push and pull between separate tiers of production quality and marketing power. In the post-YouTube phase of web programming of the late 2000s and early 2010s, however, festivals and award shows provided spaces for recognition across styles and levels of clout. Indie TV festivals award the best web series for mastering the art of storytelling but also provide a space for producers to recognize each other, to meet and share stories, advice, and resources. The following section shows how these newly formed organizations tried to balance open and legacy television, independent creators and institutionally sanctioned projects. They fostered innovation while serving the interests of a broader base of producers than their more established peers.

Festivals for Recognition: Hollywood Meets Indie, Indie Meets Hollywood

"If you've never been to CAA, it's amazing," festival codirector Zanca told the audience during a screening at the 2011 ITVFest. The festival scheduled several panels and screenings at the headquarters of Creative Artists Agency (CAA), Hollywood's leading firm representing the top creatives in the business. CAA's headquarters is a large glass building fronted by a majestic staircase and boasting a cavernous, white marble lobby. The building is imperious, and security is tight—I had to open my trunk to park, which cost a hefty twenty dollars an hour. It appeared to me that the festival's directors wanted to host events at CAA's Century City location for its glamour and for the possibility that agents and managers might check out some web content. Most of the other panels, screenings, and workshops took place at an independent theater miles away in West Hollywood. Like Drai's and other ritzy festival locales like the W and Renaissance Hotels, CAA served the festival's mission to bring independent television closer to Hollywood's nebulous center.

Festivals serve multiple functions, especially for a new medium, like web series, still in search of artistic and institutional standards, best practices, and recognition. They are places where deals get done or started, where industry workers watch and learn about other projects and marketing tactics, and where awards establish value and artistic hierarchies. For dispersed production communities like web series creators, they also serve as meeting places, where people congregate, catch up, and share tragedies and success stories. ITVFest also took on the additional role of positioning web television as the next big thing. As a testament to television's complexity, and the fragmentation of Hollywood production, web series festivals bring together individuals from all corners of the market: from new entrants with very little clout to executives of prominent web networks and series and television executives from the legacy channels. The constituent diversity means that web festivals negotiate between competing interests and discourses. They are dynamic, innovative organizations. Each festival chooses a small set of goals, and each festival has a different mission.

Independent television creators lack the hundreds of festivals independent film directors have, but they have a few.[101] From 2010 to 2015, I counted thirty festivals and conferences that acknowledged web series in some way.[102] Most of those were new organizations designed to bring together web series creators outside Hollywood, like Austin Webfest, New Orleans Video Access Center's Web Weekend, Seattle Web Fest, and the Long Beach Indie Film Festival. The most prominent of all the festivals is the New York Television Festival (NYTVF), which started in 2005 and bills itself as the first TV festival of its kind. In 2011, when I attended, the heavily curated festival screened just fifty pilots—short- and long-form—to a cumulative audience of about fifteen thousand. NYTVF also served as a premiere event for a number of legacy television pilots—that year it screened NBC's *Prime Suspect* remake and Logo's gay reality show franchise, *The A-List: Dallas.* It also had the clearest connections to the industry. Every year it hosts a number of panels and prizes in collaboration with networks like Fox, MTV, IFC, Syfy, and many others with which web series producers annually score development deals (Al Thompson's black sci-fi drama *Odessa* won a deal with Syfy in 2011).

For those who did not make it into NYTVF, a number of festivals showcased a wider swathe of indie web shows, including ITVFest, LAWEBFEST, and HollyWeb Festival. Sometimes individual festivals arose for a specific purpose, as in 2010 when *Drama Queenz* creator Dane Joseph produced the Out of the Box Festival in New York to showcase gay and lesbian web series. A few festivals experimented with the standard format of screenings and panels. Celebrate the Web was probably the best known and most successful of these. Started in 2010 by Jenni Powell (*The Guild*), Kim Evey (*The Guild, Gorgeous Tiny Chicken Machine Show*), and Stephanie Thorpe (*After Judgment, Hurtling through Space at an Alarming Rate*), the festival changed format and location each year. It usually included a pilot competition in which creators write, shoot, and edit a pilot in seven days, which is then judged by audiences and industry executives. The festival partnered with larger web companies like Machinima, YouTube's VidCon conference, IAWTV, and the SAG-AFTRA union, the largest for actors.

Since the middle of the twentieth century, film and TV festivals have grown in size and number, becoming vital parts of the economies for filmed entertainment, primarily for cinema. The earliest film festivals in Europe were largely free and open to the public—they served nationalist purposes, and selections were gleaned from national commissions and studios. This changed in the 1950s, after the break-up of the studio system and concurrent with the rise of auteurism and art film. Independent film rose in America and around the world, partially resulting from lighter, 16mm cameras and mobile sound technology, creating demand from art house theaters and festivals to curate and distribute new cultural products. Festivals were founded on theories of artistic excellence, but this was mainly in service of positioning them for the market: "[F]or commercial cinema to be consecrated as artistic and legitimate it needed a means of establishing valuation of artists and artworks outside of the terms of the mass market."[103] Nevertheless, many festivals have open markets for the buying and selling of films, and have since Cannes created the Marché fifty years ago. In the United States, studio disinvestment in independent production and the stable marketability of high-budget indies made film festivals ever more vital to the theatrical distribution market. "While film festivals are not studios, through their markets and production and coproduction forums, they are becoming places where connections, negotiations, and financing of films take place," writes Cindy Wong.[104] This may explain why independent television creators started to create their own festivals: finding it hard to get television's attention, they opted to follow cinema, which arguably had more success bringing outsiders in from obscurity, very often through festivals.

ITVFest had some success bringing Hollywood to independent television, and vice versa, though gleaning a clear narrative is impossible. Panels throughout the festival feature a wide array of speakers. In 2011, Terence Carter, head of drama development for Fox and responsible for their mega-hit *Glee*, sat on a panel next to Emelyn Stuart, producer of the popular indie black web show, *12 Steps to Recovery*. BET executives held a panel about their new web shows with producers from the indie production *Asylum*, created by Dan Williams. Web series creators can work on studio projects or are signed by large agencies, and the industry's B-list actors create shows as well. Here the distinction between new and veteran producers starts to blur. At a screening of workplace shows, the producers and their budgets varied in clout and size. Jay Thomas, a veteran actor, premiered a pilot, *The Talker*, shot for $8,000 (with favors from actor-friends), while a team of independent filmmakers showed their $150,000 show, *The Video Guys*, originally a feature film. The other two shows came from a group of new actors utilizing members of their acting class and its studio, and Al Thompson showed one of his many pilots, a comedy called *Tilt-a-World* set in an amusement park. Meanwhile, web video networks represented at the festival filled the void between independent producers and network executives.

Peter Hyoguchi of Strike TV sat on a panel discussing Strike TV's deal with Metacafe getting fans to fund a pilot, and Machinima, a YouTube multichannel network, hosted a panel about one of its branded series, a zombie comedy called *Bite Me*, produced for $400,000 and sponsored by billion-dollar video game brands Xbox and Capcom. Often the only thing panelists and their shows had in common was an ambivalent relationship to legacy television; thoughts about what a web series is and should be varied widely on the basis of position. Corporate players expressed their proximity to legacy models: "We don't call this stuff web series. We don't call it new media. . . . We call them shows," Machinima's vice president of development, Andy Shapiro, said at his panel. "It's more like a traditional network than you would think." Indie creators meanwhile stressed their various strategies for cutting costs and the ways their stories built on or innovated legacy network stories.

Festivals also curate ancillary and informal spaces for producers to exchange information, trade stories, and gossip. Producers meet with development executives but also with each other and the press. While attending the 2011 festival, I was regularly invited to have drinks or dinner with creators. Some hosted premiere parties and promotional events for their shows, as the indefatigable *East WillyB* producers did one night at a local Latin bar downtown. The web series market's premier news outlet, *Tubefilter*, scheduled their regular "meet-up" during the festival, bringing together YouTube and Blip executives to discuss distribution trends, with cocktails afterward. During drinks, producers mingled and discussed stories they could not share publicly on Facebook, on Twitter, or with the press. One writer revealed details of a web distribution deal with a cable network that he did not take, because the budget they offered was too low, with too much money allotted for executive salaries. At an impromptu dinner I attended with a group of black producers whose shows screened at the festival, producers relayed information about what kinds of projects brands and network executives were interested in—black female romantic comedies, one person said—and strategies for booking mainstream actors on a low budget. Backroom discussions such as these create value outside of the festival and build consensus and mutual understanding for a developing art form and dispersed production community.

Award Shows: Negotiating Value in an Open Market

Efforts to create venues to value independent television started early, as market players saw the need to create exclusive spaces to counteract the openness of the form. Following legacy television and film, they believed that web video needed similar hierarchies to elevate indie production—a mission that has never been without detractors for the ways awards might miss or overshadow innovative productions. These tensions occasionally forced new media insitutions to open processes for recognizing series, reinventing the ways Hollywood structures artistic and cultural value.

If festivals largely operated out of view from the public and press, award shows for web series arose in the late 2000s to let critics, fans, and distributors know what open TV market players deemed the best of the field. Award shows give producers and distributors bragging rights, a way to communicate their cultural and artistic significance in an ever-crowded marketplace. So in 2010, after nominees were announced for the second annual Streamy Awards, Sony's Eric Berger boasted: "We're thrilled that the Academy chose to recognize the talented individuals who worked so tirelessly to make these shows successful," he said in a release.[105] The "Academy" is not the Academy of Motion Picture Arts and Sciences (of the Academy Awards) nor the Academy of Television Arts and Sciences (of the Emmys), but the International Academy of Web Television (IAWTV), then the adjudicating body for the Streamy Awards. *The Bannen Way*, a series from the Sony's web channel, Crackle, received thirteen nominations at the Streamy Awards in 2010, including Best Drama.

Sony had good reason to promote its nomination. The first annual Streamy Awards, held in 2009, successfully established web series as a serious form. The first winners included a number of names familiar to legacy television aficionados, including producer Joss Whedon and actor Neil Patrick Harris (*Dr. Horrible's Sing-Along Blog*), writers Jane Espenson and Ronald D. Moore (for *Battlestar Galactica*'s web series, *The Face of the Enemy*), actress Rosario Dawson (for her NBC web series *Gemini Division*) and actor Paul Rudd and director David Wain (for My Damn Channel's *Wainy Days*). At the same time, beloved independent series like *The Guild* and *You Suck at Photoshop*, along with a number of prominent series from YouTube creators, were just some of the numerous smaller-budget shows nominated. Many of the 2009 nominees eventually transitioned to linear television, including *Children's Hospital* (on Cartoon Network) and *The Onion News Network* (on IFC). In 2010, media reports framed the Streamys as immature: "The awards are only two years old, and the ceremony at the Orpheum was filled with a raucous crowd of twenty-somethings who were mostly there for having produced no-budget entertainment," wrote *The Wrap's* Sharon Waxman.[106] Still, close observers could see that the Streamys were essential to positioning web programming as the new television.

The second annual Streamys in 2010 was not a success, and reports of the web series market's immaturity increased. Technical and creative issues during the event created a rift in the community, exposing the challenges of recognition in the open TV market. As with the 2011 ITVFest the following year, the issue came down to overreaching and underperforming aspirations of Hollywood legitimacy, with tensions fueled by web creators' insecurity about the medium's maturity and leadership. Complaints about what went wrong at the ceremony were wide ranging, but the general consensus was that the Streamys presented web video as an immature medium for "boys" who could not make it in Hollywood. Samuel Axon wrote that "the ceremony took a path that earned its writers comparisons to 4chan users and out-of-control YouTube commenters almost immediately after it began. Rampant misogyny and sexism, naked streakers, and dozens of penis and vagina jokes gave credibility only to the old adage that the Internet is just for pornography."[107] Tech issues exacerbated the show's questionable writing, which included jokes about masturbation, a five-minute sketch on vaginal rejuvenation, and a salute to a fictional porn entrepreneur. Sponsors such as Trident gum, financing a web series about two nominees on a road trip to the awards, reportedly asked for their money back.[108]

The debates over the immaturity of the 2010 Streamys reflected back on the web series as a new medium whose openness challenged its value. Creators saw the Streamys as having an "attitude" problem, indulging the inferiority of web video: "[T]he Streamys seemed to be making a big play for introducing web video to the mainstream audience, playing deliberately to those expectations—while simultaneously pointing out . . . that this is still a secondary industry to the TV and film world," wrote Liz Shannon Miller.[109] Exacerbating the problem was the presence of a number of legacy media stars in the audience and among the winners and presenters, like Lisa Kudrow, whose show *Web Therapy* was eventually picked up by Showtime and ran for four seasons. The Streamy producers' failure to grasp that the web has its own virtues was evident in the format of the awards show, which journalists claimed strived too hard for Hollywood glamour in style while devolving into early-YouTube-style crass humor in substance: "The problem is that the International Academy of Web Television . . . was founded in part to fight that very perception," wrote Axon.[110] Both *Tubefilter* and the IAWTV ultimately realized these contradictions and immediately issued apologies, while announcing that it would restructure the Streamys in what some characterized as an internal power shake-up.[111] Indeed, the IAWTV broke away from the Streamys several months later and created its own more indie-friendly show, the IAWTV Awards, held in Las Vegas.[112]

The International Academy of Web Television was founded in 2008 to advocate for the space and generate public awareness of its quality programming.[113] This mission was reflected in its first set of directors, comprised of individuals from new media companies like Digitas and *Tubefilter*, web producers like Felicia Day, and people from large agencies like ICM (International Creative Management).[114] Membership was initially invite-only and included respected individuals from the press, web networks, and popular shows.[115] The IAWTV and the Streamys started with a top-down approach in a bid for legitimacy that frustrated those left out of the process.[116] This was the case because the IAWTV initially modeled itself after legacy television and film academies, proclaiming that "just as the Academies of Motion Picture and Television Arts and Sciences had humble beginnings, so do we. While our industry may be in its early stages, it is growing at an exponential rate."[117] The IAWTV positioned growth as an unquestionable good as it marked a trajectory to Hollywood legitimacy.

The top-down approach did not last long, and the way the IAWTV perceived its "humble beginnings" changed in subsequent years: the membership rolls went from invite-only to screened applications (where applicants were asked to list industry contacts as referrals) to open enrollment for anyone willing to pay the ninety dollars in annual dues.

Open enrollment came partially in response to the 2010 Streamys and an explicit attempt to differentiate the academy from the legacy film and television institutions. In a widely read blog post, Jack Ferry, an IAWTV membership committee member, argued that the Streamys debacle depressed interest in the IAWTV: "The biggest issue the IAWTV will face will be attracting new members (and retaining current ones). That is, getting (and keeping) people *in*, not keeping them *out*."[118] But the shift also represents an innovative critique of Hollywood's recognition institutions:

> These academies [Academy of Motion Picture Arts and Sciences, Academy of Television Arts and Sciences] are much like the industries they represent. They're designed to keep the general public out. A side effect is that, by-and-large, within the organization, fresh blood (and the change that represents) is feared, not embraced. So every year, the median age of their membership continues to rise.[119]

In other words, if indie TV represented the future of TV, they had to recognize and value it differently. Indeed, a *Los Angeles Times* study two years later confirmed the startling lack of diversity in Hollywood's awards-granting institutions: in 2012, the median age of the Motion Picture Academy was sixty-two, and voters were 94 percent white and 77 percent male.[120] Three years later, black Twitter users spread the hashtag #OscarsSoWhite in protest of a nearly all-white crop of nominees.

In its bid to reshape the web's institutions, the IAWTV opened enrollment in 2010 and created the IAWTV Awards, whose first low-key ceremony was held at the decidedly un-Hollywood Consumer Electronics Show in January 2012. Like the Streamys, the IAWTV Awards mixed high- and low-budget programming; while most of the awards went to *The Guild* and web series from established web networks like Machinima, My Damn Channel, and Atom, self-distributed shows like *Anyone but Me* and *Pretty* also took home honors: "[T]he spread of shows recognized represents a pretty good mix of productions backed by major players and genuinely independent shows," journalist Liz Shannon Miller wrote.[121] In keeping with the nature of the venue—a tech industry conference—the academy also hosted a number of panels "to educate and build the web tv community."[122]

The IAWTV's actions—hosting at a tech conference, including education panels—contrasted with the Streamys, which announced in 2011 that it was partnering with Dick Clark Productions to produce a new show and possibly broadcast it on television.[123] The show debuted on VH1 in September 2015, and most awards went to leading YouTube creators and spreadable scripted series like *Video Game High School* and *Epic Rap Battles of History*. The kind of scripted series that dominate this book were represented by the new "Best Indie Series" category, won by Sasha Winters and Emma Jane Gonzalez for their Vimeo series *Eat Our Feelings*, an innovative series that combines a sitcom about single Brooklynites with a vegan-friendly cooking show. Meanwhile, the IAWTV awards focused on scripted comedies and dramas, giving awards out for directing, acting, production design, and cinematography to crtically lauded shows like LGBT dramedy *Out with Dad* from Jason Leaver, *Producing Juliet* from *Anyone but Me* writer Tina Cesa Ward, feminist "social web series" *Whatever, Linda*, and transmedia vlog series *The New Adventures of Peter and Wendy*. Yet in 2016 it became a division of the Caucus for Producer, Writers & Directors, an invite-only group of influential Hollywood players, to which IAWTV members could potentially gain access. IAWTV chair Tina Cesa Ward said in a statement that the move creates "a bridge between new media and traditional producers, writers and directors like never before."[124]

While it is still too early to know what impact either the IAWTV or Streamys will have on television, it is clear that new media institutions must constantly balance between embracing and challenging legacy structures—from networks to festivals and award shows. Both award shows represent non-Hollywood producers' efforts to create recognition networks for their own work. There have been other awards that web series creators could apply for, including the Webbys (run by AOL), handing out awards since the mid-1990s; the Emmys (Daytime and Primetime), which hand out various "new media" awards; and the Writers Guild, bequeathing new media awards since shortly after the 2007–2008 strike (eventually followed by the Producers Guild in 2012). For these organizations not born of indie TV's community of producers and executives, web series often find themselves at the bottom of the list. Value is always hard to pin down, and the web series community has learned that discerning what value the web brings to the mainstream is vexing.

In the tortuous process of working through its value, these organizations change television development, reorienting recognition to those with the fewest resources by offering spaces for them to make claims to representation.

Conclusion: Reinventing Legacy Development through Independent Distribution?

The quest to reinvent the way legacy television develops, distributes, and confers value on production consistently draws new entrepreneurs. Consider the fascinating case of Mobcaster. Aubrey Levy did not start Mobcaster to emulate television. Once an actor and writer based in New York, Levy had experience with the development process: one of his scripts attracted the interest of an agency (Endeavor) interested in developing it for broadcast. The experience was not positive. Levy said he had to rewrite the script "eighty times" over the course of six months to please "eighty different people," only to end up with a product no better than the original: "We had to please so many constituents just to get it sold to network." Levy's pilot never sold, and he went to work for HBO on digital strategy and distribution for the channel's transmedia GO initiative, which eventually made HBO content accessible across devices.

Levy decided to do something about it. He created Mobcaster, a crowdfunding and distribution site that debuted in 2011. Mobcaster attempted to reinvent television development from conception to release. First, a writer creates a pitch video for the pilot of a twenty-two- or forty-four-minute show; Levy approves the pitch for Mobcaster after reading a full pilot script. Once a pitch goes up on the site, users fund the pilot. If the campaign is successful, the pilot goes into production and is released on Mobcaster, after which users can fund a full, six-episode season of the show. Unlike other crowdfunding sites like Kickstarter and Indiegogo, Mobcaster also functions as a television network, releasing shows that audiences fund. Shows can then raise funds for subsequent seasons, or attract interest from television, which can pick up shows because they are written in the right format. Mobcaster takes a minority position as a producer, and content creators retain the intellectual property rights. When I spoke to Levy, Mobcaster was just beginning, but one show, *The Weatherman*, which I had seen the year prior at the New York Television Festival, had raised over $70,000 for its full season (their half-hour pilot was already shot). Levy said that independent television festivals were crucial venues for him to find shows worthy of distribution. "We are an independent TV channel. We're just in a crowdfunding phase," he told me.

The problem with the open TV market during this period, for Levy, includes the lack of distributors with resources to license and market programs, well-respected exhibitors, and clear pathways to sustainable series development. Independent film has the festival circuit and theatrical distributors, and short-form video has YouTube. "There's never been an independent outlet for television," he said. Mobcaster is targeting the missing middle, but doing it in a way television never has: shifting development power from executives to fans. The problem of television distribution is systemic for Levy. "It's a system built around finding one *Modern Family* or one *Lost* that pays for the rest," he says. Television's distribution systems are the legacy of industrialization: large, cost heavy, and ultimately more concerned with delivering profits than producing art that creators or fans want. Mobcaster wanted to rewrite the distribution equation for television, making it smaller scale but more flexible and open, the ultimate goal of every web series institution profiled in this chapter.

Years later, Mobcaster had not fully reinvented television development. *The Weatherman* pilot made it through production and set itself up in development at 20th Century Fox, with Wellesley Wild (*Ted*) under his overall deal.[125] Other series made their funding goals, but never released the pilot, either to keep it exclusive—as is the case with Dinner for One's *Life Sucks*—or for lack of time to make it—as is the case with *Nico's Nickel*, according to the show's Facebook page. All of Mobcaster's campaigns met their targets, ranging from $3,500 to $85,00, but by 2015 the site featured no series and stopped accepting submissions for new shows. Meanwhile, other distributors picked up where Mobcaster left off, particularly Seed & Spark, which focused on crowdfunding and building audiences for new film and TV.

Companies like Mobcaster reveal how networked distribution, supported by technology, passionate entrepreneurs, and discontent with legacy media's inequality, opens up spaces for radically rethinking series distribution and development. Unlike with previous alternative distribution projects, Levy's intent was never to upend the legacy system. "I see the inefficiency in the system, and we're trying to bring efficiency to the system. We're trying to disrupt the process without destroying the world," Levy said. In other words, even as Mobcaster challenged the development process, it was ultimately a project in support of television as a medium. Levy sought to widen legacy television's scope, integrate more producers—when I interviewed him he was talking to over one hundred producers to get programs on the site—and their fans. This move to expand television is far from new, with deep roots in the initially anticorporate alternative video movement of the 1960s and 1970s.[126] That utopian movement, similarly spurred by cheaper, lighter production technologies and new distribution channels (cable), started as an effort to decentralize TV but soon found its most vanguard ideas and producers usurped into the structure:

> At first, guerrilla television aimed at creating a distinct, parallel system to broadcast TV, but when that dream proved difficult to realize, it turned into a reform movement to "remake" television into something new, vital, peculiarly electronic, and responsive to the news and expectations of a generation raised on the medium. In the process, guerrilla television became entwined within the system it claimed could not be reformed, propelled from cable to public to network television and eventually devoured by the parent that spawned it.[127]

Whether web series distributors can avoid a similar fate remains to be seen. Answers about how cozy new media distributors should get with legacy television varied depending on whom I spoke to.

The United States media market, particularly during the conglomeration that accelerated in the 1990s, is harsh for independents and compels them to aspire to inclusion in the power structure. Most end up relying on—being paid by—larger institutions and structures at some point. The entrepreneurs discussed in this chapter, unlike purveyors of guerilla television of the 1960s and 1970s, started with legacy television and film as models for releasing independently produced content. When the establishment is the model for the alternative, the real question arises: do independent creators actually want to create a substantially different system?

In the networked era, independent subscription channels are debuting to curate indie TV for paying fans. Instead of relying on legacy development's resources or advertisers' financing, like many of the cases in this chapter, indie TV producers are increasingly becoming entrepreneurs and making their own destinations in collaboration with established fan bases. When I spoke to Black & Sexy TV's Numa Perrier and Dennis Dortch in the fall of 2014, they were deep in development with HBO for their first series, *The Couple*, with Spike Lee attached as an executive producer. But HBO development is slow and, Perrier said, "[W]e aren't putting all our eggs in that basket." The team had built a sizable following by releasing free videos on YouTube and had just released their first crossover episode with their two most popular black romantic dramedies: Perrier, Lena Waithe, & Ashley Blaine Featherson's *Hello Cupid* and Perrier and Dortch's *Roomieloverfriends*. They asked fans to pay for the episode, and it sold well. They soon moved new episodes of Black & Sexy to VHX, an indie VOD and subscription platform purchased by Vimeo in 2016. By that time Black & Sexy had over a dozen original series, many with legacy TV–length episodes running over twenty minutes. They were making enough from subscription to keep production going and license exclusive releases. Following their lead and the lead of lesbian-focused tello, new black queer subscription channels debuted on VHX in the mid-2010s, including Lamont Pierre's The Arthouse, built off the success of black gay drama *Freefall*; Michelle Daniel's Between Women TV, founded on the success of Atlanta's black lesbian drama *Between Women*; and Sean Anthony Torrington's SLAY TV, off the success of *No Shade*.

Sustainability in the indie space may continue to prove elusive. All of the distribution strategies outlined in this chapter in various ways rely on tried-and-true practices of legacy television and film industries. Far from radically reinventing distribution for a new media moment, most independent television organizations operate from the view that legacy media works because it is financially stable and culturally relevant. Independent networks from Blip to Babelgum sought brand-friendly content they could curate for viewers uninterested in sifting through the vast array of indie programs online. Festivals and awards shows modeled most of their elements on film, and courted recognition from Hollywood powerbrokers, even, at times, at the expense of the independent producers who composed the bulk of their supporters. Distribution is key to success in American media, but independent distribution rarely delivers sustainable success, even in moments of tremendous media change. If independent production thrives, it must choose between the constant change, innovation, and instability open distribution requires or the exclusionary, corporate-driven institutions that support large-scale productions. If there is a third way, it may stem from the likes of Black & Sexy TV: on the margins and at small scale, with programming supported directly by the communities that the distributor represents. Their role in discovering diverse new talent and adapting business strategies to support their artistic goals points to their value in the open TV market. The next chapter investigates the consequences of corporate web TV distributors' pursuit of sustainability and profitability, how they are integrating big data into development to secure big budgets for producers and mass targeting for brands and fans.

5

Scaling Open TV

The Challenges of Big Data Television

How do distributors profit from the Internet's vast swathes of fans and producers? They harness big data to develop big productions or a large number of producers for big audiences. In 2012, one year before the premiere of *House of Cards*, which established Netflix as the premier home of big data television, YouTube-based multichannel network Machinima.com proposed an extension of a corporate franchise, *Halo 4: Forward unto Dawn*. The action- and special effects–heavy teen drama series was a prequel to the complex, intergalactic first-person shooter game, which sold tens of millions of copies and grossed roughly $3 billion for Microsoft Studios. Microsoft had been trying to make a feature-length studio movie of *Halo* for most of the 2000s, but the film stalled in Hollywood, as the industry saw many game adaptations fail. Instead of investing the $100 million necessary to make and market a blockbuster film in cinemas, Microsoft bet they could harness pent-up fan demand for a film adaptation by spending less—a reported $10 million—and releasing it online as a web series. *Halo 4: Forward unto Dawn* was perceived to be a moderate success; millions of Machinima fans watched.

Machinima—short for "machine" and "cinema"—is a popular niche on YouTube, with thousands of channels under its purview. *Red vs. Blue*, a scripted series set in *Halo*'s universe, was for years one of the longest-running and most successful scripted web series, premiering in 2003 on Machinima.com and running until at least 2014. Machinima.com debuted in 2000 as a community for creators of short films captured in game play. As the site grew, it migrated to YouTube and became a business incorporating machinima creators and the gaming fans who followed their work. By signing up thousands of machinima creators—by 2013 Machinima reported roughly seventy-five hundred—the multichannel network achieved "scale" by accumulating gamers and their fans, then selling them to advertisers and, eventually, venture capitalists. As noted by Jordan Levin, former CEO of the WB Network, who sold his youth-focused digital studio Generate to multichannel network Alloy Digital, "[S]cale seems to be very critical to get people comfortable with increasing their spend in this space and make our business work as a larger enterprise."[1] Microsoft helped Machinima grow from a network of "produsers"—game users who produced content from their play—to a television network with high-production-value programming.

Halo was a key moment in the growth of so-called multichannel networks (MCNs), media distributors who acquire or license multiple YouTube channels. The Machinima network grew by taking advantage of the scale it achieved by signing thousands of both amateur and professional creators of gameplay videos. By 2014, gameplay videos reached over three billion monthly views. YouTube's most popular creator in 2016, Felix Kjellberg (aka PewDiePie), made them for over fifty million subscribers, the first channel to reach that number.[2] Machinima's gameplay video vertical, Respawn, inaugurated in 2009, was one of the first of such ventures, reaching one billion views by 2013.[3] Indie producers supplied nearly all the content on Respawn and throughout the Machinima network. A few grossed over $100,000 a year from a cut of the in-stream ad revenue. But most creators did not make nearly as much and signed away ownership of their videos to Machinima. By aggregating creators' audiences and their intellectual property (IP), Machinima reached millions, generating billions of monthly views.

Given these conditions, why did gameplay video creators sign up? The multichannel network offered some services to users: marketing and promotion of their work, better ad rates (CPMs, cost-per-mille or one thousand impressions), audience-management tools, production resources, and help orchestrating deals with Hollywood studios. It made sense for Machinima to invest in talent development, since it also took a cut of their revenue. It also made sense for the MCN to have talent compete for resources and attention. As its monthly views broke three billion, the network instituted a tiered user system called "Level Up Talent."[4] Only 2 percent of Machinima's producers received "Black Level" treatment: their own talent manager to orchestrate advertising deals and product development. The more popular and professional a creator's work was, the more marketing and development they received.

Yet *Halo* marked Machinima's shift away from developing indie creators toward courting corporate Hollywood studios and game developers with fan-proven intellectual properties. In 2012, the network launched a vertical, Prime, to brand series with the highest production and intellectual-property value, notably franchise extensions like *Knight Rider*, *Battlestar Galactica: Blood and Chrome*, *Mortal Kombat: Legacy* and *Legacy 2*, and *Street Fighter: Assassin's Fist* and *Resurrection*, all of which reportedly amassed three hundred million views.[5] Even as Machinima attracted eight-figure investments from venture capital firms and Google, indie-friendly Respawn felt the brunt of the company's successive layoffs after *Halo*'s premiere.[6] By 2014, fans noticed the changes, particularly after the departure of Respawn's founding creators.[7] Viewership declined, and in 2015, Machinima closed Respawn.[8] At the same time, Machinima focused on relaunching Prime "to find real talent in our network and get them to the place where they can deliver those tentpoles to us," vice president of programming and development Andy Shapiro told *Tubefilter*.[9] The focus on developing "tentpoles" (high-value productions that galvanize fan loyalty, often franchise properties) from top talent reflected Machinima's struggle to compete with legacy TV networks and studios in developing intellectual property. Indeed, in 2014, Microsoft Studios stopped creating web original programming altogether and set up *Halo* in development at premium subscription channel Showtime.[10] Meanwhile, in 2016, YouTube finally decided to organize and curate gaming content, launching a gaming site organizing over twenty-five thousand creators and a live-streaming option to compete with Twitch, then owned by Amazon. After receiving investments from Google and venture capital firms, Machinima faced a buy-out offer by Warner Bros. in 2016.

Machinima's quixotic quest to become "the HBO for gaming video"[11] forces us to question how corporate web TV distributors use indie production and networked distribution to achieve scale and how this pursuit disadvantages indie producers, their fans, and even their sponsors. Gameplay videos were an indie innovation. YouTube creators of gameplay videos could build large fan bases faster and at lower cost than producers of more complex scripted narratives. Game interfaces provided the set, costumes, cinematography, and camera. One user could direct and act the story or narrate instructions. Game fans eagerly consumed fictional and informational machinima videos. By modifying existing intellectual property published by game corporations, indie producers created both a new art form and the demand for it. As Hector Postigo notes,

> Video gameplay commentators engage with the notion of independence as a "promise" for a particular form of creative labor. Video game commentators have come to call themselves "directors," the term denoting their transition from hobbyist—providing footage of their gaming experience on YouTube—to conscientious craftsperson—creating and purposefully formulating a novel entertainment experience. . . . In other words their form of independence did not reproduce the narratives produced by established media players, but borrowed them as raw material for their own form of entry into the industry. They created a whole new ideal of what the video game experience can be: a spectator sport.[12]

By bridging spectatorship and production, gameplay commentators made YouTube careers out of a hobby, growing communities into audiences for views and revenue. Consistent fan attention professionalized their creative expression. Seeing these innovations, corporations seized the fruits of this labor—fan attention and aspirations of creative ownership—to gain access to a greater share of the television advertising market.

In their quest for big investments, licensing, and sponsorship deals, corporate web TV networks like Machinima are increasingly marginalizing the indie creators who helped them grow in favor of larger players who could fund programming at legacy television's scale. But multichannel networks were not alone in extracting value from independent producers and fans of web TV. Cable TV networks like Comedy Central and IFC licensed indie productions cheaply to fill official websites with original programming, test new programs before transitioning them to cable, and give advertisers another space to promote their brands. Advertising-supported corporate networks like Yahoo and AOL primarily worked with Hollywood veterans to market web TV to large user bases.

Directly funded by TV fans, subscription networks like Netflix and Amazon were most successful in growing the web TV market initially but worked almost exclusively with Hollywood studios and producers. This made sense, since companies like Netflix financed original productions directly from subscribers who paid for access to large libraries of legacy programming. By some measures, this development system worked. Netflix's *House of Cards* took the mantle of the web's first blockbuster hit until *Orange Is the New Black* surpassed its audience, both estimated in millions.[13] From 2012, when Netflix and Amazon announced original programming plans, until 2014, both companies' stocks grew dramatically, reaching all-time highs. Yet original series from corporate subscription networks did not reflect the incredible diversity of indie web original production, where new genres like gameplay videos were in constant creation and where producers historically marginalized by their race, gender, and sexuality had greater control over their narratives.

The growth of the web TV market opened opportunities for indie creators, but inequalities persist. From the 2000s to the 2010s, for low cost, indie creators supplied open networks with original, native programming, taking advantage of the creative freedom to forge meaningful connections among creative producers, fan communities, and (eventually) brands as sponsors. Corporations looking to leverage web distribution to disrupt the television business harnessed these innovations to enrich Hollywood studios and their producers, corporate advertisers, media and marketing conglomerates, and deep-pocketed investors. They sold the idea of "open TV innovation" without investing in those who had made it open. In their book-length study of major online video distributors, Stuart Cunningham and Jon Silver found the market slowly maturing, as independents continued to produce great programs but distribution oligopolies coalesced outside of Hollywood: "[R]eference to industry history indicates that, like all large-scale corporations, they are likely to use market power to seek to limit competition and corral users inside walled gardens."[14] Tech innovation in content access and delivery drove corporate web TV development.[15] Ad-supported networks like AOL and Yahoo used algorithms to manage and profit from ad sales and fan activity at scale; user-generated networks like YouTube used algorithms at the expense of developing producers, ceding this function to multichannel networks; and subscription-supported networks like Netflix and Amazon used algorithms to manage consumer demand, harnessing these efficiencies to enrich Hollywood studios and producers. Understanding how these larger players pursued market dominance puts this book's story of how independents opened TV into sharp relief:

innovation led by indie operators during the 2000s and 2010s might have just been a moment in transition before evolving technologies, policies, and business practices allowed big data-driven distributors to solidify control over the way we access TV and who gets to produce it.

Scholars are only beginning to understand how big data and algorithms affect cultural production and distribution. In this chapter I contribute preliminary insights to our understanding of what Ted Striphas calls "algorithmic culture," in which algorithms may be privatizing the way we assess and understand social dynamics, or "the forms of decision-making and contestation that comprise the ongoing struggle to determine the values, practices and artifacts—the culture, as it were—of specific social groups."[16] Examining the actions of corporations developing television for large-scale networked distribution offers a glimpse into the "knowledge logics" of algorithms and big data. This portends, in Tarleton Gillespie's words, "where and in what ways the introduction of algorithms into human knowledge practices may have political ramifications."[17] I consider how big data and its management change web TV network operations, the cultural and political consequences of what Philip Napoli describes as the institutional response to algorithms: "[W]e see strong parallels between the functioning of algorithms and established understandings of the functioning of institutions."[18] I find that the growth of web TV production marks a shift away from independent producers and marginalized communities to corporate intermediaries acting like legacy TV distributors: securing "big buys" from investors, sponsors, and studios. Their strategies raise vexing questions about the ethics and value of adapting and updating mass media frameworks to networked distribution. Internet protocols facilitate many-to-many connections, which foster innovation. But what happens when control over those connections shifts away from the indie producers who facilitate their creation to those who aggregate and profit from them?

Scaling Sales: Selling Masses of Producers and Fans to Brands

Many of TV's newest corporate distributors—chiefly AOL, Yahoo, and Hulu in this period—developed programs to attract brands' advertising campaign funds away from legacy networks. To succeed in a competitive, concentrated U.S. media market, they needed scale. Corporate advertisers historically want large audiences to remember their brands and buy their products. Before the introduction of cable and the Internet, this was relatively easy. Nearly every American home had a television set, and viewers had limited options. Cable channels complicated this system, but not until after 2000 did a critical mass of cable channels attract enough advertising to develop full slates of original programming. As soon as cable networks started to compete meaningfully with broadcast networks in ratings and financing, new competitors sprouted online to compete for viewer attention and corporate advertising funds.

The web offers opportunities but also unique challenges to new television distributors. By the mid- to late 2000s, a majority of Americans had access to broadband, but their attention was spread across the millions of content publishers.[19] Since the 1960s, advertisers have been accustomed to paying for attention through commercials or spots. Yet online, publishers reported, viewers spent minutes, not hours, on web pages. Video addressed this problem. By 2014, viewers spent over five hours a month on Google's sites, the bulk on YouTube. Other networks like Facebook, AOL, and Yahoo averaged about an hour; still, according to Nielsen, American adults spent over four and a half hours *every day* watching live and time-shifted legacy television.[20] This, along with problematic metrics for digital video, is the big reason why legacy networks continued to command revenue across broadcast and cable at the beginning of the networked era.

But advertisers were concerned about viewer attention to TV commercials, given the plethora of new media options. Increasingly they doubted whether the time they pay for on linear television was worth the high cost. Digital networking addressed advertisers' concerns over consumer attention by targeting them individually at the moment they accessed the video, instead of taking up space in programs where viewers may or may not be in the room, let alone watching the TV screen. This presumed efficiency made digital distribution attractive to brands frustrated with passive or elusive television fan attention. Yet, the immense volume of digital information and entertainment produced its own issues with attention and efficiency, suppressing prices for content producers and distributors. Rates were lower than for TV because intermediaries like advertising networks and exchanges served millions of ad impressions in seconds, decreasing the value of any one ad and any one viewer's attention. Meanwhile, publishers of all types of media—news, social media platforms, search engines, and web video networks—were competing with each other by selling their ad supply and audiences on the same market. There was not enough demand for the enormous supply of media products, ads, and audiences online. Advertising rates online were lower than on legacy television—approximately seven dollars per one thousand online impressions versus twenty-five dollars for linear television—in the early 2010s.[21]

Low advertising rates pushed web TV networks toward big data so they could aggregate online impressions, the unit of audience attention. Web TV publishers pursued different strategies to achieve scale. Facebook became a major video distributor by hosting the videos its one billion users uploaded to newsfeeds alongside status updates about their lives; by 2017 the social media giant moved into live video and programming from the likes of *Buzzfeed* and MTV (Nicole Byer). Companies like Yahoo and Google attracted hundreds of millions of users by offering search services to make navigating the web more efficient. Multichannel networks signed up thousands of producers who did the work of attracting millions of fans. Subscription networks offered paying viewers access to large libraries of content and information, which required billions in licensing fees to maintain.

Each scaling strategy made the new digital distributor a singular destination for audiences to access information and entertainment, but each one's strategy—search algorithms, content curation, and licensing—could be copied by competitors. The power of original programming, then, was its ability to "brand" a network and encourage viewer loyalty. Branding is a cultural practice, and scripted stories convey narratives about culture and society, giving the distributor its own identity that audiences can understand and connect to.[22] The more a network invests in programming, the more attention it can cultivate. Web TV distributors were aggressive in their monetization strategies so they could offer the most "high-quality" programs to users and gain an early foothold in the open TV market. In the process, corporate web TV networks betrayed the constituencies who historically created the most value in the open TV market—fans and independent producers.

Selling Fans at Scale: Up-Front Financing for Real-Time Bidding on Our Attention

How do you replicate liner TV networks' power to sell audiences in a networked TV market? In 2013, AOL debuted a new strategy for financing web television at scale: "programmatic" advertising, or what the company called merging "culture and code." Programmatic merged automated ad sales built on networked distribution's many-to-many flows with one-to-many campaign planning, the hallmark of legacy TV upfronts. In programmatic, advertising agencies and marketing conglomerates identified the types of users brands want to see ads and the specific times they want the ads delivered. Marketing and advertising firms analyzed data on users that they received from publishers (like Hulu or AOL), advertising networks, and exchanges, and, with proprietary software, constructed reportedly anonymous user identities by tracking them across sites.[23] In one scenario, advertising and marketing firms negotiated with publishers like AOL the price for their audiences and served the ads when the user visited the site at the right time. For instance, cold medication brand Zicam made programmatic buys for flu season, targeting users who searched for symptoms or broadcast feelings on social media. "This business requires us to be data driven," Jordan Rednor, CEO of Zicam's creative agency, Protagonist, told the *Wall Street Journal*.[24] Television fans and their private behavior were the data. Programmatic buying privileged advertisers' demands for user information at the expense of the affective or cultural desires driving users to sites. Because it was designed for advertisers, marketing firms predicted that programmatic would grow significantly; *eMarketer* estimated that almost half the display (banner) market, or $10 billion, and 12 percent of the digital video market, or $700 million, would be delivered using programmatic buying.[25]

AOL was uniquely positioned to bridge the legacy and networked processes of ad sales, which explains why it was eventually purchased by telecommunications giant Verizon. Like broadcast and cable networks, new TV distributors produced and licensed original series while also selling their audiences to advertisers. Unlike the broadcast and cable channels whose audiences were rated by Nielsen, an independent auditor, publishers like AOL had their own data and ad technologies to manage data on fans. These technologies were called demand- and supply-side platforms (DSP and SSP). DSPs catered to brands and ad agencies who bought ads, and SSPs catered to distributors like AOL who sold ad space. DSPs and SSPs managed the buying and selling of our attention, negotiating the distributor's supply of ad impressions with the advertiser's demand for data on our identities and behavior. The distributors' supply-side platforms organized user identities and set rate floors (at a certain price point, a TV distributor would rather reserve space for its own ads). Demand-side platforms found the cheapest, most accurate users for brands to target. An extension of advertising and video networks and exchanges, DSPs and SSPs were vital parts of the sociotechnical system of networked television distribution: "[T]hey play an essential role in determining where and when television content is available—and to whom—one that aligns neatly with more traditional concerns of media scholars about the terms on which we access and participate in our culture."[26] In 2013 AOL purchased Adap.TV, a platform for the buying and selling of video impressions (units of attention), for just over $400 million, and AOL quickly rose to the top of video ad sales, serving roughly three billion video ad impressions in a month. Historically, demand- and supply-side platforms competed and kept prices low, but AOL's Adap.TV functioned on both sides, allowing brands and marketers to buy ad inventory from AOL more efficiently.

Despite industry-wide uncertainty over what constitutes a "view" of an advertisement[27] and distrust over platforms' transparency, programmatic buying soared. At its second annual Programmatic Upfront in 2014, AOL CEO Tim Armstrong reported a nearly tenfold increase in programmatic sales, with over one third of all ad sales coming from programmatic buying.[28] AOL moved more aggressively into content licensing, promotion, and monetization, forging a deal with NBC to license its broadcast, cable, and web programs, and a ten-year deal with Microsoft taking on its search engine and ad sales.[29] Then Verizon purchased AOL for over $4 billion, largely on the promise of its advertising technology and the potential profits of combining that with Verizon's consumer data (real-time location, demographic). "That will be our key sustainable competitive advantage for a long time to come because it's a persistent data record that not only provides me with information around content consumption but also the context that somebody's in and the behaviors they have," AOL's chief technology officer Seth Dempsey told *Advertising Age* shortly after the Verizon-AOL merger closed.[30] The following year, Verizon also purchased Yahoo.

Unfortunately, AOL had not produced a compelling original series, and its advertising revenue paled in comparison to Google's and Facebook's. AOL still struggled to sell its inventory, despite immense scale. Networked television distributors needed guaranteed viewership of ads to grow the video market. Amid industry-wide skepticism over the accuracy of online view counting, releasing culturally relevant programming could assuage brands' concerns about the value of online video. If the shows were innovative and engaging, viewers must be paying attention, no matter the precise mechanics of ad delivery. But AOL was neither Amazon, home to art house directors, nor YouTube, home to indie innovators. Armstrong's Programmatic Upfront presentation boasted *Huffington Post Live*—a live news channel featuring interviews with individuals too "niche" for cable—and reality show *Candidly Nicole*, starring Nicole Ritchie, as AOL's signature programs. Unable to woo brands with programming, AOL orchestrated a snazzy event in Tribeca on a par with what marketers were used to at the upfronts: personal invites from AOL Platforms' CEO Bob Lord, concierge and car services, live music in gallery-like event spaces with floor-to-ceiling windows, and luxury food, including oysters, truffles, and cheeses, with some services extended to executive assistants for ease of communication.[31]

For years corporate web networks produced glitzy events to convince marketers to invest in online video. In lieu of robust brand investment for producing and marketing big shows with high production values like the major TV and film distributors, web networks needed both independents (to show real connections to fans) and established producers (to confer mainstream legitimacy) to make the case for big data television. The tensions between indie creativity and mass attention were visible at digital marketing events like the NewFronts, started in 2008 as a space for publishers to present programming to brands and marketers in New York. When I attended in 2012, lead participants included Hulu, YouTube, MSN (Microsoft Network), Yahoo, AOL, and Digitas. Each touted Hollywood stars first, then independent series creators. Hosted by comedian J. B. Smoove, the 2012 NewFronts featured Heidi Klum— who spoke to a largely uninterested audience about her AOL show—

Kristin Chenoweth, and *CSI* creator Anthony Zuiker, who belted out an ironic "I hate television!" at the beginning of his presentation. Yet the day began by showcasing indie entrepreneurs, including a panel with Chenoweth, Felicia Day, whose *Guild* was entering its fifth season with Microsoft, and YouTube's most successful makeup guru, Michelle Phan. Then CNN anchor Piers Morgan interviewed the two women about their success, which they attributed directly to fans connecting with their authenticity. Day said authenticity is so important that she "guards it":

> I know my audience. . . . My fans will be always serviced. I always do things with them in mind. And I reach a very high-tech, gamer audience. My show literally fills a room that networks can't at Comic-Con. And this is literally through bare bones, no PR, no anything! Just being on amazing platforms that reach audiences.

Here, Day bases her success on a deep connection to her fans, free from the pressures of corporate marketing. As I demonstrated in the second chapter, as an owner of her intellectual property, she was being honest. The sincerity of her labor inspired fan support and attention, empowering her to protect it. Yet Microsoft was still interested in using Day for public relations, cutting a commercial starring Day introducing Microsoft to marketers that morning. Throughout the day, the New-Fronts programmers featured trailers for web originals, including some independents like *Perks*, *The Lizzie Bennet Diaries*, and *Downsized*, perhaps due to the fact that the event was coproduced by *Downsized* creator Daryn Strauss, who also founded Digital Chick TV to promote women as web producers. Indie creators were symbolically important to pitching web series development as a viable alternative to television marketing, because they invested time in experimenting with and producing for fans via the web.

By contrast, panelists representing NewFronts corporate partners touted their scale and the Hollywood producers making their shows. YouTube's Jamie Byrne, global head of content strategy, spoke of the site moving beyond "individual videos" to "channelizing the platform" for its vast audience: "We're going to go from hundreds of channels to thousands of channels . . . serving underserved audiences." Yahoo's head of originals and video programing Erin McPherson touted the network's seven hundred million total users and their "blockbuster" strategy, releasing postapocalyptic dramas from Zuiker and Jerry Bruckheimer (*Cybergeddon*) and Tom Hanks (*Electric City*). McPherson termed this "TV on steroids." Zuiker compared Yahoo's scale to that of billboards: "Once you have the ability to control traffic, the promotability over the course of time and power of that reach far outweighs a billboard on Sunset [Boulevard]."[32] Despite being promoted to tens of millions of users daily, Zuiker's *Cybergeddon* did not catch on. Instead, Yahoo's subsequent successes relied on riffs on and direct purchases of legacy television: in *Burning Love*, a spoof of *The Bachelor* produced by Ben Stiller; in hiring Katie Couric to host new news programs; and in picking up the sixth season of NBC's *Community*. Hulu's Andy Forssell, then vice president of content, who would serve briefly as Hulu's CEO, focused the most on creators, promoting series from film and television veterans Richard Linklater, Seth Meyers, and Morgan Spurlock. AOL's Janey Balis, senior vice president and head of sales strategy, marketing, and partnerships, discussed the *Huffington Post* Streaming Network's twelve hours of live daily programming, its one million daily Facebook referrals, and *Huffington Post* receiving its 150 millionth comment that very day. Three years later, at the 2015 NewFronts, AOL promised forty-five times more episodes than in 2014, a whopping thirty-six thousand, mostly, it appeared, by repackaging *Huffington Post Live* programs and soliciting content from citizen journalists.[33]

TV fans had greater choice and control, and corporate web networks used their freedom from linear cable to meet fans' demands and needs—or at least they claimed to do so. Chiefly, they pitched open TV as access to their programs across platforms, all the time, to capture as much attention as possible for metrics and data. The flexibility and openness of web TV was undeniably attractive for fans, and legacy networks were compelled to follow. Web distribution eventually lured legacy networks like HBO, CBS, FX, and NBC, which created "over-the-top" (Internet-delivered, cable subscription–free) destinations and charged users for unlimited access to programming. HBO offered access to nearly all its programming, CBS to new shows, and NBC to its comedy archive. Web networks like Yahoo and AOL, long beholden to new media users, already offered these services and touted them. Before the sixth-season premiere of *Community* through the Yahoo Screen app on devices like Roku, viewers saw a brief reminder of every platform on which they could see *Community*: online at screen.yahoo.com; on Roku, Apple TV, and Xbox devices; and on mobile devices through the Yahoo Screen app.

Freed from the linear cable line-up and eager for data, web TV distributors were quite accommodating to users, whose attention they needed to aggregate and sell for profit. But large ad-supported networks took shortcuts to attain mass audiences. Finding independent producers too difficult to develop and market to corporate brands and new fans, companies like Yahoo sought legacy properties like *Community*, whose sizable, attentive fan base and independent-minded producers were recognizable to television's biggest funders. To secure these series and their fans, networks like Yahoo gave some creators greater control over narratives. In an interview with *Vulture*, *Community* creator Dan Harmon sang Yahoo's praises:

> You're working for a company that bothered to buy the show, where at NBC, it was always the problem child. There was a clear, sometimes even spoken feeling about *Community* at NBC after year one that it was a show that they wanted to either "solve" or get rid of. . . . [B]ecause Yahoo is so supportive of the show, I have to admit that my anxiety is now more about whether or not I'm going to let them down.[34]

Harmon's creative license depended heavily on Yahoo's need to attract and sell his fans, which he got through NBC.

Would Yahoo have continued to guarantee creative ownership to other show producers? The answer hinges on the critical question of whether web-based, networked distribution is fundamentally different from linear, network distribution: whether the decentered nature of digital networking disempowers cultural distributors as it empowers creative producers and those who support their work consistently, the fans. But Harmon was already empowered by the industry; despite his gripes about NBC, *Community* remained one of network TV's most experimental shows, allowing Harmon the creative time and marketing support to build strong associations with millions of fans. Web networks have not invested in web-grown producers in the same way, despite their many attentive fan bases.

The open TV market challenged the ad-supported business model through the mid-2010s. Licensing original programming for web distribution proved prohibitively expensive for Yahoo, and the company shuttered Yahoo Screen and debuted Yahoo View in 2016. Yahoo View took over Hulu's model of re-airing recent legacy TV episodes free and ad supported. Meanwhile Hulu, following the success of Netflix and Amazon, transitioned to a subscription-only service. Hulu's owners in Disney (ABC), Comcast (NBC), and 21st Century Fox (Fox) injected $750 million into the platform in 2013, allowing it to order series like *Casual* from newcomer Zander Lehmann, along with the *The Mindy Project* and *11.22.63* from veterans Mindy Kaling and Bridget Carpenter, respectively. Yet Hulu's biggest moves were securing licensing deals for legacy TV shows *Seinfeld* and *Empire* in 2016 and announcing a "cable package" the next year, distributing legacy channels live via the web.[35] Hulu's development slate, in terms of the status of its producers and the format of its narratives, started to look a lot like that of its legacy owners. "[Hulu's owners] have accepted the notion that the bigger we can build the show, the better it is likely to do on Hulu, not the opposite," Gary Newman, cochairman of Fox Television Group, told *Variety*.[36] Legacy television's inequalities persisted in an open TV market where the pursuit of fan attention at scale trumped developing new and diverse affective connections between a broader base of producers and their fans.

Selling Producers at Scale: Depressing the Value of Indie Labor and Fans for Profit

With so many producers making online video and brands reluctant to invest in them, corporate web distributors amassed large swathes to profit from advertising or fan subscription at a large scale. Nowhere was this dynamic more visible than with YouTube. YouTube's very name implies empowering creators and their fans, but the company could not avoid the challenges of scaling their labor and attention. Some of YouTube's most seasoned and respected partners criticized the company in public for not supporting "YouTubers" or "YouTube creators"—the stars, producers, and entrepreneurs who started their own channels and coaxed tens of millions of people to subscribe. They griped that YouTube had become more focused on raising revenue from the fruits of their labor than on investing in those who supply the platform with content.

By aggregating videos from millions of producers, YouTube profited from their labor without having to invest in it. Creators continually labored for views. In summer 2013, investor Jason Calacanis penned a much-discussed diatribe against YouTube's nearly fifty-fifty revenue split between creators and itself: "Since YouTube doesn't have to create any content, just aggregate it, they don't need to worry about the individual profitability of any one brand. Things can be dying and soaring and going sideways throughout their ecosystem, but as long as they have a ton of traffic and control the relationships with advertisers, they win."[37] Here, Calacanis identifies the advantages of scale in digital distribution. In YouTube's earliest years, small groups of producers could develop a following. YouTube was interested in growing the network and showcased work from indie creators without large subscriber bases. In 2008, I spoke to YouTube entertainment editor David McMillan, when one of his jobs was curating work for the site's homepage. He spoke of YouTube as actively nurturing connections between new TV producers and fans: "We try to add some diversity. . . . We think there are videos that don't go viral but are worthy of being seen. . . . YouTube, when it does work well, is a place for people to communicate back and forth." However, even then McMillan saw production-value standards rising: "The early vloggers probably had the benefit of there being not a lot out there . . . [Now] you're just competing with so much content." With more producers investing their own time to produce for YouTube, they increased standards and volume, decreasing YouTube's interest in any one channel. Seven years later, YouTuber Akilah Hughes critiqued YouTube's lack of interest in its black stars, from its choices for its first global marketing campaign (including Vietnamese makeup guru Michelle Phan; Latina Bethany Mota, and white Rosanna Pansino); poor comment moderation ("subscriber gap"); and lack of diversity at its annual convention, VidCon, where one star, Adande Thorne, held twenty-four hours of fan meet-and-greets outside the convention center because he was not invited.[38] Realizing that they had forsaken smaller, diverse creators,

YouTube started mentoring and production programs for black- and woman-identified creators in 2016.[39]

One of those early vloggers, and a VidCon cofounder, Hank Green, described the climate as YouTubers against YouTube, MCNs, and advertisers: "[They] all want viewership consolidated. It's easier to buy and sell a few large properties than many small ones. These institutions control how a HUGE number of dollars are spent so there is less incentive to create niche content."[40] Green, who with his brother John founded the Vlogbrothers channel offering educational content for millions of passionate fans of John's young adult novels, contrasts the pursuit of mass profits with the challenges indie creators face attracting fans, whose attention is valuable to advertisers. This was not Green's first critique of how YouTube managed the creator-fan relationship. He publicly criticized YouTube for adjusting the way it counts subscribers and openly advocated for creators to stop relying on advertising and pursue direct fan sponsorship.[41]

Creator discontent with YouTube grew. After penning his screed against YouTube's lopsided ad-revenue split with creators, Calacanis proposed a YouTube Bill of Rights to protect creators, including more transparency on who was advertising on YouTube, a better revenue split from AdSense (Google's advertising network), and more investment from Google in its creators. In 2016 Green started the Internet Creators Guild as a nonprofit to advocate for web producers. The Vlogbrothers even started an off-YouTube platform called Subbable, offering fans the chance to directly support creators (it eventually sold to its bigger competitor Patreon). That year YouTube, for its part, started offering paid channels for fans to support monthly, but only to select, corporate users at first. The early results of this premium strategy were mixed, with a number of partners publicly expressing their disappointment at fan adoption of individual subscriptions.[42] The debut of competitors like Patreon, VHX, Vimeo, and Vessel cast doubt on whether YouTube offered the service to enough channels in time. In 2015, seeing the market shift rapidly, YouTube relaunched YouTube Red to allow fans to subscribe to YouTube's own original programming, produced at the length of legacy TV programs.

As it worked to consolidate, YouTube fractured, first losing creators to rival aggregators like Vessel, Vimeo, social media platforms, and, most significantly, new start-ups in multichannel networks. Multichannel networks stepped into the online video market to do what YouTube avoided: manage creators' careers and help them sell to brands and advertisers. MCNs pursued scale by aggregating independent producers and their fans. Denise Mann shows how this pursuit of scale exploited independents to attract Silicon Valley and Hollywood investors.[43] In 2009, firms invested less than $100 million in multichannel networks; by the end of 2012 investments jumped to almost $500 million.[44] By 2014, $1.65 billion had been invested, matching the amount Google spent on YouTube just eight years prior.[45] Creators like Hank Green decried this escalation of investment as losing sight of the independent spirit that attracted fans and independent producers to YouTube in the first place. Of course, some creators had leverage as they sought value from YouTube, MCNs, and major brands. As pay-off for their labor, YouTubers grew their subscriber bases as MCNs rose to power to aggregate their fans; by 2016, analytics company VidStatsx estimated that at least two thousand channels had over one million subscribers.[46] Moreover, the growth of competing social media platforms, particularly Twitter, Snapchat, Instagram, Facebook, and Vine, gave YouTubers alternative platforms to leverage fans' attention. Ultimately, though, distributors had the upper hand because they aggregated creators and their fans, but fan loyalty rested with creators first, so both YouTube and the MCNs needed to support these sincere connections to continue to profit from their labor. This tension fueled controversies as producers and distributors pursued capital in a constantly changing market.

YouTube's staggering growth, coupled with its lack of investment in independents, enriched multichannel networks. We can find evidence of this through the stories of the site's most high-profile creators. Known for his viral video commentary show =3, Ray William Johnson became the most-subscribed YouTuber in 2011 with almost four million subscribers, surpassing Korean American comedian Ryan Higa. Johnson held the spot throughout 2012, growing his channel to six million subscribers. Even as his popularity grew, competitors were angling for his spot. Competition and the need for production support led Johnson to sign with Maker Studios two years earlier. Maker offered marketing support, audience development, and talent management. But in the fall of 2012, Johnson left Maker, claiming that the multichannel network wanted him to sign a contract giving Maker 40 percent of his AdSense revenue and over 50 percent of =3's intellectual property, among other allegations: "Youtube-based networks are built around exploiting Youtube channels for profit, and I totally understand that."[47] Johnson realized that he gave away too much of his value for the marketing and development support multichannel networks offered.

In January 2013, Ian Hecox and Anthony Padilla's dude comedy channel SMOSH, which sold to MCN Alloy Digital, surpassed Johnson as the most-subscribed channel on YouTube. Eager to find a new backer for his work, Johnson entered a partnership with independent network Blip, itself transitioning away from curating independent web series to promoting creators with bigger fan bases and cheaper productions. In an ironic twist, MCN Maker Studios then purchased Blip for less than $10 million. One year later, Disney purchased Maker Studios for $675 million. By 2015, Johnson was the twenty-seventh most-subscribed YouTuber and back to the place he'd tried to escape. Maker's PewDiePie took the top spot, with the top thirty comprised of MCNs like Machinima and VEVO (its channels for studio musicians like Rihanna and Justin Bieber), a sprinkling of long-producing YouTubers like SMOSH and the Fine Brothers (represented by Fullscreen), and a handful of indies.

How did Maker, a studio with less name recognition, beat indie heavyweight Johnson in attracting fans? Like Machinima before them, Maker built its network on signing up as many creators as possible, leveraging scale to increase its chances of finding a hit. At the time of the Disney acquisition, Maker Studios reported 5.5 billion views a month across 55,000 channels.[48] Disney purchased Maker for its "great access to data and algorithms you wouldn't have unless you had volume," CEO Bob Iger told *Variety*.[49] Even though Maker described its pursuit of scale as empowering YouTubers, nowhere did Iger mention the indie creators who built Maker into the "United Artists" for online video, as the *New York Times*, the *Wrap*, and then chief operating officer (and eventual head of Maker) Courtney Holt all described it.[50] By contrast, Johnson built his fan base by covering independent YouTube productions. Commentary shows, extending enduring TV genres like "fail" videos (think *America's Funniest Home Videos*), were very popular on YouTube. Competition in the genre was stiff, but fans for offbeat YouTube videos were plentiful.

Both Johnson and SMOSH benefited from starting their channels on YouTube when the site had fewer professionally produced videos and did not invest in multichannel networks. Early on, YouTube incentivized original production, starting with the 2007 partner program. Originally invitation-only, the partner program allowed creators the option of putting ads on their videos for a majority cut of the display and video advertising revenue, split with YouTube. SMOSH and Maker Studios cofounder Lisa Donovan were among the very first partners. It was not until 2012 that YouTube opened the partner program to all YouTube creators. Digital advertising rates were low, so partners needed to attract millions of views to make a living. By the time anyone could join, partners had a small suite of advertising technologies with different ways to view ads (pre-roll, post-roll, skippable, or banner) with different price points for each one. Creators who worked assiduously to populate their channels with original programming could attract enough fan attention and generate six-figure incomes from their attention to ads. Most creators made negligible amounts. Multichannel networks stepped in, offering creators better rates and more program development support.

To stem rising discontent from its reported ten thousand partners, YouTube decided in 2010 to create a Partner Grants program to directly fund "eligible partners," based largely on metrics of scale "such as video views, subscribers, growth rate, audience engagement and production expertise."[51] The program offered creators $1,000 to buy equipment at B&H Photo, up to $5 million.[52] The program saw few hits. Yet among a select group of first recipients was the musical parody series Key of Awesome, the marquee channel of Next New Networks (NNN), one of YouTube's first multichannel networks, which YouTube purchased months later for a reported $50 million. Unlike the MCNs it preceded, NNN managed comparatively few channels, just sixty at the time of its acquisition, which cumulatively garnered two billion views and six million subscribers.[53] Its success developing channels like Key of Awesome and Barely Political (producer of famed viral video, "Obama Girl") stemmed from its nurturing of a small group of independents in its Next New Creators program. In buying NNN, YouTube found a shortcut to developing its base of independent producers. Under Google, NNN spearheaded the YouTube Next program, where small groups of producers received production support from YouTube; workshops at Google's New York and Los Angeles headquarters; the Creator Playbook, a comprehensive guide to YouTube best practices for producers; and the programming and production resources at Google's first studio in Culver City, YouTube Space LA.

Soon after, in 2012, YouTube pledged a bigger investment in channels through its Original Channels Initiative, its first attempt to invest in wide-scale production. Google selected one hundred channels to receive $100 million to support further production; Google pledged an additional $300 million the following year to provide marketing support to the channels. After much fanfare, including top billing at the 2012 NewFronts, YouTube shut down and removed all mention of the program two years later, in 2013.[54] The program was flawed from the start. First, only a sprinkling of indie YouTube creators were represented, including the Fine Brothers (for their transmedia series *MyMusic*), the Vlogbrothers, Michelle Phan, Felicia Day (Geek & Sundry), Philip DeFranco (*Sourcefed*), and EQAL (departing from its scripted beginnings in *lonelygirl15* in favor of reality lifestyle programming). Many of the channels were not "homegrown" YouTubers but rather mainstream media corporations interested in increasing their online video presence, including Electus (from former NBC cochair Ben Silverman and InterActiveCorp), Hearst Magazines, Meredith Corporation, Lionsgate, Red Bull, *Slate*, and WWE. The rest of the channels were multichannel networks—Machinima, Maker, Clevver, Big Frame, Alloy—and celebrities largely unfamiliar with YouTube channel development—Pharrell Williams, Shaquille O'Neal, Madonna, Tony Hawk, and Amy Poehler (*Smart Girls at the Party*). Most significantly, the Original Channels Initiative funding was not direct investment in production but an advance of future advertising sales. Channels had to generate a lot of views at low ad rates to continue getting funding. Most missed their targets.

YouTube focused its smaller NNN investment on raising production standards and developing best practices for a slightly broader base of creators. When I visited YouTube Space LA in 2013, I met its head, Liam Collins, former NNN chief operating officer. A bright and spacious lobby featured a giant video screen, couches, and tables. Young people moved about excitedly, carrying equipment at times but mostly talking to each other. Collins said he worked with Google to make the space welcoming to creators, from offering regular workshops and classes to making sure security was as hands-off as possible:

> After we got acquired, we immediately started advocating for this. Because at Next New Networks we always had some production space. Our feeling was that we always want to be friendly to talent. And one way we can do that is by being closer to them. And really the only way to be authentic when you're trying to give talent and channel builders advice on how to build their channels is to be doing it yourself. We came in advocating that if YouTube wanted to move more in that direction of being able to counsel its creators on how to build their channels we would need some production facilities of our own.

We can see glimpses of Collins's rhetoric of nurturing creators manifest in the inaugural group of twenty-three YouTubers offered access to the studio. The Space received residency applications on an ongoing basis and judged applicants on their commitment to YouTube, their willingness to collaborate with other channels, and their resources (team, basic skills to complete their projects). When the YouTube Space opened, Freddie Wong and Dave Days, each with millions of subscribers, were its primary residents, but creators like Nikki Limo, with just thousands of subscribers, were also invited. When I met Limo she was editing a comedy series on racial profiling in acting. She spoke of the value of being in a professional studio that YouTube's top creators regularly visited: she collaborated with top YouTubers like KassemG and Grace Helbig in her show (without needing to pay). Collins noted that the open editing environment promoted learning: "When some members of my team and I were at Next New Networks we were YouTube partners, and one of the ways we found that people really learned from each other was by being in open space together," he said. The Space gave creators access to high-tech soundstages, green screens, and facilities for live programming.[55] Yet when I visited in 2013, the vast majority of the Space's soundstages were taken up by shooting for the second season of Freddie Wong's *Video Game High School*. YouTube did not announce the identities of the residents, so it was unclear to what degree Google was upholding more open access to its facilities, which have subsequently opened in London, Tokyo, and São Paolo.

By the time YouTube opened its Partner program and studio Space to the public, it had already missed a big opportunity to invest in and grow production on its platform, and investors chased MCNs and their YouTuber clients. An estimated two hundred multichannel networks were offering marketing and support for tens of thousands of creators.[56] Networks like Big Frame attracted creators by understanding their challenges producing independently for a vast network like YouTube: "These guys are starring in the video, doing the lighting, music, editing and uploading, and that's just what 20 percent of their time is spent on. . . . They have to be their own marketing company, as well," Big Frame cofounder Sarah Evershed told *USA Today*.[57] Big Frame made a name for itself by partnering its clients—among them comedian DeStorm Power and director Mike Diva—with big media companies like Disney, 20th Century Fox, and BBC America to support marketing campaigns. The company's cofounders, Evershed and Steve Raymond, were vocal opponents of malpractice among multichannel networks, and penned a "challenge" to their peers to value creators, fans, and sponsors over views. Multichannel networks' focus on leveraging scale led to "bad contracts," with low, fixed CPMs, no right of contract termination, and "unsustainable growth rates"—networks signing up hundreds of channels per month.[58] Penna and Raymond published this critique on the same day they launched a new initiative to brand Big Frame's top channels (of 160) as "Forefront," which *Variety* reporter Andrew Wallenstein characterized as a shift away from talent management to "marketing at scale."[59] Two years later, after taking on some debt, Big Frame and its three hundred channels with thirty-nine million subscribers sold for $15 million to youth-focused multichannel network AwesomenessTV; Awesomeness itself had been acquired by Steven Spielberg's DreamWorks Studios, which committed it to "aggressive growth," in direct opposition to Big Frame's mission of serving a small number of talented producers.[60]

Multichannel networks were best at serving top creators, whose large fan bases they could leverage to get meetings with major advertisers and Hollywood studios. The lengthy and complex process of negotiating deals in Hollywood could lead to big payoffs but also corruption. Collective Digital Studio, an offshoot of management firm the Collective, showed this in 2011 when it negotiated one of the biggest YouTube-to-TV deals licensing Dane Boedigheimer's *Annoying Orange* to cable channel Cartoon

Network. *The Annoying Orange* was a deceptively simple narrative series about an orange with a CGI face who annoys the fruits and vegetables around him; conceptually it recalled *Fred* by Lucas Cruikshank, who ran effects on his voice to sound like an annoying preteen. *Fred* ran on cable channel Nickelodeon for years as series and movies. As with Cruikshank before him, Boedigheimer's idea skyrocketed his channel to the top ten of YouTube's most subscribed, with two million subscribers and nearly one billion views at the time of the deal. The simple concept—one character, no serial plot—allowed Collective to license *The Annoying Orange* for commercials and other campaigns. Even as his YouTube channel fell in the rankings, Boedigheimer appeared in the press as a new media marvel.[61] Yet in 2014, Boedigheimer sued Collective for not paying any revenue from the licensing of *The Annoying Orange*; the suit alleged that the Collective was in financial ruin and did not have the funds to pay him.[62]

Focusing on top creators made sense for multichannel networks working to secure large investments and keep growing, but the practice made skeptics of many of YouTube's creators, who desperately sought production support. After MCN Revision3 sold to Discovery Communication for a reported $30 to $40 million, they worked to solidify their relationship with affiliated producer Philip DeFranco, who had been vlogging on YouTube since 2006. Revision3 paid him "six figures per month," most of which he reportedly invested back in his ventures.[63] A year after the Discovery deal, Revision3 purchased DeFranco Creative and installed him as a vice president. DeFranco signed because Revision3 had given him access to brand integration and ad sales: "[I]f you have 10,000 people in your network, how can you actually help them? The focus, it's not there. With Revision3, you don't have to go to a third party and [risk] getting ripped."[64] DeFranco clearly felt attended to by Revision3, enough to sign over the channels he spent seven years building. Yet as Revision3 courted DeFranco, it lost Benny and Rafi Fine, who left the network for Fullscreen months after the DeFranco acquisition. Fullscreen beat out Revision3 by offering direct production financing: "A handful of us have found these type of deals but they are very hard to come by, and not all of Fullscreen's competitors are trying to make those type of deals," Rafi Fine told *Variety*.[65] After joining Fullscreen, the Fine Brothers started producing the work of other creators, selling series to cable channels and developing a feature film.[66]

Usually reserved for top creators, production support is critical in an economy where independent producers must constantly create work to keep fan attention. Fullscreen made its name by offering some of this, representing leading YouTube stars, like violinist Lindsey Stirling and talk show host Michael Buckley, as a "helpful mediator between You-Tube and Hollywood talent agencies" as well as between established and emerging YouTubers to encourage collaboration and resource sharing.[67] The MCN supported creators directly and publicly through grant programs: $5 million to one hundred creators in 2011; $1 million in marketing grants in 2012; $10 million for original programming in 2014.[68] On the strength of its scale and its talent management unit, headed by former Creative Artists Agency executive Larry Shapiro, Fullscreen sold to Otter Media (backed by producer Peter Chernin and AT&T) for a reported $300 million.[69] At the time of sale Fullscreen had signed 50,000 creators with 450 million subscribers contributing four billion views monthly. In 2016, Fullscreen launched "fullscreen," a subscription media platform with original programming.

What happened to multichannel networks once they sold to major investors and media conglomerates? They focused on growth, and in the case of Maker Studios, increasing the value of their investors' intellectual property while cutting costs (jobs). In the months after selling itself to Disney in 2014, Maker Studios focused on owning its own platform in Maker.TV, growing its subscriber base through deals, servicing Disney, and trimming staff. Cofounders and siblings Lisa and Ben Donovan left months after the deal was finalized and 10 percent of the staff lost their jobs.[70] Maker announced seven new series at its NewFronts presentation following the acquisition, four from its YouTube stars (Chester See, Shay "ShayCarl" Butler, Joseph Garrett, and P'Trique); two from TV and film veterans Morgan Spurlock, Keegan-Michael Key, and Jordan Peele; and one, its biggest production, in partnership with *Nylon* magazine.[71] To grow its gaming vertical Polaris, the network partnered with the third most popular gaming network on YouTube—it was already partnered with the top two, PewDiePie and Stampylongnose.[72] Aside from Maker's clear growth potential as YouTube's fastest-growing multichannel network, Disney got an instant YouTube competitor with its own player in Maker.TV (formerly of Blip TV), where it could market content from ABC, ESPN, and the Disney Channel;[73] Maker's 2015 presentation at the NewFronts revealed its work for Marvel, ESPN, and ABC's Lincoln Square Productions.[74] Later that year Disney deputized fourteen Maker creators to live-stream an unboxing of toys for its newest franchise, *Star Wars*, for which Disney paid $4 billion.[75] Maker provided Disney with a necessary cost savings; right before announcing its purchase of Maker, Disney fired seven hundred employees, or roughly one quarter, in its Interactive Division.[76] Two years later, Disney cut thirty Maker jobs in a "strategic adjustment."[77]

YouTube started regulating the MCN-creator relationship in 2013 with new features and rules designed to benefit creators large and small, but the policies stoked resentment among many smaller channels. According to YouTube's Help resource, "MCNs are not affiliated with or endorsed by YouTube or Google,"[78] but Google had to acknowledge the growing role of MCNs on the site—and, by extension, its own inability to manage and invest in YouTubers. Yet Google's intervention was motivated primarily by its need to maintain relationships with major copyright holders, particularly musicians. In the summer of 2013, the National Music Publishers Association sued Fullscreen over its use of unlicensed copyrighted music in its videos; NMPA had just settled with Maker Studios.[79] Two months later, YouTube instituted new rules for MCNs and their channels, including creating a button for smaller channels to acknowledge their discontent with an MCN (though YouTube will not intervene in contract disputes) and showing comparisons between MCN and YouTube Partner ad rates in YouTube Analytics reports.[80] YouTube representatives said the site worked with MCNs on the rules, yet months later when YouTube started implementing the rules, Maker distanced itself from the "unpartner" button in a message to its channels: "Maker does not use this feature for communication about its contracts and this button is not a legal notice."[81]

The biggest policy shift was YouTube creating two tiers of MCN status: "Managed" and "Affiliate" channels. Videos from Managed creators received exemption from copyright review; YouTube would hold the MCN responsible. Affiliate channels bore responsibility for their intellectual property rights management and were subject to a copyright review process from YouTube that took from a few hours to a few days, during which, initially, YouTubers would lose out on ad revenue. By creating tiers in this new "monetization review" process, YouTube made explicit the rising divide between top and emerging creators on MCNs.[82] Small creators decried the expected delays in the release of their programs and the higher bar it set for getting boutique service from MCNs. Under the rules, by taking on "managed" channels, MCNs agreed to penalties across its networks for copyright violations and to take on full liability in litigation. Smaller creators feared this made it less likely that MCNs would expand their upper tiers: "The fact that smaller channels are those who have the most to lose with these changes is plain to see. It brings up the idea that starting a successful YouTube channel just became that much harder."[83]

In December 2013, YouTube implemented its Content ID system on the smaller Affiliates, screening their videos for matches in a database of twenty-five million reference files for copyrighted content.[84] Gaming channels were hardest hit.[85] The day MCNs announced the changes, YouTube gameplay video creator MaskedGamer, who by 2015 had four hundred thousand subscribers, uploaded a video in response, writing in the "info" section, "I've never subjected my network to a single copyright strike, yet I'm not big enough or trustworthy enough to receive 'Managed' status, which would continue to provide me with the key benefit that I joined the network for—instant monetization without any oversight or scrutiny by Google/Youtube."[86] MaskedGamer evokes a feeling of being policed by YouTube and undervalued by MCNs. The rise of new MCN competitors shows that this feeling was widespread. The month YouTube implemented the new Content ID system, a new MCN called Freedom! premiered. Started by George Vanous after he sold his gaming MCN, TGN, to BroadbandTV, Freedom! promised creators a "no lock-in" contract (you can leave anytime) and Managed status if you did not receive any violations in your first videos. In a year and a half it reported over forty-five million daily views by signing up over fifteen hundred new channels every day.[87] Nevertheless independent forums on YTalk, and essays by smaller creators, warn creators about Freedom! on the basis of its ability to promote, monetize, and legally defend so many channels.[88]

The Content ID controversy shows the pitfalls of YouTube's pursuit of legitimacy from major rights holders to secure big buys from advertisers and fans. After asking YouTubers for feedback on the policy, YouTube addressed the concerns of smaller creators by allowing them to profit temporarily from videos accused of infringing copyright; meanwhile, YouTube reported paying out $2 billion to major rights holders through Content ID.[89] To make it easier for creators to find MCNs right for them, YouTube also introduced a certification program available only to partners as a way to establish quality standards for networks.[90] Completing the program made channels eligible for inclusion in a "Service Provider Directory" of certified networks organized by services (talent management, caption and translation, production, music licensing, etc.) that creators could search to find representation. After years of supporting false copyright claims, YouTube finally agreed to legally defend creators for fair use in 2015, but it started by supporting just four channels.[91]

YouTube's primary goal is increasing revenue, not catering to new and smaller creators. When Google advertising chief Susan Wojicki stepped in as CEO of YouTube, she spoke of how the site "gives a voice to people who would otherwise not have a voice."[92] Yet, like the MCNs, YouTube's major initiatives promoted the site's cream of the crop—notably the global marketing campaigns of Phan, Mota, and Pansino, along with *VICE News*, Maker's *Epic Rap Battles of History*, and the third season of Freddie Wong's *Video Game High School*. At the 2014 NewFronts, Google announced its "preferred" content initiative, where it reserves ad slots for the top 5 percent of its creators. Brands could buy Nielsen-rated audiences in bulk and with guarantees of minimum levels of viewership.[93] Google publicly announced the top 1 percent across fourteen content verticals (Comedy, Cars, News, Music, etc.); the 385 channels boasted considerably more indie creators than YouTube's one hundred premium channels years prior, and YouTube reported nearly selling out of preferred ad inventory.[94] In 2015 YouTube reported that top advertisers increased their spend by 60 percent compared to 2014.[95] By 2016 the strategy appeared to be working when marketing conglomerate Interpublic Group gave YouTube its biggest up-front deal to date by shifting $250 million of its $5 billion TV ad spending budget to the company, bringing ads from Johnson & Johnson, Fiat, Coca-Cola, and others to online video.[96] In its pursuit of top advertisers, YouTube increased its censorship of content, removing videos that it deemed not "ad-friendly," even from creators like DeFranco: "I'm not going to censor myself. . . . Feels a little bit like getting stabbed in the back after 10 years," he tweeted.[97]

At the same time, however, Google reorganized YouTube's content division to directly develop original programming for the first time and structure their network like a traditional broadcast or cable channel. YouTube picked MTV executive Susanne Daniels to head programming, with NNN founder, Tim Shey, heading scripted content and NNN's former vice president of programming and development, Ben Relles, as head of comedy. The development team funded top creators and brokered deals with Hollywood studios.[98] YouTube Red debuted in 2016 with long-form originals and feature-length movies from top producers like PewDiePie (*Scare PewDiePie*), AwesomenessTV (*Dance Camp, Foursome*), Fine Brothers (*Sing It*), BlackBoxTV (*Fight of the Living Dead*), Rooster Teeth (*Lazer Team*), and *Buzzfeed*'s Quinta Brunson and Try Guys (*Broke* and *Squad Wars*). Red released at least twenty-five originals in 2016 to around 1.5 million subscribers, far less than its competitors.[99] By 2017 it planned to release its first drama and biggest program investment: an extension of the *Step Up* dance film franchise executive produced by movie star Channing Tatum.[100]

Managing thousands of producers is precarious. YouTube and its multichannel networks replicated hierarchies of media production, the very inequalities driving millions of creators to produce for an open-upload site like YouTube in the first place. In their bid for market dominance on YouTube, "MCNs produce a new overflow they cannot contain themselves" and "decelerated the momentum for aesthetic creation," according to Patrick Vonderau, so creators flocked to new apps in the video economy.[101] Rather than invest in new and upcoming creators, Google invested in MCNs (including Machinima) and tech platforms that managed large amounts of creators, as seen in its purchase of FameBit, a self-service platform connecting brands and YouTubers. In its first decade, YouTube dramatically grew its valuation without investing in indie creators; multichannel networks organized them for the company and profited handsomely from indie labor. When YouTube finally stepped in, they did so to protect major rights holders and the most popular producers it feared losing to competitors like Vessel, designed for direct-fan support, and Maker.TV, a multichannel backed by a major media conglomerate in Disney. Meanwhile, the indie creators who attracted fan attention to YouTube still hustled for views and suffered low ad rates due to lack of representation and their ongoing marginalization on the site.

Scaling Fandom: Selling Masses of Fans on Open TV

Mobilizing masses of fans eager to see legacy TV open its distribution technologies and practices generated considerable economic value by the mid-2010s. Subscription networks like Netflix enjoyed stable, robust revenue and budding relationships with major producers and intellectual property owners. Media fans would pay distributors for on-demand access to TV and movies. Monthly and yearly subscriptions made a small number of web TV distributors much richer and freer than their ad-supported competitors like Hulu and YouTube.

We can see the shift in power from advertisers to fans in the story of Jason Kilar and Vessel. Kilar started Vessel after running Hulu, seeing the massive popularity of YouTube, and observing the critical acclaim of Netflix. Hulu's original programs had yet to impress critics, but the partially ad-supported network commanded high CPMs because it had "premium" content; it licensed the bulk of its programs from legacy networks for next-day distribution. Hulu's own original series, initially, were lackluster; before releasing *Casual* and picking up Fox's *Mindy Project, East Los High*, an indie drama for the Latino market addressed in chapter 3, was arguably its most critically noteworthy show, and it was developed outside of Hulu. As I have shown, brand investment in digital video was slow to finance slates of original TV series comparable to the programs of Hulu's owners—ABC, NBC, Fox, and other network partners. YouTube found itself in the same predicament, but it delivered innovative and engaging programming because of its broad base of producers and their fans.

Kilar's pitch for Vessel was simple. It would be like YouTube, supported primarily by subscribers, with advertising functioning as secondary support. Videos on Vessel would premiere exclusively to paying subscribers, whose $2.99 per month fees were split with Vessel and its premium partners. After the first "window," the exclusivity ended, and the video was available to the public with advertising. Kilar wooed top YouTubers by offering better representation to advertisers, a more favorable revenue split than Google, and a curated site for quality programming. Kilar bet that by creating a walled garden for online video, he could deliver fifty-dollar CPMs, nearly twice the TV average and several times YouTube's average. In the initial agreement Kilar said creators kept 70 percent of advertising revenue, whereas Vessel split 60 percent of the cumulative subscription revenue among creators on the basis of popularity. When Vessel premiered in early 2015, Kilar had secured $135 million in investments from venture capital.[102] With partner Rich Tom, Hulu's former chief technology officer, Kilar lined up support for advertising from Corona Extra, Chevy, Land Rover/Jaguar, and Unilever's Axe, Dove, Suave, and St. Ives.[103] Yet in 2016, Vessel sold to Verizon, which quickly closed the service to utilize its underlying technology and software.[104]

Kilar and Tom's bid to marry YouTube and Netflix's business models shows how advertisers' reluctance to fund native web programming put pressure on ad-supported networks' revenue, making it difficult for them to create "mainstream" programs and achieve scale. Some television fans happily subscribe to networks directly for web original programming so long as networks offer access to hours and hours of information and entertainment. For Netflix, this meant spending billions every year to license legacy television series and films from Hollywood studios. For Amazon, this meant providing discounts and expedited shipping on a broad range of products, from media (books, DVDs, music) to hardware, software, and everyday wares. To augment their licensing deals and keep subscribers paying, Amazon and Netflix have developed original programming. This was not new. Amazon and Netflix were following the business models of cable and premium cable networks like HBO. As Netflix's head of content, Ted Sarandos, told *GQ*, "The goal . . . is to become HBO faster than HBO can become us."[105] Netflix increased original programming dramatically after its first original in *House of Cards*. In 2016, CEO Reed Hastings promised the company's eighty million global subscribers six hundred hours of originals, nearly double the number of hours in 2014 and costing upwards of $6 billion, more than Time Warner, owner of HBO; not to be outdone, HBO announced the same number of original programming hours for 2016.[106] In 2014, Netflix surpassed HBO in subscription revenue, but HBO was more profitable, because it owned more of its programs and had a stable subscriber base buoyed by legacy deals with linear cable providers like Comcast.[107] Amazon helped expand the bubble, doubling its own programming spend in 2016.[108]

The pressure to satisfy subscribers forced web networks to devise complex algorithms to make development decisions based on user behavior. Devising and revising systems to understand what captures user attention is a labor- and resource-intensive process, requiring large data sets and complex math. In a thorough analysis of the Netflix Prize, a competition to refine Netflix's recommendation system, Blake Hallinan and Ted Striphas identify key shifts in our understanding of culture resulting from the tech industry's reliance on algorithms: "from 'great works' to more tepid forms of art, from personal to pre-personal renderings of cultural identity, and from a court of human appeal to an algorithmic one."[109] The authors suggest that Netflix's algorithmic growth strategy, producing recommendations to engage customers so they can produce more data and continue to cycle, means that "issues of quality or hierarchy get transposed into matters of fit."[110] Presumably, if a user doesn't like horror, Netflix will never or rarely market its original horror series to those customers, no matter how many Emmys it wins. It is still unknown what effects, if any, this programming strategy has on television culture. What is clear is how vastly it differs from the kinds of intimate, idiosyncratic associations among producers, sponsors, and fans characteristic of the dynamics of the indie TV market identified throughout this book.

Early on, Netflix calculated recommendations through "factoring," a mathematical process allowing for the simplification of numerical meanings and relationships (its 1–5-star scale). This quantitative recommendation system raised issues of privacy. Early on, Netflix settled a lawsuit from a lesbian whose viewing preferences exposed her sexuality. Netflix later successfully lobbied for an exemption from federal privacy law.[111] Netflix was reluctant to adapt systems to expressions of cultural identity, if only to reduce costs; for example, Netflix spent years fighting a suit from the National Association of the Deaf demanding that the site provide closed captioning consistent with the Americans with Disabilities Act.[112]

Netflix eventually shifted to collecting and using more nuanced information on fans' use of its site to develop original programming. The company focused on technical interactions with the platform: "tracking when users start, stop, rewind, fast forward, and pause videos, in addition to logging the time of day of viewing, the user's location, the device on which the streaming occurred, whether the user watched a program from beginning to end, what if anything she or he watched next, and more."[113] Moreover, programmers competing to refine Netflix's original algorithm asserted that "sex, age, race, and other broad classifications fail to capture the more subtle factors relevant to decisions people make about the cultural goods they will consume."[114] Today, Netflix runs A/B testing—trying out different designs and recommendations on similar users—on a global scale to encourage viewing.[115]

Engineering and design mattered more than culture to Netflix. Culture mattered only inasmuch as it fit into the 76,897 content categories the *Atlantic* estimated Netflix had in 2014, with such types as "Mother-Son Movies from the 1970s" and "Movies directed by Otto Preminger."[116] As Tod Yellin, vice president of product innovation, told *Wired* in early 2016, "That mountain [of data] is composed of two things. Garbage is 99 percent of that mountain. Gold is one percent. . . . Geography, age, and gender? We put that in the garbage heap. Where you live is not that important."[117] To Netflix, behavior inferred identity, but identities were most valuable in their precise interactions with Netflix's large library and systems, not in relationship to the culture at large. In an extensive article describing how its algorithms work, Netflix vice president of product innovation Carlos Gomez-Uribe and chief product officer Neil Hunt focused on how its algorithms interacted with each other, the site's design, and users' past behavior; yet the reported downsides of this approach hinged on material and cultural realities, including account sharing, language disparities, differences in program options across countries, presentation bias ("feedback loop" where highly recommended videos get higher engagement), and challenge of integrating new users into the system.[118] Nowhere do Gomez-Uribe and Hunt mention gender, race, sexuality, class, disability, religion, or the many other sociological categories research has shown are relevant to cultural production and reception.

Does big data television create "a problem of knowing too much," as Nick Marx writes, contrasting open TV development with the broadcast executive's perennial "problem of knowing"?[119] Historically, development executives limit producers' creative freedom so programs meet the "lower common denominator," minimizing executives' problem of knowing what audiences want. Hallinan and Striphas characterize Netflix's strategy as aiming for "low-hanging fruit." Freed from the allure of broad appeal, Netflix could presumably empower creative producers by supplying data to support unconventional ideas for niche audiences. As Matt Sienkiewicz writes about the critically acclaimed *BoJack Horsemen*:

In the age of big data, "television" outlets such as Netflix have embraced the possibility that even the most counterintuitive combinations—say a talking animal animated sitcom that will by the end of season one include a very serious story of cancer, death, shame and forgiveness—might succeed, provided there are some statistics speaking in its favor.[120]

Yet amid BoJack's clear narrative innovation Sienkiewicz nevertheless finds legacy network–driven calculation in its creativity, describing it as "culturally omnivorous" enough to suggest that Netflix developed it to entice fans to find connections to other shows in its Hollywood-based library; a similar argument might be made of *Stranger Things*, an effective reimagining of 1980s horror. This is a different kind of engagement with fandom but one nevertheless focused on streamlining storytelling to meet a network's needs.

Like many corporate networks, Netflix's development process was hidden, so we had no way of knowing to what degree big data influenced its programming strategy. Critics hailed Netflix's innovations in serial storytelling. Yet as Jennifer Fuller noted, Netflix's predecessors in ad-supported and subscription cable established the strategy of developing "edgy" series in response to competition for fan attention.[121] Racial and sexual representation were key to this script because niche networks must show willingness to take more "risks" than broadcasters to "draw critical attention ('buzz') and boost subscriptions."[122] Netflix's original programming had some cultural diversity, from the lesbian, queer, and trans women of color in *Orange Is the New Black*, Lana and Lilly Wachowski's queer- and transwoman-led *Sense8*, Frank Underwood as a polyamorous queer figure in *House of Cards*, black gay characters on *The Get Down* and *The Unbreakable Kimmy Schmidt*, and a black superhero in the Marvel series *Luke Cage* to *Jessica Jones*, a woman fighting male oppression. Each program twisted formulas from past and contemporary critical hits: *Orange Is the New Black* built on HBO's *Oz* with a nearly all-female cast; *Sense8* one-upped Amazon's *Transparent* by situating trans representation in the sci-fi genre; *House of Cards* queered the dominant form of the white male antihero made iconic in HBO's *Sopranos* and AMC's *Breaking Bad*; and the Luke Cage series was Marvel's first black-led franchise, after years of the studio licensing its top, white characters for blockbuster films and broadcast series.

Even with algorithms, Netflix's programming was substantially derivative. Its earliest notable shows were adaptations: *House of Cards* an adaptation of the British series of the same name; *Orange Is the New Black* an adaptation of a book of the same name; and *Arrested Development* picked up from Fox, *The Killing* from AMC, and *Longmire* from A&E. As of this writing Netflix had announced adaptations, spin-offs, or continuations of *The Office, Lemony Snicket's A Series of Unfortunate Events, Full House, Gilmore Girls, Puss in Boots, Wet Hot American Summer, Inspector Gadget, One Day at a Time, Dear White People, She's Gotta Have It*, three Marvel series in addition to *Luke Cage*, starring Jessica Jones, Iron Fist, and Daredevil, and *The Defenders*, featuring all four Marvel characters. Of those, four—*Dear White People, She's Gotta Have It, Luke Cage*, and *One Day at a Time*—had creators of color, the latter two outnumbered by white men among executive producers.

At least a dozen more of Netflix's shows were originals, but mostly from Hollywood veterans like Aziz Ansari, Bill Burr, Ricky Gervais (*The Office*), Tom Fontana (*Oz*), Eli Roth, Tina Fey, and Robert Carlock (*30 Rock*), and established producers like Harvey Weinstein, Judd Apatow, Baz Luhrmann, Shawn Ryan, and Joe Swanberg. Hollywood studios profited handsomely from Netflix licensing original programs. DreamWorks Animation secured a commitment to supply three hundred hours of original programming exclusively to Netflix.[123] In addition to four thirteen-episode seasons for individual characters, Marvel secured a shorter eight-episode miniseries for *The Defenders*.[124] Morgan Stanley estimated that major studios, including Disney, NBC Universal, Time Warner, Fox, and CBS would receive 30 percent of Netflix's content spending in 2016, almost twice what it spent on originals (where production companies are more likely to be independent); at 11 percent, Disney commanded the highest share.[125]

Amazon was less aggressive than Netflix and distinguished itself through its open, competitive piloting process and by producing, under its Amazon Studios, series and films from auteurs with indie cred, including Garry Trudeau, Spike Lee, Woody Allen, and Jill Soloway, veteran of *Six Feet Under* whose feature *Afternoon Delight* premiered at Sundance. Many of Amazon's TV pilots had producers with credits on wide-release films and legacy network shows, though Amazon initially had less critical success than Netflix. Its early acclaim mostly came from

Transparent, though *Catastrophe* (created, written, and starring Rob Delaney and Sharon Hogan), *Mozart in the Jungle* (adapted from oboist Blair Tindall's memoir by Roman Coppola, Jason Schwartzman, and Alex Timbers), and *The Man in the High Castle* (adapted from Philip K. Dick by *X-Files* writer Frank Spotnitz) all found Emmy nominations or critical acclaim. "The studio's initial programming strategy had less to do with producing innovative shows than it did with promoting an innovative way of choosing shows," *New York*'s Adam Sternbergh wrote in his profile of the network.[126] Yet, Amazon exempted high-profile producers from having to make pilots, notably David E. Kelley (*Ally Mc-Beal*, *The Practice*) and his drama *Trial*, starring Billy Bob Thornton and William Hurt. Prime's original programming grew in popularity over 2015, increasing subscriptions by 50 percent that year.[127]

Diversity was hard to find among Amazon's and Netflix's producers, similarly to legacy networks. Netflix's series creators were mostly white, cisgender, and straight. This is particularly notable for its earliest series with leads of color, including *Unbreakable Kimmy Schmidt*, *The Get Down*, and *Orange Is the New Black*. Speaking to *Fresh Air*'s Terry Gross, *Orange Is the New Black* creator Jenji Kohan (*Weeds*) said she got the green light for her show, among the most diverse in TV history, by confirming the undesirability of minority leads:

> You're not going to go into a network and sell a show on really fascinating tales of black women, and Latina women, and old women and criminals. But if you take this white girl, this sort of fish out of water, and you follow her in, you can then expand your world and tell all of those other stories. But it's a hard sell to just go in and try to sell those stories initially.[128]

Kohan explicitly centers white identity as critical to anchoring her series and allowing her to "expand" the perspective. Whether *Orange Is the New Black* expands perspectives on identity is debatable; the series's greatest representational breakthrough, a regular role for trans actor Laverne Cox, was limited by her comparatively few storylines. Cox's Emmy nomination was as a guest star, an award not featured in the main telecast. Unlike *Transparent*'s Soloway, who hired transgender artist Our Lady J as a writer for the second season, Kohan did not believe that a producer's identity necessarily related to their art, so her show had no trans writers: "I have trouble with, like, what you are in life shouldn't automatically make you what you do in your art."[129] Kohan conforms to Hollywood's identity-blind ideologies that privilege the mainstream as neutral—cisgender, white, straight people can write any type of character. Shortly after the show's fourth-season premiere, filmmaker Matthew Cherry tweeted a photo of Kohan's nearly all-white writing room, retweeted over two thousand times amid vigorous online discussion over that season's representation of racialized, gendered, and sexual trauma.[130] Critic and activist Ashleigh Shackelford wrote in a widely circulated essay,

> This show is no longer a show that needs to stand on its first season, using Piper's white privilege to garner attention for more interesting stories of people of color in the background. *Orange Is the New Black* is in Season 4 and is using every trick in the white supremacist handbook to exploit and gain attention with the pain of our bodies and experiences, while utilizing satire and "true life" plots to disguise it.[131]

Shackelford here implies that the show, like Netflix, uses diversity to attract buzz and attention without a focus on sincere writing. Netflix's lack of sensitivity to representational politics resulted in controversies over its narratives of race and ethnicity, particularly regarding indigenous people. Indigenous actors walked off Adam Sandler's Netflix original movie after reading racially insensitive jokes in the script; on-set video recorded a producer telling the actors they were "overly sensitive."[132] A number of critics took issue with representations of race and ethnicity in *Kimmy Schmidt*, particularly the stereotypes of indigeneity and the whitewashing of that identity through the casting of Jane Krakowski as Native American.[133]

Amazon, for its part, was more proactive in promoting gender representation, ordering half of its series from women in 2015 and giving Soloway an overall deal.[134] Soloway used *Transparent* and her studio Topple to bring trans, femme, and intersectional people into production and development.[135] Yet in 2016 Amazon faced a public controversy after canceling *Good Girls Revolt*, a (white) feminist period series; creator Dana Calvo claimed the show was critically acclaimed and delivering returns but was canceled because Amazon Studios head Roy Price was "representative of the Amazon culture in that he's just impenetrable."[136]

In general, streaming TV distributors either matched or trailed already-lagging broadcast and cable distributors in representations of race and gender behind and in front of the camera. According to the University of Southern California's Institute for Diversity and Empowerment at Annenberg, Netflix, Amazon, and Hulu marginally improved on-screen representations of women (38 percent of characters versus 33 percent across film and TV) and underrepresented minorities (29.4 percent versus 28.3 percent across platforms) during the 2014–2015 season.[137] Behind the camera, streaming distributors had slightly more show creators who were women (25 percent versus 22.6 percent on average), but fewer directors (11.8 percent) and writers (25.2 percent) than for legacy TV.[138] Only 11.4 percent of directors came from racially underrepresented backgrounds, and only 2 percent of streaming series had a racially balanced cast, compared with 12 percent across platforms.[139] Film and TV distributors, across legacy and web platforms, lagged behind in full representation of race and gender.

Why weren't Netflix, Amazon, Hulu, and the other corporate web distributors developing programs from a broader base of producers, including independent web series creators?[140] The lack of racial diversity among its producers was particularly frustrating given the hype over the efficiencies of its data-driven development processes, which presumably minimize the risks legacy networks avoid by making it easier to target niche communities by identity and interest. At issue might be perceptions of which audiences are valuable, which has plagued legacy TV for its entire history.

Paradoxically, at the same time that Netflix and Amazon virtually ignored indie creators,[141] legacy networks started to develop series from creators who had built substantial fan bases online:[142] HBO offered development deals to Black & Sexy TV's Numa Perrier and Dennis Dortch, Issa Rae, and *Twenties'* Lena Waithe, while Comedy Central developed Abbi Jacobson and Ilana Glazer's *Broad City* and continued to invest in its online division, CC Studios, from which it picked up *Idiotsitter*, costarring Jillian Bell of its hit *Workaholics*. Fox developed a scripted series with Vine and Instagram star Andrew "King Bach" Bachelor, while ABC ordered a season of the web series *Downward Dog*, after a pilot.[143] In an unprecedented deal, Katja Blichfeld and Ben Sinclair signed with HBO for a six-episode series order for *High Maintenance*, after its online distributor Vimeo produced its fifth and sixth cycles. In this context, the composition of Netflix's programming and its producers raises questions as to whether the networks' over sixty million subscribers were getting the open, innovative television they were being sold.[144]

Who Will Open TV?

Before the Federal Communications Commission set rules for the open Internet in 2015, Netflix played a key role in contentious debates over net neutrality, becoming a symbol of free and open access to information via the web. As a corporation, however, it was most invested in maintaining its subscriber base at the lowest cost to shareholders. Netflix positioned threats to subscribers' service as threats to open television, when in fact it was primarily a threat to its bottom line. In 2010, Netflix's content delivery network (CDN), Level 3, alleged that Comcast, an Internet service provider (ISP), was charging a new fee to account for the amount of traffic Netflix takes up on its networks, anywhere from 20 percent to 33 percent of all downstream traffic.[145] Web video analysts disagreed on who was to blame, but the majority blamed Comcast for appearing to throttle web television to get more money from web TV networks and their contractors. Stacey Higginbotham, an analyst of web infrastructure, wrote, "[T]he very threat that Level 3 alleges Comcast made—essentially that Level 3 could accept the proposed fee or Comcast wouldn't deliver Level 3's content—should lead to concern."[146] Three years later, Level 3 accused Verizon of throttling traffic as well, but soon after, Netflix started moving away from working with CDNs and developed Open Connect to make deals with ISPs directly, a business decision to avoid potential fees.[147] Netflix purchased traffic services from CDN Cogent before cutting a deal with Comcast directly with its Open Connect. Their traffic improved when they paid Comcast. As the company said in a filing to the Federal Communications Commission (FCC) urging the commission to deny Comcast's proposed—and failed—merger with Time Warner Cable, "The degraded viewing quality for Comcast subscribers also resulted in a sharp increase in calls to Netflix customer support. Those calls made clear that Comcast was well aware of the degradation of Netflix traffic and was directing its subscribers to contact

Netflix."[148] Netflix characterizes Comcast as deliberately manipulating Internet traffic for profit, threatening the open TV system.

In 2015, in its net neutrality order, the FCC reclassified the Internet as a telecommunications service and issued clear rules for Internet traffic, including no blocking, throttling, or paid prioritization of content. Supporting innovation in web television is at the core of the rules. In the report, the FCC introduces the new rules with references to Netflix's downstream traffic, Amazon's Golden Globes for *Transparent*, HBO's and CBS's streaming services, and ESPN's online offerings brokered by DISH: "[C]arefully-tailored rules to protect Internet openness will allow investment and innovation to continue to flourish."[149] Free Press called the rules "the biggest victory for the public interest in the FCC's history."[150] The Electronic Frontier Foundation (EFF) called it a "win," with a few loopholes ISPs could exploit.[151]

Lost in the excitement over Netflix's growth and the FCC's regulation of web traffic are the indie producers who have created the bulk of web television. The FCC's report contains scant reference to independent production, save a reference to comments provided by Vimeo about the effect of paid prioritization on indie filmmakers without resources to pay for distribution.[152] We know the likes of Issa Rae actively lobbied the FCC for net neutrality, but the rules primarily govern the relationship between corporate web TV distributors like Netflix and cable/Internet providers like Comcast. Nowhere is there discussion about regulating or prioritizing sites like YouTube and Vimeo, where most independent creators upload their videos, or rules ensuring ease of use and compability for new video distributors who might want to challenge the established companies explored in this chapter. In the meantime, the rules left open the possibility for "more subtle forms of discrimination online" from providers like AT&T, which worked around the rules through practices like "zero-rating," or *not* charging users for specific content, particularly via mobile.[153] In 2017, after the election of President Donald J. Trump, anti–net neutrality FCC commissioner Ajit Pai assumed the chairmanship, threatening already-compromised rules and forcing companies like Vimeo to again lobby for openness.

In this book I have spotlighted the production of television for the web to expand our understanding of innovation beyond corporations who can distribute TV at large scale and negotiate with conglomerates, as Netflix clearly can. Scale benefits companies that need to reach, retain, and quickly monetize the attention of masses on a consistent basis. But peer-to-peer distribution potentially shifts the mass media logic of scale. I argue that during the 2000s and 2010s independent producers fostered innovation by developing television through decentralized networks, organizing producers, fans, and sponsors on a smaller scale and generating significant cultural impact.

The open TV market is at odds with corporate media's distribution strategies, which constrain creativity and diversity in search of reliable profits. Internet distribution does not change this fundamental truth. The heart of the television revolution is the opportunity independent cultural makers have to reach audiences large or small without interference from large institutions. Today the growth of the web has seen the rise of new corporations and continued dominance of old ones, all serving various gatekeeping functions in television development. Netflix and Amazon work with elite talent but give fans more flexibility. YouTube and Vimeo are open to nearly all producers but curate and cultivate precious few. Most legacy media companies invest in digital networks even as they are slow to change the linear TV businesses that make them most of their money.

Those of us who believe in an open television market must advocate for more than an open web where consumers can get corporate-distributed series on demand. *Open TV* spotlights the independents who make television in the hopes that we will include them in our assessments of the health of the U.S. media market. I hope web distribution fosters an ethics of consumption for television. Artistic diversity is necessary for democracy. In addition to net neutrality rules that preserve open access to distribution—the lost dream of amateur radio operators, independent film and television studios, and alternative video and video art producers—we must demand and ensure equality and diversity in production and technological development. We must hold corporations with access to capital accountable for the way they develop television, as well as the way they manage production and distribution in service of profit. Digital cables alone cannot guarantee the dream of America fully represented on television. If television continues to be open, it will be so because we demanded it, and independents showed us the way.

Epilogue

Open TV (beta) in the Networked Era

June 2016: a lone shooter slaughtered fifty queer people, mostly black and Latina/o, at Pulse, a dry nightclub in Orlando, in the worst mass shooting in U.S. history. They lost their lives at last call. They stayed out late to drink, kiss, and dance, in search of love and sex. Conflicting reports suggest that the shooter, Omar Mateen, had connections to the queer community via mobile apps, lovers, and Pulse. On the day of the massacre, Mateen's father told the press that the sight of two men kissing angered his son, and soon after, photos with the hashtag #TwoMen-Kissing spread widely through social media in protest of homophobia. Dylan Marron, who played the gay Latino lead in this book's opening case study *Whatever this is.*, produced a video for Hearst's Seriously.TV called "Men Kissing Men," featuring just that. Garnering over thirteen million views on Facebook, the video stated that for every homophobic comment, one dollar will be donated to the OneOrlando Fund, benefiting survivors and the victims' families. The hashtag died down after a Puerto Rican man claimed to be Mateen's lover and said his rampage might have been motivated by revenge against the queer Latinx community, not domestic terrorism, a narrative that dominated mainstream news coverage.

I learned about the attack in Japan, where I was presenting on my current research project: Open TV (beta). By mid-2016, Open TV occupied nearly all my time, and I had been touring conferences showing clips and trailers of pilots and series centering queer, black, brown, and femme lives, including the Latinx community. I started the platform both to address corporate television's inconsistent interest in stories told by intersectional artists and to further explore the challenges of independent TV distribution chronicled in chapter 4. Distributing series gave me access to data about how series and platforms develop in networked economies. I was constantly talking about the limits of the open TV market, and the possibilities for a sustainable alternative. As I fought back tears, trying to make sense of the carnage, it struck me that we all have a role in the struggle for liberation, but American television has not embraced its role.

I started this book with Marron's gay Latino character resisting his friend's failure to recognize and act on racism on set. The story resonates with me because Ari's feeling of invisibility mirrors American television's neglect of queer people of color in representation, their lack of interest in #TwoBrownMenKissing or #TwoBlackMenKissing.[1] I can count on my hand the number of times in my life when two black or brown men have kissed each other on legacy television. On HBO's *True Blood*, Lafayette briefly had a Latino boyfriend, a *"brujo"* or masculine-spectrum witch, but by the last season even the writers had to acknowledge how little story they'd given Lafayette—his big finale moment is a rant to his white friends that they never pay attention to him. Years later, on *Empire*, lead black gay character Jamal (Jussie Smollett) kissed his "down low" producer, but some fans reacted negatively on Twitter and Smollett publicly apologized, albeit with shade. As I processed what happened in Orlando I thought not only of whether the shooter had representations of #TwoMenKissing to alleviate his fear of difference but also of what representations of queer black and brown people Americans could see to imagine their lives and the loss.

The pursuit of big scale haunts legacy television, instilling a fear of cultural difference in executives. The web, meanwhile, allows for smaller-scale productions to appear, and at times thrive. It embraces difference for its relevance to diverse lives. I designed Open TV (beta) to acquire data on the value of small-scale distribution, what I call "small data," to communities historically excluded from development. I spent most of 2016 developing and promoting two new shows for Open TV (beta): Ricardo Gamboa's *Brujos*, a fantasy series about gay Latino PhD students who are witches, and Fatimah Asghar's *Brown Girls*, a dramedy about a queer Pakistani writer and her friend, a singer and black woman. The writers and producers of those series mostly hail from Chicago and from the racial and sexual communities they represent in their series. Both series imagine love between and among brown people with original music produced and performed by brilliant women of color Jamila Woods and

Sadie Rock. At conferences and talks throughout 2016 I showed a teaser for *Brujos* with the lead couple kissing and making love to the delight of queer and straight, Latino and white audiences alike.

From 2015 to 2016 Open TV (beta) exhibited queer and intersectional web television in over thirty instances, mostly in Chicago, drawing together diverse communities to celebrate art and lives historically underrepresented and underresourced. I started to see how using television—serial storytelling—to create space for queer people of color online and in Chicago encourages collaboration across identities and art forms, productive conversation among intersecting communities, and professional advancement for emerging artists to tell even more ambitious stories. Chicagoans are eager to connect with one another and use art to do so. These spaces give people a place to celebrate and understand specific cultural and social identities. After seeing a space curated for queer Latinos subjected to violence, I was reminded of the value of intersectional art and local community, even at small scale. As scholar and video/performance artist Malik Gaines wrote in a brief essay for *BOMB* in response to the tragedy at Pulse in Orlando, "In our field of representation, we rehearse [violence's] efficacies. I've seen so many murders on TV. . . . It would be remarkable if this violence could serve to help us think about intersectionality better, not just fuel our drive for dissensus around difference."[2]

The burgeoning networked TV distributors are not focused on improving on legacy television's performance in representing culture, least of all intersectionality. Research by Stacy Smith at the University of Southern California suggests that the new digital-first distributors like Netflix do no better on diversity than the old, behind or in front of the camera, in terms of gender or race. Moreover, their strategies of branding channels with "edgy" representations of race and sexuality mirror those of cable channels, which eventually forsook minority-led programs for "broader" series.[3]

Instead of focusing on cultural representation, the likes of Netflix and Amazon are intent on improving legacy TV's organizational and technological efficiency and effectiveness by reinventing the pilot process and series-release conventions (binge viewing). Furthermore, every major TV distributor is now networked. Strategies for program development, delivery, and financing are converging as networked television distributors pursue dominance in, and attempt to constrain, an open, digital market. As of this writing, YouTube, Hulu, and their competitors announced legacy TV subscription services with programming from broadcast networks alongside YouTube original content. Subscription-based Amazon Prime has announced that it is offering ad-supported distribution for independents, even as it courts premium channels to offer subscriptions through Prime. Legacy premium subscription channels from Starz, Showtime, HBO, and little-known gay network Here all announced that subscribers could access programming through third parties like Amazon and in apps from Apple TV to Roku: premium TV for cord cutters. Meanwhile, Hulu and Netflix cut deals with Cablevision and Comcast, respectively; now linear TV subscribers can access web content through cable interfaces. Live-streaming via the web has grown considerably with Amazon's Twitch platform, and social media platforms such as Facebook, Twitter, Tumblr, and YouTube have also announced live TV platforms. Ad-supported linear channels, from broadcasters like CBS and NBC to their offspring in Hulu to multichannel networks like VEVO and Fullscreen, have all announced subscription services on demand, via apps and websites. Vimeo, after years of investing in Vimeo On Demand for films and series, purchased VHX for its subscription business. Legendary Pictures announced that Felicia Day's Geek & Sundry and Chris Hardwick's Nerdist, formerly YouTube networks, would merge into a subscription streaming service, Alpha. Cable TV distributors announced online studios to cultivate new talent, including Turner (Super Deluxe), IFC (Comedy Crib), Comedy Central (CC Studios), and MTV (on its site and through Snapchat). Plaforms like Crackle and Vine that started with short-form content ordered long-form series, while multichannel networks are becoming "multiplatform networks" focused on organizational and tech innovation.[4] Telecommunications provider Verizon reinvested in networked TV programs, purchasing both AOL and Yahoo after ordering six series from New Form Digital, an independent studio collaborating with YouTube and other creators that produced twenty-five pilots, sold eighteen shows, and released four series by 2015.[5] More platforms, including Snapchat and fullscreen, are signing agreements with Nielsen for ratings, while Facebook and Apple entered the original programming business, hired legacy executives, and bought legacy shows. Award shows like the Emmys and Gotham Awards announced new and expanded categories to recognize short-form television, while film festivals like Sundance and the Tribeca Film Festival have started to curate and cultivate markets for indie TV.

No matter how these developments unfold, we have entered the networked era, characterized by a convergence of old network and new networked business strategies for developing original TV programming enabled by networking technologies: subscription, ad-supported, on demand, spreadable, sponsored, user-generated, short- and long-form, exclusive and nonexclusive distribution all emerge as options for amassing revenue and cultivating fans. The next seismic shift may be the deregulation of the set-top box, the device most Americans use to access hundreds of cable channels. President Obama publicly supported breaking this market open in early 2016, arguing that doing so will advance innovation. If cable operators like Verizon, AT&T, and Comcast lose their oligopoly over how Americans access linear television, it will blow the doors to TV distribution wide open to tech companies like Apple, Google, and Amazon, which have their own original and licensed programs as well as connected devices that can redesign the way we access TV.[6]

What is missing from this new era is a critical focus on cultural specificity and the scale best suited to represent it. When TV is liberated from linearity and the bureaucracies that support it, what will take its place? As the industry focuses on increasing efficiency through big data, I argue that we as scholars need to focus on the small and the local, on analyzing and sustainably developing sources of innovation before venture capital takes interest. As we can get TV anywhere and everywhere, we will need to grapple with what stories we see, what we don't see, and why—not to mention who can access them and how.

In just over one year, Open TV (beta) seemed to fill a void, however small. I originally intended to limit my project to a series of pilots about artists exploring alternative relationships, then called *Wide Open*. I was inspired by Brooklyn's burgeoning indie TV market: how *High Maintenance* used a series of short films to tell the story of New York's blossoming creative community and its discontents, and how *The Outs* used local screenings to build a community around its programs, targeting Brooklyn's gay men. I intended to produce and release these pilots online and in Chicago, getting both local/qualitative and online/

quantitative reception data. This data would not only offer rare insight for scholars on the intricacies of television development but would also serve as useful information for artists as they develop their careers. Then, as I was editing the first pilot, a beautiful show made its way into my inbox: *You're So Talented* by Sam Bailey, a drama about a young black woman searching for a sense of self and an artistic calling. Sam wanted me to write about it on my blog *Televisual*, but I had to distribute it. I had no more time for blogging while on the tenure track at Northwestern. Sam's series was beautifully shot, sincerely acted, and featured local actors and locales.

I debuted Open TV (beta) with *You're So Talented* in March 2015. The next month the Tribeca Film Festival selected it to participate in its second annual New Online Work program. Two months later, the Voqal Fund, working with a member-based organization, Chicago Filmmakers, granted Sam $19,000 to produce the second season, which we released in February 2016. On the basis of this success, Sam solicited commercial work, courted representation to package her work for a long-format, and prepared for her second web series, this time as director: *Brown Girls*. That summer both *Brown Girls* and *Brujos* received funding and went into production thanks to a combined $29,000 from the same grant that funded *You're So Talented*'s second season, along with thousands more crowdfunded by fans.

By June 2017 I had released twelve original series and eleven pilots, along with a raft of ancillary videos documenting Chicago's cultural life. All but one was shot in Chicago, and all had local premieres before going online. The Open TV programming slate rivals any larger network in diversity. Our artists are gender-nonconforming, transgender, black, Latinx, gay, lesbian, and queer-identified. Over twenty hours of programming led to more than 600,000 plays on Vimeo with total production budgets near $100,000, cobbled together from grants, crowdfunding, and my own personal investment. We had shown in such diverse spaces as artist-run and nonprofit galleries; the University of Chicago, Northwestern University, and the School of the Art Institute of Chicago; community-based agencies like TransTech Social Enterprises (designed to train trans people for work in tech) and Global Girls Studio (a youth empowerment agency); curated spaces like Soho House Chicago and a private dance class at the Dance Center; along with local bars. We collaborated with the Art Institute of Chicago for the premiere of an experimental docu-series by a local artist at Woman Made Gallery, a local nonprofit. Legacy and new film, TV, and art institutions even gave us recognition, including *You're So Talented*'s selection as an honoree at the Tribeca Film Festival's New Online Work program, its nomination at the Independent Filmmaker Project's Gotham Awards, and its eventual distribution on fullscreen's subscription network. In 2017 Open TV premiered its second cycle with *Brujos*, *Brown Girls*, and *Afternoon Snatch* at the Museum of Contemporary Art Chicago. Months later, after premiering on *Elle* magazine, trending on Twitter the night of its release, and screening in over a dozen cities, *Brown Girls* sold to HBO. Weeks after that announcement, the show received an Emmy nomination for Outstanding Short Form Comedy or Drama—the only indie in the category.

Beyond the numbers and accolades, however, I could see queer people, trans people, and people of all colors come together to have serious discussions around art and culture. I could see how local web television allows people to both leave their homes and connect with strangers—instead of locking themselves indoors to binge Netflix—while also allowing those who cannot make local events a chance to share their favorite artists with friends on social media. I could see how Open TV (beta)'s small-scale approach was encouraging local artists to produce programs that could benefit their own and others' careers in theater, television, and performing arts, aided by sources of funding in grants, sponsors, and donors. Knowledge of the project spread through Open TV's local and online networks of artists. By focusing on local and community-driven projects, I became aware of numerous quality, diverse programs in all stages of production. Achieving diversity is far less challenging when you are connected to the communities you want to represent. By mid-2017, when I started to solidify the programming cycle for 2018, I had dozens of programs I could develop, a number with functioning production teams, clear and culturally specific artistic visions, growing fan bases, and access to funding. That my team and I were able to accomplish so much in so little time convinced me of the value of intersectional, artistic, and small-scale development, even as bigger networked distributors pursued mass targeting and customization with abandon.

Throughout 2016 a very different community of people used networked distribution to challenge legacy television: the so-called alt-right, emboldened by the rise and election of Donald J. Trump. The "alt-right" was a rebranding of white supremacy, and I had never seen hate take over the mainstream so clearly and quickly in my life. Scholars and journalists will spend years trying to uncover how this happened, from the spread of "fake news" through social media to the particularities of America's outdated electoral system, but as a television scholar I locate legacy television as another cause. It was through legacy TV, particularly NBC, that Trump rose to promince in the 1980s and 1990s. After his off-camera comments with *Access Hollywood*'s Billy Bush about "grabbing pussy" came to light, more clips of him and Bush on that show started to circulate. For over a decade, from 2004 until he announced his candidacy in 2015, he honed his brand on NBC's *Apprentice*. In late 2016, *Variety* reported that Trump would keep his executive producer credit in *Celebrity Apprentice* after assuming the presidency, making him the first TV producer president.

All of this occurred during what many scholars have identified as a color-blind era in TV. In the networked era, we have to be honest and critical about who is making media, why, for whom, and how their identities influence its production and circulation. We can no longer afford to be blind to the particularities of identities and how they express themselves. We must name white supremacy and combat it with intersectionality, a rigorous analysis of cultural differences and connections. Only by attending to cultural differences and the ways power and scale structure expression can we grapple with what kind of media system America needs. Television and media scholars can find guidance by reaching outside the discipline to black, Latinx, Asian American, American, gender, queer, and performance studies. Performance studies of culture connect individual and community-based expression to political, social, and economic realities by engaging ethnography, history, law, and theory as methodological tools. Their work undergirds my critique of networked television's performance across cultural, organizational, and technological contexts.

Television has always been fraught. It has never fully represented America. Yet the Internet opened up the possibility that TV could not only be more efficient in production and more effective in reaching audiences but also more specific and more sincere in its representations. As networked technologies continue to transform TV, raising new problems and presenting possibilities, let us never forget television's legacy in delivering stories that bring us together and make us more aware of who we are and have yet to become. As Pat Aufderheide wrote on the effects of the 1996 Telecommunications Act,

> The notion of a protected electronic commons has been quashed, by corporations aspiring to be at once the shapers of culture and the delivery systems of it. The sheer abundance of communications options is unlikely to lead, in itself, to formations of electronic commonses. The promise that burgeoning communications systems will create an abundance of access, making governmentally protected spaces and activities unnecessary, turns out to be hollow as the electronic universe expands. It is not merely that corporations are developing new services and striving to develop propriety gates and pathways through that electronic universe. In order to make use of any such common or public spaces, people have to have something to say, someone to talk to, and something that can happen. They need habits, knowledge, history, resources.[7]

Let us demand more than convenience from TV. We must demand that TV represent our cultural complexity and human fallibility. We must continually push TV, in its stories as well as its business practices and technologies, to open.

NOTES

INTRODUCTION

1 In this book, I will shift tenses quite a bit. When writing about events that have happened—production, distribution, and exhibition of specific series—I will use past tense. In all other instances—including analysis of series narratives and the market—I will use present tense, to reflect their persistent relevance at the time of this book's publication.

2 Max Kessler, "Adam Goldman, Creator of *The Outs*, Talks *Girls*, Grindr, and How He Created the Best Web Series Ever," *Paper*, June 26, 2012, www.papermag.com; Matt Miller, "Why Fans of *Girls* and *Master of None* Should Be Watching *The Outs*," *Esquire*, March 30, 2016, www.esquire.com.

3 John Sherman, "The New Normative: Queer Politics in *The Outs*," *Los Angeles Review of Books*, May 17, 2016, lareviewofbooks.org

4 *Work It* was a very short-lived ABC show about two straight men who dress like women because women supposedly find employment easier to secure in the new economy (a laughable premise given Hollywood's own diversity problems).

5 Adam Goldman, "The Outs," *Kickstarter*, March 27, 2012, www.kickstarter.com/projects/236250953/the-outs.

6 The most-funded film/video project on Kickstarter before Hollywood producers started using the site was Freddie Wong's web series, *Video Game High School*, a record that would be overtaken the following year by another web series from animation outfit Frederator Studios. See Sam Gutelle, "'Bee and Puppycat' Raises $872,133, Breaks Kickstarter Record," *Tubefilter*, November 14, 2013, www.tubefilter.com.

7 Janet Wasko, *Hollywood in the Information Age: Beyond the Silver Screen* (Cambridge, MA: Polity Press, 1994), 4.

8 I will generally refer to viewers of open TV programs as "fans," to reflect that the vast majority of people must actively seek out these productions (because producers frequently do not have marketing budgets to reach them) and frequently engage with them (liking, commenting, sharing) because of the affordances of digital platforms. I will use the term "audiences" and "viewers" to refer to the industrial construction of this activity—in other words, how producers and the market frame engagement to describe or specify program value.

9 Timothy Havens, Amanda Lotz, Serra Tinic, "Critical Media Industry Studies: A Research Approach," *Communication, Culture, and Critique* 2, no. 2 (2009): 234–53.

10 Ibid., 247.

11 John Thorton Caldwell, *Production Culture: Industrial Reflexivity and Critical Practice in Film and Television* (Durham, NC: Duke University Press, 2008).

12 I have been particularly inspired by Dick Hebdige, *Subculture: The Meaning of Style* (New York: Routledge, 1979); John Jackson, *Real Black: Adventures in Racial Sincerity* (Chicago: University of Chicago Press, 2005); and Esther Newton, *Mother Camp: Female Impersonators in America* (Chicago: University of Chicago Press, 1972).

13 Devorah Heitner, *Black Power TV* (Durham, NC: Duke University Press, 2013); Alisa Perren, *Indie, Inc.: Miramax and the Transformation of Hollywood in the 1990s* (Austin: University of Texas Press, 2012); David Hesmondhalgh, "Indie: The Institutional Politics and Aesthetics of a Popular Music Genre," *Cultural Studies* 13, no. 1 (1998): 34–61; Denise Mann, *Hollywood Independents: The Postwar Talent Takeover* (Minneapolis: University of Minnesota Press, 2008); Henry Jenkins, *Textual Poachers: Television Fans & Participatory Culture* (New York: Routledge, 1992); Ramon Lobato, *Shadow Economies of Cinema: Mapping Informal Film Distribution* (London: Palgrave Macmillan, 2012); Susan J. Douglas, *Inventing American Broadcasting, 1899–1922* (Baltimore, MD: Johns Hopkins University Press, 1989); Judy L. Isaksen, "Resistive Radio: African Americans' Evolving Portrayal and Participation from Broadcasting to Narrowcasting," *Journal of Popular Culture* 45, no. 4 (2012): 749–68; Michael Keith, *Signals in the Air: Native Broadcasting in America* (Westport, CT: Praeger/Greenwood, 1995) and *Voices in the Purple Haze: Underground Radio and the Sixties* (Westport, CT: Praeger/Greenwood, 1997); Robert Hilliard and Michael Keith, *The Broadcast Century and Beyond* (Burlington, MA: Focus Press, 2005); Deirdre Boyle, *Subject to Change: Guerilla Television Revisited* (New York: Oxford University Press, 1997); S. Craig Watkins, *Representing: Hip Hop Culture and the Production of Black Cinema* (Chicago: University of Chicago Press, 1998).

14 Perren, *Indie, Inc.*; Michael Z. Newman, *Indie: An American Film Culture* (New York: Columbia University Press, 2011).

15 "Above" and "below the line" is a way of organizing labor or production that arose during the twentieth century. Above-the-line producers are typically creative leaders like writers, directors, and lead actors, whereas below-the-line workers compose the majority of the crew who execute producers' vision. As will be shown in chapter 3, indie productions frequently confound these distinctions. I position this kind of labor as "off the line."

16 Andy Plesser, "Web Originals to See $250 Million in Production Budgets in 2013, IAWTV Chair," *Beet.tv*, January 10, 2013, www.beet.tv.

17 IAWTV, Press release, "Web Series Grow 150% from 2011 with Record Number of New Releases, Representing $135MM+ Industry," International Academy of Web Television, November 5, 2012.

18 More about YouTube's premium channel initiative will be discussed in chapter 5. Google initially put its investment at $100 million, essentially an advance to stu-

dios that they would have to pay back in advertising generated through views and sales. Google later doubled that investment but also cut the number of channels considerably, leading prominent independents to balk. See Claire Cain Miller, "YouTube to Serve Niche Tastes by Adding Channels," *New York Times*, October 7, 2012, www.nytimes.com; Chase Hoffberger, "Hank Green Sounds Off on You-Tube's '$300M Hole,'" *DailyDot*, April 1, 2013, www.dailydot.com.

19 Visible Measures stopped ranking web series that year. See Visible Measures, "The Top 10 Most Watched Web Series," *Visible Measures*, August 2010, www.visible-measures.com.

20 While all the above could refer to scripted and nonscripted (or reality) video projects, this book will focus almost exclusively on scripted web series. Focusing on scripted content emphasizes labor-intensive and deliberate production and marketing: producers must carefully craft a message, assemble a team, and deliver it to users. This approach unfortunately deemphasizes a number of important creations, most notably vlogs (the domain of YouTube), which are cheaper and thus even more diverse and successful.

21 For more on efforts to include new media and video game writing in the Writers Guild, see chapter 5 in Miranda Banks's history of the WGA: Miranda Banks, *The Writers: A History of American Screenwriters and Their Guild* (New Brunswick, NJ: Rutgers University Press, 2015), 195–232.

22 The *Hollywood Reporter* reported that the Emmys had interest in web content as early as 2005, but a disagreement between New York– and Los Angeles–based academies delayed the decision for years, until the Hollywood-based Academy of Television Arts and Sciences relented and designated three areas of competition, partly in response to the success of web dramas like *Quarterlife*. Debra Kaufman, "Broadband Content Has a Place at the Emmys," *Hollywood Reporter*, May 20, 2008, www.hollywoodreporter.com.

23 Jude Dry, "Short Form Emmy Nominations: 'Children's Hospital' Leads, Few Independents Honored," *IndieWire*, July 14, 2016, www.indiewire.com; Jude Dry, "Emmys 2016: 'Her Story' Nomination Is the Cinderella Story Trans Creators Needed," *IndieWire*, July, 21, 2016, www.indiewire.com.

24 David Hesmondhalgh, "User-Generated Content, Free Labour, and the Cultural Industries," *Ephemera* 10, no. 3/4 (2010): 280–82; David Hesmondhalgh and Sarah Baker, "'A Very Complicated Version of Freedom': Conditions and Experiences of Creative Labour in Three Cultural Industries," *Poetics* 38, no. 1 (2010): 4–20.

25 Amanda Lotz, "How to Spend $9.3 Billion in Three Days: Examining the Upfront Buying Process in the Production of US Television Culture," *Media, Culture & Society* 29, no. 4 (2007): 550.

26 Josef Adalian, "Why Fox's Kevin Reilly Is Canceling Pilot Season," *Vulture*, May 6, 2014, www.vulture.com.

27 Ibid.

28 Estimates range from two thousand to three thousand. See Amy Chozick, "The Math of a Hit TV Show," *Wall Street Journal*, May 2, 2011, www.wsj.com.

29 Ibid.

30 Anthony Crupi, "Cable Upfront Haul Passes the US$10 Billion Mark," *Adweek*, October 21, 2013, www.adweek.com.

31 David Dayen, "The Real World of Reality TV: Worker Exploitation," *In These Times*, October 14, 2014, inthesetimes.com; John Vanderhoef, "Guilds Struggle to Organize Reality TV," *Carsey-Wolf Center: Media Industries Project*, December 2, 2013, www.carseywolf.ucsb.edu.

32 A practice some broadcast networks are starting to follow, most notably Fox. See Nellie Andreeva, "Fox's Abolishment of Pilot Season: Practical Guide to How Will It Work," *Deadline*, January 13, 2014, deadline.com.

33 Internet Advertising Bureau, "IAB Internet Advertising Revenue Report 2014: Full Year Results," *Internet Advertising Bureau*, April 2015, www.iab.net.

34 Lotz, "How to Spend $9.3 Billion in Three Days," 556.

35 Lotz, "How to Spend $9.3 Billion in Three Days."

36 Maureen Ryan, "TV Peaks Again in 2016: Could It Hit 500 Shows in 2017?" *Variety*, December 21, 2016, variety.com.

37 Film LA, *2016 Television Pilot Production Report* (Los Angeles: Film LA, 2015).

38 Film LA, *2013 Television Pilot Production Report* (Los Angeles: Film LA, 2013).

39 Vicki Mayer, "Who Benefits from Film and Television Tax Incentives," *Wall Street Journal*, January 15, 2015, blogs.wsj.com.

40 Film LA, *2016 Television Pilot Production Report*.

41 Todd Gitlin, *Inside Prime Time* (New York: Pantheon, 1983), 14.

42 Ibid., 26.

43 Ibid., 29; William T. Bielby and Denise D. Bielby, "'All Hits Are Flukes': Institutionalized Decision Making and the Rhetoric of Network Prime-Time Program Development," *American Journal of Sociology* 99, no. 5 (1994): 1287–1313.

44 Glen Creeber, *Serial Television: Big Drama on the Small Screen* (London: British Film Institute, 2004); Jason Mittell, *Complex TV: The Poetics of Contemporary Television Storytelling* (New York: NYU Press, 2015).

45 This has been the case historically, but inequalities have been exacerbated as writing staffs cut back and are more egregious given the possibilities of redistributing programs equitably across multiple channels. See James S. Ettema, "The Organizational Context of Creativity: A Case Study from Public Television," in *Individuals in Mass Media Organizations: Creativity and Constraint*, eds. James S. Ettema and David Charles Whitney (Beverly Hills, CA: Sage, 1982), 91–106; Joseph Turow, "Unconventional Programs on Commercial Television: An Organization Perspective," in *Individuals in Mass Media Organizations: Creativity & Constraint*, eds. James S. Ettema and David Charles Whitney (Beverly Hills, CA: Sage, 1982), 107–29.

46 Patricia Aufderheide, *Communications Policy and the Public Interest* (New York: Guilford Press, 1999), 49.

47 Ibid.

48 Aufderheide, *Communications Policy and the Public Interest*, 83.

49 Brian Steinberg, "How TV Tuned in More Upfront Ad Dollars: Soap, Toothpaste, and Pushy Tactics," *Variety*, July 27, 2016, variety.com; Rick Porter, "CBS Wins the 2015–16 TV Season, Plus a Guide to Network Spin on the Ratings," *TV by the Numbers*, May 25, 2016, tvbythenumbers.

50 Darnell Hunt, "Turning Missed Opportunities into Realized Ones," *2014 Hollywood Writers Report*, 2014, www.wga.org; Darnell Hunt, "Renaissance in Reverse?" *2016 Hollywood Writers Report*, 2016, www.wga.org.

51 Darnell Hunt and Anna-Christina Ramón, *2015 Hollywood Diversity Report: Flipping the Script* (Los Angeles: Ralph A. Bunche Center for African American Studies at the University of California, February 2, 2015), www.bunchecenter.ucla.edu.

52 Denise D. Bielby and William T. Bielby, "Hollywood Dreams, Harsh Realities: Writing for Film and Television," *Contexts* 1, no. 4 (2002): 21–27; NAACP Hollywood Bureau, *Out of Focus—Out of Sync: Take 4; A Report on the Television Industry* (NAACP Hollywood Bureau, 2008), courses.washington.edu; Aymar Jean Christian, "The Black TV Crisis and the Next Generation," *Flow* 18, no. 5 (2013), flowtv.org; Beejoli Shah, "In the White Room with Black Writers: Hollywood's 'Diversity Hires,'" *Defamer*, December 20, 2013, defamer.gawker.com.

53 NAACP Hollywood Bureau, *Out of Focus—Out of Sync.*

54 Darnell Hunt, "WGAW 2015 TV Staffing Brief," *Writers Guild of America, West*, March 3, 2015, www.wga.org.

55 Maureen Ryan, "Peak Inequality: Investigating the Lack of Diversity among TV Directors," *Variety*, November 10, 2015, variety.com.

56 Maureen Ryan, "FX CEO John Landgraf on the 'Racially Biased' System and Taking Major Steps to Change His Network's Director Rosters," *Variety*, August 9, 2016, variety.com.

57 NBC's strategy, which allowed them to weather the multichannel transition, included ordering shows like *Will & Grace, Friends, Frasier,* and, later, *The Office,* to make the channel a "'premium brand'—one with an audience of young, wealthy city dwellers," the *New York Times* reported in an extensive 1998 report showing how broadcasters were increasingly focusing on young, affluent viewers. For most of the 2000s, NBC would boast the high percentage of its upper-income viewers to advertisers as a way of hedging declining ratings. Other scholars have argued that while networks have historically targeted upscale viewers, increasing market competition in the 1990s forced broadcasters to refine their demographic to one that incorporated gays and lesbians but left out those who were not white:

    [I]n the mid-1990s, the quality demographic that has become the most widely sought after isn't simply upscale adults but, more specifically, "hip," "sophisticated," urban-minded, white, college-educated, upscale eighteen to forty-nine year olds with liberal attitudes, disposable income, and a distinctively edgy and ironic sensibility, a group basically comprised of segments of the aging yet still socially progressive and upwardly mobile baby boomers and the youthful twenty- and thirty-somethings that follow in their wake.

See Ron Becker, "Prime-Time Television in the Gay Nineties: Network Television, Quality Audiences, and Gay Politics," *Velvet Light Trap*, Fall 1998, 38; Bill Carter, "Shrinking Network TV Audiences Set Off Alarm and Reassessment," *New York Times*, November 22, 1998, A1.

58 Stuart Cunningham, *Hidden Innovation: Policy, Industry, and the Creative Sector* (Brisbane, Australia: University of Queensland Press, 2013), 4.

59 Ibid., 7.

60 Lotz, "How to Spend $9.3 Billion in Three Days," 557.

61 Ratings for individual series, while rising, cannot match them—programs like AMC's *Walking Dead* and Netflix's *Orange Is the New Black*, along with sports, aside.

62 Henry Jenkins, Sam Ford, and Joshua Green, *Spreadable Media: Creating Value and Meaning in Networked Culture* (New York: NYU Press, 2013); Amanda Lotz, *The Television Will Be Revolutionized* (New York: NYU Press, 2007); Teresa Rizzo, "Programming Your Own Channel: An Archaeology of the Playlist," in *TV Futures: Digital Television Policy in Australia*, ed. Andrew Kenyon (Melbourne, Australia: Melbourne University Press, 2007), 107–31; Ethan Tussey, "Connected Viewing on the Second Screen: The Limitations of the Living Room," in *Connected Viewing: Selling, Streaming, and Sharing Media in the Digital Age*, eds. Jennifer Holt and Kevin Sanson (New York: Routledge, 2014), 202–16.

63 Lotz, "How to Spend $9.3 Billion in Three Days," 555.

64 Cunningham, *Hidden Innovation*.

65 Ibid.; Edmund Phelps, *Mass Flourishing: How Grassroots Innovation Created Jobs, Challenge, and Change* (Princeton, NJ: Princeton University Press, 2013).

66 Paul Stoneman, *Soft Innovation: Economics, Product Aesthetics, and the Creative Industries* (New York: Oxford University Press, 2010).

67 Ibid.

68 Andrew Currah, on the basis of interivews with 150 executives, describes the problem well in his analysis of film studios' responses to file sharing:

> These executives have powerful incentives to protect the existing spatial and temporal structure of "release windows," which is currently dominated by a physical commodity form—sales of the "digital versatile disc" (DVD) format. As we will see, this strategic behaviour is rational and fiscally advisable in the short-term (as it seeks to minimize risk and maximize quarterly earnings); but it is suboptimal and potentially damaging (to consumers, creators and even the oligopoly) in the long-term.

Andrew Currah, "Hollywood versus the Internet: The Media and Entertainment Industries in a Digital and Networked Economy," *Journal of Economic Geography* 6, no. 4 (2006): 442; Jason Potts and Stuart Cunningham, "Four Models of Creative Industries," *International Journal of Cultural Policy* 14, no. 3 (2008): 233–47.

69 Though Catherine Squires reminds us that innovation is key to black contributions to media generally. S. Craig Watkins, *Representing: Hip Hop Culture and the Production of Black Cinema* (Chicago: University of Chicago Press, 1998), 68;

Catherine Squires, *African Americans and the Media* (Malden, MA: Polity Press, 2009), 3.

70 What communication scholars have variously called "co-creation" or "co-development." See John Banks and Mark Deuze, "Co-Creative Labour," *International Journal of Cultural Studies* 12, no. 5 (2009): 419–31; Gernot Grabher, Oliver Ibert, and Saskia Flohr, "The Neglected King: The Customer in the New Knowledge Ecology of Innovation," *Economic Geography* 84, no. 3 (2008): 253–80; Jason Potts et al., "Consumer Cocreation and Situated Creativity," *Industry and Innovation* 15, no. 5 (2008): 459–74; William Uricchio, "Beyond the Great Divide: Collaborative Networks and the Challenge to Dominant Conceptions of Creative Industries," *International Journal of Cultural Studies* 7, no. 1 (2004): 79–90.

71 Josh Quiggin, "Blogs, Wikis, and Creative Innovation," *International Journal of Cultural Studies* 9, no. 4 (2006): 481–96.

72 I am sympathetic to critiques of Australian creative industries policies that locate innovation primarily in the market and thus minimize the importance of the state in supporting art for the public good. The inequality in American media's production (overproduction and oversupply of media workers) and distribution markets (high sale value for television series and films) makes the situation quite distinct and, I assert, changes innovation in a country where there is little corporate or state support for independent production. For a critique of Australian media industries policy, see Justin O'Connor, "Creative Industries: A New Direction?" *International Journal of Cultural Policy* 15, no. 4 (2009): 387–402.

73 Gina Neff, *Venture Labor: Work and the Burden of Risk in Innovative Industries* (Cambridge: Massachusetts Institute of Technology Press, 2012), 4.

74 Mariana Mazzucato, *The Entrepreneurial State: Debunking Public v. Private Sector Myths* (New York: Anthem, 2013), 7.

75 Christina Dunbar-Hester, *Low Power to the People: Pirates, Protest, and Politics in FM Radio Activism* (Cambridge: Massachusetts Institute of Technology Press, 2014); Bill Herman, *The Fight over Digital Rights: The Politics of Copyright and Technology* (New York: Cambridge University Press, 2013); Jenkins, Ford, and Green, *Spreadable Media*; Derek Johnson, *Media Franchising: Creative License and Collaboration in the Culture Industries* (New York: NYU Press, 2013); Vicki Mayer, *Below the Line: Producers and Production Studies in the New Television Economy* (Durham, NC: Duke University Press, 2011).

76 Angela McRobbie, *Be Creative: Making a Living in the New Culture Industries* (Cambridge, MA: Polity Press, 2016), 14.

77 Aymar Jean Christian, "The Problem of YouTube," *Flow* 13, no. 8 (February 11, 2011), flowtv.org.

CHAPTER 1. DEVELOPING OPEN TV

1 Staff, "Net Enters TV Age: 2 Webcasters Try Launching Online Networks," *Variety*, October 3, 1996, 8.

2 Ibid.

3 John Geirland and Eva Sonesh-Kedar, *Digital Babylon: How the Geeks, the Suits, and the Ponytails Tried to Bring Hollywood to the Internet* (New York: Arcade, 1999).

4 Jennifer Holt, *Empires of Entertainment: Media Industries and the Politics of Deregulation, 1980–1996* (New Brunswick, NJ: Rutgers University Press, 2011).

5 Parts of this chapter come from material previously published in *First Monday*. See Aymar Jean Christian, "Real Vlogs: The Rules and Meanings of Personal Online Videos," *First Monday* 14, no. 11 (2009), firstmonday.org.

6 Tim Wu, *The Master Switch: The Rise and Fall of Information Empires* (New York: Random House, 2010).

7 John Ellis, *Seeing Things: Television in the Age of Uncertainty* (New York: Tauris, 2002).

8 Henry Jenkins, *Convergence Culture: Where Old and New Media Collide* (New York: NYU Press, 2006).

9 Caldwell, *Production Culture*.

10 Mayer, *Below the Line*.

11 Lotz, *The Television Will Be Revolutionized*.

12 Jason Mittell, *Genre and Television: From Cop Shows to Cartoons in American Culture* (New York: Routledge, 2004), 5, emphasis in original.

13 Creeber, *Serial Television*; Jason Mittell, "Narrative Complexity in Contemporary American Television," *Velvet Light Trap* 58 (2006): 29–40.

14 Jane Feuer, "Narrative Form in American Network Television," in *High Theory/ Low Culture*, ed. Colin MacCabe (Manchester, UK: Manchester University Press, 1986), 101–14; Sarah Kozloff, "Narrative Theory and Television," in *Channels of Discourse, Reassembled*, 2nd ed., ed. Robert C. Allen (Chapel Hill: University of North Carolina Press, 1992), 61–100.

15 Max Dawson, "Television's Aesthetic of Efficiency: Convergence Television and the Digital Short," in *Television as Digital Media*, eds. James Bennett and Niki Strange (Durham, NC: Duke University Press, 2011), 206.

16 Kathryn Zickuhr and Aaron Smith, "Home Broadband 2013," *Pew Research Center*, August 26, 2013, www.pewinternet.org; Aaron Smith, "Trends in Broadband Adoption," *Pew Research Center*, August 11, 2010, www.pewinternet.org.

17 Barbara Klinger, *Beyond the Multiplex: Cinema, New Technologies, and the Home* (Berkeley: University of California Press, 2006).

18 William Boddy, *New Media and Popular Imagination: Launching Radio, Television, and Digital Media in the United States* (London: Oxford University Press, 2004), 57.

19 Arlene Dávila, *Latinos, Inc.: The Marketing and Making of a People* (Berkeley: University of California Press, 2001); Herman Gray, *Watching Race: Television and the Struggle for Blackness* (Minneapolis: University of Minnesota Press, 2004); Katherine Sender, *Business, Not Politics: The Making of the Gay Market* (New York: Columbia University Press, 2004); Joseph Turow, *Breaking Up America: Advertisers and the New Media World* (Chicago: University of Chicago Press, 1997).

20 Ien Ang, *Desperately Seeking the Audience* (New York: Routledge, 1991), 2; James S. Ettema and D. Charles Whitney, *Audiencemaking: How the Media Create the Audience* (New York: Sage, 1994); Jenkins, *Textual Poachers*; David Morley, *Television, Audiences, and Cultural Studies* (New York: Routledge, 1992).

21 Lotz, *The Television Will Be Revolutionized*, 38.

22 "A Second 'Homicide' Shifts Content to Web," *USA Today*, March 24, 1998, 10D.

23 Ibid.

24 Jim Hu, "NBCi President, Other Execs Leaving Portal Company," *CNET*, January 2, 2002, news.cnet.com.

25 Rex Weiner, "Break-in at WWW Hot 'Spot,'" *Variety*, June 12, 1995, 7. One other article noted the connections between web soaps and traditional print writers: Robert Bowden, "Fiction Becomes Reality on the World Wide Web," *Tampa Tribune*, March 15, 1996, 1. This connection is probably best seen in the Lifetime web drama, *In the House of Dreams*, which was written by a popular novelist.

26 Given its time period, videos were short, usually less than a minute, and took quite a bit of time to load.

27 Virginia Rohan, "Soaps on Line: Tune in Tomorrow; Same Place, Whatever Time," *Record*, February 18, 1996, E01; G. Spring, "See 'Spot' Duo Run to New Deal for NBC, Online," *Electronic Media*, February 12, 1996, 40. In terms of staff, *The Spot* started with a small group of about five people working after hours at the agency and grew to almost seventy in 1996. Antonia Zerbisias, "Cyberscapes: The Internet's Infant 'Episodic Websites' Are Starting to Draw Crowds—and Advertisers," *Toronto Star*, August 18, 1996, B1.

28 Rohan, "Soaps on Line."

29 Stephen Lynch, "Online Mystery Soon Unfolds," *Orange County Register*, October 18, 1995, A01.

30 Ibid.; Michele Hilmes, *Hollywood and Broadcasting: From Radio to Cable* (Chicago: University of Illinois Press, 1999).

31 Marc Graser, "Play or Pay: Networks Eye New Website Uses," *Variety*, September 14–20, 1998, 27; "NBC's Development Deal with 'The Spot' Creators," *Newsbytes*, February 7, 1996.

32 "A List of Some Broadcasters' On-Line Ventures," *Associated Press*, December 14, 1995.

33 Rex Weiner, "Net Gain: CAA Hits 'Spot,'" *Variety*, January 4, 1996, 1.

34 Gitlin, *Inside Prime Time*, 14.

35 Janet Wasko, *Hollywood in the Information Age: Beyond the Silver Screen* (Cambridge, UK: Polity, 1995), 8.

36 Rohan, "Soaps on Line."

37 Glenn Gamboa, "Soaps Emote on Command for Users of the Web," *Akron Beacon Journal*, August 18, 1996, E1.

38 Colin Covert, "As the Web Site Turns," *Variety*, March 14, 1996, 1E.

39 Gamboa, "Soaps Emote."

40 Zerbisias, "Cyberscapes."

41 Robert C. Allen, *Speaking of Soap Opeas* (Chapel Hill: University of North Carolina Press, 1985).

42 Ibid., 4.

43 Jenkins, Ford, and Green, *Spreadable Media*.

44 Louisa Ellen Stein, *Millennial Fandom: Television Audiences in the Transmedia Age* (Iowa City: University of Iowa Press, 2015), 161, 167.

45 Philip Fine, "Cyber-soaps on the Net: Will They Really Wash? Episodic Programs on the Internet Have Attracted Hollywood Money and Talent, but Most of the Suspense Lies in Waiting for Still Pictures to Form On-screen," *Globe and Mail*, November 2, 1996, C21.

46 Kate Stalter, "Layoffs Hit 'Spot': 12 Let Go at Internet Co. American Cybercast," *Variety*, November 22, 1996, 3.

47 Kate Stalter, "Cybercast in Search of Cybercash," *Variety*, January 13–19, 1997, 150.

48 Art Kramer, "Out, Digital 'Spot': Web Serial Opera May Get the Wash," *Atlanta Journal-Constitution*, January 9, 1997, 07C.

49 Jim McClellan, "Cyberlife UK: Soap Bubble Bursts," *Guardian*, January 23, 1997, 13.

50 Jennifer Gillan, *Television and New Media: Must-Click TV* (New York: Routledge, 2011), 39–46.

51 Richard Helm, "NBC Pioneers TV Drama on the Net: Leading U.S. Network Experiments with Web Sites That Complement Prime-Time Schedule," *Gazette*, August 1997, B8.

52 George Mannes, "NBC TV Works Second Shift on Web," *Daily News*, December 21, 1997, 50.

53 Geirland and Sonesh-Kedar, *Digital Babylon*, 245.

54 Ibid., 204.

55 Ibid., 223.

56 Microsoft also provided technological support to numerous media companies, from BET to NBC. Denise Caruso, "Microsoft Morphs into a Media Company," *Wired*, June 1, 1996, www.wired.com.

57 Michele Matassa Flores, "MSN to Cancel Its 'Shows,' Lay Off 50 Workers," *Seattle Times*, February 26, 1998, community.seattletimes.nwsource.com.

58 Jay Sherman, "Online Efforts a Tangled Web: Showbiz-Silicon Valley Alliance is Probed at Internet World," *Hollywood Reporter*, March 11, 1998.

59 Linton Weeks, "The Moving Pixel Show: Internet Video Companies Are Starting to Roll," *Washington Post*, February 16, 1999, C01.

60 Ibid.

61 Michele White, *The Body and the Screen: Theories of Internet Spectatorship* (Cambridge, MA: MIT Press, 2006).

62 Weeks, "The Moving Pixel Show," C01.

63 Sam Gutelle, "Comedy Central Launches CC Studios for Digital Content," *Tubefilter*, January 31, 2013, www.tubefilter.com.

64 Nick Marx, "'The Missing Link Moment': Web Comedy in New Media Industries," *Velvet Light Trap* 68, no. 15 (2011): 14–23.

65 Mittell, "Narrative Complexity."

66 "AtomFilms Brands Its Comedy Shorts: 'Definitely Not Hollywood'; Leveraging the Internet to Find Tomorrow's Talent for Today's Consumers," *Business Wire*, September 22, 1999.

67 Richard Katz and Martin Peers, "AtomFilm Secures Biondi, WB Funding," *Variety*, May 26, 1999, 12.

68 Marc Graser, "Web-First Content Finds Friendly Market," *Variety*, June 27, 2000, A2; Frank Houston, "Hollywood Flirts with Short Films on the Web," *New York Times*, June 15, 2000, G13.

69 Peter M. Nichols, "Now Playing, Short Stories at a Web Theater Near You," *New York Times*, December 30, 2000, B9.

70 Marc Graser, "Net Set Gets Fest-Friendly," *Variety*, October 4–10, 1999, 37. Atom-Films was not the only one. Icebox reportedly gave away stock and cuts of offline revenue to producers, though it's unclear whether this was a cost-cutting measure implemented in its final months before closing up. Neil Strauss, "Where Funny Zombies Like to Eat Human Brains," *New York Times*, May 27, 2000, B17; Tim Swanson, "Icebox Melting Sans Cash," *Variety*, February 8, 2001, 1.

71 Klinger, *Beyond the Multiplex*, 195.

72 Marc Graser, "IFilm Starts TV Series for IFC on Independents," *Variety*, August 23, 2000, 6.

73 Klinger, *Beyond the Multiplex*, 205.

74 Ibid.

75 Ibid.; Jill Feiwell, "Toonspotting: A Guide to the Web," *Variety*, May 30, 2000, A10.

76 Paul Glader, "Internet Animators Star in a New Medium, the 'Webisode,'" *Associated Press*, July 3, 2002; Tim Swanson, "Keeping Broadband Hope Alive," *Variety*, February 26–March 4, 2001, 18.

77 Graser, "Web-First Content Finds Friendly Market," A2.

78 Amy Harmon, "Slowly and Saucily, Internet Animations Nibble at TV's Turf," *New York Times*, October 30, 2000, A1.

79 Michael Schneider, "TV Toppers Fret over Toon Boom," *Variety*, January 31–February 6, 2000, 47.

80 Amy Harmon, "Coming to Grips with the Web: Reluctantly Cooperating in the Redefining of Fun," *New York Times*, December 11, 2000, C5.

81 Marc Graser, "Dot-Com Dough: Only Top-Tier Talent Taps the Till," *Variety*, September 4–10, 2000, 1.

82 Marc Graser, "Sign Here Please," *Variety*, October 2–8, 2000, 48.

83 Tim Swanson and Marc Graser, "Heavy Hits $3 Mil in Financing," *Variety*, March 1, 2001, 6.

84 Marc Graser, "H'w'd Clicks on Content," *Variety*, June 7, 2000, 1.

85 Lotz, *The Television Will Be Revolutionized*, 94.

86 Richard Covington, "Net TV: New Stage for Video Creativity," *International Herald Tribune*, July 5, 2000, 13.

87 Graser, "H'w'd Clicks on Content."

88 Marc Graser, "Lessons Learned," *Variety*, January 22–28, 2001, 18.

89 Marc Graser, "Z.com Joins Net Casualties," *Variety*, February 13, 2001, 5.

90 Stuart Elliott, "The Convergence of Hip: Calvin Klein's Newest Campaign Features a Crucial Internet Component," *New York Times*, November 18, 1998, C7.

91 Ann Donahue, "Itsy Bitsy Dials 'Net Coin," *Variety*, October 24, 2000, 4; Wendy Jackson Hall, "Content Providers Question Next Big Move," *Variety*, November 10, 2000, A4.

92 Michael McCarthy, "More Star-Studded Ads Hit Small Screen Web Films, Strike Threats Give Commercials Appeal," *USA Today*, April 6, 2001, 8B.

93 The trend was sometimes called "mini-movies" and was credited with helping encourage theaters to use digital projection. McCarthy, "More Star-Studded Ads," 8B; Amy Harmon, "Using a Hard Drive to Show Films in Theaters," *New York Times*, November 14, 2002, 5. For a definitive account of how new media interacted with cinema at this time, see Klinger, *Beyond the Multiplex*.

94 Vera H-C Chan, "Now Showing on the Web: Internet Films Changing the Ways Movies Are Made," *Contra Costa Times*, May 6, 2001, C03.

95 James Curtis, "Brands Are Now Looking beyond Traditional TV Ads and Sponsorship to Connect with Audiences," *Marketing*, September 11, 2003, 20; Scott Donaton, *Madison and Vine: Why Entertainment and Advertising Industries Must Converge to Survive* (New York: McGraw-Hill, 2004).

96 "10 Best Web Series or Films," *Advertising Age*, 2004, 26; Angela Phipps Towle, "Diversify and Conquer," *Hollywood Reporter*, June 11, 2004, 37–40.

97 Brian Steinberg, "Have You Ever Noticed How Internet Ads Are More Creative? Seinfeld, Superman Reunite in American Express Pitch as Web Campaigns Intensify," *Wall Street Journal*, March 30, 2004, B3.

98 John Hayes, American Express's chief marketing officer. Ibid.

99 Robert W. McChesney, *Communication Revolution: Critical Junctures and the Future of Media* (New York: New Press, 2007).

100 Bree Brouwer, "YouTube CEO Susan Wojcicki Discusses Her Plans for the Site," *Tubefilter*, October 6, 2014, www.tubefilter.com.

101 Eleftheria Parpis, "David Carson on *The Spot*," *Adweek*, June 12, 2006, www.adweek.com.

102 Dan Glaister, "Hollywood Writers Threaten Internet Breakaway: Plan to Circumvent Studios as Strike Deadlock Goes On: Talkshows Due Back on Air without Key Creative Staff," *New York Times*, December 29, 2007, 25.

103 Edward Wyatt, "As Writers' Strike Looms, Stakes Are Higher for TV Than Film," *New York Times*, October 18, 2007, C9.

104 Seeing competition from a range of media, legacy distributors reduced costs with reality television while increasing investments in key scripted shows designd to be tent poles and critical darlings. Jason Mittell documents many of these series in *Complex TV: The Poetics of Contemporary Television Storytelling* (New York: NYU Press, 2015).

105 Creeber, *Serial Television*; Mittell, "Narrative Complexity."

CHAPTER 2. OPEN TV PRODUCTION

1 For a grad school class on "Ethnographic Imagination" I made pilots for a series called *MEET*, about two people who are trying to meet up after talking online. I held the camera and my colleague, Rocio Nuñez, handled the boom and assisted in directing. My late friend Jiwon Lee starred alongside Brett Bumgarner, another grad student friend.

2 We completed postproduction after I was hired at Northwestern University and used my research funds to pay an editor an appropriate, if still modest, amount, in exchange for allowing him to use his brand at the end of each episode.

3 David Hesmondhalgh and Sarah Baker, *Creative Labour: Media Work in Three Cultural Industries* (New York: Routledge, 2013).

4 In 2014, Above Average and UCB Comedy extended their partnership. Sam Gutelle, "Upright Citizen Brigade YouTube Channel Joins Above Average Network," *Tubefilter*, May 12, 2014, www.tubefilter.com.

5 Ilana Glazer, "How Two Broads Braved the Web (*Broad City*)," *Televisual*, April 29, 2013, tvisual.org.

6 Aymar Jean Christian, "15 Web Series That Could Be the Next *Broad City*," *IndieWire*, April 2, 2014, www.indiewire.com.

7 Caldwell, *Production Culture*, 36.

8 Johnson, *Media Franchising*; Denise Mann, "It's Not TV, It's Brand Management TV: The Collective Author(s) of the *Lost* Franchise," in *Production Studies: Cultural Studies of Media Industries*, eds. Vicki Mayer, Miranda Banks, and John Thorton Caldwell (New York: Routledge, 2009), 99–114.

9 Michael Curtin and Kevin Sanson, *Precarious Creativity: Global Media, Local Labor* (Los Angeles: University of California Press, 2016).

10 Mark Deuze, *Media Work* (Cambridge, UK: Polity, 2007), 173.

11 Michael Curtin, "VFX Labor Unrest Points to Broader Trends in Hollywood," *Carsey-Wolf Center: Media Industries Project*, June 7, 2013, www.carseywolf.ucsb.edu.

12 John Thorton Caldwell, "Para-Industry: Researching Hollywood's Blackwaters," *Cinema Journal* 52, no. 3 (Spring 2013): 157–65.

13 Mayer, *Below the Line*, 3.

14 Mike Schramm, "BlizzCon 2009: WoW.com Interviews Felicia Day," *Engadget*, August 24, 2009, www.engadget.com.

15 Felicia D. Henderson, "It's Your Own Fault: How Post-Strike Hollywood Continues to Punish Writers for Striking," *Popular Communication* 8, no. 3 (2010): 235.

16 John Thorton Caldwell, "Breaking Ranks: Backdoor Workforces, Messy Workflows, and Craft Disaggregation," *Popular Communication* 8, no. 3 (2010): 222.

17 Miranda J. Banks, "*I Love Lucy*: The Writer-Producer," in *How to Watch Television*, eds. Ethan Thompson and Jason Mittell (New York: NYU Press, 2013), 244–52.

18 Horace Newcomb and Robert Alley, "The Producer as Artist: Commercial Television," in *Individuals in Mass Media Organizations: Creativity and Constraint*, eds.

James S. Ettema and David Charles Whitney (Beverly Hills, CA: Sage, 1982), 69–89; Turow, "Unconventional Programs."

19 Josh Heuman, "'Independence,' Industrial Authorship, and Professional Entrepreneurship: Representing and Reorganizing Television Writing in the FCC Media Ownership Reviews," *Cinema Journal* 52, no. 3 (2013): 120–44.

20 Ibid.

21 Newcomb and Alley, "The Producer as Artist," 88.

22 Janet Staiger, "Hollywood Mode of Production, 1930–1960," in *The Classical Hollywood Cinema: Film Style and Mode of Production to 1960*, eds. David Bordwell, Janet Staiger, and Kristin Thompson (New York: Columbia University Press, 1985), 548–79; Alan Paul and Archie Kleingartner, "Flexible Production and the Transformation of Industrial Relations in the Motion Picture and Television Industry," *Industrial and Labor Relations Review* 47, no. 4 (1994): 663–78.

23 Guy Standing, *The Precariat: The New Dangerous Class* (London: Bloomsbury Academic, 2011) and *Work after Globalization: Building Occupational Citizenship* (Northampton, MA: Edward Elgar, 2009); Stephen Wood, *The Transformation of Work: Skill, Flexibility, and the Labour Process* (New York: HarperCollins, 1989); Charles F. Sabel and Jonathan Zeitlin, eds., *World of Possibilities: Flexibility and Mass Production in Western Industrialization* (Cambridge UK: Cambridge University Press, 2002).

24 David Stark and László Bruszt, *Postsocialist Pathways: Transforming Politics and Property in East Central Europe* (Cambridge UK: Cambridge University Press, 1998), 7.

25 Aymar Jean Christian, "Indie TV: Innovation in Series Development," in *Media Independence: Working with Freedom or Working For Free?*, James Bennett and Niki Strange (New York: Routledge, 2014), 159–81; Michael Piore and Charles Sabel, *The Second Industrial Divide* (New York: Basic Books, 1984); Joshua Cohen and Charles Sabel, "Directly-Deliberative Polyarchy," *European Law Journal* 3, no. 4 (1997): 313–42; Susan Helper, John Paul MacDuffie, and Charles Sabel, "Pragmatic Collaborations: Advancing Knowledge While Controlling Opportunism," *Industrial and Corporate Change* 9, no. 3 (2000): 443–88.

26 Imogen O'Rorke, "WoW! How *The Guild* Beat the System," *Guardian*, December 22, 2008, 6.

27 Maureen Ryan, "Felicia Day Slays the Internet with 'The Guild,'" *Chicago Tribune*, July 13, 2010, featuresblogs.chicagotribune.com.

28 Wagner James Au, "NewTeeVee Pick: *The Guild*," *NewTeeVee*, October 31, 2007, gigaom.com.

29 Ibid.

30 Joli Jenson, "Fandom as Pathology," in *The Adoring Audience*, ed. Lisa A. Lewis (New York: Routledge, 1992), 9–29; Gus Mastrapa, "How Felicia Day Recruited Millions for Her Guild," *Wired*, September 29, 2009, www.wired.com.

31 Peter Larsen, "'The Guild' Plays by Its Own Rules," *Orange County Register*, June 14, 2009, K.

32 Mary Kirby-Diaz, *Buffy and Angel Conquer the Internet: Essays on Online Fandom* (Jefferson, NC: McFarland, 2009).

33 Joseph Turow, *Niche Envy* (Cambridge, MA: MIT Press, 2006).

34 Mayer, *Below the Line*, 47, emphasis in original.

35 Mastrapa, "How Felicia Day Recruited Millions for Her Guild."

36 Gina Trapani, "How Dr. Horrible's Felicia Day Gets Things Done," *Lifehacker*, August 4, 2008, lifehacker.com.

37 Rich Mbariket, "Web Series Creators Wearing Many Hats: Good or Bad for Production?" *Web Series Network*, June 14, 2011, webseriesnetwork.com.

38 Daisy Whitney, "Web Video Stays above SAG Fray," *Television Week*, October 2008, 4.

39 Ruth Livier, "Green-lit by the Neutral Net (Ylse)," *Televisual*, May 15, 2013, tvisual.org.

40 Dan Cox, "Guilds Sketch Guidelines for High-Tech Talent Deals," *Variety*, December 27–January 2, 1993, 74; David Robb, "Guilds Split on Handling of New Media," *Hollywood Reporter*, February 7, 1994.

41 Lauren Horwitch, "Are You Ready for the New Media?" *Backstage*, March 30, 2006, www.backstage.com.

42 Whitney, "Web Video Stays above SAG Fray."

43 A notable exception for contemporary television is *Louie*, which has a famously low budget, for which its creator, Louis C.K., gets creative control before final cut. Thomas Attila Lewis, "TV Junkie Interview: Louis C.K., Mastermind of FX's 'Louie,'" *LAist*, March 8, 2011, laist.com.

44 Caldwell, *Production Culture*, 201.

45 Ibid., 198.

46 Mastrapa, "How Felicia Day Recruited Millions for Her Guild."

47 Schramm, "BlizzCon 2009."

48 Andrew Wallenstein, "Triple 'Guild' Play for Microsoft," *Hollywood Reporter*, November 24, 2008, www.hollywoodreporter.com.

49 Elizabeth Ellcessor, "Tweeting @feliciaday: Online Social Media, Convergence, and Subcultural Stardom," *Cinema Journal* 51, no. 2 (2012): 48.

50 Susan Murray, *Hitch Your Antenna to the Stars: Early Television and Broadcast Stardom* (New York: Routledge, 2005).

51 Mastrapa, "How Felicia Day Recruited Millions for Her Guild."

52 Day told *NewTeeVee*, "I didn't want it to be so obscure that people who didn't play MMORPGs would be turned off by the 'inside' nature of the material." Au, "NewTeeVee Pick: *The Guild*."

53 Day has referred to the marketing power of her gamer identity explicitly: "So, hopefully there's an authenticity to it because I am a gamer." Matthew Price, "Online Program 'The Guild' to Debut in Comic Book Series," *Oklahoman*, October 2, 2009, newsok.com.

54 Mastrapa, "How Felicia Day Recruited Millions for Her Guild."

55 Ellcessor, "Tweeting @feliciaday," 56.

56 Trapani, "How Dr. Horrible's Felicia Day Gets Things Done."

57 Ibid.

58 Liz Shannon Miller, "Is Kickstarter the Best Solution for Independent Creators?" *NewTeeVee*, October 2, 2011, gigaom.com; Yancey Strickler, Eli Dvorkin, and Elisabeth Holm, "$100 Million Pledged to Independent Film," *Kickstarter*, January 3, 2013, www.kickstarter.com/blog/100-million-pledged-to-independent-film.

59 Mike Schramm, "The Guild Comic Book, and Other News from the SDCC Panel," *WoW Insider*, July 24, 2009, wow.joystiq.com.

60 Felicia Day, *You're Never Weird on the Internet* (New York: Touchstone, 2015); Titan Books, *The Guild: The Official Companion* (London: Titan Books, 2013).

61 Schramm, "BlizzCon 2009."

62 Brian Stelter, "For Xbox, Focus Shifts from Game to Video," *New York Times*, January 19, 2010, B1.

63 Emily Nussbaum, "Taster's Choice: 'High Maintenence' and 'My Mad Fat Diary,'" *New Yorker*, June 6 and 16, 2014, www.newyorker.com.

64 Ann Marie Baldonado, "Friends and Favors: 'High Maintenance' Creators Share Their Secret to Success," *Fresh Air*, NPR, March 4, 2015.

65 Drew Grant, "'High Maintenance' Creators: It's Not TV, It's Art!" *New York Observer*, November 13, 2014, observer.com.

66 Nellie Andreeva, "Ingrid Jungermann to Adapt Her Web Series 'Fo th 7th' as Comedy for Showtime," *Deadline*, April 22, 2016, deadline.com.

67 Hunt and Ramón, *2015 Hollywood Diversity Report*, 18.

68 Ibid., 19.

69 Ibid., 19–20.

70 Carolina A. Miranda, "It's a Hit in More Ways Than One; Industry Buzz Surrounds Pot-Based 'High Maintenance' Internet Comedy," *Los Angeles Times*, April 19, 2015, E8.

71 Alicia Montgomery, "Sex and Another City: For Brown Girls," NPR: *Tell Me More*, May 27, 2010, www.npr.org; Latoya Petersen, "A Web Series for Women That Stands on Its Own," *Jezebel*, June 18, 2010, jezebel.com.

72 Karman Kregloe, "Interview with Carmen Elena Mitchell, Creator of *The Real Girl's Guide to Everything Else*," *AfterEllen*, March 19, 2010, www.afterellen.com.

73 Aymar Jean Christian, "Is Hulu Winning the Web Video Wars?" *Televisual*, July 29, 2010, televisual.org; Aymar Jean Christian, "Rise of the Black Network? Online and On-Air, Growing Alternatives to YouTube and BET," *Black Web 2.0*, October 15, 2010, www.blackweb20.com; Aymar Jean Christian, "BWE: A New Web Network Targeting Black Women," *Televisual*, June 22, 2011, tvisual.org

74 When it was active, KoldCast provided distribution for independent filmmakers, while Rowdy Orbit focused on series by and about people of color. Aymar Jean Christian, "Beyond 'Black Hulu': Rowdy Orbit's Ambitious Bid to Build a Web Series Market," *Televisual*, December 7, 2009, televisual.org.

75 Toby Miller, "Television and Citizenship: A New International Division of Cultural Labor," *Communication, Citizenship, and Social Policy: Rethinking the Limits*

of the Welfare State, eds. Andrew Calabrese and Jean-Claude Burgelman (Lanham, MD: Rowman & Littlefield, 1999), 279–92.

76 Christian Fuchs, "Labor in Informational Capitalism and on the Internet," *Information Society* 26 (2010): 186.

77 Rosalind Gill, "Life Is a Pitch: Managing the Self in New Media Work," in *Managing Media Work*, ed. Mark Deuze (Thousand Oaks, CA: Sage, 2011), 249.

78 Streamy Awards, "Streamy Awards Announce Official Call for Entries and 12 New Categories for 2010 Show," *Streamy Awards*, December 15, 2009, www.streamys.org.

CHAPTER 3. OPEN TV REPRESENTATION

1 John Fiske, *Television Culture* (London: Metheun, 1987).

2 Patricia Hill Collins, *Black Feminist Thought: Knowledge, Consciousness, and the Politics of Empowerment* (New York: Routledge, 2000); Jenkins, Ford, and Green, *Spreadable Media*.

3 Jonathan David Jackson, "The Social World of Voguing," *Journal for the Anthropological Study of Human Movement* 12, no. 2 (2002): 36; Madison Moore, "Walk for Me: Postmodern Dance at the House of Harrell," *Theater* 44, no. 1 (2015): 4–23.

4 *Glee* featured a segment with *Sex and the City*'s Sarah Jessica Parker singing "Let's Have a Kiki"; *Looking* promotional videos featured a guide to "gay" vernacular by New York comic Eliot Glazer; and *Drag Race* drew heavily from black gay subcultural vernacular since its producer, star, and host, RuPaul Charles, grew up artistically in it.

5 Stuart Hall, "What Is This 'Black' in Black Popular Culture?" in *Black Popular Culture*, eds. Michele Wallace and Gina Dent (Seattle: Bay Press, 1992), 24.

6 Jasmine Nicole Cobb and Robin R. Means Coleman, "Two Snaps and a Twist: Controlling Images of Gay Black Men on Television," *African American Research Perspectives* 13 (2010): 82–98.

7 Peter Brooks, *The Melodramatic Imagination: Balzac, Henry James, Melodrama, and the Mode of Excess* (New Haven, CT: Yale University Press, 1995).

8 Hall writes,

> In its expressivity, its musicality, its orality, in its rich, deep, and varied attention to speech, in its inflections toward the vernacular and the local, in its rich production of counternarratives, and above all, in its metaphorical use of the musical vocabulary, black popular culture has enabled the surfacing, inside the mixed and contradictory modes even of some mainstream popular culture, of elements of a discourse that is different—other forms of life, other traditions of representation.

Hall, "What Is This 'Black,'" 27.

9 Jackson, *Real Black*, 15, emphasis in original.

10 These findings were first published in a chapter for S. Craig Watkins's collection on the innovation economy. See Aymar Jean Christian, "Intersectional Production as Innovation in Networked Comedy," in *Rethinking the Innovation Economy,*

ed. S. Craig Watkins (New York: Routledge, in press). Several series appear in multiple lists because they are intersectional. There are other databases for these series, notably several YouTube, Facebook, and Twitter pages counting black web series, including www.facebook.com/BlackWebSeries and twitter.com/blackweb-series.

11 Vincent Terrace, *Internet Lesbian and Gay Television Series, 1996–2014* (New York: McFarland, 2015).

12 Jillian Báez, "Latina/o Audiences as Citizens: Bridging Culture, Media, and Politics," in *Contemporary Latina/o Media: Production, Circulation, Politics*, eds. Arlene Dávila and Yeidy Rivero (New York: NYU Press, 2014), 267–84; Beretta E. Smith-Shomade, *Pimpin' Ain't Easy: Selling Black Entertainment Television* (Berkeley: University of California Press, 2008); Gray, *Watching Race*; Sender, *Business, Not Politics*.

13 Gray, *Watching Race*.

14 Devorah Heitner, *Black Power TV* (Durham, NC: Duke University Press, 2013); Gayle Wald, *It's Been Beautiful: Soul! and Black Power Television* (Durham, NC: Duke University Press, 2015).

15 Susan J. Douglas, *The Rise of Enlightened Sexism: How Pop Culture Took Us from Girl Power to Girls Gone Wild* (New York: Times Books, 2010), 4.

16 Ibid., 5.

17 Felicia D. Henderson, "The Culture behind Closed Doors: Issues of Gender and Race in the Writers' Room," *Cinema Journal* 50, no. 2 (2011): 145–52.

18 Kristen Warner, *The Cultural Politics of Colorblind TV Casting* (New York: Routledge, 2015), 62–94.

19 Emily M. Drew, "Pretending to Be 'Postracial': The Spectacularization of Race in Reality TV's *Survivor*," *Television and New Media* 12, no. 4 (2011): 326–46; Jennifer Esposito, "What Does Race Have to Do with Ugly Betty? An Analysis of Privilege and Postracial(?) Representations on a Television Sitcom," *Television and New Media* 10, no. 6 (2009): 521–35; Hollis Griffin, "Never, Sometimes, Always: The Multiple Temporalities of 'Post-Race' Discourse in Convergence Television Narrative," *Popular Communication* 9, no. 4 (2011): 235–50.

20 Sarah Banet-Weiser, "What's Your Flava? Race and Postfeminism in Media Culture," in *Interrogating Postfeminism: Gender and the Politics of Popular Culture*, eds. Yvonne Tasker and Diane Negra (Durham, NC: Duke University Press, 2007), 224.

21 Catherine Squires, *The Post-Racial Mystique: Media and Race in the Twenty-First Century* (New York: NYU Press, 2014), 170.

22 Warner, *Cultural Politics of Colorblind TV Casting*, 73.

23 Suzanna Danuta Walters, *All the Rage: The Story of Gay Visibility in America* (Chicago: University of Chicago Press, 2001).

24 Michael Warner, *The Trouble with Normal: Sex, Politics, and the Ethics of Queer Life* (Cambridge, MA: Harvard University Press, 2000), 44.

25 GLAAD's annual reports of LGBT representation on television consistently identifies white gay men as overrepresented in scripted narratives. For more information, see "Where We Are on TV Report," 2015, *GLAAD*, www.glaad.org/publications.

26 Sender, *Business, Not Politics*.

27 Herman Gray, *Cultural Moves: African Americans and the Politics of Representation* (Berkeley: University of California Press, 2005).

28 Ibid., 2.

29 Stuart Hall, *Representation: Cultural Representations and Signifying Practices* (New York: Sage, 1997); Gray, *Cultural Moves*.

30 Gray, *Watching Race*; Jennifer Fuller, "Branding Blackness on US Cable Television," *Media Culture Society*, 32, no. 2 (2010): 285–305; Tom Long, "Black Programs Dwindle as Networks Chase Cash: Abandoned African-American Shows Kickstarted Fox, WB, UPN," *Detroit News*, April 14, 2002, 1A; Kristal Brent Zook, *Color by Fox: The Fox Network and the Revolution in Black Television* (London: Oxford University Press, 1999).

31 Beejoli Shah, "In the White Room with Black Writers: Hollywood's 'Diversity Hires,'" *Defamer*, December 20, 2013, defamer.gawker.com; Claude Brodesser, "Mfume Wields Hollywood Influence," *Variety*, February 11, 2000, Special Section; NAACP Hollywood Bureau, *Out of Focus*; Michael Schneider, "NAACP: Eye Talks, Trio Walks," *Variety*, November 30, 1999, 1.

32 Anne Bergman, "WGA Fights for Writers in More Than One Arena," *Variety*, February 27, 2001, A10; Christopher Grove, "Diversity Executives Strive to Make Color Adjustment," *Variety*, September 14, 2001, A8; Richard Horgan, "Women and Minorities Change the Odds," *Variety*, December 3, 2002, A6.

33 Warner, *Cultural Politics of Colorblind TV Casting*, 132.

34 John Edward Campbell, "Outing PlanetOut: Surveillance, Gay Marketing, and Internet Affinity Portals," *New Media and Society* 7, no. 5 (2005): 663–83; Megan Mullen, *The Rise of Cable Programming in the United States: Revolution or Evolution?* (Austin: University of Texas Press, 2003).

35 Sender, *Business, Not Politics*, 141.

36 Katherine Sender, "Neither Fish nor Fowl: Feminism, Desire, and the Lesbian Consumer Market," *Communication Review* 7, no. 4 (2004): 407–32; Katherine Sender, "Dualcasting: Bravo's Gay Programming and the Quest for Women Audiences," in *Cable Visions: Television beyond Broadcasting*, eds. Sarah Banet-Weiser, Cynthia Chris, and Anthony Freitas (New York: NYU Press, 2007), 302–18.

37 Smith-Shomade, *Pimpin' Ain't Easy*; Squires, *African Americans and the Media*, 256.

38 Ariana Huffington, "Introducing HuffPost BlackVoices: Covering Black America's Split-Screen Reality," *Huffington Post*, August 4, 2011, www.huffingtonpost.com; Matthew Fleischer, "AP Profiles *Awkward Black Girl* Creator Issa Rae," *FishbowlLA*, September 9, 2011, www.adweek.com.

39 Stephanie Dunn, *"Baad Bitches" and Sassy Supermamas: Black Power Action Films* (Urbana-Champaign: University of Illinois Press, 2008).

40 Aymar Jean Christian, "Robert Townsend: The Future of Television, Importance of Social Justice, and Working with Committed Collaborators," *Televisual*, December 14, 2010, tvisual.org.

41 Mittell, "Narrative Complexity."

42 Beretta E. Smith-Shomade, *Shaded Lives: African-American Women and Television* (New Brunswick, NJ: Rutgers University Press, 2002).

43 Brande Victorian, "Crunk Feminist Collective Calls Out *Awkward Black Girl* for 'Tranny,' 'No Lesbo' Phrases," *Madame Noire*, December 6, 2011, madamenoire. com.

44 "Open Letter to Our Friends @awkwardblkgrl," *Crunk Feminist Collective*, December 3, 2011, crunkfeministcollective.tumblr.com/post/13668840994/open-letter-to-our-friends-awkwardblkgrl.

45 See Victorian, "Crunk Feminist Collective Calls Out *Awkward Black Girl*."

46 Diana Scholl, "Issa Rae on the Mis-Adventures of *Awkward Black Girl* and Creating the Black Liz Lemon," *Vulture*, December 11, 2011, www.vulture.com.

47 Helena Andrews, "Embracing the Awkward, One Webisode at a Time," *Root*, July 6, 2011, www.theroot.com.

48 Issa Rae, *The Misadventures of Awkward Black Girl* (New York: Atria, 2015), 70.

49 Jenna Wortham, "The Misadventures of Issa Rae," *New York Times Magazine*, August 4, 2015, www.nytimes.com.

50 Issa Rae, "People on the Internet Can Be Hella Racist," *xojane*, March 29, 2012, www.xojane.com.

51 According to Patricia Hill Collins,

> Hair texture, a female feature that is far more malleable, also matters greatly in re-creating femininity in the context of the new color-blind racism. Because a good deal of women's beauty is associated with their hair, this aspect of women's physical appearance takes on added importance in the process of constructing hierarchies of femininity. . . . Some authors claim that hair texture has long been more important than skin color in racial politics.

> Patricia Hill Collins, *Black Sexual Politics: African Americans, Gender, and the New Racism* (New York: Routledge, 2004), 195. See also Kobena Mercer, "Black Hair/Style Politics," *new formations* 3 (1987): 33–54.

52 It is important to note that *Awkward Black Girl* prefigures the rise of dark-skinned, natural-haired actors like Viola Davis in *How to Get Away with Murder* and Lupita Nyong'o in *12 Years a Slave*. There was clearly pent-up desire from black women to see natural hair represented in media. *Awkward Black Girl* was not the only web video property to tap into the desire of black women to see natural hair in the media. Natural hair stylists and experts proliferated on YouTube at the same time. See Jamila Bey, "'Going Natural' Requires Lots of Help," *New York Times*, June 8, 2011, www.nytimes.com.

53 Diana Scholl, "Issa Rae on the Mis-Adventures of *Awkward Black Girl* and Creating the Black Liz Lemon."

54 HBO did air one series starring a black woman, Jill Scott: *The No. 1 Ladies Detective Agency*, which lasted one season.

55 Jada Yuan, "'Awkward Black Girl' Goes to Hollywood," *New York*, October 10, 2015, www.vulture.com.

56 Tamar Jeffers McDonald, *Romantic Comedy: Boy Meets Girl Meets Genre* (London: Wallflower Press, 2007).

57 Christelyn Karazin, "The New, NEW Black Woman: Issa Rae!" *Beyond Black & White*, February 4, 2012, www.beyondblackwhite.com.

58 Britni Danielle, "Werk! Issa Rae Gets Fab for *Edge* Magazine," *Clutch*, March 5, 2012, www.clutchmagonline.com.

59 Issa Rae, "I Just Got This Shirt and I Can't Wait to Rock," *Issa Rae*, August 29, 2011, blog.issarae.com/post/9577513203/i-just-got-this-shirt-and-i-cant-wait-to-rock.

60 Megan Mullen, "The Fall and Rise of Cable Narrowcasting," *Convergence* 8 (2002): 62–83.

61 Thomas Streeter, "Blue Skies and Strange Bedfellows: The Discourse of Cable Television," in *The Revolution Wasn't Televised: Sixties Television and Social Conflict*, eds. Lynn Spigel and Michael Curtin (New York: Routledge, 1997), 221–42.

62 Thomas Streeter, "The Cable Fable Revisited: Discourse, Policy, and the Making of Cable Television," *Critical Studies in Mass Communication* 4, no. 2 (1987): 174–200.

63 This has been well documented. For a good survey of the politics of cable regulation, see Patrick Parsons, *Blue Skies: A History of Cable Television* (Philadelphia: Temple University Press, 2008).

64 Smith-Shomade, *Pimpin' Ain't Easy*, 33.

65 Melvin Patrick Ely, *The Adventures of Amos 'N' Andy: A Social History of an American Phenomenon* (New York: Free Press, 1992); Angela M. S. Nelson, "Black Situation Comedies and the Politics of Television Art," in *Cultural Diversity and the U.S. Media*, eds. Yahya R. Kamalipour and Theresa Carilli (Albany: State University of New York Press, 1998), 79–88.

66 Smith-Shomade, *Shaded Lives*, 70.

67 Ibid., 72.

68 Squires, *African Americans and the Media*, 253.

69 Avtar Brah and Ann Phoenix, "'Ain't I a Woman?': Revisiting Intersectionality," *Journal of International Women's Studies* 5, no. 3 (2004): 73–86; Collins, *Black Feminist Thought*.

70 Beretta E. Smith-Shomade, "Narrowcasting in the New World Information Order: A Space for the Audience?" *Television and New Media* 5, no. 1 (2004): 69–81.

71 Issa Rae's personal account on Facebook can be found at www.facebook.com/issarae112 and the Facebook page for her show *Awkward Black Girl* can be found at www.facebook.com/awkwardblackgirl.

72 Issa Rae's personal Twitter account can be found at twitter.com/issarae. Her show *Awkward Black Girl* also has a Twitter account at twitter.com/awkwardblkgrl.

73 Issa Rae's blog at blog.issarae.com highlighted the show's merchandise with t-shirts stating "I'm Awkward . . . And Black" or "I'm Awkward . . . And Mixed" available through the blog's online store at store.awkwardblackgirl.com.

74 Issa Rae, "Ridiculously Awesome Awkward Black Girl Fan Art," *Issa Rae*, August 22, 2011, blog.issarae.com.

75 Issa Rae, "What Better Way to Celebrate Black History Month," *Issa Rae*, February 10, 2012, blog.issarae.com.

76 Examples include a *Daily Show* interview with George Lucas on his big-budget black war movie, *Red Tails* (Issa Rae, "First Viola, Then Steve McQueen, Now George Lucas Blasts Hollywood: A Change Gon' Come? (Thanks, Rob)," *Issa Rae*, January 15, 2012, blog.issarae.com/post/15891230169/first-viola-then-steve-mcqueen-now-george-lucas); an article on female comic writers (Issa Rae, "Ladies Making Comics: How Media Clearly Reflects the Sexism and the Racism We Cannot See In," *Issa Rae*, August 24, 2011, blog.issarae.com/post/9355654519/ladies-making-comics-how-media-clearly-reflects-the); and an excerpt from Indian American writer and actress Mindy Kaling from *The Office* (Issa Rae, "Just Read: 'Is Everyone Hanging Out without Me (and Other Concerns)' by Mindy Kaling," *Issa Rae*, January 2, 2012, blog.issarae.com/post/15193378046/just-read-is-everyone-hanging-out-without-me).

77 Issa Rae, "Black Folk Don't Like to Be Told They're Not Black," *Huffington Post*, August 4, 2011, www.huffingtonpost.com; Rae, "People on the Internet Can Be Hella Racist."

78 Issa Rae, "ABG College Tour," *Issa Rae*, n.d., accessed February 27, 2017, blog.issarae.com/ABGCollegeTour.

79 See Issa Rae, "Nothing Made You Happier Than Seeing This When Walking into a Classroom as a Kid," *Issa Rae*, January 22, 2012, blog.issarae.com/post/16296550787/calinative-lol-yuuuup.

80 Issa Rae, "How *Awkward Black Girl* Raised over $44,000 through Kickstarter," *Huffington Post*, August 10, 2011, www.huffingtonpost.com.

81 "CONTEST: VIBE x *Awkward Black Girl*—Win a Walk-On Role!" *Vibe*, April 3, 2012, www.vibe.com.

82 Issa Rae, "Hey Everyone I'm a Fan First," *Issa Rae*, April 18, 2014, blog.issarae.com/post/83114165922/hey-everyone-im-a-fan-first-everyday-i-am.

83 For more information, see the website *The Black List* at blcklst.com.

84 Yuan, "'Awkward Black Girl' Goes to Hollywood."

85 The Tribeca Now program, in which I participated as a member of its advisory committee, embedded the fourth episode on its website: tribecafilm.com/online/tribecanow.

86 Aymar Jean Christian and Khadijah Costeley White, "One Man Hollywood: The Decline of Black Creative Production in Post-Network Television," in *From*

Madea to Media Mogul: Critical Perspectives on Tyler Perry, eds. TreaAndrea Russworm, Karen Bowdre, and Samantha Sheppard (Jackson: University Press of Mississippi, 2016), 138–58.

87 Joshua Cohen, "Indie Drama 'Anyone but Me' Hits 10 Million Views," *Tubefilter*, August 9, 2011, www.tubefilter.com.

88 See *Anyone but Me*, homepage, n.d., anyonebutmeseries.com.

89 Ibid.

90 Eve Kosofky Sedgwick, *Epistemology of the Closet* (Berkeley: University of California Press, 2008), 71.

91 Lisa Duggan, *The Twilight of Equality? Neoliberalism, Cultural Politics, and the Attack on Democracy* (New York: Beacon Press, 2004).

92 Sedgwick, *Epistemology of the Closet*, 71–72.

93 Sender, *Business, Not Politics*.

94 Ibid., 311.

95 It should be noted that *The L Word* premiered soon after *Sex and the City* was concluding its run on HBO, a boon for competitor Showtime.

96 Susan Driver, *Queer Girls and Popular Culture: Reading, Resisting, and Creating Media* (New York: Peter Lang, 2007); Larry Gross, "Gideon Who Will Be 25 in the Year 2012: Growing Up Gay Today," *International Journal of Communication* 1 (2007): 121–38; Mary Gray, *Out in the Country: Youth, Media, and Queer Visibility in Rural America* (New York: NYU Press, 2009).

97 Aymar Jean Christian, "Web Series Spotlight: 'It Gets Betterish' Hates Lady Gaga," *Televisual*, November 17, 2011, tvisual.org.

98 Lisa Parks, "Flexible Microcasting: Gender, Generation, and Television-Internet Convergence," in *Television after TV: Essays on a Medium in Transition*, eds. Lynne Spigel and Jan Olsson (Durham, NC: Duke University Press, 2004), 133–56.

99 Ben Aslinger, "Creating a Network for Queer Audiences at Logo TV," *Popular Communication: The International Journal of Media and Culture* 7, no. 2 (2009): 110.

100 Liz Shannon Miller, "*Anyone but Me* Plans "Web-a-Thon" to Fund Third Season," *NewTeeVee*, June 14, 2010, gigaom.com.

101 Trish Bendix, "*Anyone but Me*: Interlude 1," *AfterEllen*, February 16, 2009, www.afterellen.com; Grace Chu, "The 'Anyone but Me' Premiere Party Sets the Pace for Season 2," *AfterEllen*, December 9, 2009, www.afterellen.com.

102 Miller, "*Anyone but Me* Plans 'Web-a-Thon' to Fund Third Season," 2010.

103 Aymar Jean Christian, "Move Over, Oprah! Maurice Jamal Is Starting His Own Network," *AfterElton*, October 19, 2010, www.afterelton.com.

104 Ibid.

105 Christin Mell, "A Network for Creatives and Fans," *Televisual*, April 18, 2013, tvisual.org

106 Ibid.

107 For an example of the formulas of web comedy, see Streeter Seidell, "I Waste People's Time Online. How? Don't Ask Me," *New York Times*, April 20, 2008, 2.

108 East WillyB, "*East WillyB* Buzz Clip," *YouTube*, March 21, 2011, www.youtube.com/watch?v=Q-T0e2XjaRw&feature=channel_video_title.

109 Following Arlene Dávila's work, I use "Latino" and "Hispanic" interchangeably. "Hispanic" is generally thought to be a more conservative term, used by the U.S. Census but connected to Spanish colonialism (the imposition of "Spanish-language" on subjugated populations). "Latino" is a younger term with activist connotations. But both are "equally guilty of erasing differences while encompassing highly heterogeneous populations and can be equally as appropriated for a range of politics." Dávila, *Latinos, Inc.*, 15.

110 Juan Piñón and Viviana Rojas, "Language and Cultural Identity in the New Configuration of the US Latino TV Industry," *Global Media and Communication* 7, no. 2 (2011): 129–47.

111 Ibid., 93.

112 Ibid., 162.

113 Angharad Valdivia, "Latinas as Radical Hybrid: Transnationally Gendered Traces in Mainstream Media," *Global Media Journal* 3, no. 4 (2004): www.globalmediajournal.com.

114 Mary Beltrán, *Latina/o Stars in U.S. Eyes: The Making and Meanings of Film and TV Stardom* (Urbana: University of Illinois Press), 157.

115 Ibid., 163.

116 Viviana Rojas, "The Gender of Latinidad: Latinas Speak about Hispanic Television," *Communication Review* 7, no. 2 (2004): 125–53; Jesús Salvador Treviño, "Latino Portrayals in Film and Television," *Jump Cut: A Review of Contemporary Media* 30 (1985): 14–16.

117 Frances Negrón-Muntaner, *The Latino Media Gap: A Report on the State of Latinos in U.S. Media*, Center for the Study of Ethnicity and Race at Columbia University, December 2015, latinodonorcollaborative.org, 16.

118 Ibid.

119 Ibid., 3, 16.

120 Allison Perlman and Hector Amaya, "Owning a Voice: Broadcasting Policy, Spanish-Language Media, and Latina/o Speech Rights," *Communication, Culture, and Critique* 6 (2013): 143.

121 América Rodriguez, "Commercial Ethnicity: Language, Class, and Race in the Marketing of the Hispanic Audience," *Communication Review* 2, no. 3 (1997): 283–309.

122 Dávila, *Latinos, Inc.*, 88.

123 YlseShow, "Behind the Scenes: Featurette 1," *YouTube*, March 3, 2010, www.youtube.com/watch?v=G4EN_EWWZus&feature=player_embedded.

124 YlseShow, "Season 1: Trailer," *YouTube*, March 3, 2010, www.youtube.com/watch?v=XWDmYXTmVvk&feature=related.

125 Dávila, *Latinos, Inc.*, 218–19.

126 Mark Asch, "And Here's *East WillyB*, a Web Series about Latino Williamsburg," *L Magazine*, April 18, 2011, www.thelmagazine.com; The Complex, "New Latino Web Series: *East WillyB*," *Sinuous Magazine*, April 6, 2011, www.sinuousmag.com;

"*East WillyB*: Moving on Up, without Moving," *Fox News Latino*, April 15, 2011, latino.foxnews.com: "Tr3s Exclusive: Introducing *East WillyB*," *Tr3s: Blogamole!* April 13, 2011, blogamole.tr3s.com/2011/04/13/tr3s-exclusive-introducing-east-willyb.

127 Bernadette Marie Calafell, *Latina/o Communication Studies: Theorizing Performance* (New York: Peter Lang, 2007), 127.

128 Ibid., 127.

129 Sam Gutelle, "Univision Goes Short-Form with a New Destination Called Udisea," *Tubefilter,* December 2, 2015, www.tubefilter.com; Todd Spangler, "Mitú Raises $27 Million from AwesomenessTV, Verizon, and WPP," *Variety*, January 13, 2016, variety.com.

130 Mullen, "Fall and Rise of Cable Narrowcasting."

131 Diana Veiga, "Talking with Thursday: Issa Rae, Tracy Oliver, and the Misadventures of *Awkward Black Girl*," *A Work in Progress*, August 4, 2011, aworknprogress.com.

132 Robert E. Weems Jr., *Desegregating the Dollar: African-American Consumerism in the Twentieth Century* (New York: NYU Press, 1998).

133 Isaac Julien and Kobena Mercer, "De margin and de centre," *Screen* 29, no. 4 (1988): 2–11.

134 Rosemary Hennessy, "Queer Visibility in Commodity Culture," *Cultural Critique* 29 (1994–1995): 32.

135 Dávila, *Latinos, Inc.*, 238.

136 Smith-Shomade, *Pimpin' Ain't Easy*.

CHAPTER 4. OPEN TV DISTRIBUTION

1 A version of the letter was posted to LA WebFest's Facebook page: Michael Ajakwe Jr., "Everybody Wants to Know Why We Added an 'Exclusivity Clause' to Our Rules in 2015," Facebook, February 6, 2015, www.facebook.com/lawebfest/posts/782449365125671.

2 For the most complete report on the controversy, see Chris Hadley, "LA WebFest Strikes Back against Competition: Creators Caught in Crossfire," *Snobby Robot*, February 10, 2015, snobbyrobot.com.

3 Anthony Anderson, Anacostia Series Twitter account, Twitter, February 6, 2015, twitter.com/ANACOSTIASERIES/status/563844553330163713.

4 Allen Weiner, "The L.A. Web Festival Scene Is in Need of Some Less Selfish Thinking," *Daily Dot*, February 11, 2015, www.dailydot.com.

5 Lisa Gifford, "What the Hell Is Going On in LA?" *Where I Say Stuff*, February 6, 2015, lisagiffordwriter.wordpress.com.

6 See Ed Robinson, "Fact Checking LA Webfest's Exclusivity Clause: An Open Letter to Creators," *Pairings*, n.d., www.pairingstheseries.com.

7 Jason Leaver, "An Open Letter to the LAWEBFEST," *Out with Dad*, February 5, 2015, www.outwithdad.com.

8 Jonathan Robbins, Facebook, accessed February 2015, www.facebook.com/ClutchOfficialFanPage/posts/899384193445433.

9 Michael Ajakwe Jr., "Welcome to LAWEBFEST 2015," Facebook, February 6, 2015, www.facebook.com/lawebfest/posts/782449365125671.

10 Leesa Deen, "Chapter 93: #Clausegate," *Adventures of a Web Series Newbie*, February 13, 2015, chilltowntv.wordpress.com.

11 As of early 2015, we had 463 Twitter followers, 575 Facebook likes, and 77 YouTube subscribers. Starting in August 2013, when we started publishing the series in earnest, we had around 100 likes. By targeting fans of black web series about women (chiefly, Issa Rae and the Black & Sexy TV network) and classic black television shows from Derek, Rhonney, and Teresa's youth (*A Different World, Girlfriends*), we were able to grow that to around 550 likes by November. Social media engagement led to a small increase in views, but none of our episodes save two reached over 1,000 views—the first at over 2,500, and "Space Disco Chump," for which we experimented with "buying" views to see if perception might influence reality. The increase in real views was negligible—most of the surplus 5,000 views came from Russia, far from our actual fan base. In all, YouTube counted 14,000 views across episodes and nearly as many minutes watched; 70 percent of the minutes and 80 percent of our views occurred during our release period, comprising most of 2013.

12 Sergio Mims, "Comedy Web Series 'She's out of Order' Gets Online Distribution Deal," *Shadow and Act*, September 10, 2014, blogs.indiewire.com/shadowandact.

13 Brian Stelter, "Online Video Start-Ups Seek to Carve Out a Place beside YouTube," *New York Times*, June 5, 2011, www.nytimes.com.

14 Ryan Lawler, "Blip Gets into the Original Content Game, with a New Studio and Three Exclusive Series," *Techcrunch*, June 28, 2012, techcrunch.com.

15 Janko Roettgers, "Shrinking Pains: Blip Upsets Publishers by Removing Countless Videos," *Gigaom*, December 2, 2013, gigaom.com.

16 Stelter, "Online Video Start-Ups."

17 Douglas Kellner, *Television and the Crisis of Democracy* (Boulder, CO: Westview, 1990).

18 Thomas Streeter, *Selling the Air: A Critique of the Policy of Commercial Broadcasting in the United States* (Chicago: University of Chicago Press, 1996).

19 Joseph Turow, *The Daily You: How the New Advertising Industry Is Defining Your Identity and Your Worth* (New Haven, CT: Yale University Press, 2011), 114.

20 Karen Petruska, "Television beyond the Networks: First-Run Syndication of Original Content in the 1970s," *Velvet Light Trap* 75 (2015): 39.

21 Lotz, *Television Will Be Revolutionized*; Turow, *Breaking Up America*.

22 Turow, *The Daily You*.

23 Donaton, *Madison and Vine*.

24 Joseph Jaffe, *Life after the 30-Second Spot: Energize Your Brand with a Bold Mix of Alternatives to Traditional Advertising* (Hoboken, NJ: Wiley, 2005).

25 Patricia Aufderheide, *Communications Policy and the Public Interest* (New York: Guilford Press, 1999); Mara Einstein, *Media Diversity: Economics, Ownership, and the FCC* (Hillsdale, NJ: Erlbaum, 2004); Holt, *Empires of Entertainment*.

26 Ellis, *Seeing Things.*

27 Alisa Perren, "Rethinking Distribution for the Future of Media Industry Studies," *Cinema Journal* 52, no. 3 (2013): 170.

28 Josh Braun, *This Program Is Brought to You By . . . : Distributing Television News Online* (New Haven, CT: Yale University Press, 2015), 3.

29 Axel Bruns, *Blogs, Wikipedia, Second Life, and Beyond: From Production to Produsage* (New York: Peter Lang, 2008); David Gauntlett, *Making Is Connecting: The Social Meaning of Creativity, from DIY and Knitting to YouTube and Web 2.0* (Cambridge, MA: Polity, 2011); Jean Burgess and Joshua Green, *YouTube: Online Video and Participatory Culture* (Cambridge, MA: Polity, 2009).

30 Joshua Green and Henry Jenkins, "Spreadable Media: How Audiences Create Value and Meaning in a Networked Economy," in *The Handbook of Media Audiences*, ed. Virginia Nightingale (Hoboken, NJ: Willey-Blackwell, 2011), 109–27.

31 Braun, *The Program Is Brought to You By . . .* , 10.

32 Matthew Hindman, *The Myth of Digital Democracy* (Princeton, NJ: Princeton University Press, 2009).

33 Chris Atton, *Alternative Media* (Thousand Oaks, CA: Sage, 2002); Rodney Benson, "Commercialism and Critique: California's Alternative Weeklies," in *Contesting Media Power: Alternative Media in a Networked World*, eds. Nick Couldry and James Curran (Lanham, MD: Rowman & Littlefield, 2003), 111–28.

34 Nick Couldry and James Curran, "The Paradox of Media Power," in *Contesting Media Power: Alternative Media in a Networked World*, eds. Nick Couldry and James Curran (Lanham, MD: Rowman & Littlefield, 2003), 3–16.

35 Newman, *Indie,* 3.

36 Aymar Jean Christian, "Who Wins When TV and the Web Converge? Nielsen and the Problem of Web Ratings," *Televisual*, October 24, 2011, televisual.org.

37 Yochai Benkler, *The Wealth of Networks: How Social Production Transforms Markets and Freedom* (New Haven, CT: Yale University Press, 2006); Bruns, *Blogs, Wikipedia, Second Life, and Beyond*; Clay Shirky, *Here Comes Everybody: The Power of Organizing without Organizations* (New York: Penguin, 2008).

38 Cindy H. Wong, *Film Festivals: Culture, People, and Power on the Global Screen* (New Brunswick, NJ: Rutgers University Press, 2011), 136.

39 Kylie Jarrett, "Beyond Broadcast Yourself™: The Future of YouTube," *Media International Australia* 126, no. 1 (2008): 132–44.

40 Burgess and Green, *YouTube.*

41 Will Wei, "Meet the YouTube Stars Making $100,000 Plus per Year," *Business Insider*, August 19, 2010, www.businessinsider.com.

42 Marc Hustvedt, "The Web Series Identity Crisis," *Tubefilter*, September 3, 2010, news.tubefilter.tv.

43 Liz Shannon Miller, "The Lessons YouTubers Teach Us," *NewTeeVee*, August 30, 2010, newteevee.com.

44 Christian, "Is Hulu Winning the Web Video Wars?"

45 "Strike.TV and Koldcast.TV Enter into Content Distribution Partnership," *PR Web*, December 16, 2008, www.prweb.com.

46 Miranda Banks, "The Picket Line Online: Creative Labor, Digital Activism, and the 2007–2008 Writers Guild of America Strike," *Popular Communication* 8, no. 1 (2010): 20–33.

47 Ibid., 27; "Strike TV Workshop Reminder," *United Hollywood*, January 7, 2008, unitedhollywood.blogspot.com.

48 Other reports have estimated attendance at three hundred. John Burton, "Film and Television Writers Plan 'Strike TV' Internet Programming," *World Socialist Web Site*, January 14, 2008, www.wsws.org.

49 *Dr. Horrible* remains an ideal within the industry. Professionally produced with famous actors, it eventually made money through DVD sales, along with other deals with Hulu, Netflix, and the CW. See Cynthia Littleton, "Joss Whedon Says He Made More Money from 'Dr. Horrible' Than the First 'Avengers' Movie," *Variety*, October 10, 2016, variety.com.

50 Burton, "Film and Television Writers."

51 Marc Hustvedt, "Strike TV Delays Launch Date, Rethinking Distribution Strategy," *Tubefilter*, September 25, 2008, news.tubefilter.tv; Marc Hustvedt, "Strike TV Signs Content Deal with YouTube and Joost, Set for October 28 Launch," *Tubefilter*, October 13, 2008, news.tubefilter.tv.

52 "Shoot First, Get Advertisers Later," *United Hollywood*, February 26, 2008, unitedhollywood.blogspot.com.

53 Liz Shannon Miller, "Online Celebrities or Mainstream Celebrities: Who Should You Cast?" *NewTeeVee*, November 19, 2008, newteevee.com.

54 Liz Shannon Miller, "Strike.TV: Still Stuck in the Year 2008?" *Gigaom*, January 19, 2010, gigaom.com.

55 "Video Ads Beat TV in Recall, Likability: Nielsen," *MediaBuyerPlanner*, April 20, 2010, www.mediabuyerplanner.com.

56 Ryan Lawler, "Online Video Viewers: The Young, the Hip, and the Well Off," *NewTeeVee*, April 5, 2010, newteevee.com; Mary Madden, "The Audience for Online Video-Sharing Sites Shoots Up," *Pew Research Center*, July 2009, www.pewinternet.org.

57 Elliott, "Convergence of Hip," C7.

58 Daisy Whitney, "Web Video Evolves in Bid for Ad Money: Next Gen User Gen," *TV Week*, September 24, 2007, 1.

59 Craig Rubens, "TubeMogul's (Biased) List Shows New Media Kicking A$$ Online," *NewTeeVee*, June 25, 2008, gigaom.com.

60 Reports abounded, and the debate persisted for years. In 2008, *Advertising Age* wrote, "On average, the cost-per-thousand rates for network-sold inventory are less than a 10th the CPMs publishers were able to charge when selling it themselves. Because of this price differential, some publishers complain that ad networks drive down prices." Abbey Klaassen, "Ad Networks Appear to Drive Down CPMs," *Advertising Age*, August 11, 2008, adage.com.

61 Justin Kroll, "New Media a Lab for *Valemont*," *Variety*, April 24, 2010, www. variety.com; Aymar Jean Christian, "Verizon Wireless Enrolls at Valemont U," *BusinessWeek*, October 12, 2009, www.businessweek.com.

62 Staci D. Kramer, "Sony's Grouper Rebrands as 'Crackle'; Hangs Future on Fame and Studio Connections," *Gigaom*, July 16, 2007, gigaom.com.

63 Ryan Lawler, "Who Knew? Joost Makes a Better Ad Network Than a Video Portal," *Gigaom*, April 14, 2010, gigaom.com.

64 Richard MacManus, "Content Farms: Why Media, Blogs, & Google Should Be Worried," *ReadWriteWeb*, December 13, 2009, www.readwriteweb.com; Mike Shields, "Rise of the Generators," *MediaWeek*, April 25, 2010, www.mediaweek. com.

65 Providing a useful analogy, in 2007 DoubleClick's David Rosenblatt compared the exchange marketplace to eBay. Louise Story, "DoubleClick to Set Up Exchange for Buying and Selling Ads," *New York Times*, April 4, 2007, www.nytimes.com. For a guide to ad networks versus ad exchanges, see *Advertising Age*'s guide, adage.com/adnetworkexchangeguide.

66 Turow, *Niche Envy*.

67 Wayne Friedman, "Online Video Trumps TV in Engagement, Ad Shifts," *MediaDailyNews*, June 5, 2013, www.mediapost.com; Lucia Moses, "Some Question Just How Great Online Video Engagment Is," *Adweek*, September 16, 2013, www. adweek.com.

68 Alex Dobuzinskis, "Stars Tune-in to Web Video, Advertisers Still Shy," *Reuters*, September 26, 2008, mobile.reuters.com.

69 Beecher Tuttle, "IKEA's Hit Web Show: An Entertaining Ad," *Wall Street Journal*, September 7, 2012, online.wsj.com.

70 Staff, "Illeana Douglas Assembles The Web's Most Beloved Hit Show—No Allen Wrench Required," *Fast Company*, September, 2010, www.fastcompany.com.

71 Dobuzinskis, "Stars Tune-in to Web Video."

72 Steve McClellan, "Media Agency Report Cards '08," *Mediaweek*, March 16, 2009, www.adweek.com.

73 Andrew Hampp, "If You Build a Web Series around It, Will They Come?," *Advertising Age*, August 9, 2010, 13.

74 Matthew Manarino, "Wilson Cleveland Has a Bright Idea for Web Video," *Video Ink*, October 10, 2013, www.thevideoink.com.

75 Tanya Lewis, "Small Business-Themed Web Series Helps Drive Extra Sales," *PR Week*, January 1, 2013.

76 "Wilson Cleveland: How Can I Break into Branded Entertainment?," *Writers Guild of America East Channel*, January 19, 2012, www.youtube.com/watch?v=PYKLiTPw2qo.

77 Sarah Banet-Weiser, *Authentic™: The Politics of Ambivalence in a Brand Culture* (New York: NYU Press, 2012).

78 "Wilson Cleveland."

79 Manarino, "Wilson Cleveland Has a Bright Idea for Web Video."

80 Marc Hustvedt, "Spherion-backed 'Temp Life' Re-Staffs for New Season," *Tubefilter*, September 10, 2009, www.tubefilter.com.

81 Vanessa Williams, "Washington Native's Web Soap Opera 'Anacostia' Has Loyal Fan Base," *Washington Post*, November 3, 2011, www.washingtonpost.com

82 Competing telecommunications behemoths like AT&T started sponsoring their own web series years later, with *Daybreak* and *Away We Happened* spin-offs of legacy TV programs CW's *The Flash* and MTV's *Teen Wolf*. Sprint similarly worked with NBC's *Heroes*, and sponsored its own indie series, See Hampp, "If You Build a Web Series around It, Will They Come?"

83 See "Stage 9 Digital Media," *Imdb.com*, n.d., www.imdb.com; "NBC Universal Digital Studio," *Imdb.com*, www.imdb.com.

84 "Fox Digital Studios," *Imdb.com*, n.d., www.imdb.com.

85 Turow, *The Daily You*.

86 Liz Gannes, "My Damn Channel, the Funny or Die Clone," *NewTeeVee*, July 31, 2007, gigaom.com.

87 My Damn Channel, "My Damn Channel Launches Branded Network on Yahoo! Video," *PRNewswire*, August 25, 2008, www.prnewswire.com.

88 Gary Gentile, "Web Sites Attract Striking Writers," *Associated Press*, November 27, 2007, www.msnbc.msn.com.

89 The digital arm of Fox Television Studios, 15 Gigs, later went to My Damn Channel to help distribute a web series it had developed months before and placed on YouTube and Hulu to little avail. Christian, "Is Hulu Winning the Web Video Wars?" "If you're going to be lost in somebody's sea, there's a lot of effort lost in putting it up there," Barnett said when interviewed about the site's deal with the studio.

90 Aymar Jean Christian, "Will My Damn Channel Grow into YouTube's Biggest Comedy Network?," *IndieWire*, January 28, 2013, www.indiewire.com.

91 Liz Shannon Miller, "Why Web Video Vet My Damn Channel Is Now Omnivision, and Why It's Not Going Anywhere," *Gigaom*, April 15, 2014, gigaom.com.

92 Ryan Lawler, "Babelgum Shutters 2 European Offices," *NewTeeVee*, November 20, 2009, newteevee.com.

93 Benjamin Toff, "*Quaterlife* Is a Ratings Flop," *New York Times*, February 27, 2008, mediadecoder.blogs.nytimes.com.

94 Aymar Jean Christian, "If a Social Network Dies . . . ," *Splice Today*, June 16, 2009, www.splicetoday.com.

95 Aymar Jean Christian, "*Quarterlife* Has Passed, after a Brief Second Life on Ning," *Televisual*, May 10, 2016, tvisual.org

96 Will Richmond, "Howcast Is Innovating in Crowded How-to Video Market," *VideoNuze*, August 2, 2010, www.videonuze.com

97 Steve Lekowicz, "An Open Letter to ITVfest 2011," *Wren Forum*, August 6, 2011, www.lekowicz.com.

98 Ibid.

99 Alex Ben Block, "Dick Clark Productions Joins Tubefilter to Produce Streamy Awards," *Hollywood Reporter*, August 5, 2011, www.hollywoodreporter.com.

100 Christian, "Who Wins"; Jason Lynch, "With Its Total Audience Measurement Rollout Delayed, Nielsen Will Share More Connected TV Data," *Adweek*, March 23, 2016, www.adweek.com.

101 Aymar Jean Christian, "Web Video/Series Festivals and Conferences," *Televisual*, October 12, 2010, televisual.org.

102 Aymar Jean Christian, "Web Series Festivals," *Televisual*, October 2010, updated August 2015, tvisual.org.

103 Newman, *Indie*, 55.

104 Wong, *Film Festivals*, 145.

105 Sony, "Crackle.com Garners Most Streamy Award Nominations for a Video Network or Production Company," *PR Newswire*, March 1, 2010, www.prnews wire.com.

106 Sharon Waxman, "Exclusive: YouTube CEO Chad Hurley Defends Net Neutrality," *Wrap*, April 12, 2010, www.thewrap.com.

107 Samuel Axon, "The Streamy Awards: How to Unwreck the Car [Opinion]," *Mashable*, April 13, 2010, mashable.com.

108 Liz Shannon Miller, "How the Webventures of Justin & Alden Survived the Streamy Awards," *NewTeeVee*, June 1, 2010, gigaom.com.

109 Liz Shannon Miller, "The Streamy Awards: A Producer's Apology and Its Three Fails," *NewTeeVee*, April 12, 2010, gigaom.com.

110 Samuel Axon, "The Streamy Awards."

111 Liz Shannon Miller, "Can the Streamy Awards and the IAWTV 'Rebuild the Trust'?" *NewTeeVee*, April 27, 2010, gigaom.com.

112 Liz Shannon Miller, "IAWTV Dumps Streamys for Its Own Awards Show," *NewTeeVee*, November 9, 2010, gigaom.com.

113 For more information, see International Academy of Web Television, "Mission Statement," *Iawtv.org*, n.d., iawtv.org.

114 IAWTV, press release, "International Academy of Web Television Names Inaugural Chairman and Board of Directors," *Iawtv.org*, December 14, 2010, iawtv.org.

115 Jamison Tilsner, "Transparency: The Streamys and the IAWTV," *Tubefilter*, March 4, 2009, www.tubefilter.com.

116 Rick Rey, "Hoping for More Transparency from the Streamy Awards," *Reymerica*, January 23, 2009, blog.rickrey.com.

117 IAWTV, press release.

118 Jack Ferry, "IAWTV: The Case for Open Enrollment," *Jack Ferry*, October 6, 2010, www.jackferry.com.

119 Ibid.

120 John Horn, Nicole Sperling, and Doug Smith, "Oscar Voters Overwhelmingly White, Male," *Los Angeles Times*, February 19, 2012, www.latimes.com.

121 Liz Shannon Miller, "The IAWTV Awards Nominees Mix Up the Professional and Independent," *NewTeeVee*, December 18, 2011, gigaom.com.

122 Patrick Bardwell, "IAWTV Awards Educational and Industry Panel Videos Are Online," *Iawtv.org*, February 2, 2012, iawtv.org.

123 Block, "Dick Clark Productions."

124 Not a Gossip Girl, "International Academy of Web Television (IAWTV) Finds New Home as a Division of the Caucus #IAWTVNews," *Red Carpet Report*, December 19, 2016, www.redcarpetreporttv.com.

125 Leslie Goldberg, "'Ted' Writer, Sandy Grushow Team for 'The Weatherman' Remake at Fox," *Hollywood Reporter*, October 22, 2014, www.hollywoodreporter.com.

126 Boyle, *Subject to Change*; Stephanie Tripp, "From TVTV to YouTube: A Genealogy of Participatory Practices in Video," *Journal of Film and Video* 64, no. 1 (2012): 5–16.

127 Boyle, *Subject to Change*, xiv.

CHAPTER 5. SCALING OPEN TV

1 Andrew Wallenstein, "Alloy Acquires Digital Studio Generate," *Daily Variety*, January 5, 2012, variety.com.

2 Stuart Dredge, "YouTube Gaming Levels Up: 3.5bn Monthly Views for Top 100 Channels," *Guardian*, June 13, 2014, www.theguardian.com.

3 Sam Gutelle, "YouTube Billionaires: Machinima Respawn Scores Elite Viewcount," *Tubefilter*, July 25, 2013, www.tubefilter.com.

4 Michelle Castillo, "Machinima Rebrands with a TV-Leaning Strategy," *Adweek*, November 10, 2014, www.adweek.com.

5 Todd Spangler, "'Knight Rider' Reboot from Justin Lin Set at Machinima," *Variety*, October 25, 2016, variety.com.

6 Matthew Manarino, "Is Machinima Respawn on the Chopping Block?" *Video Ink*, September 20, 2013, www.thevideoink.com.

7 Rom Morgan, "What Happened to Machinima on YouTube?" *Tubechum*, August 8, 2014, tubechum.com.

8 Andrew Wallenstein, "Machinima Cuts Staff, Shuts Some Channels after New Financing," *Variety*, February 20, 2015, variety.com.

9 Sam Gutelle, "Fullscreen Will Invest $10 Million in Original Programming," *Tubefilter*, June 26, 2014, www.tubefilter.com.

10 Cynthia Littleton, "Showtime Near Deal to Partner with Xbox Studios on 'Halo' Series," *Variety*, May 2, 2014, variety.com.

11 Nathan Ingraham, "With HBO Partnerships, Machinima Wants to Be the HBO of Gaming Video," *Verge*, July 18, 2013, www.theverge.com.

12 Hector Postigo, "Playing for Work: Independence as Promise in Gameplay Commentary on YouTube," in *Media Independence: Working with Freedom or Working for Free?*, eds. James Bennett and Niki Strange (New York: Routledge, 2014), 203.

13 Jessica Gelt, "'Orange Is the New Black' Is Netflix's Most Watched Original Series," *Los Angeles Times*, October 21, 2013, articles.latimes.com; Andrew Wallenstein, "'House of Cards' Viewing Soars on First Day of Season 2," *Variety*, February 14,

2014, variety.com; Andrew Wallenstein, "'Orange Is the New Black' Trending Stronger Than 'House of Cards,'" *Variety*, June 15, 2014, variety.com.

14 Stuart Cunningham and Jon Silver, *Screen Distribution and the New King Kongs of the Online World* (New York: Palgrave McMillan, 2013), 5. We can also think of Tim Wu's *Master Switch* as a framework for this transition.

15 As they succinctly put it, "[I]f content is *king*, then distribution is *King Kong*. The power and profitability in screen industries have always resided in distribution." Ibid., 4.

16 Ted Striphas, "Algorithmic Culture," *European Journal of Cultural Studies* 18, no. 4–5 (2015): 406.

17 My understanding of the activites of the networks in this chapter suggests that they fit within Tarleton Gillespie's typology of "public relevance algorithms," which "produce and certify knowledge" in specific ways, through patterns of inclusion, cycles of anticipation, the evaluation of relevance, entanglement with practice and the production of calculated publics. Tarleton Gillespie, "The Relevance of Algorithms," in *Media Technologies: Essays on Communication, Materiality, and Society*, eds. Tarleton Gillespie, Pablo Boczkowski, and Kristen A. Foot (Cambridge, MA: MIT Press, 2014), 168.

18 Philip Napoli, "Automated Media: An Institutional Theory Perspective on Algorithmic Media Production and Consumption," *Communication Theory* 24 (2014): 348.

19 James G. Webster, *The Marketplace of Attention: How Audiences Take Shape in a Digital Age* (Cambridge: MIT Press, 2014).

20 "ComScore Releases January 2014 US Online Video Rankings," *Comscore*, February 21, 2014, www.comscore.com; Glenn Enoch, *The Total Audience Report: Q3 2015*, Nielsen, December 10, 2015, 13.

21 Leslie Kaufman, "Chasing Their Star, on YouTube," *New York Times*, February 2, 2014, www.nytimes.com.

22 Sarah Banet-Weiser, *Authentic™: The Politics of Ambivalence in a Brand Culture* (New York: NYU Press, 2012).

23 Turow, *The Daily You*.

24 Mike Shields, "Cold Medication Brand Zicam Ditches Upfront, Takes Full Programmatic Plunge," *Wall Street Journal*, 2014, blogs.wsj.com.

25 "Digital Display Advertising: Nine Things to Know for 2015," *eMarketer*, February 11, 2015, www.emarketer.com.

26 Braun, *The Programs Is Brought to You By . . .* , 10.

27 Mike Shields, "The Push for Web Ad Viewability Proving to Be Nightmare for Publishers Early On," *Wall Street Journal*, January 27, 2015, blogs.wsj.com.

28 ONE by AOL, "AOL Programmatic Upfront—Tim Armstrong," *Vimeo*, vimeo.com/108928112.

29 Sydney Ember, "AOL and NBCUniversal Announce Partnership to Share and Develop Content," *New York Times*, April 28, 2015, www.nytimes.com; Tim Peterson, "Microsoft, AOL Sign 10-Year Search, Display Deal to Rival Google's Ad Dominance," *Advertising Age*, June 29, 2015, adage.com.

30 Tim Peterson, "Loaded with Data, Verizon's AOL Looks Up at Giants—and Takes Aim," *Advertising Age*, September 28, 2015, adage.com. See also Mike Shields and Ryan Knutson, "AOL's Tim Armstrong Aims to Build Digital-Ad Empire at Verizon," *Wall Street Journal*, March 30, 2016, www.wsj.com.

31 Rachel Kirkpatrick, "AOL Shifts Focus for a C-Suite Upfront Event," *B-to-B Events*, January 8, 2015, www.eventmarketer.com.

32 Andrew Wallenstein, "Zuiker Pushes H'wood-Silicon Valley Ties," *Variety*, April 30, 2012, variety.com.

33 Peterson, "Loaded with Data," 2015.

34 Lucas Kavner, "Dan Harmon on *Community*'s New Season on Yahoo, Base-Level Anxiety, and the Future of Broadcast TV," *Vulture*, March 17, 2015, www.vulture.com.

35 Cynthia Littleton, "Hulu Sets Mammoth 'Seinfeld' Licensing Deal," *Variety*, April 28, 2015, variety.com; Todd Spangler, "Hulu Live TV Service Launches with 50 Channels for $40 Monthly, *Variety*, May 3, 2017, variety.com.

36 Keach Hagey and Shalini Ramachandran, "Hulu Courts TV Networks in Bid to Catch Up to Netflix," *Wall Street Journal*, June 17, 2015, J1.

37 Jason Calacanis, "I Ain't Gonna Work on YouTube's Farm No More," *Launch*, June 2, 2013, www.launch.co.

38 Akilah Hughes, "YouTube Rarely Promotes Black YouTube Stars, Even during Black History Month," *Fusion*, April 8, 2015, fusion.net.

39 Akilah Hughes, "Last Year I Accused YouTube of Failing to Promote Black Talent: Here's What Happened Next," *Fusion*, April 7, 2016, fusion.net; Tambay Obenson, "YouTube Launches Global Production Program That Puts Women in Front of and behind the Camera," *IndieWire*, March 2, 2016, www.indiewire.com.

40 Hank Green, "You Can't Make It on YouTube Anymore: At Least, Not Alone," *Medium*, December 1, 2014, medium.com.

41 Hank Green, "The $1,000 CPM," *Medium*, April 5, 2015, medium.com; Sam Gutelle, "Hank Green Is Pissed Off about YouTube's Constant Changes," *Tubefilter*, July 17, 2013, www.tubefilter.com.

42 Todd Spangler, "YouTube Pay Channels Aren't Taking Off Yet, Some Partners Say," *Variety*, July 17, 2013, variety.com.

43 Denise Mann, "Welcome to the Unregulated Wild, Wild, Digital West," *Media Industries Journal* 1, no. 2 (2014), www.mediaindustriesjournal.org.

44 Eva Knoll, "From MCN to Next-Generation Media Company, Part 1: Funding," *Enders Analysis*, December 1, 2014, 3.

45 Ibid.

46 Sam Gutelle, "There Are Now 2,000 YouTube Channels with at Least One Million Subscribers," *Tubefilter*, April 4, 2016, www.tubefilter.com.

47 Ray William Johnson, "Ray William Johnson: Why I Left Maker Studios," *New Media Rockstars*, December 11, 2012, newmediarockstars.com.

48 Marc Graser, "Bob Iger Explains Why Disney Bought Maker Studios," *Variety*, May 6, 2014, variety.com.

49 Ibid.

50 Holt, who hails from legacy media and said he had to "throw out" 30 percent of what he learned from it, told Bloomberg TV's *Money Moves*: "The founding team that built this business built it on a premise of talent-first, and I'll tell you traditional media is not always built that way." "Is Maker Studios This Generation's United Artists?" *Money Moves*, Bloomberg TV, New York, NY: April 30, 2013; Claire Cain Miller, "Actors in Smaller Studios, Making Pictures for the Smaller Screen," *New York Times*, April 10, 2011, www.nytimes.com; Lucas Shaw, "How Maker Studios Is Turning YouTube Cynics into Believers," *Wrap*, September 17, 2012, www.thewrap.com.

51 George Strompolos, "Investing in the Future of Video: YouTube Announces Partner Grant Program," *YouTube Official Blog*, July 9, 2010, youtube-global.blogspot.com/2010/07/investing-in-future-of-video-youtube.html.

52 Liz Shannon Miller, "YouTube Partner Grants Aren't That New and Aren't That Easy to Get," *Gigaom*, July 12, 2010, gigaom.com.

53 Fred Seibert, "Here Comes YouTube Next," *Next New Reblog*, May 7, 2011, next-newblog.tumblr.com/post/3709043588/here-comes-youtube-next.

54 Sam Gutelle, "YouTube Has Removed All References to Its Original Channels Initiative," *Tubefilter*, November 12, 2013, www.tubefilter.com.

55 Aymar Jean Christian, "Four Ways YouTube's The Space Could Help the Company Survive the Netflix Wave," *IndieWire*, March 20, 2013, www.indiewire.com.

56 Fruzsina Eördögh, "The YouTube Industry Has a Transparency Problem," *ReadWrite*, November 28, 2012, readwrite.com.

57 Jefferson Graham, "More Stars Than You See in the Sky—on YouTube?" *USA Today*, April 12, 2012, usatoday.com.

58 Steve Raymond and Sarah Penna, "A Challenge to YouTube Multichannel Networks," *Big Frame blog*, December 12, 2012, www.bigfra.me.

59 Andrew Wallenstein, "Big Frame Brands Top Channels Together as Forefront," *Variety*, December 12, 2012, variety.com.

60 Joshua Cohen, "AwesomenessTV to Acquire YouTube MCN Big Frame for $15 Million in Cash," *Tubefilter*, April 2, 2014, www.tubefilter.com.

61 Anita Hamilton, "YouTube to Boob Tube: Dane Boedigheimer's Annoying Orange TV Show Has Kids Hooked," *Time*, December 3, 2012, business.time.com.

62 Eriq Gardner, "YouTube Star Claims the Collective Withheld Money from 'Annoying Orange' Show (Exclusive)," *Hollywood Reporter*, December 23, 2014, www.hollywoodreporter.com.

63 Eördögh, "YouTube Industry."

64 Mike Shields, "How YouTube's New Arrangements with MCNs Work," *Adweek*, October 30, 2013, www.adweek.com.

65 Andrew Wallenstein, "How Fullscreen Landed One of YouTube's Hottest Properties: The Fine Bros," *Variety*, December 3, 2013, variety.com.

66 Alex Ben Block, "Nickelodeon Greenlights Fine Brothers' First TV Series," *Hollywood Reporter*, April 30, 2014, www.hollywoodreporter.com; Sam Gutelle, "Maker

Studios Now Partnered with Top Three YouTube Gaming Channels," *Tubefilter*, August 28, 2014, www.tubefilter.com; Todd Spangler, "YouTube's Fine Bros. Developing Teen Comedy Movie," *Variety*, December 4, 2014, variety.com.

67 Andrew Hampp, "With NBCU Digital Studio Closure, What's Next for Network-Backed Web Series?," *Advertising Age*, July 11, 2011, adage.com; Jessica E. Vascellaro, "Building Loyalty on Web: Online Video Programs Remix Promotional Tactics to Draw Regular Audiences," *Wall Street Journal*, March 28, 2011, www.wsj.com.

68 Hampp, "With NBCU Digital Studio Closure"; Sam Gutelle, "The Fine Bros Begin Funded Content Initiative with Video from the Kloons," *Tubefilter*, November 11, 2014, www.tubefilter.com; Gavin O'Malley, "Fullscreen Commits $1M to Promote Online Video," *Media Post*, November 30, 2012, www.mediapost.com.

69 David Lieberman, "Peter Chernin, AT&T's Otter Media to Buy Fullscreen YouTube Network," *Deadline*, September 22, 2014, deadline.com.

70 Sam Gutelle, "Maker Studios Co-Founders Lisa and Ben Donovan Leave the Company," *Tubefilter*, August 8, 2014, www.tubefilter.com; Wallenstein, "'Orange Is the New Black.'"

71 Todd Spangler, "Maker Studios Launches Maker.tv, Tees Up Original Series from Morgan Spurlock and YouTube Stars," *Variety*, May 6, 2014, variety.com.

72 Gutelle, "Maker Studios Now Partnered."

73 Andy Fixmer, "Disney Expects Maker Studios to Become Next Marvel, Pixar, or Lucasfilm," *Mashable*, September 10, 2014, mashable.com.

74 David Lieberman, "Maker Studios Will Develop Online Videos with Marvel and Other Disney Units," *Deadline*, April 28, 2015, deadline.com.

75 Bree Bouwer, "Maker Creators to Unbox 'Star Wars' Toys in Global Live Streaming Event," *Tubefilter*, August 26, 2015, www.tubefilter.com.

76 Ronald Grover and Malathi Nayak, "Disney Overhauls Troubled Interactive Unit, Lays Off 700," *Reuters*, March 6, 2014, www.reuters.com.

77 Geoff Weiss, "Disney-Owned Maker Studios Confirms Layoffs amid 'Strategic Adjustments,'" *Tubefilter*, July 29, 2016, www.tubefilter.com.

78 YouTube on the same page offers guidelines and suggests legal representation for those interested in partnering with MCNs: support.google.com/youtube/answer/2737059?hl=en.

79 Todd Spangler, "Fullscreen Sued by Music Publishers Group over Songs in YouTube Videos," *Variety*, August 6, 2013, variety.com.

80 Shields, "How YouTube's New Arrangements with MCNs Work."

81 Sam Gutelle, "YouTube's MCN Affiliate Channels Will Be Subject to Monetization Review," *Tubefilter*, December 6, 2013, www.tubefilter.com.

82 Matthew Manarino, "Is YouTube Completely Changing Network/Creator Relations?" *Video Ink*, October 30, 2013, www.thevideoink.com.

83 Dave Sandige, "New YouTube Rules Rub Content Creators up the Wrong Way," *Playstation Universe*, December 10, 2013, www.psu.com.

84 Todd Spangler, "YouTube Copyright Crackdown Hits Multichannel Network Affiliates," *Variety*, December 12, 2013, variety.com.

85 Stephen Totilo, "YouTube Channels Crippled by Copyright Claims," *Kotaku*, December 10, 2013, kotaku.com.

86 Ohmwrecker/Maskedgamer, "Surprise! MCN Partnered Youtubers Get Screwed: Managed vs Affiliate Maker RPM Polaris," *YouTube*, December 5, 2013, www.youtube.com/watch?v=DB9pCFzZfLg&feature=share.

87 The company publishes its earnings and growth reports on its website: *Freedom!* "Earnings Report," n.d., docs.google.com/spreadsheets/d/1vUdfo9GRTT-KsieuWFkFaEMZWWvFUywy1tUvH5YHHaY/pubhtml#.

88 Chris Bellum, "A Warning about George Vanous/Freedom," *YTtalk*, September 8, 2014, yttalk.com; Hachil, "Freedom! Partnership Review, *Hachil.blogspot.com*, March 31, 2014, hachil.blogspot.com.

89 Y. T. Spencer, "Note from YouTube's Policy Team," February 24, 2016, productforums.google.com/forum/#!topic/youtube/x3aGmn_MsqI; Sam Gutelle, "YouTube to Change Content ID Policy to Let Creators Profit from Disputed Videos," *Tubefilter*, April 28, 2016, www.tubefilter.com.

90 YouTube Help, "About YouTube Certification," accessed July 13, 2016, support.google.com/youtube/answer/6145904?hl=en.

91 Sam Gutelle, "YouTube Pledges Legal Support for Video Creators Who Claim Fair Use," *Tubefilter*, November 19, 2015, www.tubefilter.com.

92 Brouwer, "YouTube CEO."

93 Sahil Patel, "DCNF: Here Comes Google Preferred, Which Makes YouTube Sound Like TV," *Video Ink*, April 30, 2014, www.thevideoink.com.

94 Sam Gutelle, "YouTube: We've Almost Sold Out Our Google Preferred Ad Inventory," *Tubefilter*, October 14, 2014, www.tubefilter.com.

95 Greg Jarboe, "YouTube: Mobile Watch Time, Programmatic Ad Revenue on Increase," *Reel SEO*, October 26, 2015, www.reelseo.com.

96 Suzanna Vranica, "Interpublic to Shift $250 Million in TV Ad Spending to YouTube," *Wall Street Journal*, May 4, 2016, www.wsj.com.

97 Aja Romano, "YouTube's 'Ad-Friendly' Content Policy May Push One of Its Biggest Stars off the Website," *Vox*, September 2, 2016, www.vox.com.

98 Todd Spangler, "YouTube, to Keep Its Stars Happy, May Fund Content and Arrange Hollywood Hookups," *Variety*, July 14, 2014, variety.com.

99 Andrew Wallenstein, "Susanne Daniels: How YouTube Red Will Turn Its Homegrown Stars into TV Talent," *Variety*, February 3, 2016, variety.com.

100 Brooks Barnes, "YouTube Red Buys 'Step Up,' Its First Big-Budget TV Drama," *New York Times*, June 23, 2016, www.nytimes.com.

101 Patrick Vonderau, "The Video Bubble Multichannel Networks and the Transformation of YouTube," *Convergence: The International Journal of Research into New Media Technologies* 22, no. 4 (2016): 361–75.

102 Sam Gutelle, "Vessel Brings Total Funding to $134.5 Million with $57.5 Million Series B Round," *Tubefilter*, April 17, 2015, www.tubefilter.com.

103 Sam Gutelle, "Here's Everything You Need to Know about Vessel, Jason Kilar's New Online Video Platform," *Tubefilter*, January 21, 2015, www.tubefilter.com.

104 A statement from Verizon highlighted Vessel's "technical strengths" in "content discovery, recommendation, OTT subscription management, and user experience management." Geoff Weiss, "Vessel to Close Service at Month's End Following Acquisition by Verizon," *Tubefilter*, October 27, 2016, www.tubefilter.com.

105 Nancy Haas, "And the Award for the Next HBO Goes to . . . ," *GQ*, February 2013, www.gq.com.

106 Jeremy Bowman, "HBO Promises 600 Hours of New Original Content—Should Netflix Inc. Be Worried?" *Motley Fool*, March 13, 2016, www.fool.com; Joe Nocera, "Can Netlix Survive in the New World It Created?" *New York Times*, June 15, 2016, www.nytimes.com.

107 This was partly a result of deals with cable operators to lower and discount fees for subscribers. Todd Spangler, "Netflix Now Pulls in Almost as Much Revenue as HBO—but HBO Is Far More Profitable," *Variety*, February 5, 2015, variety.com.

108 Eugene Kim, "Amazon Is Doubling Its Investment in Video as It Steps Up the War against Netflix," *Business Insider*, July 28, 2016, www.businessinsider.com.

109 Blake Hallinan and Ted Striphas, "Recommended for You: The Netflix Prize and the Production of Algorithmic Culture," *New Media and Society* 18, no. 1 (2014): 14.

110 Ibid., 6.

111 Ibid.; Brendan Sasso, "Thanks to New Law, Netflix Adds Facebook Sharing Features," *Hill*, March 13, 2013, thehill.com.

112 Tori Smith Ekstrand, "Should Netflix Be Accessible to the Deaf?" *Atlantic*, April 16, 2015, www.theatlantic.com.

113 Hallinan and Striphas, "Recommended for You," 12.

114 Ibid., 7.

115 Brian Barrett, "Netflix's Grand, Daring, Maybe Crazy Plan to Conquer the World," *Wired*, March 27, 2016, www.wired.com.

116 Alexis Madrigal, "How Netflix Reverse Engineered Hollywood," *Atlantic*, January 2, 2014, www.theatlantic.com.

117 Ibid.

118 Carlos A. Gomez-Uribe and Neil Hunt, "The Netflix Recommender System: Algorithms, Business Value, and Innovation," *ACM Transactions on Management Information Systems* 6, no. 4 (2015): article 13:1–19.

119 Nick Marx, "Industry Lore and Algorithmic Programming on Netflix," *Flow* 21, no. 6 (2015), flowtv.org.

120 Matt Sienkiewicz, "Neighed to Order: The Case of *BoJack Horseman*," *Flow* 21, no. 6 (2015), flowtv.org.

121 Fuller, "Branding Blackness on US Cable Television."

122 Ibid., 286.

123 Todd Spangler, "Netflix Adding 5 Kids' Series, including 'Danger Mouse' and 'Inspector Gadget' Remakes," *Variety*, February 25, 2015, variety.com.

124 Merrill Barr, "Marvel's Scope Is Far Larger Than Anyone Realized," *Forbes*, November 7, 2013, www.forbes.com.

125 Andrew Wallenstein, *Variety*'s editor-in-chief, leaked the data on his Twitter account: October 27, 2015, twitter.com/awallenstein/status/659040941613961216.

126 Adam Sternbergh, "The 'Moneyball' Network," *Vulture*, May 6, 2015, www.vulture.com.

127 Nathan Ingraham, "Amazon Prime Memberships Grew by Over 50 Percent in 2015," *Engadget*, January 28, 2016, www.engadget.com.

128 Terry Gross, "'Orange' Creator Jenji Kohan: 'Piper Was My Trojan Horse,'" *Fresh Air*, August 13, 2013, www.npr.org.

129 Moze Halperin, "Dissecting Jenji Kohan and Jill Soloway's Clash over Trans Representation on TV," *Flavorwire*, October 14, 2014, flavorwire.com.

130 Aran Isha, "Go Ahead, Guess How Many Black Writers Work on 'Orange Is the New Black,'" *Fusion*, June 22, 2016, fusion.net.

131 Ashleigh Shackelford, "*Orange Is the New Black* Is Trauma Porn Written for White People," *Wear Your Voice*, June 20, 2016, wearyourvoicemag.com.

132 Joe Otterson, "Adam Sandler's 'Ridiculous Six' Producer Tells Native American Actors to Leave Set 'If You Are Overly Sensitive'" (video), *Wrap*, April 27, 2015, www.thewrap.com.

133 Meghan O'Dea, "The Unbreakable Kimmy Schmidt Has a Race Problem," *Medium*, March 7, 2014, medium.com; Gabe Bergado, "The Dong Problem: How 'Unbreakable Kimmy Schmidt' Deals with Race," *Daily Beast*, March 9, 2015, www.thedailybeast.com; Libby Hill, "What's Up with the Native American Subplot on *Unbreakable Kimmy Schmidt*?," *Vulture*, March 10, 2015, www.vulture.com.

134 Natalie Jarvey, "Amazon's 'Transparent' Scores Third Season, Creator Jill Soloway Signs Overall Deal," *Hollywood Reporter*, June 25, 2015, www.hollywoodreporter.com; Inkoo Kang, "50% of Amazon's Next Pilots Created by Women; Tig Notaro, Anna Camp, Christina Ricci to Headline," *IndieWire*, September 23, 2015, www.indiewire.com.

135 Diana Tourjee, "48 Hours on the Game-Changing Set of *Transparent*'s Second Season," *Buzzfeed*, December 1, 2015, www.buzzfeed.com.

136 Bryn Elise Sandberg and Lesley Goldberg, "'Good Girls Revolt' Creator Slams Amazon over Cancellation: 'They Run Some People Out,'" *Hollywood Reporter*, December 7, 2016, www.hollywoodreporter.com.

137 Stacy Smith, Marc Choueti, and Katherine Pieper, *Inclusion or Invisibility? Comprehensive Annenberg Report on Diversity in Entertainment*, Institute for Diversity and Empowerment at Annenberg (IDEA) (Los Angeles, CA, USC Annenberg School for Communication and Journalism, 2016), 2, 7.

138 Ibid., 4, 5.

139 Ibid., 7, 10.

140 Though I should mention that *Ask a Slave* creator Azie Dungey found employment as a writer for *Kimmy Schmidt*.

141 Elizabeth Wagmeister, "Netflix Orders Scripted Series 'Haters Back Off' Based on YouTube Star Miranda Sings," *Variety*, January 24, 2016, variety.com; Geoff Weiss,

"Netflix Taps Digital Heartthrob Cameron Dallas to Headline New Reality Series," *Tubefilter*, June 22, 2016, www.tubefilter.com.

142 For more web-to-TV series deals, see Aymar Jean Christian, "How Does a Web Series Jump to TV," *IndieWire*, February 25, 2015, www.indiewire.com.

143 Wagmeister, "Netflix Orders Scripted Series 'Haters Back Off' Based on YouTube Star Miranda Sings"; Laura Prudom, "ABC Orders Comedies 'Downward Dog,' 'Imaginary Mary,' 'Speechless,' and 'Second Fattest Housewife,'" *Variety*, May 12, 2016, variety.com.

144 In 2016, the tide seemed to turn. Netflix ordered a series by YouTube star Colleen Ballinger-Evans, known for her character Miranda Sings, and reality series fared better, as when Hulu released a docu-series with Freddie Wong and Netflix with Cameron Dallas.

145 Brian Stelter, "Netflix Partner Says Comcast 'Toll' Threatens Online Video Delivery," *New York Times*, November 29, 2010, mediadecoder.blogs.nytimes.com.

146 Stacey Higginbotham, "Forget Net Neutrality; Comcast Might Break the Web," *Gigaom*, November 29, 2010, gigaom.com.

147 Ben Popper, "Verizon Says Level 3 Is Looking to Get a 'Free Ride' for Its Massive Netflix Traffic," *Verge*, July 21, 2014, www.theverge.com; Zachary Seward, "The Inside Story of How Netflix Came to Pay Comcast for Internet Traffic," *Quartz*, August 27, 2014, qz.com.

148 Markham Erickson, et al., "Petition to Deny Netflix, Inc. in the Matter of Applications of Comcast Corp. and Time Warner Cable Inc. for Consent to Transfer Control of Licenses and Authorizations before the Federal Communications Commission," MB Docket No. 14-57, August 25, 2014, apps.fcc.gov.

149 Federal Communications Commission, "In the Matter of Protecting and Promoting the Open Internet," GN Docket No. 14-28. February 26, 2015.

150 "Net Neutrality," *Save the Internet*, n.d., www.savetheinternet.com.

151 Kit Walsh, "Today's Net Neutrality Order Is a Win, with a Few Blemishes," *Electronic Frontier Foundation*, March 12, 2015, www.eff.org.

152 Federal Communications Commission, "In the Matter of Protecting and Promoting the Open Internet," 55.

153 Danny Kimball, "Sponsored Data and Net Neutrality: Exemption and Discrimination in the Mobile Broadband Industry," *Media Industries* 2, no. 1 (2015), www.mediaindustriesjournal.org.

EPILOGUE

1 Alfred Martin finds that broadcast networks in general obscure gay kisses: Alfred L. Martin Jr., "It's (Not) in His Kiss: Gay Kisses and Camera Angles in Contemporary US Network Television Comedy," *Popular Communication* 12, no. 3 (2014): 153–65.

2 Malik Ganies, "We Are Orlando," *BOMB*, June 24, 2016, bombmagazine.org.

3 Fuller, "Branding Blackness on US Cable Television"; Stacy Smith et al., *Inclusion or Invisibility?*

4 Stuart Cunningham, David Craig, and Jon Silver, "YouTube, Multichannel Networks, and the Accelerated Evolution of the New Screen Ecology," *Convergence: The International Journal of Research into New Media Technologies* 22, no. 4 (2016): 376–91.

5 Todd Longwell, "Company of the Year: New Form Digital," *Video Ink*, December 31, 2015, www.thevideoink.com.

6 Though Verizon, AT&T, and Comcast all have or have made investments in their own original programming (Go90, Hulu, sponsored series), which they have pursued as a branding strategy and defense against competitors like Google that provide both access (fiber optic cables) and original programming (YouTube). Verizon in particular has been aggressively buying and developing original series.

7 Pat Aufderheide, *Communications Policy and the Public Interest*, 106, 109.

Aymar Jean Christian is Assistant Professor at Northwestern University and Fellow at the Peabody Media Center. His work on television has been published in numerous journals, including the *International Journal of Communication*, *Cinema Journal*, and *Continuum*. He leads Open TV (beta), a platform whose partners have included the Museum of Contemporary Art Chicago and City of Chicago. He has juried the Gotham Awards, Streamy Awards, and Tribeca Film Festival, among others.

9 781479 815975